Colección Támesis

SERIE A: MONOGRAFÍAS, 209

A COMPANION TO THE
LIBRO DE BUEN AMOR

Juan Ruiz's *Libro de Buen Amor* is one of the major literary accomplishments of the Iberian Middle Ages, and has generated an extensive secondary bibliography. Its uniqueness and diversity have thrilled and perplexed readers, and its influence is felt in modern letters. The current volume contains a series of essays that offer new scholarly insights into the *Libro*, in tribute to the late G. B. Gybbon-Monypenny and his *'Libro de buen amor' Studies*, and contextualize the *Libro* for a fresh generation of readers. The Preface addresses the critical legacy of the articles in Gybbon-Monypenny's Tamesis volume, and assesses trends in *Libro* scholarship. The articles offer surveys and new insights on the context and socio-political milieu of Juan Ruiz (Louise M. Haywood), the *Libro*'s metrics (Martin J. Duffell), its use of traditional wisdom (Barry Taylor), and its transmission (Jeremy Lawrance), the central episodes of Don Amor and Doña Endrina (Alan Deyermond, Dorothy S. Severin), and the application to the *Libro* of modern critical approaches, drawing on Mikhail Bakhtin, folklore studies, chaos theory, and reader-reception theory (Elizabeth Drayson, Laurence de Looze, Louise O. Vasvári).

A COMPANION TO THE
LIBRO DE BUEN AMOR

Edited by

Louise M. Haywood
and
Louise O. Vasvári

TAMESIS

First published 2004 by Tamesis, Woodbridge

ISBN 1 85566 094 6

Tamesis is an imprint of Boydell & Brewer Ltd
PO Box 9, Woodbridge, Suffolk IP12 3DF, UK
and of Boydell & Brewer Inc.
668 Mt. Hope Avenue, Rochester, NY 14620, USA
website: www.boydellandbrewer.com

A CIP catalogue record for this book is available
from the British Library

Library of Congress Cataloging-in-Publication Data

Companion to the Libro de buen amor / edited by Louise M. Haywood and Louise O. Vasvári.
    p. cm. – (Colección Támesis. Serie A, Monografías ; 209)
Includes bibliographical references and index.
ISBN 1–85566–094–6 (hardback : alk. paper)
1. Ruiz, Juan, fl. 1343. Libro de buen amor. I. Haywood, Louise M. II. Vasvári, Louise O.
(Louise Olga), 1943- III. Ruiz, Juan, fl. 1343. Libro de buen amor.
PQ6430.A1L533 2004
861′.1–dc22

                                                                                                    2004009424

This publication is printed on acid-free paper

Printed in Great Britain by
Antony Rowe Ltd., Chippenham, Wiltshire

CONTENTS

NOTES ON CONTRIBUTORS

Alan Deyermond, FBA, Corresponding Fellow of the Medieval Academy of America and of the Real Academia de Buenas Letras de Barcelona, is Research Professor at Queen Mary, University of London. He founded the Medieval Hispanic Research Seminar at Westfield College in 1967, and is the author of *La literatura perdida de la Edad Media castellana*, I: *Épica y romances* (1995), *Point of View in the Ballad* (1996), and *The 'Libro de Buen Amor' in England* (2004). He was President of the Asociación Internacional de Hispanistas, 1992–95, and in 1994 was awarded the Premio Elio Antonio de Nebrija.

Elizabeth Drayson is Lecturer in Spanish at New Hall and Peterhouse, and is Affiliated Lecturer in the Department of Spanish and Portuguese (University of Cambridge). Her special interests are the Middle Ages and translation studies, and she has published a translation and edition of the *Libro de Buen Amor*. She is currently writing a history of the reception of the legend of King Roderick and La Cava.

Martin J. Duffell is an Honorary Fellow of Queen Mary, University of London, where he is engaged in research and an Honorary Companion of the University of Manchester. He is the author of *Modern Metrical Theory and the 'Verso de arte mayor'* (1999), and of many articles on historical and comparative metrics. He served as Editor-in-Chief of *Hispanic Research Journal* from 1998–2002, and is a member of the Advisory Board of the journal *Rhythmica* (Univ. of Seville). He has recently completed a history of English metre, and is currently working on its Spanish equivalent.

Louise M. Haywood is University Senior Lecturer in Medieval Spanish Studies at the University of Cambridge, and Fellow of Trinity Hall. She is the author of *The Lyrics of the 'Historia troyana polimétrica'* (1996), and of over twenty articles on medieval topics, co-author of a course-book on translation, and editor of *Female Voices / Cultural Contexts* (2000). Current interests are the treatment of body, place, and humour in the fourteenth century.

Jeremy Lawrance is Professor of Spanish at the University of Manchester. His main research interests lie in medieval and Renaissance Spanish literature and culture, and he has published extensively in these areas, and has edited texts by Alfonso de Cartagena (1979), Alfonso de Palencia (with R. B. Tate, 1998), and Francisco de Vitoria (ed. and trans. with Anthony Pagden, 1991). He is currently working on a study of the presentation of Islam in medieval and Renaissance literature.

Laurence de Looze is Associate Professor of Comparative Literature at the University of Western Ontario, Canada. He is the author of *Pseudo-Autobiography in the Fourteenth Century* (1997) and of numerous articles on French, Icelandic and Spanish medieval literature, the editor and translator of Jean Froissart's *La prison amoureuse* (1994), and is currently completing a book on the manuscript versions of Don Juan Mannel's *Conde Lucanor*. He also writes fiction and has published further translations.

Dorothy S. Severin, OBE, is Gilmour Professor of Spanish at the University of Liverpool. She has published extensively on *cancionero* poetry and on sentimental romance, but is best known as a critic and editor of *Celestina*. Her editions (1969 and 1987) are widely used, and she has published many articles and four monographs: *Memory in 'La Celestina'* (1970), *Tragicomedy and Novelistic Discourse in 'Celestina'* (1989), *Witchcraft in 'Celestina'* (1995), and *Animals in 'Celestina'* (with Vicenta Blay Manzanera, 1999).

Barry Taylor is curator of Hispanic Collections, 1501–1850, at The British Library. His publications include *Cultures in Contact in Medieval Spain: Historical and Literary Essays Presented to L. P. Harvey* (ed. with David Hook, 1990), *Latin and Vernacular in Renaissance Spain* (ed. with Alejandro Coroleu, 1999), *Alonso de Cartagena* (?), *Cathoniana confectio* (ed. and trans., 2004), and over thirty articles on Don Juan Manuel, Juan de Mena, and wisdom literature in Old Spanish, Old Catalan and Latin.

Louise O. Vasvári, Fulbright Professor in Linguistics (Oetvos Lorand University, Budapest, Hungary), has recently retired from her post as Professor of Comparative Literature and Linguistics at the State University of New York at Stony Brook, and now splits her time between Budapest and New York. She has edited Juan de Mena's *Laberinto de Fortuna* and the *Tratado sobre el título de duque* attributed to him, *The Heterotextual Body of 'Mora Morilla'* (1999), and has published widely on medieval literature, translation theory, and applied linguistics, including over a dozen articles on the *Libro de Buen Amor*, on which she is now writing a monograph.

In memory of
G. B. Gybbon-Monypenny, 1923–2002

SCHEMA OF THE PLOT OF THE *LIBRO DE BUEN AMOR*

	Exemplum
E	Endrina
En	Endrina
FG	Ferrand Garçia
G	Garoça, nun
M	Melón / Archpriest
Nebuc	Nebuchadnezzar
T	Trotaconventos
Va	Vieja

Dueñas	Elaboration	Other Main Episodes
Prefatory material 1: Religious	1–43	
Invocation 1		
Prose sermon		
Invocation 2 + Marian lyrics		
Prefatory material 2: Secular	44–76	
Greeks & Romans		
Nature of Man		
Dueña I (La cuerda)	77–104	
E Wounded lion		
E Roaring earth		
		Vanity of Worldly Things (inverted) + 105–14
Dueña II & Go-between (Cruz cruzada & Ferrand Garçia)	115–22	
		Astrology + E 5 Astrologers 123–65
Dueña III (La encerrada)	166–8	
E thief and loyal dog		

Debate with Don Amor   181–649
Dream-vision sequence
Vision of Amor
Expression of scorn +

Sins of Love: Cobdiçia
              Sobervia
              Luxuria

E Young man with three wives
E Frogs desired a King
E Mastiff & reflection
E Horse & ass
E Virgil

Dueña IV (Doña Endrina)
(181–649 and 653–909)

Invidia
Gula
Ira y vanagloria
(Nebuc.; Samson; Saul)
Açidia

E Eagle's feathers
E Peacock & crow
E Lion & horse

E Angry lion
E Trial of wolf and fox
Parody of Canonical Hours
E Mole & frog

Vituperation of Love

Love's Response
Ovid's advice on appropriate beloved
On go-between
Love service

E Two lazy suitors
E Don Pitas Payas

Properties of Money
Sobriety
Moderation

E Drunk hermit

Lover alone
Vision of Venus
Complaint to Venus about Doña Endrina

Address to audience 650–52
Venus's Response: need for cunning

Doña Endrina and Don Melón   653–909
En & M: dialogue
Finds go-between: dialogue
Va & En: dialogue; lover is don Melón de la Huerta
Va   E Buzzard & swallow
En   E Wolf & kids; pig & litter
Va & M: dialogue; entices
Va & Doña Rama   + Va & En
Meeting M and En; resolution

Warning to Women +   E Lion & ass

SCHEMA OF THE PLOT OF THE *LIBRO DE BUEN AMOR* – cont'd

Dueñas	Elaboration	Other Main Episodes
Dueña V (La guardada) 910–44		
search for go-between (Urraca) unlike FG		
	Names of Go-between; lady dies	
	La Vieja 945–49	
Serranas = Women VI–IX 950–1042		
(La Chata, Gadea de Riofrío, Menga Lloriente, Alda de la Tablada)		
		Santa María del Vado + lyrics (compassion lyric (*horae*); Wounds) 1043–60
		Allegorical Battle: Don Carnal / Doña Cuaresma 1067–1314
		Burlesque epic challenges
		Archpriest as character / narrator with Don Jueves Lardero
		Parodic enumeration of opposing armies
		Cuaresma's victory; Carnal's capture
		Carnal's escape, flight, corralling of an army, victory
		Triumphal procession of Don Carnal and Don Amor
		Archpriest's visit to Don Amor's tent
Dueña X (La biuda loçana) and Trotaconventos 1315–20		
Dueña XI (Garoça, monja) and Trotaconventos 1321–1507		
T and G debate:		
G E Snake		
T E Greyhound & its master		
G E Town mouse & country mouse		
T E Sapphire in the midden		

T	E Ass & the lapdog	
G	E Fox plays dead	
T	E Lion & mouse	
G	E Fox & raven	
T	E Hares	
G	E Thief & the Devil	

Description of Archpriest; G accepts him as 'buen servidor' and dies

Dueña XII (la mora)   1508–12

Catalogue of instruments   1513–19
Death of Trotaconventos: apostrophe to Death; epitaph   1520–78
Arms of the Christian   1579–1605
Virtues of small women   1606–17

?Dueña XIII & Go-between   1618–25
(Doña Fulana & Don Furón)

Concluding Material
On the Interpretation of the Book   1626–49
2 × Gozos

Escolares   1650–1728
Ave María + 3 × Loores
Against Fortune
Clérigos de Talavera
Ciegos × 2

E	*Exemplum*
En	Endrina
FG	Ferrand Garçía
G	Garoça, nun
M	Melón / Archpriest
Nebuc	Nebuchadnezzar
T	Trotaconventos
Va	Vieja

Introduction: Reading the
Libro de Buen Amor Thirty Years On

LOUISE M. HAYWOOD AND LOUISE O. VASVÁRI

The present collection of studies is the second volume published by Tamesis to be dedicated to the *Libro de Buen Amor*, the first being the *'Libro de buen amor' Studies*, edited by G. B. Gybbon-Monypenny (1970a), who died before we were able to complete this volume.[1] He had kindly agreed to write a Preface for us and it is with great sadness, therefore, that we undertake this task ourselves. That collection of eleven articles, whose authors had their university education in Britain or Ireland (although two were teaching in the United States and one in the West Indies), was, surprisingly, the first ever published on the work of Juan Ruiz and has continued to make a significant impact, particularly on anglophone *Buen Amor* studies.[2] Partly because of this fact and partly because of the comprehensive range of topics covered, its articles have been among those most cited in *Libro* scholarship. Although the two editors of the present volume are a full generation apart in age, each grew up intellectually with that 1970 collection as a major source of inspiration. Was it, then, perhaps out of an 'anxiety of influence' that in 1999, while together at a conference in Santander, they realized that, thirty years on, there was an urgent need for an equally comprehensive, but now more theoretically-oriented, re-vision of the state of scholarship on the *Libro*? In the meantime, the project, having taken longer than expected, has also brought us into a new century, so that it is fitting that in this new volume we also attempt to look back Janus-like over the development of *Libro* scholarship over those thirty years, as well as to anticipate what direction future scholarship might profitably take.

Let us begin by reviewing from the perspective of a new century the achievements and limitations of that 1970 collection, and, to some degree, the earlier scholarship with which it was in dialogue, as well as suggesting selected follow-up studies with which these articles could now be re-read. Our aim, by this method,

---

[1] Contributors chose whether to capitalize *Buen Amor*, depending on whether they interpret the title as Good Love's Book or a book about good love (see Lawrance and Drayson, this volume). Note that editions and works cited are listed separately.

[2] In the light of the pseudo-autobiographical nature of the *Libro*, we shall refer to the author as Juan Ruiz and the protagonist as the Archpriest.

is not one of criticism but to begin to chart the course of the *Libro de Buen Amor*'s critical reception.

The first article, 'Juan Ruiz's Manipulation of Rhyme: Some Linguistic and Stylistic Consequences', by Kenneth W. J. Adams, is dedicated to analysis of rhyme schemes, which he considered a prime element of composition in the *Libro*. Compared to earlier *cuaderna vía* works, such as the *Libro de Alexandre* and the works of Gonzalo de Berceo, Adams found in the *Libro* a much greater variety of rhymes, with fewer of them being facile and monotonous. Further, compared to earlier works, the *Libro* has a superabundant vocabulary, with many new items making their first textual appearance in Spanish, with some 700 appearing only in rhyme position, and 500 of them only once. In his article, Adams essentially treats the work as a linguistic document. Adams also points out that a host of humorous place and personal names appear in the work exclusively in rhyme position but he does not develop this idea in detail. His study, which has not been superseded, was complemented by Francisco Ynduráin's (1973) study on rhyme schemes and developed, from a more literary perspective, by Louise Vasvári's study (1988–89) of the obscene-naming conventions in the Melón / Endrina episode, all found in rhyme position.[3]

Janet A. Chapman, in 'Juan Ruiz's "Learned Sermon"', analysed the *Libro*'s Prose Prologue within the tradition of the learned sermon, and concluded that the author was acquainted with pulpit oratory and the arts of preaching, as were his contemporaries, like Geoffrey Chaucer. Chapman closely studies the learned *divisio intra* structure, which analyses a Biblical versicle phrase by phrase, in the Prose Prologue. By way of contrast she mentions the *divisio extra* popular sermon – in which a topic is discussed with reference to a range of examples – but does not study Juan Ruiz's use of popular sermon in the Digression on Sin (on which see, later, Gerli 1981–82 and 1982, Vasvári 1985–86). While she notes that Pierre L. Ullman's study (1967), then recently appeared, fails to consider the potential comic effects of the prologue, she herself is nevertheless reluctant in concluding anything more than that Juan Ruiz was not composing a serious sermon. Sander L. Gilman's (1974) work on the parodic sermon, however, offers an important corrective to this view.[4]

A. D. Deyermond's 'Some Aspects of Parody in the *Libro de Buen Amor*' has been the most frequently quoted article to emerge from the 1970 collection. Deyermond attributes the recognition of the role of parody as a central feature of the *Libro* in great part to Félix Lecoy's *Recherches* (1938; a work which Deyermond subsequently re-edited in 1974, with a valuable bibliographical introduction). Deyermond points to six episodes as particularly clear examples of parody: the debate of the Greek and Roman, the Don Ximio trial, the canonical hours, the *serranas* episodes, the battle of Don Carnal and Doña Cuaresma,

---

[3] On further ludic uses of rhyme see also Johnson 1990.

[4] For later studies see Kinkade 1970 and 1973, Nepaulsingh 1974, Zink 1976, Deyermond 1979–80, Cátedra 1982, Koopmans 1984, Koopmans and Verhueyck 1987, Russell 1991, Bataillon 1993, Brown 1998: 116–17, and Saperstein 2000.

and the Lament for Trotaconventos, and, in particular, her epitaph. He concludes that most of the parodies were either ecclesiastical or of love literature, and that the two methods most favoured were reversal and incongruous associations. He does not discuss parody on the semantic level, such as *double entendres* and homonyms. The area of research developed in this influential article by Deyermond has probably been the one which has seen the most dramatic development in subsequent years, begun by John K. Walsh (1979–80b, 1983), who hinted at the need for a methodology for the recuperation of the layers of humour and parody which have been shed in the six centuries between the creation of the *Libro* and our reading of it. See also Dayle Seidenspinner-Núñez (1981) and Monique De Lope (1984), whose study was informed by Mikhail Bakhtin's theory of carnivalesque, not available in the Western languages until the late sixties (see Vasvári, in this volume).

Peter N. Dunn, in 'De las figuras del arçipreste', re-examines the personal portrait of the Archpriest described by Trotaconventos, by placing it in the literature of medical discourse, which was grounded in anatomical theory and astrological medicine; on which see Amasuno, Haywood, and Morros (all in press). He concludes that the description is that of a man whose sanguine temperament should promise amorous success but instead rendered him helpless by some contrary influence. Like Chapman's study, which also uses extra-literary discourses to elucidate the work, Dunn's study qualifies as an incipient form of New Historicism. Like some other studies in the collection, his is cautious. For example, he suggests that the protagonist being dubbed *valiente* should be understood as '*audax*', when from Latin the term is attested with the meaning of 'priapic' (see our discussion of Tate, below).[5]

In his '"Buen Amor": Its Meaning and Uses in Some Medieval Texts', Brian Dutton revisits an issue which by 1970 already had over half a dozen articles dedicated to it, including his own earlier 1966 semantic analysis. He discusses how Juan Ruiz used *buen amor* in both senses in which it was current at the time: courtly love, love of God, or either, according to context. The first part of the article is an extra-textual examination of the term, while the second analyses its use within the *Libro*. Dutton concludes that the term means *loco amor* when referring to courtly love but, although he gets close (118), he does not go so far as to consider that in the mouth of Trotaconventos it is further perverted to suggest prostitution.[6]

G. B. Gybbon-Monypenny points out in '"Dixe la por te dar ensienpro": Juan Ruiz's Adaptation of the *Pamphilus*' (1970b) that previous studies of this key episode were piecemeal, or concerned with giving it a didactic interpretation, or with claiming that Juan Ruiz increased the social realism of the episode compared to its Latin predecessor. Gybbon-Monypenny thinks that these earlier studies were on the right track but did not go far enough. He sees the episode as

---

[5] See, further, Goldberg 1986 and Mary F. Walker 1990.
[6] See the further rich bibliography on this term, cited in Vasvári below.

concerned with building the role of Trotaconventos and generalizing about the activities of go-betweens, and altering the social and civil attributes of the heroine from a virgin in the *Pamphilus* to a widow (see further, Vasvári 1992b). He concludes that the emphasis on Trotaconventos's cynicism and her greater virtuosity in the *Libro*'s version serves a didactic purpose, although he ultimately fails to decide if the author is being ironic about this didactic tradition. Walsh (1979–80a) underlined the importance of the episode from a different aspect, positing that, in the evolution of the *Libro* from a performance text, this episode was the first item in the poet's repertoire. Seidenspinner-Núñez (1981) attempted a detailed line-by-line analysis of the Melón / Endrina episode in relation to its source, while others have focused on the significance of Juan Ruiz's choice of ridiculous-sounding horticultural names for the protagonists, which can hardly signal social realism (Clarke 1972, Gilman 1983, who calls the piece 'a tender and humorous garden allegory' (247), Cantarino 1989; and, in contrast, Vasvári 1988–89, who finds the names carnivalesque, a position criticized by Dagenais 1992 and 1992–93, and Hook 1993; Ramírez Pimienta 1998 offers no new insights).[7]

Rita's Hamilton's 'The Digression on Confession in the *Libro de buen amor*' quotes Lecoy's poor opinion of this episode, where he judged Juan Ruiz to be summarizing definitions found in Gratian's *Decretum*, reproducing what he had learned in his theological studies about the sacrament of penance and the jurisdictional question of who can hear confession. In calling attention to the ambiguity of the Church's teaching on the sacrament of penance Juan Ruiz treats scornfully the friar who had the doubtful privilege of giving Don Carnal absolution. Although this digression is placed within the carnivalesque episode of the Confession of Don Carnal, Hamilton suggests that in this passage, more than any other section of the work, the voice of the narrator may possibly be that of Juan Ruiz.[8]

Kemlin M. Laurence, in 'The Battle of Don Carnal and Doña Cuaresma in the Light of Medieval Tradition', sees this episode primarily as an imitation of the thirteenth-century *Bataille de Charnage et de Cuaresme*. Her interest is in studying what Juan Ruiz owed to previous literary tradition rather than in what he added, seeing the work as part of anti-clerical satire. She criticizes Anthony N. Zahareas (1965) for his insistence on the parodic aspects of the episode, which she deems anachronistic. However, subsequent studies have borne out Zahareas's reading, even though he, too, was working without knowledge of Bakhtin's work on carnival. The lack of discussion of the oral tradition is precisely what caused

---

[7] For further studies on the Latin *comoedia* tradition, see Elliott 1984, who underlines the bawdiness and sexual explicitness of the genre; Thomson & Perraud 1990, Parker 1991, Allen 1992, Gerli 1992, Kinkade 1996, and Burkard 1999. See also Deyermond and Severin in this volume on different aspects of this episode, and Haywood, below, on *Pamphilus* and Latin narrative.

[8] See Gurevich 1988: 24–26, Cherchi 1993, and the new study of Gratian's *Decretum* (Winroth 2000).

Laurence's study to be superseded by the mid-1980s (De Lope 1984, Márquez Villanueva 1990, Mintz 1997, and Vasvári, in this volume).

Ian Michael's 'The Function of the Popular Tale' catalogues thirty-five tales that occupy over one fifth of the work; he aims to go beyond motif-index classifications. He points out the uncertainty of relying only on written versions and paying insufficient attention to the author's artistic treatment. Although Michael shows that the tales are unevenly clustered around ten points in the text, arguing that they were grouped in this way because they occur at moments of argument and debate, he relates the technique only to the use of *exempla* by medieval preachers, but not to the agonistic or disputative style characteristic of oral discourse. Michael also analyses the many tales in the Digression on Sin without taking into consideration the parodic nature of the frame *recuestas* between the protagonist and Don Amor. He therefore has difficulty with the tales not matching their application. Nevertheless, he concludes that Juan Ruiz 'does not provide sufficient grounds for thinking he deliberately wished to subvert the firm moral values of the time' (1970: 218). See the article by Barry Taylor in this volume for a philologically farther-reaching analysis of popular tales and proverbs (and compare also Schwarzbaum 1989).

Taking as his starting point the contradictory opinions of Ramón Menéndez Pidal (1957: 212), for whom the realistic and caricaturesque narrative portions of the *serrana* episodes contrasted sharply with the idealized lyrical portions, and María Rosa Lida de Malkiel's contrary opinion (1959: 45), R. B. Tate, in 'Adventures in the *sierra*', sets out to re-examine the episode to see if these conflicting textual interpretations might be reconciled. First, he examines the passage to determine its relation to the larger work and concludes that, with no mutual references 'except perhaps that of 950a, a somewhat distant echo of 76c, and the fact that we may associate the time of year, March (951a), with the opening of the mountain-passes at Guadarrama' (219), it is independent. He then examines each of the four parts of the larger episode, and finds each to be a balance of a lyric *zéjel* preceded by a narrative 'prologue' of variable length in *cuaderna vía*. Questioning the methodology of Lida de Malkiel (1961) and Pierre Le Gentil (1949), who treated the whole section as a sequence, he proposes to work outwards from the lyrics to the context, in order not to contaminate his analysis. He concludes that there are more resemblances among the four narratives than among the lyrics, and that in all of the former the *serrana* is wilful, dominating, ugly or stupid, sexually experienced, or comical; they thereby cohere to themes in the rest of the *Libro*. The relation of the lyrics to their narratives, on the other hand, varies widely, with the last two lyrics, in particular, being neither crude nor caricature. The inappropriate fit he finds between the two sections leads Tate to the conclusion that the lyrics must have been composed before the narratives, but it still leaves the problem of how to situate the whole passage within the larger work, for which he finds no convincing solution, remarking in passing that neither does Roger M. Walker (in the following article).

Tate's article is focused on structural relationships and does not delve into an analysis of the *serrana* within the broader wild-woman tradition, or offer a stylistic analysis. His method of analysis means he did not realize the semantic suggestiveness of some key terms which, in turn, led him to underestimate the level of crude suggestiveness in the lyric portions. Like Dunn, above, Tate interprets *valiente* too tamely in a key passage; at the beginning of the second lyric, in speaking of the *serrana valiente* (987b), Gadea de Riofrío, he translates the word as 'husky'. As Margherita Morreale (1963: 320) earlier suggested in relation to the *Libro*, and as is evident already in the Latin etymon *valen[tulu]s* (Pierrugues 1908: 501), whether applied to men or women, *valiente* implied sexual vigour. Erminio Braidotti (1981: 180), in an unjustly neglected semantic study, adds many more examples in other episodes, as, for example, in the *moço más valiente* (1542c), who is capable of satisfying the sexual appetite of a young widow. In modern Spanish, Gadea would then be more colloquially described as a *serrana cojonuda*, a far more fitting description for the kind of girl who does nothing but hurl sexual insults at the poor protagonist-as-pilgrim, ending with the threat to 'skin his nuts' (Vasvári 1997: 1570). Similarly, Tate's reading of the *serrana*'s words, repeated in three different variants – 'Do non ay moneda, / non ay merchandía / [. . .] Non ay mercadero / bueno sin dinero [. . .] del que no·m da algo / ni·l' dó la posada' (Blecua 1992; st. 1040bc–1041abde) – as demanding gifts from the protagonist is denotative and presents her as simply materialist rather than coarse or violent. However, *merchandía* commonly connotes 'female sexual goods for sale', as in the French farce, where two prostitutes pretending to be *mercières* discuss at length whether it would be more profitable to sell their *marchandise* to clerics or to gentlemen (Hindley 1967: 15); *posada* can also be interpreted sexually, as in the Pitas Pajas episode, where the wife 'pobló la *posada*' (78c) in her husband's absence. These are not merely semantic quibbles, but rather serve to show that the lyrics – in the *zéjel* form like many of the *Libro*'s other lyrics – do, in fact, share some of the crude flavour of the accompanying narratives, and through their erotic lexicon they can also be related to the larger work. That is not to say that Tate is not correct in his hypothesis that the lyrics were composed independently, an idea that was later brilliantly developed by Walsh (1979–80a), who considered the whole work as one of accretion. De Lope (1984) totally reinterpreted the episode in carnivalesque terms.[9]

For Walker in '"Con miedo de la muerte la miel non es sabrosa": Love, Sin and Death in the *Libro de buen amor*', the most puzzling feature of the work is its apparent dualism, with which critics have dealt by mostly ignoring one side or the other. He is struck by what he calls the 'particular poignancy' (1970: 235) of Juan Ruiz's focus on death, which he attributes to the poet's deep religious convictions and fear of death.[10] Walker argues that Juan Ruiz in his Digression on Sins means his charges against Don Amor very seriously, and wants to teach that love leads man to mortal sin, and that in spite of the gay façade of the work,

---

[9] See also Kirby 1986, Dagenais 1991, Gerli 1995, Vasvári 1997, and Burke 1998: 183–96.
[10] Walker 1970 is often read in conjunction with his 1966. In a conversation with Louise Haywood in March 1993 Walker confessed to a growing scepticism about the unitary nature of the *Libro*.

on closer examination Juan Ruiz paints a very sombre picture of the human predicament. Further, according to Walker, although Juan Ruiz may at times be seen to contradict himself, he is, in fact, never in doubt about his moral purpose. If one considers the Digression within the oral tradition of the popular sermon and the highly stylized agonistic vituperative exchanges of oral discourse, it becomes difficult to take the Archpriest's logorrhoea against Don Amor as anything but a set piece of invective, or traditional insult exchanges, a staple of oral performance within the rules of game structure (Ong 1981: 204–07; McDowell 1985, Edwards and Sinkiewicz 1990, Gerli 1992, Vasvári, below), arising from his angry state of mind during the dream-vision encounter with Don Amor (see Deyermond, below). Walker's piece is a work of traditional scholarship based on moralistic interpretation, which continues to be frequently cited, yet it has arguably stood the test of time less well than most articles in the collection (see Haywood, below).

As we stated at the outset, the foregoing observations are not meant in criticism but rather to serve as a scholarly tool for re-reading '*Libro de buen amor*' *Studies* within the context of a further thirty years of *Libro* scholarship. It is inevitable that the hindsight available from these years of additional research has provided some significant correctives, as well as a wealth of new approaches. In general, the bulk of the contributions in the volume can be characterized as breaking new ground in their time in that they venture beyond the confines of didactic interpretations and explore the comedic in the *Libro*, but, from today's perspective, they may appear overly tied to questions of textual influences. In the light of this it is curious that there is no contribution on the manuscript traditions or editorial practices. Given the lack of prominence of studies on orality and the bawdy humour of popular culture in the late 1960s and early 1970s, it is unsurprising that little attention was given to popular culture and to the interaction of oral and written modes of communication. Predominantly, the questions that were posed are the traditional ones of authorship, intent, structural unity, and literary influences.

In 1973 a second major collection of articles dedicated solely to the *Libro* appeared, this time in the form of the proceedings of over fifty papers presented in 1971 in Alcalá de Henares, dubbed by its editor, M. Criado de Val (1973a), as the Primer Congreso Internacional sobre el Arcipreste de Hita. Given its greater size, with almost twenty sections, it was possible to cover a wide range of topics, including some that have received little attention since (such el 'El *Buen Amor*: su crítica social', and 'El Arcipreste y Chaucer'). However, Criado de Val's collection has not enjoyed the scholarly impact of the earlier Tamesis volume, perhaps because of the inconsistent quality of its necessarily brief contributions. Maybe half of the articles have never again been cited, while a number of others have lived on mainly as footnotes in various editions of the *Libro*.

Curiously, and that is probably symptomatic of the level of theoretical sophistication of that period, the only group of articles from the 1973 Criado de Val collection that had any continuing impact is the section 'La huella histórica de Juan Ruiz', where no fewer than three scholars promoted the candidacy of a different Juan Ruiz as the author of the *Libro*.[11] The identification by Emilio Sáez and José Trenchs (1973) of Juan Ruiz with Juan Rodríguez de Cisneros, an illegitimate member of the Cisneros family, who was born in Moorish captivity, was the most popular of the three candidates. Their findings initially gained enthusiastic though uncritical acceptance by some scholars, but have since lost favour. The tenuous and conjectural hypotheses on which these mutually contradictory identifications of the author were based are complicated by several additional problems: the lack of reliability in naming conventions and the extraordinary frequency of many names in the fourteenth century, as well as the continued uncertainty surrounding the date of composition of the work.

To seek to identify medieval authors about whom there is no independently verifiable historical information essentially through textual clues such as personal names, toponyms, or supposed references to contemporary events tends to result, as it did in the studies in the Criado de Val collection, in a proliferation of hypotheses, often circular. Ultimately, after much conjecture based on supposed biographical details in the text by many scholars, and serious archival research by a few, such as Francisco J. Hernández (1984–85, 1988), all we know about the author of the *Libro* is that he had the cultural formation necessary to write such a work. We mention this scholarly controversy about authorship, which had yet to arise when the Tamesis volume was published and which was taken up with vigour in the Criado de Val collection and afterwards, because it exemplifies how so much scholarship got bogged down in these largely speculative discussions without documentary underpinnings (see further Márquez Villanueva 2002; and Haywood, Lawrance, and de Looze, all below).

Thirty years on . . .

If we now jump forward thirty years, it is curious to note that our collection, just as its 1970 predecessor, is now also flanked by the Proceedings of another conference on the *Libro*, which took place in May 2002 at the Ayuntamiento of Alcalá la Real (Jaén), and which, paying homage to an earlier conference (Toro Ceballos and Rodríguez Molina 1996), bills itself as the Segundo Congreso Internacional sobre el Arcipreste de Hita y el *Libro de buen amor*.[12] The Proceedings of that congress (Toro Ceballos in press) show that it covered a range of traditional philological topics, along with a few articles presenting newer theoretical approaches. However, what was less evident were studies

---

[11] For further discussion of Juan Ruiz's identity see Haywood, below.

[12] The proceedings of the Alcalá la Real congress, with a misleadingly similar title, provide useful socio-historical background on the prototypical *fronterizo* environment of Alcalá in the fourteenth century rather than dealing with the *Libro* from a literary perspective (only Rodríguez Puértolas does this). The connection with Juan Ruiz was the tenuous identification of the *Libro*'s author with Juan Rodríguez (or Ruiz) de Cisneros, born in that city about 1295.

utilizing contemporary theoretical and interdisciplinary approaches, such as cultural or gender studies, that would pose serious challenges to more traditional approaches still dominant in much of peninsular scholarship. As one North American colleague who attended that conference commented: 'All told, Juan Ruiz's *Libro* emerged from Alcalá la Real certainly as a more richly annotated work, but scarcely a different work from the one presented [either by the first Tamesis collection or] by the first Congreso Internacional over thirty years ago.'

Alan Deyermond, the only author represented in the original 1970 collection, at the 2002 Alcalá de Real conference, and in the present collection, asserted (in a paper presented on 11 May 2002 at Alcalá de Real) that a single theory is insufficient to interpret the *Libro*. We have taken this as our guiding principle, sensing the need to include a much broader range of scholarly voices in order to challenge traditional scholarship, to create a polyphony of voices and multiple reading strategies, juxtaposing and intermingling not only complementary but contradictory and seemingly even incompatible theoretical positions. In the present collection of nine essays, divided into four sections, we have attempted to present the outlines for just such an approach. The reader will note that, while the articles can profitably be read in the order in which they are printed; the first and last articles, contributed by the two editors, in somewhat medieval fashion, also frame the collection. Louise M. Haywood's initial piece on 'Contexts and Milieu' is a kind of *accessus* that provides an introductory overview of many of the key issues – authorship, dating, manuscripts, Occidental versus Oriental influences, and so on – which have been contested issues in relation to the *Libro*. Louise Vasvári's concluding article, 'The Novelness of the *Libro de Buen Amor*', picks up many of the literary and genre issues discussed in the earlier pieces – oral versus literary genres, proverbs and *exempla*, the carnivalesque elements, the paratextual episodes – and attempts to propose a (perhaps too grand) theory of what the totality of the work represents in the history of the development of European novelistic discourse, and in a broader sense of literary narrative.

The seven articles within the frame of the two editorial articles by Haywood and Vasvári offer overviews, detailed analysis, and differing theoretical approaches, and as such vary considerably in length depending on their aim and the focus of their analysis. In particular homage to G. B. Gybbon-Monypenny, we have chosen to include two articles on the Doña Endrina / Don Melón episode, which draws on the Latin *comoedia Pamphilus de amore*, and about which he wrote in '*Libro de buen amor*' *Studies*. The articles in the present volume can be paired in a variety of ways, to be read in conjunction with or in sharp contrast to other contributions. For example, Laurence de Looze's article, 'Text, Author, Reader, Reception: The Reflection of Theory and the *Libro de Buen Amor*', as its key-word-laden title suggests, is a more theoretically and comparatively oriented analysis of some of the key issues, already introduced in Haywood's article. Similarly, Lawrance's '*Libro de Buen Amor*: From Script to Print' is an extended analysis of the manuscript traditions of the *Libro*, again already introduced by Haywood. In his discussion Lawrance makes continued reference to the concept of *mouvance*, or textual instability; readers who are not familiar with this term may turn to de Looze. Lawrance also importantly reiterates throughout his paper the indebtedness of manuscript traditions to orality and offers eloquent illustrations of oral residues in textuality. Martin J. Duffell takes up the question of the *Libro*'s metric irregularity, posed by Jeremy Lawrance as a puzzle. The totality of Vasvári's article (as well as the larger *oeuvre* on which is based), though it does not mention manuscripts at all, is an exemplification of the inseparable intertextualities of oral and literate cultures so eloquently described by Lawrance. Barry Taylor's '*Exempla* and Proverbs in the *Libro de Buen Amor*' analyses in a more traditionally philological sense at its exhaustive best these same interrelations of orality and textuality in these two 'little genres' of oral-based discourse in the *Libro*. At the same time, Taylor's exhaustive and erudite definitions and catalogue of *exempla* and proverbs in the *Libro* are, once again, aptly illustrated by Vasvári in her close textual and semantic analysis of the key phrase *buen amor*.

It is the two articles at the core of the collection, Alan Deyermond's ' "Was it a Vision or a Waking Dream?": The Anomalous Don Amor and Doña Endrina Episodes Reconsidered' and Dorothy Sherman Severin's 'The Relationship between the *Libro de Buen Amor* and *Celestina*: Does Trotaconventos Perform a *Philocaptio* Spell on Doña Endrina?' which at first seem to stand most independently from the others: their in-depth analysis of the dream vision and of the discourse of magic, respectively, do not intersect with the major recurring preoccupations of the other articles, although they do interrelate with one other, both being devoted to the same episode. Their intertextual relationships are to be sought, rather, in another, comparative, direction. Deyermond's article places the episode of Don Melón and Doña Endrina in the comparative tradition of the dream vision in medieval Europe, particularly in England. Severin, in her brief article, which begs to be read in conjunction with her monograph on magic in *Celestina* (1995), manages to provide new insights by reading the *Libro de Buen Amor* through *Celestina*, at the same time as shedding fresh light on that later work. Finally, the first and last articles inside the introductory and concluding frame also paradoxically complement each other, albeit in the most dialogic fashion. In talking about *mouvance* Lawrance asserts that the chaos we find in medieval works that seems bothersome to modern readers was normal. Elizabeth Drayson's 'Chaotics, Complexity and the *Libro de Buen Amor*' offers the same opinion from the very different perspective of chaos theory. Drayson's focus on the lack of unity in the work can be compared with de Looze's different theoretical analysis, and her use of chaotics in the semantic analysis of the key term *buen amor* with the linguistic analysis undertaken by Vasvári.

Part 1: 'Contexts' comprises Louise M. Haywood's contribution, 'Juan Ruiz and the *Libro de Buen Amor*: Contexts and Milieu', and Jeremy Lawrance's '*Libro de Buen Amor*: From Script to Print'. Haywood's comprehensive overview of the work aptly illustrates her assertion that the *Libro* 'is one of the most diverse, unusual, and challenging texts any reader is like to encounter [. . .] posing many dilemmas to the modern reader'. She dedicates considerable attention to the interrelated questions of authorship, dating, and the implications of the use of a first-person narrator who is identified with the author, presumably one 'Juan

Ruiz, Archpriest of Hita'. Beginning with the question of dating, which must precede any search for a historically identifiable author, she concludes that in the present state of research we should tentatively accept the 1330–43 dating as a reasonably accurate timeframe for the work to be completed, with some sections likely to have been composed earlier. With this seemingly cautious conclusion, Haywood rejects the two-version theory, widely accepted when the 1970 Tamesis collection was published. Next, reviewing attempts to identify a historical Juan Ruiz, Haywood carefully comes down on the side of the likelihood that he existed rather than that the name was a pseudonym or some other kind of literary game. On the other hand, she leaves open the question of the sincerity of the author's pseudo-autobiographical form. In this context she reviews the arguments in favour of European versus Arabic and Hispano-Jewish models in relation to the work's autobiographical and generically heterogeneous narrative structure, in which unrelated episodes are linked through a single protagonist. She does not find convincing evidence for the possibility that the author could have been sufficiently acquainted with the Oriental sources, when among the European analogues proposed for specific episodes, the erotic pseudo-autobiography, the Latin versified tales or pseudo-Ovidian narrative, and St Augustine's *Confessions* there are structural parallels to the *Libro* from all, and most strongly from the second. In her discussion of the potential thematic unity of the work Haywood shows how such arguments ultimately rest on a didactic interpretation of the work, in stark contrast with performance-centred models in which pre-existing set-pieces are united in an over-arching structure.

Jeremy Lawrance's essay aims to convey to the modern reader the enormously misleading visual impression that a printed copy of the *textus receptus* of the *Libro de Buen Amor* gives of manuscript culture, and of how the passage from orality to script and from manuscript culture to printing modified communication as well as aesthetic appreciation. In manuscript culture every codex was unique and all texts were characterized by *mouvance*, or instability, both in the variant texts given by the manuscripts themselves, as well in the marginal notes and annotations by later readers. However, all this variation, which seems to modern readers chaotic, was by medieval standards normal and, indeed, artistic unity and authorial intent may well be inappropriate to the medieval concept of literature. Following the argument that authorship was also alien in an essentially oral-based society, Lawrance also argues that the text does not allow for the construction of the author – whose name is announced outside the frame of fiction – and narrator as the same person.

Lawrance's aim is 'to strip down the work to its matrix in scribal and oral culture', revealing the transformations it has undergone in reaching print. He traces how far the text we know today reflects this. While he finds the main scheme of the original to have followed a standard process of medieval composition he allows that two puzzles remained unanswered, having to do with both missing and extraneous passages, both of which he attributes to unbound sheets gone astray. He also attributes to *mouvance* the larger anomaly that two different dates of composition are given – a fact that led the two-version theory. Lawrance demonstrates with many examples how the *Libro* addresses both a literary and a listening audience. He surmises that performances would have lasted about two hours and would have been mixed-form, with the narrative segments read out but with sung lyrics. Taking up again the argument about the influence of Oriental elements in the frame-tale structure of the work, Lawrance concludes that it is rather orality which shapes the *Libro* at many levels: its authorial voice, language, style, and structure. Next he traces the scribal tradition of the *Libro*, discussing dialect, rubrics, and marginal annotations – the whole process showing a progressive movement from a performance text to a more readerly tradition. In the third and briefest part of his study, Lawrance traces the passage of the text from script to print, characterized by the oblivion into which the text fell in the sixteenth and seventeenth centuries. By way of conclusion he proposes that in the future inventive typographers or the use of electronic media of publication will give readers access to still new textual realities of manuscript *mouvance*.

Part 2: 'Form and Traditional Wisdom' comprises two articles, Duffell's 'Metre and Rhythm in the *Libro de Buen Amor*', and Taylor on *exempla* and proverbs. Duffell argues that the fact that the *Libro*'s metre is irregular points to the insufficiency of current hypotheses regarding *cuaderna vía* metre in dealing with it. It makes little sense to suppose that a poem, most likely intended for oral performance, is metrically irregular, for three reasons. First, scribes used metre to facilitate the copying process and so it is psychologically improbable that it would have been obliterated in copying. Second, the *Libro* is chronologically positioned at the end of the process by which exemplars of early texts which had previously been copied in highly abbreviated forms were copied with resolved abbreviations, which when expanded fully destroyed syllabic regularity. In addition, poets moved towards accentually (rather than syllabically) based patterns. Finally, irregular lines defy emendation. Duffell proposes an alternative hypothesis of accentual word stress to determine metre types of duple- and triple-time, and mixed time lines.

Barry Taylor's study, '*Exempla* and Proverbs in the *Libro de Buen Amor*', illustrates a point already much discussed in Lawrance's article, how the *Libro* exemplifies the fusion of the popular and the learned, in this case through its Latin and vernacular stories and sayings. The *exemplum*, a short story with a message made explicit either in the introduction or conclusion, appears in the *Libro* under many names, with the same terms sometimes being used for proverbs. Ruiz is conventional in his structural use of *exempla*, being truant, rather, in their application. Within the narrative frame, many are employed in agonistic exchanges. The majority are animal fables, which, just like animals appearing in illustrations and doodles in the margins of serious texts, may well have an association with low-grade humour, and it is clear that Ruiz was aware of their subversive potential, referring to one as a *juguete*. Taylor traces how Ruiz adapted his principal learned source, the Aesopic fables attributed to Walter the Englishman, which served as a school text. His adaptations include localization, familiarization, the addition of visual details, lewdness, and legal knowledge, but in other cases it is likely that he also had recourse to oral versions. If the animal fable is tinged with potential lewdness, the *fabliau*, of which there are three examples in the *Libro*, is defined precisely by its bawdiness, leading Taylor to question if there is a valid generic distinction to be made between Ruiz's use of humorous *exempla* and the *fabliaux*.

The second part of Taylor's study is devoted to the proverb, which has received far less scholarly attention than the *exemplum*. As with the latter form, the proverb has both a learned and a popular tradition, of which Ruiz uses the latter far more often, although sometimes lines that sound popular are actually translations from the Latin reformulated to fit the *cuaderna vía* rhyme. Among Ruiz's learned sources the most frequent is the *Disticha Catonis*, followed by Biblical references. As an appendix to his article Taylor offers an invaluable chart guiding readers through all the *exempla* in the *Libro*. The important final question addressed is the level of truancy in Ruiz's use of this sententious material. Taylor shows how the author achieves a parodic reinterpretation by omitting the second half of a proverb, and by attributing subversive views to an authoritative source.

The third part, 'The Doña Endrina / Don Melón Episode', comprises articles by Deyermond and Severin on the Doña Endrina episode. Deyermond points out that even by the standards of anomaly of the work as a whole, the Doña Endrina episode is highly odd, owing, among other factors, to the depiction of an adult Don Amor rather than an infant Cupid, to the odd vegetal name of the narrator-protagonist alter ego of the Archpriest as well as of the other characters, and to the fact that the seduction of Endrina is the only successful love affair depicted in the whole work. He suggests that the peculiarities of the episode might be accounted for by the fact that it is meant to be read as a dream vision; to support his argument he places the episode in the context of medieval Castilian, English, and French dream-vision poetry. He shows that, in spite of the lack of an explicit use of the term *sueño*, there are adequate verbal markers both at the beginning and at the end of the episode to signal that it is a dream vision. Deyermond's revision of the enigmatic Doña Endrina episode, which is so central to an interpretation of the *Libro*, is particularly valuable because the dream vision, even though it can be considered the paradigmatic medieval form, has not always been recognized as a discrete genre. The question might remain to what degree Juan Ruiz is parodying this highly conventional genre.

In her essay, Severin revives the question, mentioned by F. Castro Guisasola (1924) and revived by Samuel G. Armistead (1973, 1976–77), of whether there could have been a direct influence on *Celestina* by the *Libro*, which she proceeds to examine through a comparison between Celestina's *philocaptio* spell and the magic procedures used in the *Libro* by Trotaconventos to enchant Doña Endrina, and presumably other victims as well. She traces the role of a magic love potion, a wax effigy, a magic sieve, an enchanted ring and, possibly, a magical incantation in the process of enchantment in the latter episode; what does not appear in the *Libro* is the piece of clothing obtained from the victim, as in the girdle or *cordón* procured from Melibea. Precisely because the episode of enchantment does not feature in the *Pamphilus*, the common source of the two works, this could indicate a direct link between them, although the *Libro* episode only suggests in passing the *philocaptio* spell that *Celestina* will develop in such explicit detail. This contrast also shows that while Trotaconventos was a mere *hechicera*, 'sorceress', Celestina was a *bruja* or witch (as Severin showed in her 1995 study).

The fourth and final section of the volume, 'Theoretical Approaches', comprises Laurence de Looze's 'Text, Author, Reader, Reception: The Reflections of Theory and the *Libro de Buen Amor*', Elizabeth Drayson's 'Chaotics, Complexity and the *Libro de Buen Amor*', and Louise O. Vasvári's 'The Novelness of the *Libro de Buen Amor*'. De Looze raises what is perhaps the greatest challenge to *Libro* scholarship to date: to reflect theoretically on the still unresolved questions of interpretation, precisely to help us to clarify the nature of these critical issues. He begins from the premise that theoretical presuppositions had always had an implicit hold on critical reception. He notes that what was lacking was a failure of synthesis as well as a recognition that a different theoretical approach to any given question might have led to a different set of results, or, as he succinctly puts it, 'change the theory and you will change the text: it is as simple as that'. Juan Ruiz himself has stated much the same idea in his famous 'bien o mal, qual puntares, tal diré ciertamente' (1992: st. 69–70 at 70b), or, as he puts it in proverb form at the conclusion of the debate between the Greek and the Roman: 'non ha mala palabra si non es a mal tenida' (64b). De Looze examines the potential contributions of a number of newer theoretical approaches such as that of the New Philology, and of theoretical contributions of John Dagenais (1994, 1997–98), and, more importantly, of new ways of asking interrelated questions about the *Libro* – such as 'what is / are the text/s of the *Libro*?, what is the range of meanings that it can have? what is the role of the receptors of the text?' – where the aim is not to resolve these issues but to look at the new theoretical assumptions that underpin them.

De Looze next reviews issues of the authorial and narratorial voice, which could have much to contribute to the elucidation of the slippages and overlaps between narrator, protagonist, and implied author in the *Libro*. In the study of literary influences, too, the question needs to be rephrased: perhaps instead of conscious imitation there may be intertextual relations and even what Gérard Genette (1982) calls a manifest or hidden *transtextualité* between a work and a whole range of its predecessors. With such new approaches criticism can be freed from having to identify a historical Juan Ruiz and yet can still reconstruct, as Lawrance has shown, the world of clerical discourses in which he would have been active. Similarly, there would not be a need to seek organic unity in the work if it is seen as a kind of precursor to *Pantagruel* or *Don Quijote*, which seeks to challenge the horizon of expectations of its audience, thus also bridging the gap between author and reader, and from creation to reception. In the latter context de Looze discusses the active role that readers take in filling the gaps left in a text, citing theoretical work by Wolfgang Iser (1974, 1978) and Stanley Fish (1980) which has been applied to the *Libro* only by Seidenspinner-Núñez (1988–89, 1990), an approach that is complemented by Peter J. Rabinowitz's (1977) and Umberto Eco's (1979) very different treatment of the role of the reader in constructing the meaning of a work. Although many of the theoretical works cited by de Looze date from the seventies, until quite recently relatively few scholars of the *Libro* have applied theoretically diverse approaches; but such approaches are providing new impetus for the next generation of graduate students.

Elizabeth Drayson's 'Chaotics, Complexity and the *Libro de Buen Amor*' is the theoretically most unusual piece in the collection in that she attempts to offer fresh critical insights on the work by reading it for the first time through chaos theory. While chaos theory belongs to scientific discourse, in the last decade it has been applied with some success, albeit in metaphorical fashion, to the humanities. Along with de Looze and Vasvári, Drayson is critical of the still dominant scholarly discourse in which the apparent complexity or disorder of the text is seen as a problem which must be solved, reined in by a unity imposed by centrist critical paradigms. Basing herself in part on the work of Harriet Hawkins (1995), Drayson proposes that not only is the amorphous *Libro* in a state of what chaos theorists call permanent instability in terms of divergences among extant manuscripts (compare Lawrance's and de Looze's discussions of *mouvance*), and in terms of the mutability of critical opinion, but also in relation to every other aspect of the text, such as lack of conventional plot structure or its thematic and moral heterodoxy. She proposes that reading a medieval text through chaos theory can set free aspects that have by necessity gone unnoticed in other critical interpretation. The method will allow the text to become intelligible, as through it discontinuity and irregularity are seen as a result of a complex dynamic principle where seemingly random phenomena are actually repeated with slight variations over time, a complex system which can produce discord and coherence at the same time.

Drayson discusses the placement of the *exempla*, of allegory, and of the Marian lyrics within the work to illustrate its asymmetrical structure. This is followed by a focus on the imagery of the poem, such as that of food, music, journeys, including, metaphorically, the roads to sexual experience and to death to show how the same chaotic pattern operates. The seemingly chaotic repetition of the key term *buen amor* with a continually evolving meaning is central in showing this repeated progression with variation, from which the essential ambiguity but ultimately also the deep associative unity of the text arises. *Buen amor* also stands for the powerfully chaotic nature of love, which according to the Archpriest is responsible for the seven deadly sins and for the ultimate chaos, murder. The chaos of sexual passion is exemplified by the various women, referred to by Drayson as 'strange attractors', in the Archpriest's amorous adventures. While for Drayson in the Doña Endrina episode the natural sexual order is restored by the presumed final marriage, in the Archpriest's adventures in the topsy-turvy sexual world of the *serranas* chaos once again sets in. She concludes that, in the figure of Juan Ruiz, the orderly role of the priest and the chaotic persona of the lover are in conflict and, thus, the narrator figure himself represents a force of chaos in the context of the fourteenth-century Church. Drayson's approach is likely to provide an essential metaphoric framework from which modern readers will be able to grasp the *Libro*'s form and meaning.

Like Drayson's study, the final article in the collection, Louise O. Vasvári's 'The Noveless of the *Libro de Buen Amor*', is concerned with offering a theoretical explanation for the heterogeneous nature of the text, but she attempts to do so by considering the work as an example of novelized discourse (or 'novelness'), placing the work within the context of the prehistory of the novel. In the first part of the study she offers a brief outline of received notions of such a prehistory, discussing such theorists of the novel as Ian Watt (1957) and György Lukács (1971), while in the second part she applies this model to several key episodes in the *Libro*. Theoretically, her approach is indebted to Bakhtin's oeuvre but in particular to his collection of essays in *The Dialogic Imagination* (1981), where he makes a claim for the 'absolute novelty of the novel', meaning not only that it is younger than all the other genres, but that it is a metagenre, swallowing all other established rule-governed genres, with its very essence being to renew itself each time it is re-created. Most importantly, the novel does not tolerate generic monologue, insisting on a dialogue between what is admitted in a given period as literature and other discourses. 'Novelness' also 'penetrates' privileged discourses, so that ultimately it works to parody official culture.

Vasvári begins the second part of her study with, once again, a re-examination of *buen amor*, the key term of the whole work, but now from the perspective of how it sheds light on the polyphonic nature of the work. Like Drayson she finds the meanings of the term both sense-shifting and recurring, but her emphasis is on the carnivalesque deflation of its higher meaning by being applied to the naming both of the bawd Trotaconventos and of the book itself, each promiscuously open to manipulation; *buen amor* appears also in a number of proverbs, perverted sexually with the connotation of 'prostitute', and is even put into the 'mouth' of the speaking *yo libro*, which Vasvári argues derives from an erotic riddle from oral tradition. She concludes that the erotic polysemy of *buen amor* is interwoven with the oral-textual dialogism of the book.

Within generic conventions the function of the episode of Don Carnal and Doña Cuaresma, which Vasvári discusses in her final section, serves to deflate high culture. The carnival episode, by turning the armies of Carnal and Cuaresma simultaneously into edible food, sexual organs, and military combatants, demolishes the high seriousness of the epic. It is the concept of fictionality in the later Middle Ages, fused with the dethroning voice of orality, that created the novelistic discourse of the *Libro de Buen Amor*, a work which de Looze, above, called the fourteenth-century *Pantagruel* or *Don Quijote*.

Seidenspinner-Núñez (1988–89: 263) proposed that the main difficulties the *Libro* poses to a modern reader are reconstructing what Walsh in his pathbreaking study (1979–80b) called the lost context of parody, and suspending modern prejudices about medieval literature. The articles collected in this volume, reflecting a diversity of theoretical approaches and multiple reading strategies, address both of these issues. One can, nevertheless, point to the absence of articles dealing with, for example, the interrelations of Arabic and Western literary traditions (touched on by Haywood and Taylor; see Menocal 1987, López-Baralt 1992, Rouhi 1999), more work on comparative approaches (note, in this context, the chasm between French and Spanish medieval studies, as discussed by de Looze) and, in general, more in-depth interdisciplinary and transdisciplinary approaches.

A prime example of interdisciplinary approaches would be the investigation of the complex interdependence of scriptural and visual traditions, to uncover what Michael Camille (1992: xxvii) called the intervisual and not just the intertextual meanings, where images and texts do not merely reflect meaning innocently but often subvert or alter their meaning. Whereas art history uses literary texts in recovering the meaning of pictures, in the other direction we are only beginning to use pictures, church portals, misericords, and so on, as a means of recovering the meaning of literary texts (Koch 1957, Holzinger 1980, Kolve 1984, Altman 1986, Freedberg 1989; for the *Libro*, Gerli 2001–02). Some other questions which need further study include the consideration of the *Libro de Buen Amor* as precursor of picaresque (Brownlee 1994), which might, in turn, also deal more in depth with its relation to the *māqāmat* and the Latin *comoedia*. Further attention should also be given to the frame structure in a more theoretical fashion, rather than with the more traditional emphasis on balance and unity (Picone 1988, Gittes 1990, Tomassini 1990, Seagar 1991). Perhaps most notable is the absence of any attention to issues of gender and sexual politics (see, in contrast, the articles collected in Blackmore & Hutcheson 1999, Lees 1994; also see Hansen 1992, Gaunt 1995, Cox 1997) or to socio-political readings.[13] Finally, the *Libro* needs to be studied further in the context of medieval erotic discourses and as part of the history of sexuality (Baldwin 1994, Bulloch & Brundage 1996, Haug 2000, Goytisolo 2001, Dangler 2002 and the 'Return to Queer Iberia' (Donnell and Hutcheson 2001) cluster of *La Corónica*).

Although most of the articles in this collection address in some respect the interface between the written and the oral, there remains much more excavation to be done of the lost, 'low' oral, vernacular layers of culture, not so much the study of popular culture itself, but rather its meeting with official culture and the mutual influence of these traditions and the border of their contacts, in a complex contradictory synthesis which Gurevich (1988: xvii; Ginzburg 1989) called 'dialogue-conflict of the two forms of consciousness'. These were inseparably linked in a single cultural universe, with reciprocal influences which travelled from low to high as well as from high to low: in this sense the *Libro de Buen Amor* is a paradigmatic medieval text.[14]

---

[13] It should be noted that sections on gender and on time and space were included in the original proposal for the collection but the need to avoid an over-long volume prevented their inclusion.

[14] The editors would like to record their thanks to those individuals who have read and commented on all, or parts, of the manuscript of this book; particularly, to Alan Deyermond, and two anonymous referees.

Part 1: CONTEXTS

Juan Ruiz and the *Libro de Buen Amor*: Contexts and Milieu

LOUISE M. HAYWOOD

The book known as the *Libro de Buen Amor* or *del Arcipreste* is one of the most diverse, unusual, and challenging texts any reader is likely to encounter. It has a loose, largely first-person, narrative thread which recounts the failed amorous adventures of the narrator who is apparently identified with the named author, Juan Ruiz, the Archpriest of Hita.[1] It is polymetric, with *cuaderna vía* (a monorhymed four-line alexandrine) narrative verse and lyric metres, and comprises a range of materials, representing the majority of medieval generic forms: a wide range of tales, *exemplum* (plural, *exempla*; see Taylor below) which demonstrate how to behave, some in the form of Aesopic tales (for example, those used by the Archpriest in his attack on Love, 181–422) and others are *fabliaux*, comic tales depicting low-estate characters (such as Pitas Payas, 474–89); didactic, sometimes burlesque, passages (see the section on penance, 1128–72, or on the Arms of the Christian, 1579–1605); a prose, possibly parodic (Chapman 1970), sermon on the *thema* (Biblical versicle which forms the topic), 'Intellectum tibi dabo [. . .]' ('I will give thee understanding, and instruct thee in the path that thou shouldst follow: my eyes shall be fixed upon thee', Psalm 31, v. 8; after stanza 10); an extended dream-vision sequence in which the narrator's identity shifts (180–909; see Deyermond below); a carnivalesque mock epic (the Battle between Flesh and Lent, 1067–1314; see Vasvári below); and finally, lyrics, ranging from secular bawdy ('Cruz cruzada', 115–22, and *serrana*, or wild-women, lyrics, 950–1042) to sincere religious ones (on the Joys, 20–43 and 1635–49, and Sorrows of the Virgin, 1049–58).[2]

The *Libro* poses many dilemmas to the modern reader and the purpose of this essay is to provide some orientation to those new to its study, although more detailed consideration of some of these issues will be provided by other contributors to this volume. I shall begin by addressing questions of authorship, dating, and the identification of Juan Ruiz. I shall move on to consider the implications of the use of a first-person narrator who is apparently identified with the author for the interpretation of the *Libro* and its relationship to the

---

[1] For convenience I refer to the poet as Juan Ruiz and the narrator as the Archpriest.
[2] All references are to stanzas and are from Blecua 1992.

European, Arabic, and Hispano-Hebraic literary traditions, and then examine questions of narrative unity. My discussion closes with a brief overview of the social, cultural, economic, and geographical milieux in which the author and his book can be situated.

Perhaps the first question that a modern reader poses concerns the identity of the author (see de Looze below) but to address that question the *Libro*'s date of composition must be established. Two of the extant manuscripts, Salamanca (*S*) and Toledo (*T*), contain different dates given at stanza 1634, according to the Julian Calendar, as 1381 and 1368, that is AD 1343 and 1330; a third manuscript, Gayoso (*G*) has a gap at this point but is otherwise thought to belong to the same tradition as *T* (see Lawrance below). The fact that *S* contains some material absent from the *GT* branch means that some commentators have argued that the two manuscript groups represented two versions of the *Libro*. G. B. Gybbon-Monypenny carried out a thorough comparison of the manuscripts which demonstrated that *S* differed from the *GT* branch in that it has rubrics and includes the prose prologue and opening prayer, and that the text shared by the two traditions did not differ substantially except in the change of dating and in some minor additions (1962: 210, 215, and 220). He notes that Juan Ruiz's 'revision, in fact, consisted of adding odd bits of material, totalling not more than 90 stanzas, and of writing an introduction in prose' (215). Alberto Blecua (1992: lxxxi–lxxxvi) counters this argument, stating that the *GT* branch suffered from suppressions rather than having been subject to authorial revision and expansion to produce the *S* version.[3] Although the one-version theory has gained considerable favour, it seems that the evidence as it stands could be interpreted as supporting a hypothesis of alteration through either revision or omission, accidental or deliberate, on the part of the poet or copyist.

As Ian Michael has noted, there is a possibility that the date(s) given in st. 1634 could be scribal (Gybbon-Monypenny 1988: 11n) and thus internal textual evidence should be sought concerning the date of composition. The most reliable evidence concerning dating is found in *S* only in an allusion to Archbishop Don Gil in the 'Cántica de los clérigos of Talavera' (1690–1709; hereafter 'Cántica'), often taken as referring to Don Gil de Albornoz, Archbishop of Toledo (1337–50), whose Synodal Constitution of 1342 dealt with the issue of clerical concubinage and to which the 'Cántica' seems to refer (Gybbon-Monypenny 1988: 11). However, it is problematic as most authorities accept that, even if the 'Cántica' is the work of Juan Ruiz, it was possibly composed separately from the majority of the *Libro* (Blecua 1992: xviii, Kelly 1984: 34–35, 87–88, and 113–15, Hernández 1988: 10), and is possibly not intended to be seen as part of its main structure.

Henry Ansgar Kelly (1984, 1985–86, 1988) argues, from internal references to canon law, that the *Libro* is more likely to date from the 1380s when *G* was

---

[3] The case for a single version had been made as early as 1913: see Blecua (1992: liv–lvi) for a discussion of supporters of this hypothesis.

copied; however, his evidence has been convincingly challenged by Blecua (1992: xviii–xxiii), Francisco J. Hernández (1984–85) and Peter Linehan (1986–87). José Luis Pérez López (2002) argues also from internal evidence for a *terminus a quo* of 1322 for the *GT* branch and of 1342 for *S*. His dating for *S* arises from the association of the 'Cántica' with Don Gil de Albornoz's Synodal Constitution, but note my observations above about the doubtful relationship between the *Libro* and the 'Cántica'. The date of *GT* derives, first, from the argument that the date of 1330 given in *T* is a copyist's date so logically the *Libro* must have been composed earlier and, second, from three internal references, two of which are linked to legislation passed by the 1322 National Council at Valladolid convoked by Fray Guillermo de Godín, Cardinal of Santa Sabina and papal legate. The first internal reference concerns the case of the Fox and the Wolf, judged by Don Ximio, in which the Fox's lawyer makes his case against the Wolf on the authority of a 'costituçión de legado' which applies the penalty of excommunication to married laymen who kept concubines:[4]

> Otrosí le opongo que es descomulgado
> de mayor descomunión por costituçión de legado,
> porque tiene varragana pública e es casado
> con su muger doña Loba [. . .]   (337)

Pérez López construes 'costituçión de legado' as referring to the constitution of a council called by a papal legate whereas it was previously taken as a degree of excommunication which can be imposed only by a papal legate (Gybbon-Monypenny 1988: 175, Zahareas and Pereira with McCallum 1990: 114, Blecua 1992: 89). He argues that stanza 337 is an allusion to the Valladolid Council of 1322 on account of the form of the citation and its reference to the penalty of excommunication for laymen, first mentioned in the Valladolid Constitutions (2002: 107). The Council also prohibited clerical use of the tabard, repeated only once, in 1324 (Pérez López 2002: 133–37). Juan Ruiz's reference to that garment, 'so el mal tabardo está el buen amor' (18), is consequently a humorous allusion to the prohibition, which intentionally echoes his earlier use of the proverb, 'so mala capa yaze buen bevedor' (17). A third piece of evidence in favour of the early *terminus a quo* concerns the possibility that the section on Penance (1131–61) is Juan Ruiz's ironic response to the constitution promulgated at the Synod of Toledo called by Archbishop Don Juan de Aragón in 1323. The Archbishop commented on the legal ignorance of some archpriests (compare with 'Escolar só mucho rrudo, nin maestro nin doctor [. . .]' (1135) – perhaps more ironic than a commonplace expression of modesty as it is contradicted by the extensive list of authorities at stanza 1152), he discussed the competence of clergymen of varying rank to deal with sins of different magnitude (the central topic of the Penance section), and used the same Biblical allusion – admittedly a commonplace – in a context similar to that used at stanza 1145cd, 'si el çiego

---

[4] Pérez López argues that this ruling is also alluded in the 'Cántica' (1694–95).

al çiego adiestra [. . .]'.[5] The present state of research suggests that readers should bear in mind the possibility of a later date but accept 1330–1343 as a reasonably accurate time-frame during which compilation of the whole *Libro* was completed, with some sections certainly, and possibly more probably, having been composed at an earlier date.

Although the author is not named in prefatory materials (see Lawrance below), the narrator gives his name as Juan Ruiz, Archpriest of Hita, and identifies himself as author, 'yo, Joan Royz, / Açipreste de Fita, d'ella [the Virgin] primero fiz / cantar de los sus gozos siete', and later, 'yo, Johan Ruiz, el sobredicho açipreste de Hita, / pero que mi coraçón de trobar non se quita [. . .]' (Blecua 1992: 19bcd and 575ab, respectively).[6] There are two broad conclusions that can be drawn from these statements: either that the author is indeed Juan Ruiz, Archpriest of Hita, as he claims, and is writing an autobiography or confessional work either intending his confession to be taken literally or projecting himself as a specific or universal character type; or that the author uses the name and title as a pseudonym, perhaps to disguise his own identity, to invoke a type of character in the audience's imagination, or humorously to attribute the adventures to an individual known to some, or all, of his implied audience.[7]

At first, attempts to identify a Juan Ruiz, Archpriest of Hita in the diocese of Toledo, as an historical figure yielded no results as it was an extraordinarily common name. Variations on it and its Latin form – Johannes Roderici – appeared in many documents as a signatory or as an individual mentioned. Yet not one of these was also identified as the Archpriest of Hita. The response to this was to assume that the name was invented by a scribe, or that the author was having a joke at the audience's expense (Michael in press) or deliberately adopting a pseudoepigraphon (Criado de Val 1960b: 152, Moffatt 1960: 41, Kelly 1985–86: 4). None the less, since the last third of the twentieth century, a series of quite likely contenders has been advanced. First, Emilio Sáez and José Trenchs (1973) argued that Ruiz (a contraction of Rodríguez) may be identified with Juan Rodríguez de Cisneros, active in the first half of the fourteenth century. Born in Alcalá la Real in 1295 or 1296, Rodríguez de Cisneros was the illegitimate son of a Christian noble held captive by the Muslims. He was taken to Castile in his early teens by his father, entered the Church, and had a well documented and successful career, serving Don Gil,

---

[5] The Archbishop does not complete the *sententiae* but Juan Ruiz does, '[. . .], o lo quier traer / en la fova dan entranbos e dentro van caer'.

[6] Its meaning at 845a, 'que yo mucho faría por mi amor de Fita', depends on whether *fita* is being used an adjective meaning an ardent or irresistible passion, or 'lover who puts me under pressure' (Blecua 1992: 845an), as a simple toponym (Aguado 1929: 393, Richardson 1930: 114) thereby merging the identities of Don Melón and the Archpriest (Gybbon-Monypenny 1988: 845an), or as a pun (1992: 845an, and Lawrance, below).

[7] Hernández (1984–85: 15–16) suggests that some of the names may have been intended to be recognized and that there is a 'deliberate fusion of fact and fiction'. Kelly proposes that the name and title adopted by the author may be a pseudoepigraphon, deliberately alluding to the earlier life of a well-known Juan Ruiz (1988: 4). On the historicity of names see Hook 1993, Pérez López in press, and Deyermond below.

Archbishop of Toledo. This background fits well, associating Juan with the right geographical area, providing an explanation for the treatment of religious matters and for the hypothesis (discussed below) that Arabic narrative frameworks may have influenced the external structure chosen for the *Libro* since a child raised in Muslim territory, even by Christian parents, might well have had Arabic narrative patterns deeply imprinted in his memory. However, despite the existence of many documents about the ecclesiastical career of Juan Rodríguez de Cisneros, in those extant he is never alluded to in the context of Hita nor as an archpriest. Consequently, he can not be placed as having exercised the post of Archpriest of Hita, and it seems that he held higher office, as canon, about the time the *Libro* was composed.

Second, José Filgueira Valverde (1973) identified the poet with Johan Rodrigues, choral master at the Cistercian convent of Las Huelgas near Burgos, and one of a number of Johannes Rodericis whose compositions appear in the Códice Musical de las Huelgas in the first half of the fourteenth century.[8] Again such an attribution is plausible as Juan Ruiz appears to have been familiar with Burgos (Filgueira Valverde 1973: 370) and, although the manuscripts of the *Libro* contain no musical notation, he was obviously interested in music, using the metaphor of book as instrument (69–70) and a wide range of musical and instrumental terms (for example, 1513–19; see Ferrán 1973, Perales de la Cal 1973, Lanoue 1980–81); however, there is no direct link between the choral master and Hita nor is he recorded as having held an archipresbyterate.

Finally, Hernández (1984–85, 1988) published the results of his researches in the archives of the Cathedral of Toledo in which he located a late copy of a document, originally dated c. 1330, to which a Juan Ruiz, Archpriest of Hita ('venerabilis Johannes Roderici archipresbter de Fita'; 1984–85: 10) acted as a signatory. Although it is possible that the document is a forgery, no good grounds for believing this have been established. The document consists of a ruling on a dispute between the Archbishop and the confraternity of parish priests of Madrid concerning their authority and legitimate responsibilities, including the right to excommunicate; this may have had financial ramifications for the parties involved. There does seem to be some overlap between the contents of the *Libro* and the issues dealt with in the ruling: for example, in the *Libro* there is a section on financial corruption within the church (490–514), another which treats the question of which categories of churchmen have authority to hear confession and make absolution (1128–72), and the 'Cántica' deals with the issue of clerical concubinage, punishable by excommunication (1690–1709; Hernández 1984–85: 16). The coincidence of thematic overlap, name and title, and appropriate geographical and historical context suggest that this Juan Ruiz is likely to be the one named in the *Libro*; less likely, but still possible, is that our poet at some time also held the post of choirmaster at Las Huelgas; least likely, that Juan Ruiz de Cisneros may have been Archpriest of Hita.

---

[8] Daniel G. Lanoue (1980–81: 85) cites Higini Anglés's 1931 attribution of this hypothesis to Ph. Aug. Becker.

If there were an individual named Juan Ruiz holding the office of Archpriest of Hita when the *Libro* was composed, as now seems likely, then it is probable that he was indeed the author; however, the question of a medieval author who claims also to be protagonist is not so straightforward since it has been established that the 'poetic "I" ' was often used not to allude to a specific and empiric self-referring individual but rather to 'a representative of mankind' or an Everyman (Spitzer 1946: 416). The alternative, that the author is deliberately assuming the identity of some other real person, to flatter or criticize, would need to be borne out by evidence from the *Libro* itself or from its milieu and, as far as I am aware, this has not been done. The question of authorship is one of particular interest as it relates to the *Libro*'s (pseudo-)autobiographical form, its generic affiliations, and the issue of sincerity.

There are two main approaches to the *Libro*'s form, generic status, and use of the first person. In the first place, there is the view that it is an anthology of diverse types of material (Lecoy 1938: 346–47, Castro 1948: 371–74, Menéndez Pidal 1957: 144–47, Sevilla Arroyo 1988: 179) which seems to be borne out by the claim that it offers an art of composition, 'conpóselo otrosí a dar algunos leçión e muestra de metrificar e rimar e de trobar' (Blecua 1992: 11; ll. 141–42), and the fact that the majority of individual segments or episodes in the *Libro* had independent Latin or vernacular analogues, and were very possibly composed at different times (Lecoy 1938: 359–60, Corominas 1967: 96). In the second place, critics have attempted to explain its structure by recourse to European or Oriental analogues whose structure is characterized by diversity, digression, and autobiography.

Américo Castro published in 1948 an important, and very controversial, book in which he argued that the Arabic heritage of Spanish, and by extension European, literature is insufficiently acknowledged. There can be little doubt that he is right on this point, which was subsequently taken up with considerable success by a fresh generation of scholars (such as María Rosa Menocal 1987 and Luce López-Baralt 1992); however, much of his argument derives from broad general assumptions, not always well founded, about the nature of Andalusian and medieval Castilian Christian culture.[9] He argues that the form and ambiguous tone of the *Libro* is alien to European literature, and derives from the Arabic tradition, in particular from the Cordovan Ibn Hazm's *The Dove's Neck's Ring*, written in 1022; a first-person prose and verse treatise on love and lovers, hetero- and homosexual, belonging to the genre of *maqāmāt*.[10]

---

[9] For example, that Arabic culture is more tolerant of sexual matters than Christian culture, which would not tolerate a churchman's discussion of sexual love, that there is no earlier tradition of Christian autobiographical material dealing frankly with sexual love, and that Christian culture lacks the inherent tension and ambiguity of Islamic culture.

[10] Castro 1952 presents a briefer and slightly modified case in which he clarifies the fact that the relationship between the *Libro* and *The Dove's Neck's Ring* is one of structure rather than content, and responds to Emilio García Gómez's critique (1st publ. 1952; see 1971: 77–82). For a useful, and very brief, summary of the nature of the debate see Dodds 1990: 2–3. I should like to thank my colleague Dr James Montgomery for sharing his thoughts on the putative relationship between the *Libro* and the *maqāmāt*, and for bibliographical guidance.

Usually translated as 'Assemblies' or *Séances*, the *maqāmāt* is an Arabic genre, originating in the East in the tenth century, which consists of a series of rhythmic-prose comic episodes, full of word-play, verbal virtuosity, and displays of learning, linked through the participation of a central narrator and a traveller, often a trickster.[11] The genre was taken up enthusiastically by Hispano-Jews, who – María Rosa Lida de Malkiel argues (1966: 36–37) – preferred a more straightforward autobiographical structure.[12] The *maqāmāt* was a learned, essentially didactic, form in both its Eastern and Western branches, and was disseminated through performances from authorized copies, and perhaps also from memory, largely to groups of scholars.[13]

Lida de Malkiel, following an 1894 study of Francisco Fernández y González, also argued for non-Christian precedents for the *Libro*'s form in her suggestion that it was influenced by the Hispano-Hebraic *maqāmāt* (1966: 29–43).[14] She adduces in particular the example of Joseph ben Meir ibn Sabarra's *Book of Delights* (second half of the twelfth century) which has a loosely autobiographical structure and whose narrator tells of his instruction by a giant who recounts short didactic tales; however, despite the parallels with the Don Amor episode, and a number of closer parallels than Castro is able to adduce with the *Dove's Neck-Ring* (36–39), the narrator does not relate any personal amorous adventures and thus the *Book of Delights* is quite different from the *Libro*.

To sum up, Lida de Malkiel and Castro both argue that the *maqāmāt*, either Arabic or Hispano-Hebraic, offered a model of narrative structure in which often unrelated episodes are linked through the participation of a single narrator and protagonist; whilst Castro also argues that the treatment of sexual desire as a natural part of life, the *Libro*'s inherent ambiguity, and preoccupation with interpretation are all Oriental features. As there are no extant medieval European vernacular or Latin *maqāmāt*, and there do not seem to have been medieval translations, these views raise two questions. First, are there analogues closer to the tradition from which Juan Ruiz gleaned the individual materials which comprise the *Libro*?; and, second, was the cultural milieu such that the author of the *Libro* could have become sufficiently acquainted with Arabic and Hispano-Jewish culture to borrow this structure but use it as a frame for material from the medieval Christian tradition? It is certainly true that post-Conquest, the kingdom of Toledo – in which Hita was located – was an environment in which there were significant, active populations of Jews and Muslims, and that the Archpriest shows knowledge of aspects of Arabic culture (for example, 1508–12, 1513–19; see Márquez Villanueva 1973 and Martínez Ruiz 1973); however, this raises the question – first put by Alan Deyermond (1980a: 218) and yet to be satisfactorily answered – as to why the Archpriest would use a structural model with no Latin or Romance

---

[11] On the *maqāmāt* see Heinrichs 1997, Brockelmann 1999, and Drory 2000.

[12] See Drory (2000: 199–205) for a different perspective on the Hispano-Hebraic *maqāmāt*.

[13] On similarities with a possible audience for the *Libro* see Lawrance in this volume.

[14] Drory (2000: 199 and 206) suggests that the Hispano-Hebraic *maqāmāt* may have developed under influence from Christian Spanish or Occitan narrative forms.

precedent when the majority of episodes in the *Libro* derive from these languages.[15] In fact, other Arabic structural models had been assimilated into the medieval European tradition even if this does not appear to have happened with the *maqāmāt* (see Taylor below).

Since Lida de Malkiel's and Castro's proposals, three main groups of analogues from the Western tradition have been proposed. First, G. B. Gybbon-Monypenny (1957 and 1973) identified a pan-European genre that he called the erotic pseudo-autobiography, which is composed of a mixed-form narrative in which lyric material is set in a narrative frame. The main aim of the narrative is to introduce the lyrics and explain the reasons for their composition; thus the frequent use in the *Libro* of transitional phrases to introduce lyrics, some of which do not appear, could be seen to relate it to this genre. However, in other examples the protagonist is portrayed sympathetically and so if the *Libro* bears any relationship to the genre it is likely to be as a parody (Gybbon-Monypenny 1957: 75–78); nevertheless, there is a lack of evidence connecting the *Libro* to other erotic pseudo-autobiographies (Gybbon-Monypenny 1957: 74).[16]

Second, the *Libro* has much in common with the elegiac *comoedia* or Latin versified tale, and, in particular, with pseudo-Ovidian narrative in the tradition of the *Amores*, *Ars amatoria*, and *Remedia amoris* (Lecoy 1938: 289–327, Rico 1967).[17] The *comoedia* rose to prominence in the twelfth century in humanistic centres of learning, under the influence of Ovid's works.[18] It was composed in the elegiac metre, a hexameter followed by a pentameter, probably as a learned exercise, and told of an amorous intrigue in a plain everyday style, with some elements of obscenity, and no tragic components (Raby 1934: 54–69 and 126–32). The *comoedia* often comprised dramatic dialogues or monologues but was not composed for representation as a play or mime. Its author would claim its intention was moral or didactic, although this was not always the case, and there were frequently satiric elements. Juan Ruiz was certainly familiar with this tradition, as he reworked one Latin elegiac *comoedia*, *Pamphilus de amore* (twelfth century), as the Doña Endrina / Don Melón episode, and he may well have known further examples.[19] In particular, a strong case has been made for

---

[15] Lida de Malkiel argues that the explanation is to enable the first-person narration of amorous adventures (1966: 40–41); however, as has been argued, the Latin *comoedia* and (pseudo-)Ovidian narrative permit this.

[16] Gybbon-Monypenny also discusses Ulrich von Lichtenstein's *Frauendienst* (1255), Dante's *Vita nuova* (c. 1295), Nicole de Margival's *Dit de la panthère* (1290–1320), Jean Froissart's *Espinette amoureuse* (c. 1362–63) and his *Prison amoureuse* (c. 1375), and Guillaume de Machaut's *Voir-Dit* (c. 1363–65) (1957: 70–75 and 1973).

[17] Most recently, see Burkard 1999 and Morros 2003; see Haywood and Vasvári, above, for further bibliography.

[18] A. B. Cobban (1975: 16–17) notes that a number of humanistic thinkers, including Roger of Hereford, Daniel of Morley, Roger of Chester, and Abelard of Bath, travelled in Spain during the twelfth century.

[19] See Rico 1967 and Morros 2003. Peter Dronke, in an unpublished paper, suggested other pseudo-Ovidian analogues: the *Cantica componans* (c. 1200), a *prosimetrum* with long

his knowledge of *De vetula* (second half of the thirteenth century), which often circulated in manuscripts with *Pamphilus* (Rico 1967: 312 and Morros 2003). Its overall organization resembles the *Libro*'s: *De vetula* has several prefatory pieces, a prose prologue which states that its purpose is to warn against love, and two short verse prologues, and its narrative deals with an unscrupulous go-between (Rico 1967: 312–24, Vasvári 1990a).

Third, St Augustine of Hippo's autobiographical *Confessions* may have played a role in the genesis of the autobiographical structure of the *Libro* by offering material for parody (Michalski 1973, Gerli 1981–82, Brownlee 1982). The Archpriest and Augustine both depict themselves as experiencing considerable conflict between sensuality and religious belief. With appropriate guidance from his mother, Monica, and the example of St Ambrose, Augustine overcomes his weak nature; the Archpriest – in contrast – is a sinner who receives inappropriate guidance (Don Amor and Doña Venus) and succumbs to his fallen nature. The dichotomy between sensuality and religious belief reflects the contemporary trend in medieval philosophy in which a heterodox Aristotelian, that is a materialist, naturalist, view of the world is defended (Paiewonsky Conde 1972, Michalski 1973, Zahareas 1978–79, Rico 1985, Cátedra 1989). Such a view holds that what gives us pleasure must be God's creation, and therefore good and purposeful. Underlying this line of argument is an appropriate insistence on Juan Ruiz's knowledge of school dialectic in the form of the *sic et non* (Aye and Nay); this was a method of reasoning through which contradictions are explored and resolved or explained, usually as functions of human error in the face of divine perfection (Zahareas 1978–79, Rico 1985, Nepaulsingh 1986: 125–60). Other aspects of Augustinian thinking may be found in the *Libro*. First, there is a concern with correct interpretation, which seems to reflect contemporary philosophical and legal debate concerning the pedagogical aptness of instruction and stimulus to correct erroneous thinking as opposed to the use of admonition. Second, in the *Libro* the Augustinian belief that disordered love, *cupiditas*, subverts the priorities of will and leads to the misdirection of appetite towards sin is substituted for the view that it is not so much desire but the flawed nature of human mind, particularly memory, that is an obstacle to salvation (Ullman 1967, Michalski 1973, Jenaro-MacLennan 1974–79, Gerli 1981–82 and 2002).

An important, though frequently overlooked, dimension of Juan Ruiz's art is his use of humour, and related devices such as verbal play, parody, irony, and satire. Its use, excluding obscenity, was a recognized sermon technique and it was used, even in a sacrilegious or obscene way, in religious contexts as a release from the awe inspired by the sacred (Green 1963). The parodic and satiric use of lines from the Latin Hours of Our Lady with sexual or obscene associations (374–87)

narrative verse-lines and short lyric ones; Boncompagno da Signa's *Rota Veneris* (c. 1200; on which see Cortijo Ocaña 2000), a humorous didactic work within a dream-vision frame; and, the Anglo-Norman *Donnei des amants* (1180–1200), which has material drawn from the Tristan legend interwoven with animal fables and the tale of a clerk wooing a young woman.

is an example of this. The parody comes in the displacment of the serious liturgical content of the Hours towards the sphere of the erotic (Zahareas 1964–65
and 1965: 94–96) whilst the satire is aimed at the wandering thought-processes
of the insincere celebrant (Bueno 1983: 68–69). Although the subject treated is
religious observance, that in itself is not the object of the humour (Deyermond
1970); moreover the linguistic play and manipulation of the parodied Hours
within the debate between the Archpriest and Don Amor permits Juan Ruiz to
exhibit his artistry to the full (Zahareas 1964–65 and 1965: 94–96).

In point of fact debates about Juan Ruiz's use of humour concentrate around precisely this question: can humour contribute to a serious message or does it provide
an opportunity to demonstrate artistic skill? Anthony N. Zahareas (1965) has
clearly demonstrated that humour and its techniques form a central aspect of Juan
Ruiz's style which allows him to display virtuosity and a serious commitment to
his art. Alan Deyermond's examination of Juan Ruiz's 'parodic vision of the world'
(1970: 78) reveals that parody, an aspect of humour, is used either to criticize or to
entertain, and that its effect is to multiply ambiguities. From this critical base,
Dayle Seidenspinner-Núñez (1981) developed the concept of 'parodic perspectivism' to refer to the multiple perspectives, ambiguity, and shifting planes of
meaning in the *Libro*. Parody was a facet of the rhetorical device of allegory,
which – in the Middle Ages – meant denoting one thing at the literal level of the
words (*littera*) and meaning another on the figurative level (*sens*). Allegory was a
prized ornament in learned and religious contexts, and was employed to convey
didactic or scriptural meaning through reading strategies based on seeking the
good through *caritas*, Christian love, and generosity of spirit. In secular and courtly
literature it was primarily a device through which the poet displayed his skill, and
from whose decipherment his reader derived pleasure. Finally, it was burlesqued
in a comic mode, associated with popular culture, through the refusal to recognize
a significance above the literal level, thereby undermining official courtly and
religious discourse (see Vasvári below, and 1983–84). Each of these modes –
religio-didactic, courtly, and comic – is present in the *Libro*'s parodic perspectivism.
The *Libro*, therefore, is deliberately ambiguous with multiple interpretations
dependent upon the inclination of the reader to *caritas* and didactic reading, to
aesthetic pleasure and literary recreation, or to *cupiditas* and religious truancy.

The European antecedents of the *Libro*, as outlined above, appear to provide
everything needed to explain its autobiographical form. It seems clear that, as
Peter Dronke suggests in his unpublished paper, Juan Ruiz was aware of experi-
ments in mixed form and, in particular, with Latin versified tales, amongst which
feature *Pamphilus* and *De vetula*. From (pseudo-)Ovid and the *comoedia* he drew
the use of a unifying first-person narrator, the mixed narrative and lyrical form,
the use of amorous adventures, satiric elements and, consequently, the tension
between didacticism and entertainment, which may also be linked to Augustinian
attitudes to preaching and teaching (Gerli 1981–82). In addition, Juan Ruiz may
have been aware of the erotic pseudo-autobiography, whose aim was to display
the author's lyrical compositions. At the back of his mind may also have lain the
structure and content of Augustine's *Confessions* in which the tension between

religious belief and the desires of the flesh is dramatized. He drew these elements together as a broad framework in which to organize his material, including pre-composed set pieces. These conclusions are based on the best evidence available to me and must remain tentative until such time as a full study of the Arabic and, more especially, the Hispano-Hebraic *maqāmāt* has been carried out and is available to scholars working in the Western tradition. Indeed the research surveyed here points to the urgent necessity of a comparative study of mixed-form genres in Latin, the Romance vernacular, and Semitic languages.

The issue of the thematic unity of the materials brought together under the largely autobiographical narrative has proven a source of continual debate but ought, I believe, to be seen as distinct from that of form, even if the two are often linked to genre.[20] Marcelino Menéndez y Pelayo (1923: III, xxi–lxxii) suggested that the autobiographical frame links various strands: a series of moral digressions (for example, 490–514, 1528–75, 1579–1605, 1606–17), a gloss on Ovid's *Ars amatoria* in the debate with Don Amor (423–575), the reworking of the *Pamphilus* (576–891), allegorical episodes (1067–1127, 1210–65, 1266–1301), a selection of *exempla*, and juglaresque elements of extreme contrast (115–27, 1046–66, 1650–66, 1661–67, 1668–84, 1685–89, 1710–28).[21] In 1938 Félix Lecoy re-examined the *Libro* and succeeded in producing a more unitary picture of its thematic structure as being a bipartite art of loving: its first part consists primarily of the reworking of the *Pamphilus* as the Don Melón / Doña Endrina episode and its second of the Battle between Lent and Flesh. The narrator acts as a connecting thread throughout whilst the second part offers a kind of liturgical cycle on love, and each part has satellite episodes. María Rosa Lida de Malkiel, recognizing that Lecoy himself warns against the dangers of such a scheme, nonetheless rejects his analysis outright as being based on the assumption of psychological development within the narrative (1984: 28–29).

Despite this rebuttal, Roger M. Walker (1966) and Oliver T. Myers (1972) published important analyses following up Lecoy's work which support the view that the first part of the *Libro* can be read as an apprenticeship of love which moves through three failed affairs, to instruction from Don Amor and Doña Venus, and culminates in the successful seduction of Doña Endrina. Myers argues that the grouping of principal episodes in each part is broadly symmetrical and that the episode on the adventures in the Sierra (950–1042; hereafter the *serrana* section) is a central one around which the work is articulated: the work begins (1–371) and ends (1508–1634) with a series of materials, including prayers to the Virgin (20–43 and 1635–48; also see Lida de Malkiel 1966: 61–62), two named male go-betweens (Ferrand Garçía and Don Furón, 105–20 and 1618–25), and a concern with interpretation (14–18, 44–69, and 1631–32) and with brevity (297d, 421d, 422cd, 574a and 1606a). The seduction of Doña

---

[20] On the dangers of attempts to classify medieval Castilian literature generically, see Michael 1985–86 and Deyermond's response 1994, and on the *Libro*, Michael 1985–86: 516–18 and Deyermond 1994: 20–21 and 33–34, and 1980b: 114–16.

[21] I include satire with moral digressions but he treats them as separate categories.

Endrina is a triumph of love represented allegorically in the Carnal / Cuaresma section (1067–1314), and the debate with Don Amor (181–575) reflects the seduction of Doña Garoça (1332–1507).[22] Both Walker and Myers observe that there is a preoccupation with time in the second part of the *Libro*, each arguing that this reflects the preoccupations of an older man, whilst Walker adds that there is an increasing recognition of the power of death, although this is somewhat contradicted by the fact that death is mentioned around seventy times in the first part (Nepaulsingh 1986: 126–27), and Gybbon-Monypenny posits instead that 'the main plot or theme [. . .] is surely the protagonist's pursuit of the opposite sex by means of a go-between' (1962: 217).[23]

Myers envisages this structural movement as a rising and falling, 'tumescence and detumescence' (1972: 83), which he illustrates graphically (84) as the outline of a rather rugged mountain. Colbert I. Nepaulsingh correctly observes that the falling-away movement seems contradicted by the repetition of songs on the Joys or *Gozos* of the Virgin, with a seemingly upwards movement, at the end of the *Libro* (1986: 128). In Nepaulsingh's view, a second 'minor but unfortunately fatal flaw' is that Myers includes 'material that does not seem to fit the serrana episodes' as part of the central section (128). However, a number of critics have made the case for considering the *serrana* episodes and the following section (the Offering to the Virgin at Santa María del Vado, 1043–66) as a unit consisting of a contrasting pair, in line with the juxtaposition of contraries in *sic et non*. Myers himself argued that the Passion poems were 'a penitent epilogue' (1972: 80n) to the *serranas* and followed Lecoy in noting a continuity in the religious season; whereas Steven D. Kirby (1986: 161–62) emphasized a causal relationship between the two sections in which the preceding sins lead to the need to be cleansed prior to Lent; a tension which is replayed in the carnivalesque battle between Carnal and Cuaresma.[24] I have suggested that further contrasting parallels include the types of women and the varieties of love portrayed, and the purpose of journeys (Haywood 2000c: 943–44). If the poems of the Offering section are read as prayer offerings to the Virgin as their context:

> [. . .] ay un logar onrado,
> muy santo e muy devoto: Santa María del Vado;
> fui tener ý vigilia, como es acostunbrado;
> a onra de la Virgen ofreçíle este ditado   (1044)

---

[22] Luis Arturo Castellanos (1973) offers a similar set of parallel episodes to Myers but considers necessary some reordering of the contents of *S*. The lyrics after 1635 are usually taken as extraneous material: for example, see Gybbon-Monypenny 1962: 209–10.

[23] This count is based on the stanza listing at Nepaulsingh 1986: 127. A further problem with Walker's and Myers's approaches is their failure to take into account the function of humour and parody in the *Libro*. Walker 1970 redresses this balance to some extent; see also my discussion above, pp. 31–32.

[24] Gybbon-Monypenny (1962: 217) had already pointed out the chronological difficulties inherent in such an argument as the *serrana* section begins in March and precedes the struggle between Lent and Flesh, which it should logically follow.

and content, on the Seven Sorrows of the Virgin and her Compassion at Christ's suffering (Haywood 2000c), suggest then the lyrics do offer a central counterpoint to the *Gozos* (also see Morreale 1975b and 1983–84) with which the *Libro*'s external structure opens and closes, and which have thematic links to the principal concern of what constitutes good love.

Discussions of thematic unity hinge on three basic assumptions about the nature of the *Libro*, each of which has its detractors: first, that the *Libro* has a purposeful arrangement or *dispositio*; second, that *S* is the most faithful embodiment of that arrangement; and, third, that a reading or performance would be likely to be of the entire work, even if this were not carried out at one sitting. Florencio Sevilla Arroyo (1988) is amongst those who make the strongest case against the purposeful *dispositio* of the *Libro* in favour of the view that it is a miscellany.[25] He makes a robust attack on several aspects of Lecoy's argument. In the first place, he argues against the view that the first part of the *Libro* is an apprenticeship of love, as the lack of clear temporal markers undermines the notion of chronological linearity. Furthermore, several details of the *Libro* contradict the notion of an apprenticeship: the Archpriest claims always to have lived in accordance with Love (576) and therefore cannot have been won around only at the time of the debate with Don Amor; prior to receiving Don Amor's advice, the Archpriest had already used a go-between (Ferrand Garçía, 105–22); and, finally, the successful affair with Doña Endrina, which follows the advice, is an adventure of Don Melón and not the Archpriest. In the second place, Sevilla Arroyo argues that the temporal markers in the second half are too vague to consider it as a liturgical cycle of love. However, the lack of clear linearity does not contradict the view that the *Libro* comprises a series of episodes, some of earlier composition, onto which a degree of unity has been imposed through purposeful organization. Indeed, his point about the earlier use of a go-between depends on reading the love affairs in a linear fashion. It could also be argued that the Archpriest's failures, prior to his education at the hands of Don Amor and Doña Venus, were due to his inappropriate selection of go-between and beloved: compare Cruz and Ferrand Garçía, Don Amor's descriptions (428–50) of the ideals, and those later chosen by the Archpriest (on Trotaconventos, 696–700, and on Endrina, 581–84 and 653). Finally, as Alan Deyermond argues (below) Don Melón can be seen as a dream displacement of the Archpriest himself, and, even if this reading were not to be accepted, the shift in the identity of the protagonist is in line with the malleability of the 'poetic "I"' (Spitzer 1946).

Sevilla Arroyo is right, however, to argue that the unity is apparent only at some remove from the individual episodes of the work. Actually, although their arguments are framed in relation to different textual witnesses, James F. Burke (1981–82) and Richard P. Kinkade (1973), with regards to *S*, and Deyermond (1974), to two partial textual witnesses, have all pointed out the affinity of the *Libro*'s materials with preaching manuals, which suggests the possibility of private

---

[25] See Severin 1994 on the terminological problems of using the noun *cancionero*, employed by Sevilla Arroyo.

reading and public performance. John K. Walsh (1979–80a), in the abstract of an unpublished paper, suggested that if the *Libro* were regarded as a series of episodes composed for performance then many of its ambiguities would be resolved. Similarly Nicholas Round, in an unpublished paper (discussed by Lawrance below), has argued that the *Libro* can be seen as comprising a series of performance nuclei with supplementary material to allow variation in the light of differences in the audience to which it is being performed. This hypothesis also allows for the possibility of reading by a learned public and performance to both learned and non-learned audiences, and accounts for the marked tension between didacticism and entertainment. The existence of *S* in an academic context with organizing rubrics (Cátedra 1989: 44–45), and the fact that two of the fragmentary witnesses are very possibly intended for learned or clerical use (Deyermond 1974) would support the view that some members of the medieval public approached the *Libro* as a source of materials, either learned or for use in contexts like sermons. John Dagenais (1994) argues that medieval readers would not have shared modern notions of narrative unity and, instead, would have approached manuscripts piecemeal, choosing which sections to read closely, and ignoring or scan-reading others.

The poet-narrator of the *Libro* locates himself and his work geographically in the town of Hita, about 60 kilometres to the north-east of Madrid, historically and temporally in the Castile of Alfonso XI (1312–50); and by estate, as a member of the Spanish ecclesiastical establishment.[26] In the Middle Ages Hita, situated in the kingdom of Toledo (taken from the Muslims in 1085), was a major communication hub on the route north from Madrid and, like Toledo, had been an important focal point for Christians living under Muslim rule. Toledo had become the ecclesiastical and administrative seat of Castile, and had been an influential centre of learning and of the translation and dissemination of scientific and medical knowledge from Arabic, Hebrew, and Greek. The academic significance of Toledo led to the accumulation of Christian, Jewish, and Muslim scholars there.[27] Hita's first documented Jewish inhabitants had settled there around the time the *Libro* was written, and around 44% of all Jews living in the archdeaconries of Madrid and Guadalajara were resident in Hita and Guadalajara (Cantera Burgos 1973, Hernández 1988: 4–5). As a consequence Hita's community had strong Jewish and Islamic nuclei (Criado de Val 1973b: 453–54). Nonetheless Hita itself was well provided with churches, which very probably provided an above-average standard of basic education to its inhabitants, and it is likely that the Archpriest of Hita would have enjoyed a benefice at the larger of the parish churches, Santa María (Gonzálvez Ruiz in press).

The early fourteenth century was a period of considerable strife amongst the high nobility, particularly during the minority of Alfonso XI, when various factions

---

[26] For a detailed account of the ecclesiastical milieu in Hita see Gonzálvez Ruiz in press.

[27] See González Palencia 1930 for detailed information about the Mozarabs (Christians accustomed to living under Muslim rule), Franks, Jews, and Muslims living in the Toledo area in the twelfth and thirteenth centuries.

struggled to gain control of royal power (Gautier-Dalché 1970–71: 249–50, Rodríguez-Puértolas 1976). After he reached his majority, however, Alfonso XI spent a great part of his political energies on attempting to control his nobles and on centralizing the administration of the kingdom in Toledo. The Reconquest had halted in the second half of the thirteenth century, possibly as it was a period of poor agricultural production and widespread poverty, with evidence of extensive famine in 1302. Indeed there were low levels of export in 1268, 1313, and 1315, and in 1322 there were also bans on the export of leather, rabbit-fur goods, and coins. The imposition of sumptuary laws controlling the consumption of wine in 1268 and 1338 suggests that there were poor harvests (Gautier-Dalché 1970–71: 242–46).

The programmes to populate lands newly conquered to the south were not as successful as had been expected, and this led to an increasing burden of feudal dues falling on the remaining peasants, which, in its turn, caused further rural depopulation and added to the expansion of urban settlements. Higher concentrations of inhabitants in urban centres then produced increased social conflict between the towns' oligarchies, knights, and townspeople (Gautier-Dalché 1970–71: 246–49), perhaps reflecting the struggle for control of urban power structures and the effect of rural depression on the urban rich, some of whom depended for their wealth on the produce of rural land holdings. Rural depopulation then combined with epidemics, even prior to the advent of the Black Death in 1348, and with adverse climatic conditions to fuel economic regression (Valdeón Baruque 1975 and 1977).

In the thirteenth century the Spanish church had undergone a number of difficulties, many of which were economic (Linehan 1971: 101–87 and 325–26). Throughout the period, the Papacy and the monarchy struggled to control the church (Linehan 1971: 185, 324–26, Hernández 1988: 2–3). There was in addition a major clash between the mendicant Franciscan and, particularly, Dominican friars, and the older orders (Linehan 1971: 316–17). The mendicant friars were itinerant, travelling from place to place to preach, often charismatically as their very livelihood depended on it, and then often hearing the confession of lay people. Their activities posed a severe threat economically as well as in terms of their ministries to parish priests whose indignation that the mendicant friars heard confession gave rise to considerable dispute as to whether the friars were entitled to do so (Hamilton 1970: 151). This conflict was undoubtedly exacerbated by the economic crisis. In addition, concubinage was common amongst parish priests. In the 1280s there were also documented cases of friars living in open association with nuns, and the reverberations of a particularly infamous case may have led to the prohibition of friars, in particular, visiting nunneries (Linehan 1997; see also Linehan 1971: 224–28, and Dillard 1984: 127, 131–32). The type of clerical misbehaviour portrayed in the *Libro* is not entirely fanciful: priests did take mistresses, stole, took bribes, and indulged in usury and simony. It may be on account of this background that the sections on simony (492–96 and 503–507) and who is entitled to hear confession (1144–72; Hamilton 1970) appear in the *Libro*; and satiric treatments of the misdeeds of the clergy may present an attempt to bring about a change.

The early thirteenth century had marked the first wave of university foundations, notably at Palencia (1208–12; active before this date as an episcopal school)
and Salamanca (1227–28), although there was still a tendency for the school curriculum to be taught in episcopal or urban schools as well as the universities
(Linehan 1971: 171, Faulhaber 1972: 22–35, Cobban 1975), which were usually
known as *Studia generales* or *universales*.[28] In Spain most foundations were
established by a regal charter, and defined in the great Alphonsine law code, the
Siete partidas (1256–65). A *studium* comprised a guild of masters and students,
usually from a wide geographical range, offered teaching in at least one of the
advanced subjects, granted its own degrees, which may have been internationally
recognized, and held juridical authority so that its members were exempt from
secular legal authorities, except in criminal cases. The ideal path of study was for
the student to follow – either in school or at the *studium* – the *trivium* (grammar,
rhetoric, and logic) and the *quadrivium* (arithmetic, geometry, astronomy, and
music), known together as the Seven Liberal Arts, perhaps also studying the two
laws, *utrum que ius*, canon and civil, before progressing to the more advanced
study of theology or medicine. An Archpriest was usually a graduate of the
Studium generale (Kelly 1984: 43) and held at least the lowest ecclesiastical rank,
that of *coronado* or tonsured priest (Hernández 1988: 5); however, in Spain the
position of Archpriest was an unpopular one amongst the graduate clergy, of
which numbers were low, probably because it required residence in the archipresbyterate, and so others may have been appointed, such as rural priests who were
willing to stay in the diocese rather than seeking well-endowed benefices or posts
elsewhere (Kelly 1984: 64–65, Martín Martín 1996: 394–98).[29]

The Archpriest of the area would have had overall responsibility for a group
of curacies and benefices, with probably around thirty-one in Hita (Kelly 1984:
49), some of which, at any one time, would have been vacant or had an absen-
tee incumbent and so would have been the Archpriest's responsibility. His work
would have been overseen by the archdeacon, responsible in his turn to the
Archbishop of Toledo.[30] As he would have been ordained as a priest and had the
care of souls, the Archpriest would have been over the age of twenty-five. He
was required to disseminate the rulings of councils and other ecclesiastical bodies, and *ad hoc* decisions or rulings, and to collect and compile accounts of tithes
gathered in the parishes. Acting as a representative of his Archdeacon, he may
also have been required to carry out pastoral visits to ensure the correct observance of the cult and to monitor the morality of parish priests and their flocks.
The Archpriest may well have had his own chancery, perhaps with one or more
notaries, issued or authorized documents and ecclesiastical sentences, and been
called upon to mediate in or issue rulings on local matters of canon law. Although
illiteracy was common amongst the lower clergy, and occasionally also tolerated

---

[28] For a very general introduction to this topic see Gabriel 1989.

[29] For an excellent introduction to church hierarchy as it pertains to Juan Ruiz see
Gonzálvez Ruiz in press.

[30] The following summary is largely based on Kelly 1984: 36–72 and Hernández 1988.

in the higher clergy (Linehan 1971: 235), the Archpriest would have needed to be literate in Latin and the vernacular, and to have a grounding in civil and canon law. Indeed if he were not a graduate he might have been able to acquire some of the necessary expertise through the exercise of office or to enjoy the service of suitably qualified assistants.

Despite Franscico J. Hernández's observation that, 'en cierto modo, el *Libro de buen amor* es precisamente una parodia de un tratado sobre la *visita* pastoral' (his italics; 1988: 17), there is little direct evidence of the duties of an Archpriest in the *Libro* other than in the doctrinal sections and in the frequent experiences of human, and clerical, weakness. This said, the range and breadth of knowledge revealed does suggest that Juan Ruiz had the appropriate intellectual formation to have held such a post. His use of Biblical quotations and allusion (Bueno 1983: 29–30, Martín Martín 1996: 396), Latin source texts, such as Ovid, *Pamphilus*, and *De vetula*, and school texts like Aristotle (Rico 1985, Martín Martín 1996: 396) indicate a through grounding in the *trivium*; however, G. B. Gybbon-Monypenny (1988: 31–32) argues that such references to authorities may have come indirectly from the classroom or pulpit rather than from direct knowledge, and this view has recently been reinforced by M. P. Cuartero Sancho's identification (in press) of Geremia da Montagnone's *Compendium moralium notabilium* (c. 1255–1321) as a source of materials cited in the prologue and elsewhere. Juan Ruiz's discussion of musical instruments suggests familiarity with that art (Ferrán 1973, Perales de la Cal 1973), and perhaps also knowledge of its theoretical dimension (Lanoue 1980–81). His descriptions of the Archpriest (1485–1507) and other characters (428–50, 1010–20) reveal knowledge of the overlapping disciplines of astronomy, astrology, physiognomy, and medicine (Kane 1930, Michalski 1964, Dunn 1970, López-Baralt 1992: 45–68, Martín Martín 1996: 396), thereby suggesting familiarity with the *quadrivium*. Juan Ruiz shows an excellent grasp of preaching technique (Ullman 1967, Chapman 1970, Kinkade 1973, Gerli 1981–82); knowledge of a wide range of materials appropriate for sermon use (Bueno 1983: 29–52, Cuartero Sancho in press); a sound command of the specialized lexis of the churchman (Bueno 1983: 46–48 and 116, Martín Martín 1996: 399); and a sufficient knowledge of theologians such as St Augustine of Hippo, St Thomas Aquinas, and Pope Gregory IX (Ullman 1967, Jenaro-MacLennan 1974–79, Gerli 1981–82, Brownlee 1982) to manipulate their thought, and of rhetoric and liturgy to write vernacular religious lyric based on Latin prayers (Morreale 1975b and 1983–84, Haywood 2000c) and to parody religious texts (Zahareas 1964–65). His legal knowledge also seems well founded and may indicate advanced legal study or practice (Bermejo Cabrero 1973, Eugenio y Díaz 1973, Murillo Rubiera 1973, Bueno 1983: 52, Kelly 1984: 113, Gámez Montalvo 1996). Taken individually his knowledge of these subject areas need not indicate school study but taken together Juan Ruiz reveals such an impressive breadth and range of knowledge of the contemporary school and university curricula that it seems wise to infer such study.

I have argued the *Libro de Buen Amor* was composed by 1330 to 1343, with some sections having been composed as set-pieces at an earlier date. The evidence as it stands does not provide conclusive proof that it was composed in two versions and the simpler one-version theory is to be preferred. The author is likely to have been the Juan Ruiz who was Archpriest of Hita, c. 1330, and, although he identifies himself with the protagonist, the adventures should not be taken as literally autobiographical. On the basis of current evidence, the main fonts of inspiration for the confessional (pseudo-)autobiographical mixed-form narrative are, like the sources for many of the individual episodes, most probably drawn from Latin and the European vernaculars, and not from Arabic or Hispano-Hebraic. Juan Ruiz's use of ambiguity, the juxtaposition of contraries and parodic perspectivism obfuscate any single unitary, particularly serious or didactic, interpretation of the *Libro*; but this does not rule out the possibility that such readings are feasible or that Juan Ruiz intended the *Libro* to be seen as having a loose, overarching structure. Nonetheless, the *Libro* was also likely to have been read or performed piecemeal as well as a unitary whole and to have enjoyed reading learned audiences and public, possibly popular, recitation. Juan Ruiz certainly received a grounding in the school syllabus and, most likely, pursued higher study of the university curriculum, most likely in the classroom but also possibly through personal study of teaching miscellanies and other source materials. He wrote at a time of economic, political and spiritual crisis, and in a culture which was marked by the participation of members of the three faiths. The *Libro de Buen Amor* is as unique and challenging as the culture that produced it.[31]

[31] I am indebted to Alan Deyermond, who first introduced me to the *Libro*, and whose approach to it has influenced my treatment of it here.

Libro de Buen Amor: From Script to Print

JEREMY LAWRANCE

Medieval literature and 'mouvance'

To pick up a printed copy of *Libro de Buen Amor* is to encounter one of the most familiar objects in our world; but a modern book differs radically from a manuscript. For H. J. Chaytor the invention of printing 'modified the psychological processes by which we use words for the communication of thought' (1966: 1), while Hans Robert Jauss saw the milieu of script and orality as a feature of medieval otherness which no hermeneutic effort can now fully recapture (1977: 16). This chapter aims to unpack these statements and their bearing on our aesthetic appreciation of Juan Ruiz's text.

The visual contrast between the neat typeset pages of a recent edition of the *Libro* and the hand-traced leaves of its medieval witnesses provides a useful point of departure.[1] The latter are the work of men who, with cramped fingers and aching backs, toiled for months laboriously scratching out their copy with goose-quill and home-made ink. As they puzzled over the exemplar, unscrambling its many crabbed abbreviations and mistakes, they made their own errors by skipping or misreading; sometimes they skipped deliberately, or added passages of their own. Every codex was a unique artefact, 'a leisurely accumulation of heterogeneous texts' (Ivy 1958: 59). Our comfortable illusion of a regular text consisting of prose prologue, 1554 stanzas of *cuaderna vía*, and 174 lyric strophes crumbles before the bewildering *mouvance* ('textual instability') of the medieval *Libros* – not so much a single book as a clamorous tangle of voices. All three MSS include other text besides *Buen Amor*, and marginal notes by later readers (Dagenais 1994: 153–70). The most nearly complete, *S*, lacks ten of its 114 leaves; *G* and *T* are more seriously damaged, but we know they were ninety stanzas shorter than *S*. Only 351 stanzas and parts of three others are transmitted by all three witnesses. The scribes used different spellings and dialects (Blecua 1992: lxxxvi–xci). Of half-lines shared by more than one witness, some 44% show differences of wording (Gybbon-Monypenny 1972: 233–34). Besides thousands of variants the tradition poses problems about the number and order

---

[1] Of the three main MSS, *G* and *S* are reproduced in facsimile in Ruiz 1974 and Ruiz 1975, while Ruiz 1977 has plates of the relevant leaves of *T*. Quotations of *Libro* are from Blecua 1992, references are to stanzas, and translations and emphasis are my own.

of stanzas, how many lyrics were included, how much of the original it preserves, how much of it is by Juan Ruiz, and whether it transmits a single text, various versions of the same text, or a collection of disparate pieces.[2]

These are some of the questions to be considered below. They give the impression that the tradition of *Libro de Buen Amor* is chaotic, but by medieval standards it is abnormally uniform.[3] Even so, we cannot have a definitive edition. Instability was integral to medieval transmission, so a printed text is always a compromise. This by no means affects only local details of wording. The problems begin on the cover, where editors must resolve such basic questions as what to call the text and its author. Manuscripts did not have covers or title-pages and usually lacked titles, authors' names, and other paratextual signals of content.[4] The *Libro* is typical: the first page in *S* (the relevant leaves are missing in *G* and *T*) bears a scribal prayer-formula (John 19: 19) followed immediately by a heading to the first passage of *cuaderna vía*, 'Esta es la oración qu'el açipreste fizo a Dios quando començó este libro suyo', describing the following stanzas as an opening prayer. In such cases we usually try to deduce a title from the common medieval paratext of the *explicit* (scribal subscription), but *T* has none, while *G* signs off curtly with the date copying finished, Thursday 22 July 1389; our only evidence, therefore, is *S*'s *explicit*, with the claim that it is the book of the Archpriest of Hita (Blecua 1992: 569n1728f and n1709d). The author calls his text a *librete de cantares* (12c; 'little book of songs') or *romanze* (14b; 'narrative poem', also 904a, 1634b), and medieval sources always spoke of the *libro, tratado, coplas,* or *romançe* ('book', 'treatise', 'stanzas', or 'narrative poem') of the Archpriest. The first modern editors entitled the text *Poesías del arcipreste de Hita* (Sánchez 1779–90: IV, 1) or *Libro de cantares de Joan Roiz* ('Book of songs of Joan Roiz', Janer 1864).

It was Ferdinand Wolf (1859: 135–36n1) who spotted that the lines ' "buen amor" dixe al libro e a ella [Trotaconventos] toda sazón' (933b) and 'Pues es de buen amor, enprestadlo de grado: / no·l neguedes su nonbre' (1630ab) imply the denomination *Buen Amor* or 'Good Love'. Ramón Menéndez Pidal added further textual references such as 'que pueda fazer libro de buen amor' (13c), and as wisdom lies in an ugly book, 'ansí so mal tabardo está el buen amor' (18d),

---

[2] On the number and order of stanzas see Corominas 1967: 112n169 and 232n581 (st. 581 repeats 169 – or the other way round), Corominas 1967: 186–88n436 for a proposal to reverse st. 444–51 / 436–42 (and, less likely, st. 517~502, ibid. 210–12n509), presuming pages were copied back-to-front (supported by Burkard 1995), Blecua edn 1983: 167 and Blecua 1992: 120n452 and 515n452 (*S* repeats st. 611 at 452). On the authenticity, integrity, and unity of the extant *Libro* see Section 2 below; and for a discussion of *mouvance* see de Looze, below.

[3] The percentage of 44% of variant lines is about 10% less than normal (see Gybbon-Monypenny 1988: 75; for another view see Drayson, below). For a typology of the variants see Dagenais 1994: 130–49.

[4] On paratexts – cover, preface, notes, epigraphs, and other signs added around and to the text – see Genette 1987 (titles, 54–97). For their absence in medieval MSS see Deyermond 1994; on the title of *Libro*, Domínguez 1997: 108–12.

and 'lo que buen amor dize, con razón te lo pruevo' (66d). Pidal concluded that the poet has consistently referred to the *Libro* by the same significant name, thus revealing the unity he saw in it; and that this name burlesqued the didactic bent of fourteenth-century literature (Menéndez Pidal 1941: 109–14). The latter point underlines the fact that giving a book – or bawd – a nickname is different from giving a title to a text, especially one in which onomastic word-play is raised to a principle of art.[5] Jauss justly remarks that the title of a printed edition turns a book into a 'work' or a unique product of its creator, involving distinctions which are alien to the medieval concept of literature, such as that those between unintentional or intentional, didactic or fictional, traditional or individual, imitative or creative (1977: 15). Despite the felicitous coinage of our modern title (Willis 1972: xix), there is some substance in the view of critics who argue for a return to neutral *Libro del Arcipreste* (Kellermann 1951, Prieto 1980).

Similar considerations affect the issue of the *Libro*'s authorship. Once again, the MSS give no paratextual guide. The name is announced within the poem, but outside the frame of the fiction: 'por ende, yo, Joan Royz, / Açipreste de Fita, d'ella [the Virgen] primero fiz / cantar de los sus gozos siete' (19bcd). First-person narration is common in medieval fiction, but it is rare for authors to name themselves in this way. The convention is to do so within the frame of the fiction, as Guillaume and Jean appear in Fausemblant's speech on authors about love in *Roman de la Rose* 10526–67 (Guillaume de Lorris and Jean de Meun 1974: 296–97), Beatrice calls Dante by name in *Purgatorio* xxx, 55 (Dante Alighieri 1979: ii, 516), or the Man of Law blames the wind-bag Chaucer for spoiling every tale with his doggerel in *Canterbury Tales* ii (b), 46–56 (Chaucer 1988: 87). This is Juan Ruiz's method elsewhere in the *Libro*, where 'Açipreste' appears six times in speeches by fictional characters as the appellation of the narrator-protagonist (423b, 930a, 946b, 1318c, 1345a, 1484b).[6] The problem is that the text refuses to allow us to construe author and narrator as the same person. In the Endrina episode 'I' mutates into the young man-about-town Melón de la Huerta or Ortiz (st. 727, 881), though Endrina calls him 'mi amor de Hita'

---

[5] As G. B. Gybbon-Monypenny argues, 'la práctica del *buen amor* es inseparable del trato íntimo con la alcahueta, y eso es por lo que el *Libro* se llama *de buen amor*' (Gybbon-Monypenny 1988: 301n932–33). For naming a book after a pander cf. Dante on Paolo and Francesca's *Lancelot*: 'Galeotto fu'l libro e chi lo scrisse' ('the book was a Galehaut [the pander in *Lancelot*], and so was its author', *Inferno* v, 137, in Dante Alighieri 1979: i, 83). *Libro de Buen Amor* means 'Good-Love's book' rather than 'book of, i.e. about, good love' (which would properly be *del buen amor*, Deyermond 1994: 34), though Lida de Malkiel 1959: 46–47 and Joset edn 1990: 396n932b–933b give a contrary view (see also Vasvári's discussion of the term, below). The best editors are well aware of this paratextual problem, as shown by Blecua's different title-pages in his editions 1983, 1992, and 2001 (see the flyleaf of the last edition).

[6] 'Johan Ruiz' occurs again in an out-of-fiction comment at 575a but this was added by the *S*-branch (n28 below). The nearest parallel is Gonzalo de Berceo, *Milagros de Nuestra Señora*, 'Yo maestro Gonçalvo de Verceo nomnado' (Gerli 1985: st. 2; 'I, master Gonzalo, called "of Berceo" '), but this is within a fiction.

(845a). The mountain-women call him *escudero*, 'squire', or *fidalgo*, 'hidalgo' (961c, 1031b); the bawd calls him Don Polo at the start of the Garoça episode (1331c), but tells the Andalusi woman he is from Alcalá (1510c).

From the modern point of view Juan Ruiz's authorial persona is thus curiously assymetric with the first-person narrator-protagonist. Significantly, medieval readers of the *Libro* overlooked the out-of-frame name, always attributing the book to its fictional hero. Some critics conclude that 'Juan Ruiz', a very common name, was a comic pseudonym for the folkloric figure of the priapic archpriest, chosen for word-play (e.g. *cruiziava*, 'I suffered c-ruiz-ifixion for her', 112d; *ruyes*, 'you rus-tle in her ear', 396a; 'she walloped me behind the ear, *fita* ('a hit / Hita')', 977d).[7] What is at stake, however, is not the superficial question of what the author was called, but the difference between medieval reading cultures and our own. Just as paratextual titles imply modern ideas of literary structure, so an author's name on the cover of a printed book (Genette 1987: 38–53) triggers conceptions about authorship that were alien to a society which received poetry orally and therefore construed first-person narratives in a different way. In Spitzer's view (1946) the identity which fuses together the *Libro*'s first-person personae is Everyman – the guise which Juan Ruiz assumes at the critical hinge where author turns into protagonist: 'E yo, como só omne como otro, pecador, / ove de las mugeres a las vezes grand amor' (76ab).

The problems of the title-page show how transmission impinges on aesthetics. To cite Jauss once more, these paratextual aspects of medieval otherness make clear the great extent to which our modern concept of literature is formed by the printed character of transmission, the singularity of authorship, and the autonomy of the text understood as a *work* (1977: 15). This is why Raymond S. Willis lamented the 'typographical mesmerism' of the *textus receptus* (1974: 216). The following sections strip the *Libro* down to its matrix in scribal and oral culture, and then reveal the stages of its tranformation into the alien medium of print.

Genesis: the author's original

Juan Ruiz asserts that he composed his book to a firm plan.[8] Yet his text presents a singular variety of content and tone, a structure which defies simple analysis, and an unparallelled combination of forms – narrative quatrains, lyric songs, and prose prologue. The *Libro* 'is heterogeneous, ambiguous, and

---

[7] For this suggestion see Moffatt 1960: 33, Morreale 1967: 254 and 1969–71: 158, Joset edn 1990: 90n19b. In fourteenth-century usage 'Juan Ruiz' was a forename (patronymic with enclitic first-name); surnames were constructed with *de*. Fernando Colón's MS perhaps had 'Jo. Ruiz' in its *incipit* (n67 below), but the name figures in no other medieval testimony.

[8] The prologue says: '*conpuse* este nuevo libro en que son escriptas algunas maneras [. . .] del loco amor del mundo', and '*conpóselo* otrosí a dar algunos leçión e muestra de metrificar' (1992: 9; ll. 96–98, 141–42). Intentionality is reiterated at start and finish (st. 12–18, 44–70, 1626–34), and the key term is repeated in 'fue *conpuesto* el romançe' (1634).

disproportionate; structurally it is very dishevelled' (Willis 1974: 215). Examples of dishevelment are the reduplicated invocation (st. 1–10, 11–24); the story of Don Furón stuck between the brevity topos of 1606ab ('Quiérovos abreviar la mi predicaçión') and the actual end in st. 1626; many contradictions and repetitions in the plot; and a jumble of endpieces.

All this calls into question what Juan Ruiz meant by *componer*. The etymological sense is 'put together, compile'; this, with Juan Ruiz's own reference to his poem as *librete de cantares* (12c), leads critics to argue that the book is a compilation – an anthology of poems composed over time and in various circumstances.[9] The flexible pseudo-autobiographical frame is purpose-built for taking in disparate pieces, as Juan Ruiz appears to hint:

> Qualquier omne que·l oya,   si bien trobar sopiere,
> más á ý [a] añadir   e emendar, si quisiere;
> ande de mano en mano   a quienquier que·l pidiere,
> como pella a las dueñas,   tómelo quien podiere.   (1629)

> (Whoever hears it, if he knows how to compose lyrics well, there is more to add and emend if he wishes; let it pass from hand to hand to anyone who asks for it, like a ball among ladies, catch as catch can.)

Menéndez Pidal took this stanza as proof of the open-ended minstrel character of Juan Ruiz's art (1957: 209, 278–79), while Colbert Nepaulsingh saw 1626cd ('faré / punto a mi librete, mas non lo çerraré'; 'I shall put a full-stop to my little book, but I shall not close it') as expressing 'a desire not to be confined to a single beginning and a single end', and commented that 'the aesthetic function of the introductory and terminatory material is to lend an air of indecisive formlessness to the entire work' (1977: 67–68).

However, the call to 'add and emend' parodies a modesty topos common in learned prose treatises which had nothing to do with minstrels.[10] By mocking aspiring improvers with the ludicrous image of their playing ball with it like women (compare Trotaconventos's invitation to the gullible Endrina to enter her house to play at ball and other foolish games, st. 861), Juan Ruiz keeps control over his book: all can read it or enjoy it, but only experts can handle it (Zahareas 1964: 210). The rejection of closure in st. 1626–29 points to indeterminacy not of structure, but of interpretation. There is no indecisiveness in the *Libro*; it bears a deliberate name throughout, is signed and dated (19, 1634), and has a carefully posted introduction and conclusion (11–75, 1626–34) and internal

---

[9] See Lecoy 1938: 327, 346–47, Menéndez Pidal 1957: 211, Corominas 1967: 52–54, Catalán 1970: 68–71, Gybbon-Monypenny 1988: 29–30, Blecua 1992: xxviii–xxxii. On the meaning of *componer* see the well-documented study in Schaffer 1989–90: 130–44.

[10] See Catalán 1970: 72–73, Gybbon-Monypenny 1988: 445n1629ab, Joset edn 1990: 680n1629; Gómez Moreno 1983–84. Cf. 1134d and 1135d 'señores, [. . .] so la vuestra emienda pongo el mi error'; 1507c 'emiéndela [aquesta endecha] todo omne e quien buen amor pecha'.

cross-references.[11] The poem's repetitions and digressions belong to an aesthetic that incorporates oral and oriental modes of story-telling. It is purposely decentred by nesting tales within a narrative frame characterized by a lack of causal plot, but it is far from formless, as shown by comparison with a similar but less purposeful structure in Don Juan Manuel's *Conde Lucanor*.[12]

'Composing', then, meant a deliberate process of structuring; this leaves the question of how Juan Ruiz's original was put together, and how far our *textus receptus* reflects it. Medieval authors composed drafts (*notas*, *dechados*) on loose sheets (*pliegos*), then passed them to an amanuensis to write out a rough copy (*minuta*) which was later corrected.[13] Juan Ruiz refers to *pliegos* in st. 1514 and *notas* in st. 1068, 1074, 1193 (see Blecua 1992: 266n1068cd and 537n1068cd), but Spanish testimonia on the *minuta* are rare. Enrique de Villena's *Traslación de la Eneida* (1427) talks of a 'first sketch [*çeda*] or exemplar in cursive script, on which the first correction was carried out, and from that *minuta* it was then glossed'; *minuta* is explained as any 'first original which is later to be recopied [. . .] in better script and form' (Villena 1994: II, 30 and 59; my translations).

At some point a professional scribe might make a fair copy (*registro*) as exemplar for multiple copies in book-hand.[14] Juan del Encina made the three steps leading up to publication into a metaphor of the Incarnation:

> dechado para sacar
> registro muy singular
> para dar santos trasuntos

> ('the draft [infant Jesus] from which to take a singular fair copy [adult Christ] to produce holy transcripts [saints]', *Natividad trobada*, ll.808–10, in Encina 1978–83: I, 34–65, at 62)

[11] Such cross-references typically state from the narratorial perspective, 'segund vos he dicho (180a), or variants; cf. st. 152–54, 937–38, 699–700, and note a cross-reference to the 'Cruz cruzada' section at 913a (cf. st. 117), to the section on the Mortal Sins at 1583 (cf. st. 217–371); and to 'Santa María, segund dicho he, / es comienço e fin del bien', at 1626ab (cf. st. 19). See Lecoy 1938: 348–51.

[12] On the oriental features of the book's narrative technique see Spitzer 1934; Lida de Malkiel 1959: 17–28 and 1966: 30–36; Blecua 1992: xxiv–xxxiii; and the discussion in this volume (Haywood). For the comparison with *Conde Lucanor* see Seidenspinner-Núñez 1988–89.

[13] On this process see Domínguez 1997: 71–72, who cites Chaucer's *Wordes unto Adam, His Owne Scriveyn* (Chaucer 1988: 650).

[14] Thus the *minuta* of Villena's *Eneida* was copied in a 'register or original, as the exemplar for the man who was to put it into fine script' (Villena 1994: II, 8, *glosas* 1–2). The winning poem at the Barcelona Consistori de Gaya Ciència was 'asentada en el registro del consistorio', entered in the register (*Arte de trovar*, Villena 1994: I, 358), but *pliegos* of verse did not usually get such treatment; Santillana said of a bound *volumen* of his poems, 'no son de tales materias ni asý bien formadas e artizadas que de memorable registro dignas parescan' ('their content and technique do not merit the memorial of a register', *Prohemio e carta*, in Santillana 1988: 438).

Human authors could be sure of no such perfect end-product. Don Juan Manuel kept the bound *registro* of his texts under lock and key at Peñafiel to guard against scribes putting 'una razón por otra, en guisa que muda la entención et toda la sentencia' ('one word for another and so changing the whole meaning', 1994: 5), while Chaucer ruefully bad adieu to his *Troilus*, 'So prey I God that non myswrite thee, / Ne thee mysmetre for defaute of tonge' (v, 1795–96, in Chaucer 1988: 584).

Juan Ruiz probably refers to a *registro* of his poem in the line, 'estas cantigas que vos aquí robré' ('these songs I have here notarized for you', 1319b); he surely does so when he gives the year in which the *romançe* was *conpuesto* (1634b).[15] What this original consisted of can be deduced from our witnesses, which all descend from a single archetype. It comprised the closed structure mentioned above (st. 11–1634), plus a symmetrical coda of two *gozos* (st. 1635–48).[16] Once the organization of this poem was complete Juan Ruiz added the prose prologue on its intention, style, and interpretation. The prologue's last line, 'comencé mi libro en el nonbre de Dios e tomé el verso primero del Salmo [. . .] *Ita Deus Pater, Deus Filius e cetera*' (1992: 11; Prol. ll. 150–54; 'I began my book in the name of God and took the first verse of the psalm [. . .], *So God the Father, God the Son, etc.*'), confirms that st. 11 was the intended start of the book; the tense of *comencé* proves that the prologue was written last.[17] There was no precedent in vernacular poetry for such a prologue, but paratextual introductions were common in prose texts and in medieval school-books of Latin poets, where they were called *accessus ad auctores*, doors to the classics.[18] Juan Ruiz's *accessus* shows that his *registro* was made for publication beyond his own circle. It also reflects a predictable *a posteriori* rationalization of – or ironic incongruity with – the book's complex message.[19]

[15] *Robrar*, 'confirm by signing, notarize for a register' (e.g. Alfonso X, Cuenca 19 July 1273 to *escrivanos públicos*, 'que fagan las cartas e las robren e las pongan en registro', 'to draw up, notarize, and put charters in a *registro*'). For *componer* 'compile in a *registro*' cf. st. 142 (*quadernos componer*, 'compile legal ordinances'), and the subscription at the foot of the *tabla* in *Cancionero de Baena*, fol. 3ᵛ 'Johan Alfonso de Baena lo conpuso con grand pena' ('compiled it with great pains'; Blecua edn 1983: 160n3).

[16] 'Fízle [the Virgen] *quatro* cantares' (1626c; I made *four* songs for her), i.e. two opening (st. 20–43) and two final *gozos* (Nepaulsingh 1977: 67, Blecua 1992 421n1626b).

[17] Catalán 1970: 65–66; Willis 1972: xxxii. Note the distinction between the act of creation (making) and the final closure of a finished text (compiling) in Prol. ll. 95–98 '*fiz* esta chica escriptura [. . .] e *conpuse* este nuevo libro' ('I made this little writing [. . .] and composed this new book').

[18] Dagenais 1986–87b, and for a parallel in *Libro del cavallero Zifar*, Catalán 1970: 72–73n50. The authenticity of *Libro*'s prologue has been doubted. External evidence is inconclusive (Salazar's MS had it but Colón's did not, n61 and n67 below; the count of missing leaves shows that *T* did not have it but *G* did, 56 and 57 and n52 below), but why forge the first person in alluding to authorial intention: 'bien juzgar la mi entención' and 'Dios sabe que la mi intención [. . .]' (1992: 10, Prol. ll. 127–28 and 130–31)? See the discussion in Blecua 1992: xxxiii–xl, especially xxxv.

[19] For example, the prologue's schematic antithesis between mad love of the world and pure love of God has no echo in the poem except st. 904 (Ruiz 1972: xxxii–xxxvi).

The main scheme of Juan Ruiz's original is thus clear, but the tradition presents us with one major and two minor puzzles. The major one is the fact that, in line with the opening promise to give 'lyrics, notes, rhymes, and poems' as lessons in *gaya sçiençia* or poetry (1992: 11; Prol. ll. 141–44) and the closing statement that the *romance* was compiled 'por mostrar a los sinples fablas e versos estraños' (1634d; to show the simple tales and strange verses), the poem announces a number of songs with expressions such as 'Enbiéle esta cantiga, que es deyuso puesta' (80a; 'I sent her this *cantiga* which is placed below'; cf. 996b). However, on at least eight occasions the MSS fail to include the promised lyrics; this is clearly the case in st. 80, 103–04, 122, 171, 915–18, 1021 (promises three *cantigas*, of which one is included), 1319 and 1507, and there are vaguer allusions to absent songs at st. 92, 947–49, 1325, 1497–98, 1508, and 1625, and perhaps 1513–14. Given that on eleven other occasions lyrics are included, there seems little doubt that Juan Ruiz's original contained many more lyrics than our *textus receptus*.[20] Menéndez Pidal thought the missing songs were censored (1957: 211–12 and 231–32), but a simpler hypothesis is that they were inserted in the *registro* on unbound sheets and accidentally went astray. The loss is serious because the lyrics were integral to the *Libro*. They were the kernel out of which the narrative was created and, as the preserved examples show, they also explained, commented on, or subverted the concomitant episodes.[21]

The second puzzle is that two witnesses contain extra material besides the *Libro* of st. 11–1648: i.e. an initial prayer and ninety-two rubrics in *S*, and a jumble of end-pieces in *G* and *S*. The latter comprise a fragment from a Christmas carol and two *cantares de escolares* in both witnesses (st. 1649, 1650–60); two *cantares de ciego* in *G* only (st. 1710–28); and, in *S* only, an *'Ave Maria'* glosado, a linked pair of acrostic and *capfinida* Marian hymns (restoring st. 1684 to the head of 1673, in accord with Vries 1985–86), *cántica de loores*, *cantar a la Ventura* (st. 1685–89), and *cuaderna vía* fragment *De los clérigos de Talavera* (st. 1690–1709). Some of this mess was due to misplaced leaves in the archetype, which constitutes *prima facie* evidence that at least some of the endpieces were in the original. Their status and that of the initial

---

[20] The surviving lyrics are: two *gozos* (one announced, st. 19), a *troba caçurra* (announced st. 114), four *serranillas* (announced st. 958, 986, 996, 1021); two carols on Mary and the Passion (announced st. 1045; a rubric wrongly indicates a third at st. 1049, cf. 1048), and two concluding *gozos* (announced st. 1626). Félix Lecoy suggested the missing lyrics were never included (1938: 351), an idea developed variously by Willis 1974: 224, Gybbon-Monypenny 1988: 20 (but cf. 125–26n80a), Joset edn 1990: 112n80a, Blecua 1992: lxxxiv–lxxxv, and Ly 1993: 385–98; but some passages make no sense without their missing lyric, e.g. st. 90–92, 945–49 (see Corominas 1967: 94–96n92b, Catalán 1970: 68–70n40 and n42), and st. 1507.

[21] On the lyrics' role in the genesis of the book see Catalán 1970: 68–71, Willis 1972: xl–xliv, Barra Jover 1990, Blecua 1992: xxvii–xxxiii (especially xxxi and n30). For general remarks on the function of lyrics in medieval narrative genres see the study and bibliography in Haywood 1997.

prayer remains uncertain; they may be strays from authentic *pliegos*, or in some cases the work of other hands.[22] *S*'s rubrics, on the other hand, are evidently a spurious later interpolation.[23]

The third and last anomaly about the book's composition is not strictly a puzzle, though it is a good example of *mouvance*. In st. 1634 *T* gives a different year of completion (era of Spain 1368) from *S* (ES 1381); this, and the fact that *S* has twelve passages missing in the α-branch (*T*, *G*, and *P*), led to the conjecture that the two branches represent two versions of the *Libro* written in AD 1330 and 1343 respectively.[24] That poets sometimes revised their originals is not in doubt (compare the well-attested cases of Petrarch and Gower), but in the *Libro*'s case the two-version theory is disproved by the fact that both branches, *S* and α, descend from a single archetype.[25] In fact, the α-branch represents not an earlier but a later stage of the tradition, which omitted all the passages in question except st. 575. Such *mouvance* is minimal by medieval standards; α's omissions could be accidental, though it is noteworthy that most involve lost lyrics (st. 104, 915, 918, 947, 1319), blasphemous and ribald content (st. 983–984, 1016–1020), or both (st. 90–92).[26]

The only things left unexplained are st. 575 and the different dates in st. 1634. The latter could be caused by misreading roman numerals after MCCCL as XVIII instead of XXXI (Chiarini 1964: xxix–xxx), but a more likely explanation is that the *G*-branch tampered with the text to show the date when 'this book', i.e. copy, was finished ('fue acabado este libro') instead of when 'the poem' was composed ('fue conpuesto el romançe'). Such interferences in dating are very

---

[22] A leaf or two were lost in the archetype at st. 7 / 8 and 1648 / 49 (*S* lacks another at 1684 / 85). The *cantares de escolar* and *de ciego* went together, the latter on a leaf lost in the *S*-branch; cf. 'Cantares fiz algunos de los que dizen los çiegos / e para escolares' (1514ab; 'I made songs of the kind recited by blind men and scholars'). The rest were never in the *G*-branch, suggesting the archetype was already more fragmentary when *G* was copied (Blecua 1992: lxvii–lxix, 429n1649 and 567n1649).

[23] See 60 and n63 below. Germán Orduna seeks to recuperate the authentic *Libro* from this farrago (1988: 1). In his view all the pieces except the rubrics are Juan Ruiz's, but collected by an editor; Gybbon-Monypenny is less sanguine (1962: 220). The oddly-titled *cántica* of the clerks of Talavera (1690–1709), adapted in the third person from an earlier Latin satire, is suspected of being apocryphal by several critics (see Joset 1988: 21–22, 69, Joset edn 1990: 714n1690–1709).

[24] Lecoy 1938: 38–41, Menéndez Pidal 1941: 116–17, Gybbon-Monypenny 1962, Willis 1963–64, 1972: xxiv–xl, Vàrvaro 1968–69, and Catalán 1970. The extra passages in *S* are: st. 75, 90–92, 104, 111–22, *c.* nine stanzas in st. 139–329 (deduced from the number of leaves missing in *G* and *T*), 575 (with a related variant in 574cd), 910–49, 983–84, 1007, 1016–20, 1318–31, and 1472. Some scholars extend the two-version theory to include the prologue, but none has ever succeeded in explaining why the poet should have added these passages, only three of which (st. 575, 910–49, 1318–31) contribute new matter.

[25] Lecoy 1938: 47–49, Arnold 1940: 167–68, Chiarini 1964: xxv–xxx, Macchi 1968, Mignani 1969, Vàrvaro 1969–70, Blecua 1992: lviii–lxxxv. Joan Corominas 1967: 20–25 attempts to defend the two-version theory by suggesting the changes were added in the margins of the archetype itself, but this is easily disproved.

[26] For a conjecture about the obscene content of the missing lyrics see Vasvári 1990a.

common in MSS.[27] The *S*-branch's interpolation of st. 575, on the other hand, an out-of-frame comment on Love's *ars amatoria* ('Yo, Johan Ruiz, el sobredicho açipreste de Hita [. . .] nunca fallé tal dueña como a vós Amor pinta' (575ac; 'I, Juan Ruiz, the aforesaid archpriest of Hita, [. . .] never found such a woman as Love has painted for you'), evidently copied from st. 19 ('aforesaid'), is betrayed by metrical and linguistic oddities.[28] It was perhaps inserted by a minstrel as an aid to performance (see 51–52 and n36 below).

To sum up, the original of Juan Ruiz's *Libro* was compiled in 1343; it consisted of prologue, st. 11–1648 (minus 452 and 575), plus seventy stanzas at the climax of the Endrina episode and up to two dozen lyrics that have been lost. Parts may have been written separately (the author calls the book an *armario* or 'book-case' of writings in the envoi at st. 1632; see Blecua 1992: 566n1632c), but the poem is configured as a *summa*, not a miscellany (Ly 1993: 381).

Text and performance

The *Libro* was written by a literate author skilled in reading books (st. 1151). The poem draws attention to its own physical existence as a written text with spatial directions (*deyuso puesto*, *deyuso escripto*, 'written below', st. 80, 171, 958, 996), visual references to reading (st. 1021 *'veyla e ríe e calla'*, *'see* it, laugh, and keep quiet'), and images of putting the story in writing ('puse en escripto', st. 1236), notarizing poems (st. 1319), 'closing' the book (st. 1626) or covering reams of paper with it (st. 1148, it would make the poem longer than two *Manuals*; st. 1269, the description would exceed all the paper in Toledo; st. 1514, his *cantares* would not fit on ten *pliegos* or quires), allusion to an illumination (*estoria*, st. 1571), and comparisons to a lesson-book or breviary (st. 1632).[29]

At the same time, however, the poem implies a hearing audience: 'los que lo oyeren puedan solaz tomar' (12d; 'those who hear it may be entertained' (st. 12). Often it evokes the listeners' physical presence, with direct references to the ears

[27] This explanation was spotted by Sánchez (1779–90: I, 102–03); see Schaffer 1989–90: 135, Joset edn 1990: 36–37 and n43, Blecua 1992: 424n1634b, Hempel 2000: 223–29. For *acabado* 'copied' cf. the *explicit* of *G* ('este libro fue acabado'); and note the variant *'this* book (i.e. copy)' versus *'the* poem'. To say a book was *'finished* because of the evils men and women do' is odd, whereas 'composed' makes good sense. However, the interpolator forgot to change *era* to *año*, the date intended being of course 1368, not 1330 (see 55–56 below).

[28] For the evidence that this stanza is not by Juan Ruiz see Cejador y Frauca 1913: I, 209–10n3, Lecoy 1938: 329 and 330n1, Moffatt 1960: 33, 41, Corominas 1967: 230n575d, Blecua 1992: lxxv–lxxvi.

[29] St. 1514 and 1632 are bookish allusions to *Libro de Alexandre* st. 2470 and 1957 (Blecua 1992: 566n1631b). On Juan Ruiz's self-consciously literary attitude to his book see Deyermond 1980a; on allusions to scribal features such as *accessus* and *explicit*, Dagenais 1986–87a, 1986–87b, and 1989; and on the *estoria*, Blecua 1992: 406n1571c.

or to hearing (162d, 892a, 949d, 1014d). This rapport can even be encoded in the fiction of an actual performance:

> Si queredes, señores, oír un buen solaz,
> escuchad el romanze, sosegadvos en paz. (14ab)

(If you wish, lords, to hear good entertainment, listen to the poem and keep quiet.)

> La obra de la tienda vos querría contar,
> avérsevos ha un poco a tardar la yantar;
> es una grand estoria, pero non de dexar,
> muchos dexan la çena por fermoso cantar. (1266)

(I should like to tell you about the tent's craftmanship, your dinner will have to be delayed a little; it is a long story but not to be missed, many people forgo supper for a beautiful song.)

Such gambits are typical of oral literature. They link with Juan Ruiz's pose as a minstrel ('fablévos en juglería'; 1633b, 'I have spoken in minstrelsy'), like his requests for the reward of a drink or a couple of prayers (1269, 1633).[30]

Whereas in written texts the author-reader relation takes place in absence and is abstract or self-effacing, in an orally-transmitted text the speaker's formal engagement with listeners is a speech-act implying presence. Juan Ruiz foregrounds this pragmatic role of the voice by signalling decisions to tell (for example, 'dezirt'é un juïzio' (128b); cf. 181, and 1608) or not to tell ('la qual a vós, dueñas, yo descobrir non oso'; 161b, 'to you, ladies, I dare not reveal this'; cf. 1020 and 1606). As speaker he adopts a stance of authority ('pruévotelo brevemente con esta semejança'; 141d; cf. 928 and 1579) or complicity ('Veemos cada día pasar esto de fecho'; 147a; cf. 923, and the first-person plurals in the ensuing sermon, st. 1580–1605). At the same time the listeners' role is dramatized ('si villanía he dicho, aya de vós perdón'; 891c; cf. 908, 1573, and 1579).

The *Libro* thus enacts a paradoxical combination of literacy and orality. Manuel Criado de Val and Eric W Naylor saw the *mouvance* of the MSS as the product of a long, random, and perhaps collective process of minstrel elaboration (1972: ix).[31] Others interpret the addresses to an audience as mere commonplaces, opining that Juan Ruiz 'thought of his book as a manuscript in the hands of an individual reader' (Gybbon-Monypenny 1965: 236). Neither view grasps the significance of the fact that references to aural and visual reception are often simultaneous.

---

[30] For further addresses to listeners cf. st. 45, 181, 892, 904, 1301, 1629; see Menéndez Pidal 1957: 202–14, 272–84, Joset 1988: 102–10.

[31] This idea calls on Léon Gautier's notion of minstrel MSS (1878–82: I, 226, 244), which is severely questioned in Taylor 1991; none of *Libro*'s witnesses conforms to the type (pocket format, cheap paper, roughly-written text), of which Menéndez Pidal 1957: 81, 296–97, 302 could adduce from Spain only *Elena y María* (c. 1280, paper shreds, 50 × 35 mm).

In st. 1627, for example, Juan Ruiz uses the doublet *leer e oír*, 'read and hear', which was common in both prose and poetry at that time (1992: 9; Prol. l. 99, st. 427; see Crosby 1936: 90–91, 98–100); it meant that, though writing was the medium of composition and transmission, reception usually took place through group reading. In passages such as the one just referred to at st. 1627, or 'E porque major sea de todos *escuchado*, / *fablarvos* he por trobas [. . .] nin tengades por chufa algo que en él *leo*' (15ab and 16b; 'So that all may *listen* better I will speak to you in lyrics, [. . .] do not take as a trivial jest anything I *read* in it' (st. 15–16), it is clear that *leer* must mean 'read out aloud'.[32]

Such oral transmission used to be explained as a reflex of illiteracy, but in all transactions of civil and religious life fourteenth-century Iberian society was already fully dependent on writing.[33] The determining factor was not practical, therefore, but cultural, involving attitudes about what vernacular literature was and what it was for. When people wanted entertainment they chose to get it, as Ruth Crosby says, 'by means of the ear rather than the eye' (1936: 88); that is, by buying not a book but the services of a *juglar*. In Toledo the latter might be one of the Andalusi women-singers whose services Juan Ruiz envisages in the transmission of his poetry, 'fiz muchas cantigas, de danças e troteras / para judías e moras [. . .] el cantar non sabedes, oýlo a cantaderas' (1513abd; 'I made many dance-songs and carols for Jewish and Moorish women; [. . .] if you do not know one of the tunes, hear it from singing-women').[34]

What might such a reading have been like? Jean Rychner calculates that recitals lasted two hours or 1000–2000 lines (1955: 49–50). At 6726 lines excluding prologue and endpieces, the *Libro* would require three to six sessions.[35] Performance began with an opening call for attention, often a religious invocation,

---

[32] Crosby 1936, Walker 1971 and 1974: 5–11, Joset 1988: 110–12, Gybbon-Monypenny 1988: 28–29. On *leer* 'read aloud' see Menéndez Pidal 1908–11: I, 15–17, Chaytor 1966: 12n1, 15–16, and Appendix B, 144–47, Blecua 1992: 421n1627a. The colophon added to *Cantar de Mio Cid*, 'el rromanz es leído, datnos del vino' ('the poem has been read, give us some wine', 3734) evidently refers to such reading aloud (Michael 1987: 311n3733–35).

[33] Lawrance 1985 is too timid. The Archpriest assumes a well-read audience (see n41 below); even his incompetent knave Furón can read, though badly (st. 1624).

[34] For *cantaderas* see st. 408–11, 470–71, 841; Menéndez Pidal 1957: 31–36, 41–42, and *passim*. Andalusi singers were popular in Juan Ruiz's milieu, to judge by such lines as st. 1516 'çitola e odreçillo non aman *çaguh llaco*', citole and bagpipe do not love *ṣaghīr ʿalaykum* (an Arabic tune, Corominas 1967: 566n1516c; or the blessing *ṣallā llāhu [ʿalayhi wa-sallam]*, Blecua 1992: 558n1516c); and st. 1229 'cab'él el alhoraví', beside it [the rebec] the *al-ʿuraybī* (a musician of the school of the ninth-century woman-singer ʿUrayb, Menéndez Pidal 1957: 48n2, Corominas 1967: 460n1229b, Blecua 1992: 543n1229b), or 'calbi garabí', the Arabic song *Qalbī bī qalbī* (known also to Gil Vicente, Salinas, and Cervantes, Cejador y Frauca 1913: II, 136n; García Gómez 1956).

[35] See Ruiz 1972: xliv–xlv, Michael 1987: 38n42. There are breaks with suitable concluding stanzas at st. 575 (2280 lines), st. 1066 (4350 lines), st. 1634 or 1648 (6622 or 6726 lines), and intermediary ones at st. 909 or 949 (3615 or 3776 lines), st. 1314 (5342 lines) and st. 1507 (6114 lines). There is, however, no suitable place for a break in the *Libro*'s first 564 stanzas (11–574).

and ended with 'techniques of withdrawal' such as benedictions or requests for payment (Crosby 1936: 108–10); attention was held by direct addresses to the audience and by references back and forward (ibid. 106–07). These techniques are encoded in the text of the *Libro*, as we have seen; we also have an external clue in *S*'s st. 575, which Alberto Blecua suggests was a minstrel interpolation intended to close a reading of the first part of the poem, its curious parenthesis 'though my heart does not cease from poetry' being an advertisement of future sessions (1992: lxxv–lxxvi).[36]

Was *Buen Amor* recited, chanted, or sung? Narratives were commonly read out from a MS, and this was doubtless the case with Juan Ruiz's *cuaderna vía*.[37] However, mentions of songs (*cantigas, cantares, chançonetas, trobas de trotar*), musical accompaniment (st. 1228–34, 1513–17), and acoustic metaphors such as the passage in which the book becomes an instrument to be fingered for a tune (st. 70) imply singing and playing. Menéndez Pidal deduced that recitative and song were combined in a kind of *chantefable* (1957: 211–12), a mixture borne out by the *Libro*'s own language ('fablarvos he por trobas e por cuento rimado', 'I shall speak to you in lyrics *and* well-scanned rhyme', st. 15). *Chantefable* is an inaccurate term – the mixed-form narrative with inset lyrics is better designated by the Old French term *dit* – but such blends of song and recitation are well attested. An example is *Libro de Apolonio*'s description (*c.* 1250) of the enslaved princess Tarsiana taking up as a *juglaresa* (st. 426–28; Monedero 1987: 226–27; spelling regularized):

> priso una vïola   buena e bien tenprada
> e sallió al mercado   violar por soldada.
>
> Començó unos viesos   e unos sones tales
> que trayén grant dulçor   e eran naturales;
> finchiénse de omnes   apriesa los portales,
> non les cabié en las plaças,   subiénse a los poyales.
>
> Quando con su vïola   ovo bien solazado,
> a sabor de los pueblos   ovo asaz cantado,
> tornóles a rezar   un romançe bien rimado
> de la su razón misma   por ó havía pasado.

[36] Joset thinks the stanza may have been an *explicit* of an originally separate *ars amatoria* (edn 1990: 286, apparatus *ad loc.*), but that does not explain its discordant linguistic forms and crude versification; see n28 above. For comparable break-formulae cf. *Cantar de Mio Cid* 1085 and 2276 ('Here begins the *geste* of My Cid' and 'The verses of this *cantar* here come to an end'; my translations; see Michael 1987: 36–38, and 55n65 for another possible performance note in the *Cid* MS).

[37] Evidence for use of written texts in performance is documentary (e.g. Menéndez Pidal 1957: 81 and n3, a French by-law of 1372 letting *jongleurs* keep 'their *book* or fiddle, if they have one') and textual (references to *cest escript* 'this script', Rychner 1955: 35; Crosby 1936: 94 and n4; the *Cid* colophon, n32 above). *Libro de Alexandre* st. 232 calls a good *joglar*-fiddler 'ome bien razonado que *sabía bien leer*', a well-storied man who knew how to read (see Menéndez Pidal 1957: 54).

(She took a good, well-tuned fiddle and went to market to play for pennies. She began with some verses and tunes that were sweet and full of modulations. The arcades soon filled with people; there was no room left in the squares, and they began to climb on the stone benches. When she had entertained them with her fiddle and *sung* to the crowd's satisfaction, she began to *recite* them a rhymed narrative poem of the story of her own experiences.)[38]

Similarly, Juan Ruiz's contemporary Don Juan Manuel advised his prince to listen to minstrels sing (*canten*) and play instruments before him, reciting (*diziendo*) epic poems and stories of chivalry.[39] *Buen Amor* was doubtless compiled with such mixed-form performance in mind. The lyrics may have been copied with verbal indications of the melody to be used, such as the mysterious line *Quando los lobos preso lo an a don Juan en el campo* ('When the wolves have caught Don Juan in the field') which precedes the *Gozos* or *Joys of Mary* at st. 20–32 in *G*, interpreted by Cejador as the first verse of a popular tune (Cejador y Frauca 1913: I, 17 n*), or they may have had musical notation (1992: 11; Prol. ll. 142–43 'trobas e *notas* e rimas e ditados', 'lyrics, notes, rhymes, and poems').[40]

In one respect, however, the scenario differed from Tarsiana's open-air recital. The listeners for whom Juan Ruiz wrote were no vulgar crowd of market-goers, but a select and educated group with cultured tastes in courtly and clerical literature.[41] Juan Ruiz variously addresses this audience as *mancebos* 'batchelors', *clérigos* 'clerks', *amigos* 'friends', and *señores* 'lords', but its tone was set by upper-class *dueñas* 'ladies', the hearers whose response is most often solicited (st. 114, 161, 422, 892, 904, 1490, 1573) and whose presence determined the ethos of the *Libro*:

> non fuyan d'ello las dueñas   nin los tengan por lixo,
> ca nunca los oyó dueña   que d'ellos mucho non rixo.

---

[38] Menéndez Pidal 1957: 293–95; cf. also *Libro de Apolonio* at 178–79, 489, 495, 502. Calling Tarsiana by the Arabic term *mallada* (i.e. *muwallada*, 'house-slave', 505a) perhaps points to a familiar association with Andalusi *cantaderas*.

[39] *Libro de los estados* I, 59, in Juan Manuel 1991: 177. By contrast, *Libro de miseria de omne* st. 5 says, 'I will read (*leer*) it to you quite plainly, because singing (*cantar*) is not required' (Connolly 1987: 121); see Menéndez Pidal 1957: 291–93, 297.

[40] Mario Barra Jover 1990 points to a MS of *Roman de Fauvel* with musically notated lyrics, but few *dits* survive with notation (sheet-music is even rarer) and the extent to which lyrics were sung is debated; the fact that *Libro*'s lyrics had tunes need not have precluded their being appreciated in spoken or even silent reading (see Haywood 1997, Gómez-Bravo 1999, and Haywood 2000d: 134–42). A further point is raised by the *serrana* lyric (1022–42), which is attributed in Argote de Molina's MS (n67 below) to Domingo Abad, a troubadour of c. 1250 – does this mean Juan Ruiz used well-known songs or tunes by other poets?

[41] See Walsh 1979–80b, Lawrance 1984, Gybbon-Monypenny 1988: 25–30, Joset 1988: 113–14 and Joset edn 1990: 41–44. Menéndez Pidal 1957: 291–95 envisages a popular public, but this is illusory; the text demands an extraordinary range of learned cultural literacies – liturgy, canon law, scholastic debate, Latin elegy, goliardic verse, epic, and troubadour lyric (Seidenspinner-Núñez 1990: 101–03, and Haywood, this volume).

A vós, dueñas señoras, por vuestra cortesía,
demándovos perdón, que sabed que non querría
aver saña de vós.   (947c–948)

(ladies should not flee from [these ribald songs] nor take them for filth,
for no lady ever heard them without much laughter; by your courtesy,
lady mistresses, I beg your pardon, be sure I would never wish to anger
you.)[42]

Blecua links this mixed urban circle, literate but impatient of the murky logic-chopping of schoolmen, to the poet's choice of the mock-Ovidian form, content, and style which he calls *doñeguil*, 'lady-like' (st. 65, cf. 169, 581; 1992: xliii and n62).

This is as far as we need go in reconstructing how the *Libro* was performed. Speculation on the histrionic role of mime, gesture, or music is, from a literary point of view, idle; the features of orality which bear on the *Libro*'s aesthetic coherence and social function do not reside in such externals but are immanent in the text. Jauss observes that in the triangle of author, work, and public, the last is no passive part, but itself a formative energy (1982: 19). The *Libro*, as we have seen, belongs to an age when orality and literacy went hand-in-hand, 'combining the powerful ever-moving narrative needed by listeners with minute local effects that suggest a reader pausing to think or turning pages back for private perusal' (Medcalf 1981: 15). Janet Coleman points out how this intermix of orality and literacy rendered the space between narrator and audience increasingly self-conscious, permitting the author to express individuality and shifting narrative away from the 'mythic impulse' and 'tyranny of the traditional' towards more empirical forms of mimesis such as biography and realism (1981: 167–70). In literary terms, however, *Buen Amor*'s 'apparently random juxtaposition of the concepts of writing, performance, reading, and hearing' is a textual strategy which, as Michael Rössner points out, implies an audience no less fictional than the implied author (1984: 114–15; my translation); Juan Ruiz's running commentary on his own performance invokes a dialogue with this ideal listener-reader, inviting us to input meaning and realize the text's inherent potential for different readings: 'Fizvos pequeño libro de testo, mas la glosa / non creo que es chica, ante es bien grand prosa' (1631ab; 'I have made

---

[42] On the importance of the female audience see Catalán 1970: 78–82. Menéndez Pidal 1957: 57 takes Berceo's *Vida de Santo Domingo* st. 318 as evidence that damsels listened to *joglares*, while Crosby 1936: 97 finds them acting as readers at court entertainments. The *dueñas* of the *Libro* enjoy written tokens of love (80, 171, 918) – Garoça is always reading (1397) – and the Archpriest follows Ovid's advice to court with poems (*Ars amatoria* II, 275–86; Lecoy 1938: 304); his *cantiga de salva* in st. 104 and *carta* in st. 1497–98 belong to the troubadour genre of *salutz*, songs for women to read (Rieger 1987), and his *alvalá* in st. 1510 is such a missive in Arabic (*al-barā'*, Oliver Asín 1956). The women reply in kind (e.g. st. 92), which is why Furón must be literate (n33 above); one learned lady ('dueña mucho letrada', st. 96) sends a composition based on Aesop.

you a little book of text, but the gloss I do not think is small, instead it is a good long exposition').[43]

The *Libro*'s oral transmission had important effects on its style. Juan Ruiz's language has many spoken features; his diction is concrete, direct, and objective, preferring graphic images to abstract synonyms. Stock phrases and repetition are constantly used; the ubiquitous proverbs, apophthegms, fables, and *exempla* connect with traditions of wisdom literature, the primeval oral genre.[44] At the syntactic level, asyndeton and co-ordination replace subordination; grammatical clauses map closely to end-stopped metrical units of half-line and stanza, giving the *cuaderna vía* its characteristic lolloping tempo, unfolding hemistich by hemistich at a gait ideal for aural reception. Literary texts like *Buen Amor* belong to a category distinct from orally-composed poetry, but the effect of these stylistic features is similar: both readers and listeners appreciate them as playing on familiar oral traditions. From our point of view they may seem naïve, artless, or vulgar; they are often watered down in modern readings, or dismissed as padding and cliché.[45]

I have already mentioned the last respect in which the *Libro*'s oral transmission impinged upon its form, namely structure. Félix Lecoy confessed himself perplexed; there is a kind of story-line in the autobiographical frame, but it seems bolted on from outside the work, letting the poem stutter aimlessly forward while the master idea remains invisible; 'one is almost tempted to call it symbolic, except that the word too violently contradicts the poem's powerfully concrete character' (Lecoy 1938: 352–60, at 359–60; my translation). Leo Spitzer, in a ground-breaking review (1939), pointed out the anachronism of disassembling the work in this centrifugal, inorganic way, and suggested the need to approach the poem's aesthetic on its own terms. Steps were taken in this direction by studies of the structure as an open arabesque based on oriental models rather than as a closed form consisting of a central action and dynamic story-line (Castro 1954: 378–442, at 379; Lida de Malkiel 1959: 19). There are oriental elements in the use of a frame structure with embedded tales (as in contemporary texts by Don Juan Manuel), but the most important features of the *Libro*'s form belong to the

---

[43] For *Wirkung* and *Rezeption* (text-immanent effect and ideal response) in the *Libro* see Gumbrecht 1973, Rössner 1984, Seidenspinner-Núñez 1990–91, and de Looze, below. Gybbon-Monypenny's pages on ambiguity as system (1988: 61–73) come to similar conclusions by another route.

[44] Lida de Malkiel 1959: 33–34 and Taylor, below. Crosby (1936: 102) sees repetition of words, phrases, and situations as the most striking difference between medieval and modern poetry; John K. Walsh 1979–80b: 63 and n3, 83–84 and n47 calls it a 'formulaic grammar', a suggestive metaphor even if the term *formula* is misleading for texts composed in writing.

[45] Chaytor 1966: 48–82, 142–44. For 'watering down' see Bihler 1955–56: 375–76 (e.g. on the flaccid rendering of triple *sacar* in st. 1 in Brey Mariño 1966), and 66–67 and nn75–76 below. On oral syntax and the problems it poses for modern editors see Fleischman 1990; it embraces not just parataxis, but such features as the omission of articles and pronouns, anacoluthic variation of tenses, and special types of conjunction.

shared heritage of medieval orality. As Jauss points out, the problem of unity is 'an ancient crux in Romance philology' caused by applying the 'ruinous critique' of readerly notions of structure to a poetry which was originally performed in instalments – conditions which produced 'an ever-expanding cyclical move-ment' which seems to us incidental, but which was 'received by the medieval public as a succession of sequels which, in spite of constant repetition, could always develop a new element of tension'.[46] The best studies on the resulting 'flux of fancy, discontinuous, but organically unified', appear in Willis's work on the discredited two-version theory (the quotation, 1963–64: 362). He too links the form to performance, in which the *Libro* became an 'organism rendered invertebrate' by repetition, 'simultaneously present in a timeless, unstructured continuum, with no first, no last, no middle [. . .] like a pictorial scroll that can be unreeled from either spindle and viewed at any point' (Willis 1974: 224–26).

Libro de Buen Amor is thus shaped by, or for, orality at many levels: in its complex authorial voice, its traditional language and style, and above all its struc-ture. Linear in time but not in plot, working not by architectonic organization but by artful repetition of interwoven themes, it is unified but capable of separation into performable sections, poised at the historical balance-point between hearing and reading.

The scribal tradition

However it was performed or read, Juan Ruiz's book depended for its trans-mission on manuscripts deriving from the original *registro*. Besides the three surviving witnesses we have several testimonia of copies circulating in the two centuries after the poem's composition. The following remarks on this tradition are provisional; little work has been done on the MSS since Jean Ducamin described them in his pioneering edition (1901: xi–xxxi), and we still lack paleo-graphical studies or a typology of the MSS's make-up, *mise-en-page*, layout, and use.[47]

The oldest witness seems to be *T* (Madrid, BNM Vitrina 6–1), so designated because before entering the Biblioteca Nacional in 1870 it belonged to the library of Toledo cathedral. The copy was made in 1368, to judge by the interpolation in st. 1634, 'en era [of Spain] 1368' (see 47–48 and n27 above). *T* could have copied this date from its exemplar, but its script is not incompatible with the third quarter of the fourteenth century. The era of Spain (in which 1368 equalled AD 1330) was not abolished in Castile until 1383, but *era* was often used of dominical years before that time, an example being the prologue of *El cavallero Zifar*, where

---

[46] Jauss 1977: 17 (my translation); compare the modern soap-opera.
[47] The only advances since Ducamin are Vàrvaro 1968–69 and 1969–70; Catalán 1970. Dagenais 1994: 118–52 gives a useful summary.

Fernán Martínez (a near contemporary of Juan Ruiz in the Toledo cathedral chapter) says 'ES 1300' for the Jubilee year 1300, but 'ES 1339' for 1301 (Kelly 1984: 32–33 and n). The MS now consists of forty-eight worm-eaten leaves of handsome paper measuring 250×155 mm; it contains a fragment of *Buen Amor* (fols 1–37) and, in the same faded gothic script, a prose translation of the devotional *Vision of Philibert* (fols 37^v–48). Textually *T* belongs to the α-branch (Blecua 1992: lxi–lxxxi). Its *mise-en-page*, though unruled, neatly separates each stanza with a paragraph sign; the artistic aspect of the poem was evidently appreciated, though this copy does not include any lyrics.[48]

At the top of its recto pages *T* bears a medieval ink foliation in roman numerals which shows that its copy of *Buen Amor* originally consisted of 126 leaves. All but two of the first eighty-six and a further five of the remainder are lost. [49] It has been calculated that, at an average of 12.5 stanzas per leaf, its text of *Buen Amor* totalled ca 1575 stanzas, a shortfall which matches results for *G* (Gybbon-Monypenny 1962: 206n2). The first twenty-five leaves had space for about 312.5 stanzas against *S*'s 366, implying that, besides twenty-six stanzas preserved only in the *S*-branch (n24 above), it lacked the initial prayer, prose prologue, and the lyrics at st. 20–43 and st. 115–20.[50]

The second witness (Madrid, RAE ms. 19), called *G* after its eighteenth-century owner Benito Martínez Gayoso, consists of eighty-six leaves of paper measuring 225×150 mm, and bears an *explicit* dated Thursday 22 or 29 July 1389 (the date, the last digit of which is illegible due to a worm-hole in the leaf, is usually edited 'xxiii', but see Kelly 1984: 28–29). Its pages are unruled, as in *T*, but here the text is messily written in what appear to be two or three different hands. The poem is copied without verse-divisions, a *mise-en-page* which gives rise to serious errors in *cuaderna vía* such as the omission of twenty-seven single lines, a couplet (st. 1397), and even a tercet (st. 435); the skipping of a quatrain by jumping between similar line-openings ('subió en alta / otra cáthedra', st. 53c / 54c); five-line stanzas due to the repetition of a line (st. 82a) and inclusion of marginal

---

[48] Ducamin 1901: xxvii–xxx; photographs (*Libro* only) in Ruiz 1977; Octavio de Toledo 1878 edits *Filiberto*. On fol. 24 st. 1460a is copied before 1459 but not erased, and on fol. 32 two lines of st. 1551 are left blank, but otherwise the stanzas are regular. *T* has spellings often hastily classed as Leonese (Muñoz Garrigós 1977), but Blecua traces these forms to the archetype (1992: lxxxvi–xci and 536n1031c). The MS bears a set of antique corrections, of which one, an annotation on st. 1634 (fol. 37) stating that 134 years had passed since the colophon's 1368, implies a dating of 1464 or 1502.

[49] The surviving leaves are XXVI, an illegible figure (probably LXXIII), and LXXXVII–CXXVI (five missing at LXXXIX–LXXXX, LXXXXVIII, CX, CXXII, CXXXII).

[50] In 1899 binders replaced the parchment cover of 1870 (Ducamin 1901: xxvii) and repaired the leaves at the gutter, covering some with transparent film (Vàrvaro 1969–70: 549 exaggerates the damage). Losses of leaves were due to the fact that the MS was not bound; the Benedictine literary historian Martín Sarmiento recalled in 1750 that in 1727 he had seen in the library of Toledo cathedral many leaves in loose booklets, and from the foliation had found that 80 leaves were lacking, with about 50 or 60 still extant (Criado de Val and Naylor 1972: xv–xviin3; Vàrvaro 1968–69: 137).

glosses (st. 44, in Latin; st. 65).[51] Unlike *T*, however, *G* includes lyric strophes, and their layout is less disorderly than the *cuaderna vía*.

Cejador rashly took *G*'s ragged look and preference for Castilian forms instead of the archetype's original dialect as signs that this MS was closer to Juan Ruiz's original, a view shared by some subsequent editors (e.g. Corominas 1967: apparatus to 7c, 269c, etc.). The guess is not borne out by textual criticism. On the contrary, *G* marks the beginnings of a move away from the oral-oriented poetics of the original towards more readerly usages; it has occasional spaces for illuminated initials, and marginal notes indicating a rudimentary attempt to split the poem up into sections, usually in relation to *exempla* or maxims (Dagenais 1994: 156–62; Bizzarri 1999). Like *T*, it belongs to the α-branch.

From the remains of an irregular series of medieval quire signatures *G*'s original make-up has been reconstructed by Vàrvaro (1969–70) and Catalán (1970: 58–63). It lacks forty-six of its original 132 leaves, the last five of which were blank or contained matter not part of *Buen Amor*, since the *explicit* is copied on the last surviving leaf (now 86ᵛ, originally 127ᵛ). Various mistakes in the present order of pages imply that the MS was for a long time unbound. The most interesting question is whether it included the prose prologue. The present first leaf has an erasure at its head, and begins with a space for a two-line initial at st. 11 (the initial itself, like all the others in the MS, is an eighteenth-century addition); however, Ducamin noticed that there appear to be some initial leaves missing, and this is confirmed by Alberto Vàrvaro, who shows that they were three in number, making it probable that the prologue was present.[52]

The last and most nearly complete witness is *S* (Salamanca, Biblioteca Universitaria General ms. 2663), so called because it belonged to the Salamancan College of San Bartolomé.[53] It was copied before 1437 by Alfonso de Paradinas, a canon lawyer and later bishop, who became a scholar of the college in 1417.[54] Paradinas's copy is different in kind from both *T* and *G*. Neatly ruled and written, with clear spaces between stanzas and distinctive paraph-signs (*calderones*) and brackets to clarify the metrical layout of strophes, the MS is provided with a set of ninety-two rubricated section-headings. It thus imitates the *mise-en-page*

---

[51] Gybbon-Monypenny 1962: 207, Vàrvaro 1969–70: 553n10; cf. the remarks on the unmetrical layout of the MSS of *Vida de San Ildefonso*, *Mocedades de Rodrigo*, and *Libro de miseria de omne* in Lawrance 1997: 228–29 and n9. Vàrvaro 1969–70 supersedes Ducamin 1901: xvi–xxvii; Ruiz 1974 gives a facsimile.

[52] Ducamin 1901: xx, Gybbon-Monypenny 1962: 209 and n2, Vàrvaro 1968–69: 147 and 1969–70: 555 (inspection shows that this is correct, despite the denial in Willis 1972: xxv–xxvi). Vàrvaro thinks that there was also room for the initial *cuaderna vía* prayer (st. 1–10), but this seems less likely.

[53] *S* was in San Bartolomé by 1440, as shown by an inventory in Paris, BNF ms. esp. 524, fol. 56ᵛ 'el aciperste de fita en rromançe' (Cátedra 1989: 41–56, at 44n64); it has the college *ex libris* on fol. 1.

[54] For the identification of 'Alfonsus Peratinensis' (*explicit* on fol. 104ʳ, formerly CXII) see Menéndez Pidal 1941: 115–16; Vàrvaro 1968–69: 135n10. See the excellent facsimile in Ruiz 1975, and descriptions in Ducamin 1901: xi–xv, Vàrvaro 1968–69: 134–37.

of academic MSS and the visual methods of *ordinatio* developed by university stationers for legal and theological text-books, implying that this copy was intended for use in scholarly circles. Attention to textual matters is clear in a marginal correction noting the inversion of st. 710–11 on fol. XVIL (Blecua 1992: 176, apparatus *ad loc.*). The rubrics divide the text into short passages to facilitate the retrieval of *sententiae* or moral maxims, and also show an interest in the biographical fallacy (see 60 and n63 below). Scribbled on the margins are corrections, annotations, and doodles which show continued use by academic readers; on the endleaves are fragments of Latin canonical or theological texts.

A contemporary roman foliation shows that *S* originally consisted of 114 leaves of watermarked paper measuring 280 × 205 mm (Kerkhof 1993), of which 104 survive. The ten missing leaves contained 160 stanzas (ninety preserved in *G*, the rest lost at st. 765, 781, 877). Fols XXIX (including the description of the sexually desirable woman, st. 436–51) and LIX–LX (including the rape of Endrina between st. 877 / 878) may have been removed for some reason – Gybbon-Monypenny points out that *G* also appears to have had a lacuna at the second of these places (1988: 289n877–878) – but the remaining losses were accidental (Vàrvaro 1968–69: 137).

Of the other testimonia for the first century of *Libro de Buen Amor*'s scribal tradition the most important is *P* (Porto, Biblioteca Pública Municipal Ms. 785), a late fourteenth-century fragment of two leaves containing st. 60–78, 100–10, and 123–30 from a Portuguese translation of the α-branch text. This was the most luxurious of the known copies, written on parchment measuring 277 × 195 mm in double columns of fine gothic bookhand with decorated initials.[55] The conjecture that its language might be Galician (Criado de Val 1978) is not supported by orthography.[56] There was a copy of *O Acipreste de Fyta* in the library of Duarte I of Portugal by 1438, which may or may not have been the *P* version.[57]

A different story is told by nine lines of *Buen Amor* jotted down in a fifteenth-century collection of proverbs, jingles, short tales, and local saws scrawled on

[55] The leaves were used in the binding of a volume of John Damascene's *Barlaam et Josaphat* and Smaragdus's *Diadema monachorum* from the monastery of Santa Cruz, Coimbra; see Solalinde 1914, Moffatt 1956, Criado de Val and Naylor 1972: 579–97 and Lámina IV.

[56] It is plausible that a Castilian patron might have requested a version of the *Libro* in Galician – still the traditional language of lyric in late fourteenth-century Spain (Polín 1994) – implying that the book was viewed within the courtly troubadour tradition rather than that of clerical *cuaderna vía*. However, though there are many non-Portuguese forms (*priso, repiso, quiso*, st. 77; *sólo*, 78; *a las devezes*, 102; *pagés, es*, 108; *saliera*, 109; *manos*, 126; *atales, naturales, sinales, males*, 128; *tenýa*, 129), only *vylano* and *louçana* in st. 108 are typical of Galician (Solalinde 1914: 167); all are calqued on the Spanish, and the use of the digraphs *lh* and *nh* (adopted by Afonso III of Portugal's chancery c. 1265; cf. Galaico-Castilian *ll, nn* or *ñ*) implies a Portuguese scribe.

[57] Inventory in Lisboa, Arquivo Nacional da Torre do Tombo MS 1928, fol. 212ᵛ–15ᵛ (215ʳ), edited in Dias 1982: 206–08 (208); see Moffatt 1960: 36–37.

the endleaves of a Galician *Estoria d'España* from Cuenca College in Salamanca.[58] Menéndez Pidal named it the *fragmento cazurro*, 'ribald minstrel's fragment', conjecturing that it was used in performance by a *juglar* (1957: 209, 233–39 and Apéndice III, 389–92), but this is a patent misnomer; the MS's date, character, size (300 × 225 mm), and provenance preclude any possibility that it could have been a minstrel book. The jottings were notes by some scholar, perhaps to be used in sermons (Deyermond 1974), and doubtless copied from *S* in nearby San Bartolomé College.[59] The importance of the MS is that it provides more evidence for fifteenth-century study of *Buen Amor* in Salamanca, as witnessed by Paradinas's copy *S* and allusions by Alfonso de Madrigal el Tostado, and perhaps Fernando de Rojas (Cátedra 1989: 41–56, 70–72; see also Severin, below). The stanzas are copied as prose, and none is quoted complete (though one is given a spurious fourth line); it was the *Libro*'s maxims which this collector prized, not its poetry.

Reading of *Buen Amor* in scholarly circles is further evident in a fifteenth-century Aragonese miscellany of Latin rhetorical *artes* in which a marginal note to an anonymous treatise on punctuation quotes st. 553, and a gloss on Geoffroi de Vinsauf's *Poetria nova*, ll. 319–21, quotes st. 1450.[60] Diffusion of Juan Ruiz's poem in the Crown of Aragon is further confirmed by a copy in the library of Pedro Sánchez Muñoz, heir of Benedict XIII, at Penyíscola in 1483; and dissemination beyond Castile is also shown by three unattributed quotations by the Biscayan knight Lope García de Salazar in his chronicle miscellany *Libro de las bienandanzas e fortunas* (1471–76).[61]

John Dagenais interprets the emphasis on Juan Ruiz's ethical maxims in these fifteenth-century witnesses, citations, and marginalia as a 'narrowing down' to what seem 'fragmented readings' by 'bad readers' (1994: 153–213, at 168–69, 213).

---

[58] Salamanca, BUG MS 2497, fols 140^v–42^r 'Agora comencemos del libro del açipreste, toma aqueste dexenpro que vos dixere' ('Now let us begin with the Book of the Archpriest, take this *exemplum* I shall tell you'), quoting st. 547cbd, 493abd, 492abd (fol.140^v–41^r); see Criado de Val and Naylor 1972: 605–13 and Lámina VI.

[59] Corominas judges that the Cuenca jottings derive from the *S*-branch, though the inaccuracy of the copy renders it almost impossible to collate (1967: 19). It is significant that, despite the fragmentary nature of his quotations, the collector cites the book of the Archpriest, for he does not attribute any other excerpts in this way; it implies that he had a particular copy in mind (Lida de Malkiel 1959: 18–19).

[60] BNM MS 9589, fol. 1 ('nota bene in romanico optimum exemplum de distintionibus et pausis archipresbiteri Hitensis'); fol. 16^v ('juxta dictum vulgare'); Criado de Val and Naylor 1972: xxiii and 621. Charles B. Faulhaber dates the glosses c. 1508, and sees them as a 'step in the transition from Latin to vernacular culture', noting that the annotator looked on the *Libro* 'as a repository for *sententiae* rather than as a source of illustrations of literary technique' (1974–75, at 33).

[61] Monfrin 1964, §A63 'Item otro libret cubiertas verdes maltractado en paper intitulado Arcipreste de Yta'; Armistead 1973 and 1976–77 (BNM MS 1634, fol. 1, Prólogo, quoting *Libro* st. 44; fol. 190, l. 329, quoting st. 71, 73, 105). Salazar cites Ps 31:8 in the same phrase as st. 44, suggesting that his exemplar – a member of the α-branch – included the prose prologue, which uses this verse as its *thema* (see n18 above).

In truth we can deduce little about the psychology of those who copied, quoted, or doodled in margins; they may have been consummate critics who foolishly forgot that their scraps might be scanned, centuries later, for clues of literary acumen. How far the vagaries of scribal practice may mislead with regard to medieval appreciation of Juan Ruiz's art is shown by the fact that the *Libro* was often imitated by later poets, despite the gradual loss of its lyrics from the tradition (46 and n20 above).[62] Nevertheless, indications of a significant shift in aesthetic approach during the fifteenth century are given by the rubrics added to the text in the *S*-branch, and by the imitation of *Buen Amor* in Alfonso Martínez de Toledo's *Arcipreste de Talavera*.

S's rubrics or 'intertitles' (Genette 1987: 271–92) push two lines of interpretation, both inappropriate to the poetics of Juan Ruiz's text: an autobiographical reading of the first-person narrative, and a fragmentation of the poem's interwoven cyclical structure into its discrete components of parables and episodes.[63] This approach chronicles a progressive unanchoring of the work from its performance tradition – at least, one cannot easily imagine scholars performing the rubricated text in the confines of a college library. *Cuaderna vía* and entertainment by Andalusi singing-women or fiddle-playing minstrels had fallen into disuse in polite society, which preferred Italian novellas or the polyphony of Burgundian art-song performed by trained choirs of house-musicians. The mixed audience of bachelors and ladies envisaged by Juan Ruiz had been replaced by the *mâle Moyen Âge* – a masculine and largely misogynist readership of tonsured clerics and academics.

The reprobation of *loco amor* by Juan Ruiz's literary successor in the Toledo cathedral chapter, the Archpriest of Talavera Alfonso Martínez de Toledo, takes the form of an extended intertextual homage. *Arcipreste de Talavera*, as Alfonso Martínez called his book in patent tribute to his model (Toledo 1970: 38 and 40), names his predecessor only once ('the Archpriest of Hita in his treatise', I.iv, p. 54 and n4, quoting *Buen Amor* st. 206).[64] However, his text is full of reminiscences both verbal (*trotaconventos*, II.i, p. 127, cf. *Buen Amor* st. 441; *paviotas*, II.xiii,

---

[62] Santillana knew 'el libro del Arçipreste de Hita' (*Prohemio e carta al Condestable de Portugal* c. 1446; Santillana 1988: 448); on imitations in *Cancionero de Baena* and other court song-books see Lida 1940: 115–21, Deyermond 1973, Whinnom 1977–78 (cf. Corominas 1967: 342n881c, Jurado 1988), Labrador Herraiz and DiFranco 1989 (unconvincing, but see the allusion to Pitas Pajas in BNM MS 3985, mentioned on 407n20), Gerli 1990 and 1995. On Pero López de Ayala see Lida 1940: 112–15; but cf. Adams 1989.

[63] Dagenais 1994: 121–25, Domínguez 1997, Lawrance 1997. The biographical interest runs all through the rubrics, most clearly in the *explicit*'s story of Juan Ruiz's imprisonment by Gil Álvarez Carrillo de Albornoz (cardinal-archbishop of Toledo 1338–67), which is based on mentions of *presión*, 'durance', in the devotional songs at st. 1–3 and 1674.

[64] This stanza was marked by a reader in the margin of *S* (Dagenais 1994: 211). Alfonso Martínez could have seen *S* as a student at Salamanca, but he also had access to *T* in Toledo cathedral library, and, as royal chaplain of Juan II of Castile, to the MS, now lost, housed in the royal library ('de quarto de pliego, de mano, en romançe, que son las Coplas del Arçipreste de Hita, con unas tablas de papel enforradas en cuero colorado', *Libro del tesoro de los alcázares de Segovia*, 1503, in Sánchez Cantón 1950: 48, §70C).

p. 172, cf. st. 439; *troyos*, IV.i, p. 235 and 304 *s.v.*, cf. st. 699) and thematic (e.g. deadly sins, I.xxx–xxxvii, pp. 102–10, cf. *Buen Amor* st. 217–387; astrology, IV.i–ii, pp. 207–51, cf. *Buen Amor* st. 123–54; Death, IV.i, pp. 218–20 and IV.ii, pp. 246–48, cf. *Buen Amor* st. 1520–68). Alfonso Martínez constructs his book around the opposition of mad love of the world and pure love of God; he too uses copious maxims and apophthegms, humorous prosopopeia, and apologues, *exempla*, and *fabliaux* (e.g. Virgil in the basket, I.xvii, p. 77, cf. *Buen Amor* st. 261–68; see Gerli 1976: 63–67). Here, then, we have a unified reading of Juan Ruiz's *Libro* by a 'good reader', albeit one firmly anchored in a contemporary discourse of misogyny. What differentiates *Arcipreste de Talavera* from *Arcipreste de Hita* is its use of prose, its division into parts, books, and chapters, its architectonic structuring as a treatise or anatomy rather than a cyclical frame-fiction with insets. These contrasts point up a shift from the performance culture of Juan Ruiz's age to the readerly culture of the succeeding century. Even so, Alfonso Martínez de Toledo makes free use of first-person narrative and audience address, and his text retains many traces of gesture and orality. A greater prevalence of private reading did not immediately cancel out 'an oral feeling for literature' (Medcalf 1981: 15).

The gradual sea-change from oral to visual is also traceable in small local details of the extant tradition. The MS variants in st. 1299 are a good example:

> El mi señor Don Amor,   como omne letrado,
> en sola una copla   puso todo el ditado,
> por do el que lo oyere   será çertificado.

> (My lord Don Love, as a well-lettered man, put the whole caption in one stanza [=st. 1300] by which whoever hears it will be informed.)

The variants sprang from the archetype's use of a dialect form, *copra*, instead of standard *copla* 'stanza'. Puzzled, the scribes hesitated over whether aural or visual reception was envisaged; *S* took *oyere* 'hears' at face value and hence changed *copra* to *palabra* 'word', whereas the α-branch read *copra* as *copya* 'copy' and changed *oyere* to *leyere* 'reads' (*G* subsequently conjectured *copla* from the context, but retained *leyere*).[65]

A more extended case, and one with vital consequences for aesthetic appreciation of *Buen Amor*, is the scribes' treatment of metre (also see Duffell, this volume). In the light of Juan Ruiz's announcement, 'fablarvos he por trobas e por cuento rimado: / [. . .] saber sin pecado' (15bc; 'I will speak to you in lyrics and well-scanned rhymes, [. . .] an art without blemish'), it is remarkable that we cannot determine the prosody of his *cuaderna vía*. By comparison with Berceo's trim alexandrines (7 + 7 syllables) the transmitted text of *Buen Amor* seems shaggily

---

[65] Blecua 1992: lxxviii–lxxxix and 327, apparatus *ad loc*. Blecua also notes that *G*'s *ditado* 'caption' is a more noteworthy reading than *T* and *S*'s *tratado* 'treatise', 547n1299c.

irregular. Up to 20% of half-lines have eight syllables, and the witnesses unanimously transmit three half-lines of nine syllables (st. 902c, 1306d, 1511c) and two of six (st. 376c, 1484c). Rhymes are frequently unorthodox – assonantal, identical, or absent – and the treatment of caesura (mid-line break) is often odd.[66]

But to what extent were these irregularities in Juan Ruiz's original? Many are demonstrably scribal errors, and this raises a problem general in medieval poetry: namely, the phenomenon of scribes who seem unconcerned or unable to scan the texts which they copy – the *ne plus ultra* in the collapse of a performance tradition (see n51 above). The *mise-en-page* of our MSS inspires little confidence in their metrical reliability, and the practice of textual critics has been to emend to give regular measures. However, the tradition of *Buen Amor* presents us with an impasse: to discover the template of Juan Ruiz's verse we must know how to distinguish between the author's words and scribal errors, and vice versa – a vicious circle. Juan Ruiz's concern to give a lesson in prosody, writing verses 'exactly, as this art [*çiençia*] requires' (1992: 11; Prol. ll. 141–44), was singularly ill served. His verse certainly had rules, but it has proved hard to discover what they were (see Duffell, this volume).

For such situations the rascally medieval scribes must bear the blame. Before cursing them, however, we should recall the essential point: *mouvance* was not a chance consequence of manuscript transmission, but its essence. The critical problem is not medieval, but modern; a serially-printed *textus receptus* demands decisions about uniformity and fixity which did not exist in the age of script. To this point we may now turn.

From script to print

In the sixteenth century *Buen Amor* still circulated in manuscript. Columbus's bibliophile son Fernando (1488–1539) bought a copy (Askins 1986–87), the Toledan humanist Alvar Gómez de Castro (1521–86) noted some verses from a MS which had the Endrina episode intact (Sánchez Cantón 1918; Moffatt 1957), and the Cordoban antiquary Gonzalo Argote de Molina (1549–97) quoted lines from one of the *cantigas de serrana* and also possessed a *Cancionero* (or songbook) of the Archpriest, of very ancient *canciones* from the time of King Alfonso XI (Millares Carlo 1923: 145; my paraphrase).[67] Yet these men's lives spanned

[66] Chiarini 1964: xlviii–li, Blecua 1992: xci–xcvii. On rhyme see Lecoy 1938: 51–62, Chiarini 1964: liv–lxix; on caesura, Chiarini 1964: xlviii, Gybbon-Monypenny 1988: 78 and n68.
[67] Colón catalogued his copy c. 1536–39 as 'Dios padre e dios fijo e dios espiritu santo. de mano. 15206' (*Abecedarium B*, col. 487), which shows it began at st. 11 with no prologue, and 'Jo. Ruiz arcipreste obra en coplas. de mano. 15206. 4º' (*ibid.* col. 953), which is the earliest attested attribution of the poem to Juan Ruiz (n7 above). Castro's copy of thirty unattributed lines (711–829), which includes seven not elsewhere preserved, is in his miscellany in BNM MS 7896, fol. 374 (Corominas 1967: 18–19n13, Criado de Val and Naylor 1972: xxi–xxii,

the revolution of the rise of printing. As elsewhere in Europe, the bulk of what we regard as valuable in pre-fifteenth-century Spanish literature failed to cross the technological Rubicon. Of *cuaderna vía*, only a couple of penny broadsides of sententious doggerel survived the transition into print.[68]

However, one of the intriguing mysteries of *Buen Amor*'s history is a report that the bookseller Gabriel de Sancha sighted an early printed edition in London in 1786 (Sánchez 1779–90: IV, xxii). Arnald Steiger thought it probably imaginary (1964: 576–81, at 577), but Alan Deyermond has argued convincingly for its reliability (2004: 13–40). If it were ever found, this edition would revolutionize our picture of the *Libro*'s transmission; but, if it existed, it did nothing to halt the oblivion which enveloped Juan Ruiz's text in the sixteenth and seventeenth centuries. Even Argote de Molina did not mention it in the *Discurso de la poesía antigua castellana* affixed to his edition of Don Juan Manuel's *Conde Lucanor* (Sevilla: Hernando Díaz, 1575). When Francisco de Torres wrote his *Historia de la ciudad de Guadalajara* (1647, revised 1689), all he knew about Juan Ruiz was that around 1415 [*sic*] the Archipriest of Hita, whose name he could not discover, composed a great volume of verse proverbs (Whittem 1931; see Sánchez 1779–90: I, 105 and IV, vi–vii). *Buen Amor* is missing from the first comprehensive history of medieval Spanish literature, Nicolás Antonio's *Bibliotheca Hispana vetus* (Roma: Rubeis, 1696).

Juan Ruiz's poem was not rediscovered until the eighteenth century, when a group of enlightened antiquaries in the new Academies of Spanish language and history and the fledgling Royal Public (later National) Library rescued all three main witnesses, of which they made at least five MS collations (Ducamin 1901: xxxii–xliii; Vetterling 1981; Garcia 1988–89). In 1790, despite worries about the poem's obscenity, Tomás Antonio Sánchez published the text using *S* as copy (Sánchez 1779–90: IV, 1–288, 'Poesías del arcipreste de Hita', with introduction).[69] Sánchez's handsome edition is by our standards unscientific, but it opened the

601 and Lámina V). Argote de Molina quotes st. 1023–27 in notes added to his fourteenth-century MS of *Repartimiento de Sevilla* (Madrid, RB II–880, 186; see Millares Carlo 1923: 145; Criado de Val and Naylor 1972: 625), attributing them to Domingo Abad de los Romances, a minstrel of Fernando III (Sánchez 1779–90: IV, 166–67 n; Wolf 1859: 116n1; Moffatt 1960: 40, Corominas 1967: 19–20, 398n1023–27); Blecua suggests, following Alonso 1957, that the copy inventoried among the MSS in his *estudio* may actually have been our *G*, and that this may earlier have belonged to Colón (1983: 38–39; 1992: ln78 and lxxxv, n98).

[68] *Probervios en rimo del sabio Salomon* ([Burgos]: s.n., c. 1538); *Castigos y exemplos de Caton* (Medina del Campo: Pedro de Castro, 1543).

[69] Sánchez (1779–90: I, 100–06n158–64) also gives the first study of the poem, in the form of notes on Santillana's *Carta-prohemio* (see n62 above). Estevan de Terreros y Pando had earlier printed st. 1125–1234 from *T* (1758: 82–84n), with notes on *G* and *T* (60–61) and a plate of the *explicit* of *T* (Lámina 5.3 'Siglo XIV' facing p. 58). Sánchez printed Gaspar Melchor de Jovellanos's *informe* to the Real Academia de la Historia recommending that the poem be published entire (1779–90: IV, xxix–xxxii), but he nevertheless censored st. 374–87, 468–89, 516–27, 684–91, 823, 1501, and 1648–49 (which were first published by Amador de los Ríos 1861–65: IV (1863), 581, and mostly restored to the text in Janer 1864: 225n1).

way to literary studies by Ferdinand Wolf (1859), George Ticknor (1849: I, 72–79), and Count Puymaigre (1861–62: II, 63–121), laying the foundation for our consensus that *Buen Amor* is a classic.

Such consensus cannot rest on the insufficient basis of editions such as Sánchez's. Modern criticism depends on close verbal analysis, and so we require a synthetic *textus receptus* before we can start work. This is the reason for the century of editorial activity carried out since Ducamin published his recension of the three MSS (1901). The technical evaluation of this enterprise lies beyond the purview of most readers, but *Libro de Buen Amor* has been exceptionally well served; there have been five critical editions, and – a fact of great methodological significance – each marks a demonstrable step towards a superior text and a better understanding of the tradition (Chiarini 1964, Corominas 1967, Gybbon-Monypenny 1988, Joset edn 1990, and Blecua 1992; add also contributions by Aguado 1929; Lecoy 1938: 37–110; and Morreale's outstanding series of reviews). We now know that the witnesses belong to two branches, *S* and α, which descend independently from a single unbound archetype that, though close to the original *registro*, already contained errors and lacunae (e.g. the loss of announced lyrics). Logically this means two things. First, where the branches diverge, either may preserve the reading of the archetype so there can be no question of choosing a single MS as the base for a critical edition. Second, there are places where neither the archetype nor any of the surviving witnesses preserved the reading of Juan Ruiz's original. These facts underpin the activity of textual critics, who, by comparing the readings of both branches, seek to detect where errors have occurred and select which of the variants, if any, represents the original.

It may be objected that, since print-bound notions of textual fixity, authorship, and structure contradict medieval ways of reading (39–42 above), reliance on a critically-edited *textus receptus* is methodologically impure.[70] It is certainly true that Spanish philology has suffered from a historic tendency to over-edit. It is a disservice to conceal from our gaze the problematic aspects of *mouvance* – and hence the Jaussian 'otherness' of medieval literature. By comparison with Chaucer's *Canterbury Tales* (nearly 100 MSS), *Roman de la Rose* (over 300), or Dante's *Divina commedia* (over 700), the paltry surviving tradition of one and two half MSS of *Buen Amor* presents a very minor and attenuated case of textual instability (Blecua 1983: 159–68; 1991–92: 75). Even so, a critical edition involves significant choices between variants in over a quarter of the lines. Suzanne Fleischman points out, for example, that seemingly trivial variants of single letters involving gender switches or discrepancies in negatives may significantly alter meaning (1982–83: 285).[71] What readers require are editions

---

[70] Such a view is propounded by New Philology, which makes *mouvance* its object of study following Bernard Cerquiglini's dictum, 'medieval *écriture* does not produce variants, it is variance' (1989: 111). Dagenais 1994 applies the argument to *Libro*, though at several points he expressly recognizes the need for critical editions.

[71] Of Fleischman's five examples we can unhesitatingly select the correct reading of st. 391 and 1069 by sense ('vezina en vezina', 'syn amor', see Blecua 1992: 104n391d; 537n1069c)

which, without needless reconstruction or crass paratextual interference, distinguish the areas of Juan Ruiz's original which we can recover, and those where shortcomings of transmission make recovery impossible.[72]

In pursuit of the latter aim much attention has naturally been given to the problems of selection posed by the variants. In truth, however, this has only a marginal bearing on the critical problem. Modern editorial conjectures are, in methodological terms, of the same aesthetic status as medieval variants – forms of *mouvance*. Far more significant issues are raised by aspects of the printed text where modern typography is in fundamental discord with medieval aesthetics, and these are regularly disregarded by critics. We have seen above, for example, the deep implications of the seemingly simple problem of giving the text a paratextual title and author's name (pp. 40–42), or the more damaging barrier to any proper reading of *Buen Amor* posed by the inclusion in our *textus receptus* of the rubricated intertitles of *S* (60 and n63 above). By way of further illustration I conclude with two aspects of the *textus receptus* which pose special dangers to the unsuspecting reader.

I have already mentioned the editors' tendency to emend metrical irregularities – or should we say adventurous innovations? – in the transmitted text of *Buen Amor*. This has generally meant selecting variants or proposing conjectures to give perfectly isosyllabic lines (excluding combinations of seven-syllable with eight-syllable hemistichs) or perfectly isosyllabic stanzas (all sevens or all eights).[73] But wholesale emendation in this matter is almost as indefensible as non-intervention.[74] For Joset the century of effort directed at regularizing the versification in our *textus receptus* is nothing short of 'treason', expunging what may have been highly-prized forms of originality (1988: 44–45, 47). The way forward lies in approaching the problem from the point of view of reception rather than as an aspect of letter-for-letter transmission. That is to say, we should consider how, in performance, the synergy of learned regularity and popular

---

and of st. 393 by metre ('a la que matar quieres'); of st. 1237 the method of textual criticism demands the reading of *S* and *G*, although *T* is correct ('e non ál'); but st. 390 – the case which she regards as solved, by rhyme – turns out to be the problematic one (*S* 'digo digo', *G* 'dixo dixo'; see Blecua 1992: 509–10n390b).

[72] Blecua 1992 is almost faultless in this respect (the only flaw is the inclusion in the text of *S*'s intertitles), but it uses three separate *apparatus critici*, a critical introduction, and critical endnotes as well as a linguistic commentary in footnotes. Criado de Val and Naylor 1972's synoptic transcription is handier for seeing *mouvance* at a glance, but its lack of a critical text – despite its subtitle – renders it unsuitable for literary study.

[73] All critics agree that Juan Ruiz sometimes used eights, and the switches from stanzas of sevens to stanzas of eights in the Endrina episode (581–891) seem to match changes of scene in *Pamphilus*, e.g. eleven eighters at 588 = start of *actus* I; twenty-nine at 702 = start of *actus* II (Lecoy 1938: 62–82). However, though eighteen stanzas of eights are perfectly preserved in all the witnesses, Vàrvaro (1968–69: 153) found general statistics of 19% hybrid lines and over 50% hybrid stanzas.

[74] Corominas's decision to make every stanza isometric (1967: 39–68) is often excoriated, but eclecticism or non-intervention (Gybbon-Monypenny 1988: 77–78, Joset edn 1990: 38–41, Blecua 1992: xcix–c) are stop-gap solutions.

irregularity in Juan Ruiz's metre might acquire aesthetic resonance. Blecua defends the caesura-less sixes in st. 569d ('buen callar çient sueldos val en toda plaça'; 'silence is golden in every forum') as mirroring the pithy lilt of a proverb (1992: xcvii), while Joset's note on the tendency to disintegrate the quatrain with internally rhymed half-lines (edn 1990: 41 and n55) links with Wolf's insight that the end-stopped eights on the Andalusi woman in st. 1509–11 imitate a ballad (1859: 128n1; Clarke 1984). Similar is st. 653:

> Ay Dios, quán fermosa viene   Doña Endrina por la plaça,
> qué talle e qué donaire,   qué alto cuello de garça,
> qué cabellos, qué boquilla,   qué color, qué buenandança:
> con saetas de amor fiere   quando los sus ojos alça.

> (Lord, how lovely comes Lady Sloe across the square; such a figure and such grace, such a tall heron's neck, such hair, such a darling mouth, such colour, such a graceful walk. She wounds with arrows of love when she raises her eyes.)

The octosyllables, assonantal rhyme, and traditional imagery make this a perfect ballad in *romance* metre. This has an 'embossing' effect (Clarke's term), giving Endrina's entrance a punch hardly adumbrated in the meagre Latin original, 'Quam formosa, Deus, nudis venit illa capillis' ('God, how lovely she comes with uncovered hair', *Pamphilus de amore* 653).

The most vital and most neglected feature of our *textus receptus*, however, is the humble question of punctuation. This is because the thoughtless imposition of a full repertory of typographic punctuation involves a relentless trivialization of Juan Ruiz's rhythmically-modulated oral style (54 and n45 above), which is better captured by the lighter, more rhetorical pointing of medieval scribal practice.[75] Morreale reprimands editors for failing to notice the difference between the tongue-and-groove syntax of modern literary language and the staccato of Juan Ruiz's elliptical paratactic style (1969–71: 286n45). She cites the example of st. 474, which reads in *S* and *G* respectively:

> era don pitaσ pajaσ vn pyntor de bretaña
> caſoſe cõ muger moça / pagauaſe de conpaña

> Eraσ don pitaσ payaσ vñ pyntor de bretaña /
> caso cõ muğr moça pagauase de cõpaña /

A modern reader takes the subject of *pagávase* as Pitas Pajas, a pitifully anodyne reading, but the phrase is of course a wickedly euphemistic characterization of his wanton young wife. Medieval hearers would have grasped the change of

---

[75] For distortions forced on MS texts by the demands of typography see Blake 1979: 55–79 (quotation marks and italics, 57–60; orthography, obsolete letters, 62; paragraphs, 65; punctuation, 66–74; word-division and capitalization, 74–77). An example is discussed in Clarke 1971; and in de Looze, in this volume.

referent because of the audible pause at the caesura (Morreale 1969–71: 286), which in *S* is also marked by a virgule or slash. Editors have to try to make this clear – but only Corominas does so – by punctuation:

> Eras' don Pitas Pajas   un pintor de Bretaña,
> casó con muger moça;   pagávase de conpaña.

English has no choice but to revert to a construction with personal or relative pronoun: 'Once upon a time there was a painter of Brittany, Don Whistlestraws, set up house with a young woman; *she* enjoyed company', or '[. . .] woman *who* enjoyed'.

As Morreale points out, any punctuation which ignores caesura or line and stanza end is automatically suspect (2001: 198). Vital features of style hang upon the correct use and placement of commas, colons, and full stops.[76] Intrusive question and exclamation marks, inverted commas, and capital letters pose even greater threats to the poem's delicate tissue by tying down onomastic word-play (*Buen Amor* / *buen amor* being an example) or by strait-jacketing the poem's free-flowing, layered dialogue, in which the author's and narrator's voices blend seamlessly with those of the fictional characters in a singular kind of perspectivism. Readers should view such punctuation marks with caution, or, better still, ignore them.[77]

Conclusion

It follows from everything said above that the next major advance in editing *Libro de Buen Amor* will depend not on textual critics, but on the inventiveness of typographers and graphic designers or the use of new electronic media to produce texts which will give the reader easy access to the textual realities of manuscript *mouvance* described above. What might such editions accomplish? A first advantage would be to make clear the limits of certain kinds of modern critical close reading, which depend on the insecure basis of a linguistic text in which many words and phrases were already of dubious meaning for the medieval copyists. But a more liberating effect would be to open up aspects of the

---

[76] Margherita Morreale 1969–71: 287–89 lists errors in Corominas 1967, e.g. st. 1530c, st. 1589b (and see the debate on st. 904 in Corominas 1967: 348n904b *v*. Morreale 1969–71: 299). She admits an occasional colon at a stanza end (e.g. 421–22), and a semi-colon when phrases are co-ordinated in consecutive lines, but rightly condemns the widespread abuse of superfluous commas. Blecua notes the difficulty of punctuating the *Libro* owing to its special stanza-structure, which tends to take the form of apophthegm; he favours a use of the colon, contravening the Academy's rules, to recreate the book's intonation (1992: ci).

[77] Morreale (1969–71: 289, 298–99) criticizes editors who arrogate the role of *juglar* by heavy-handed use of marks of emphasis, and of capitals (ibid. 297). On the drawbacks of modern marks to punctuate Juanruizian dialogue see Lawrance 1997: 244–46.

'astounding or surprising otherness' of Juan Ruiz's literary art, thereby providing what Jauss calls an 'aesthetic bridge' to make the poem readable for a modern public (1977: 10, 13; and see de Looze, below).

Meanwhile, we should not forget that critical editions are not the only way forward. The endless process of transmission goes on in other more adventurous forms such as modernization (Brey Mariño 1966, Salvador Miguel 1985), foreign verse translation (e.g. Kane 1968, Singleton 1975), and theatrical adaptation (Criado de Val 1960a). For *Buen Amor*'s modern audience the most exciting transformation, into the medium of film, is yet to come.[78]

[78] Vetterling 1981–82 reviews Televisión Española's 1960 production, directed by Luis Fernández Santos, which divided the first-person author into three different characters (the minstrel, a youth reciting the *Libro* to a crowd; the writer, an old archpriest who comments on the action; and the lover Don Melón, 'a bewildered, round-faced man in his forties'). Vetterling judged this pedagogic version a good effort for its time; that cannot be said of the semi-pornographic films by Tomás Aznar and Javier Bayarri of 1975 and 1976. I thank the librarians of the Biblioteca Nacional, Real Academia Española, and Salamanca University for help in examining the MSS. My gratitude also to Clive Willis and Serxio Otero González for expertise in solving the problem discussed in n56 above, to Alan Deyermond and Michel Garcia for the gift of materials, and to those who read a draft of this chapter for their invaluable comments. I owe the idea in n35 above to a study by Nicholas Round shortly to be published by PMHRS (London: Dept of Hispanic Studies, Queen Mary, Univ. of London).

Part 2: FORM AND TRADITIONAL WISDOM

Metre and Rhythm in the *Libro de Buen Amor*

MARTIN J. DUFFELL

Syllabic irregularity in the 'Libro de Buen Amor'

Although the *Libro de Buen Amor* is one of the most widely admired medieval works in verse, modern editors and critics find very little to praise in its versification. This is because they write after almost half a millennium in which the first test of metrical competence in Spanish has been whether lines have the notionally correct number of syllables. Not only do Juan Ruiz's lines fail this test, they do so by a wider margin than those of most other medieval Spanish poets. Approximately four-fifths of the *Libro*'s lines are in strophes of *cuaderna vía*, a form that traditional metrics tells us should be a monorhyme quatrain made up of *heptasílabos dobles*, or *alejandrinos*. The verse design of the *alejandrino* comprises two hemistichs, each with six syllables up to and including the final accent, and each hemistich may be *grave* or *agudo*; the first hemistich may also be *esdrújulo*, 'paroxytone'.[1] A significant proportion of Juan Ruiz's *cuaderna vía* lines, at least as they appear in the surviving mansucripts, are not *heptasílabos dobles*.

The most common line length is, nevertheless, 6 + 6 syllables, but many lines have this syllable count only if we treat their adjacent vowels in a highly inconsistent manner, as the following examples (from Gybbon-Monypenny 1988) show:[2]

This chapter supports a hypothesis put forward by G. B. Gybbon-Monypenny regarding Juan Ruiz's mode of versifying (1988: 78). Gerald did not elaborate on this particular insight, but his suggestion is worked out in detail here, with what I hope is sufficient rigour for linguistic metrists, but without the specialist terminology of their discipline that often deters the general reader.

[1] It should be noted that a *heptasílabo* to Spanish metrists is a *hexasyllabe* to French writers, and that Catalan and Portuguese metrists count and name metres as the French do (see Torre 2002: 64–77). In this chapter I shall use a shorthand for line length derived from the French convention: an arabic numeral for the number of syllables up to and including the final stress; when I wish to specify *agudo* and *grave* lines, I shall suffix this numeral with the letters M (masculine) or F (feminine), respectively.

[2] In my examples separately counted syllables in the same word are divided by hyphens, and extra space is left between words in order to facilitate the reader's perception of syllable count. Uncounted post-tonic syllables are not separated from the preceding syllable, and vowels not contributing to the syllable count as a result of synaloepha (merging of word-final and word-initial vowels) are given in superscript; hiatus (separation of word-final and word-initial vowels) is emphasized by subscript [H].

(1)	que pue-da de can-tares	un li-bre-te rri-mar	(12c)
(2)	le-van-tó se [H] el griego:	ten-dió la pal-ma llana	(57a)
(3)	le-van-tó s^e el ve-llaco	con fan-ta-sí-a vana	(57c)
(4)	q^{ue} en tien-po de su vida	nun-ca la vies ven-gada	(63b)
(5)	El que fi-zo [H] el çielo,	la tie-rra [H] e [H] el mar	(12a)

Instance (1) is an example of a line with the mode (that is, the most frequently occurring number) syllable count of $6 + 6$ syllables ($6F + 6M$), but the next two lines are regular only if (2) employs hiatus between 'se' and 'el', while (3) employs synaloepha (a less likely alternative is that 'gri-e-go' in (2) becomes three syllables by diaeresis). Similarly, in (4) 'e' + 'e' requires synaloepha for regularity, while in (5) it requires hiatus. Thus, although many writers have argued that there were rules governing synaloepha and hiatus in fourteenth-century Castilian verse (for example, Clarke 1947–48: 349 and Orduna 1981: 95n4), these two instances indicate that Juan Ruiz did not always observe them.

If we wish to maximize the number of lines in the *Libro de Buen Amor* with $6 + 6$ syllables, our treatment of adjacent vowels within the same word must also be inconsistent, and must sometimes violate the norms of Castilian speech. Thus, for example, the first line of the poem can be made regular only by pronouncing the word 'jo-dí-os' as two syllables ('jo-dios'), and some editors (for example, Pons Griera 1971) omit the accent accordingly. But in the same strophe regularity requires diaeresis in 'Da-ni-el'; yet 'Da-niel' is surely a much more likely synaeresis than 'jo-dios'. The two lines concerned also show another feature that is common in Ruiz's verse and that works against a regular syllabic delivery.

(6)	Se-ñor Dios q^{ue} a los jo-díos,	pue-blo de per-di-ción	(1a)
(7)	a Da-ni-el sa-caste	del po-ço de Ba-bi-lón	(1c)

The second hemistich of (6) is 6M, but that of (7) is 7M, unless we employ a highly unlikely syncope and make 'Ba-bⁱlon' disyllabic. In later centuries Spanish poets always treated the line of 6M as the equivalent of that of 6F (as French poets had always done). This equivalence, $6M = 6F$, gives syllabic verse its distinctive primary rhythm: as Benoît de Cornulier points out (1995: 115), it ensures that in a syllable-timed delivery the final (phrasal) stresses of lines and hemistichs will occur at regular time intervals. The alternative equivalence, $7M = 6F$, is antirhythmic: it causes line-end stresses to occur irregularly, and destroys the primary rhythm to be found in any unbroken sequence of 6M and/or 6F lines. Many of Juan Ruiz's lines, therefore, are antirhythmic: he makes $7M = 6F$ as often as not, and many of the 7M hemistichs have no plausible alternative scansion, as is the case of the second in the following instance:

(8)	Pe-ro si las que-rién pa-ra por e-llas u-sar	(48a)

The practice of making $7M = 6F$ is found in the earliest surviving syllabic verse from the West of the Iberian Peninsula, which was composed early in the thirteenth century under the influence of French and Occitan models (see Hart 1998 and Parkinson in press). Making 7M = 6F is known to Hispanic metrists as the *ley de Mussafia* (named after the scholar who first published a special study of the phenomenon); but calling it a law does not mean that it was not a mistake. Poets who make 7M = 6F cannot count their syllables by ear (the way that modern Spanish poets do): the irregularity of the line-final stresses in such a system forces the poet to count syllables by eye, or on the fingers, a slow and painful process. As José Domínguez Caparros points out:

> no se han contado, en todas las épocas, las sílabas del verso como hoy acostum-
> bramos a hacerlo, y no se han utilizado de la misma forma las licencias métricas
> relacionadas con el establecimiento del numero de sílabas.   (2000: 76)

But in the *Libro de Buen Amor* it is not only *agudo* lines and hemistichs that some-times have a syllable too many; there are many hemistichs of 7F with no ambigu-ous adjacent vowels in Ruiz's *cuaderna vía*, as the following line of 6F + 7F illustrates:

> (9)   bien o mal, qual pun-tares,   tal te di-rá cier-ta-mente   (70b)

Moreover, some lines of Ruiz's *cuaderna vía* are even more syllabically irregular; for example, the following line of 8F + 5F:

> (10)   a San-ta Ma-ri-na li-bres-te   del vien-tre del dra-go   (3c)

Tomás Navarro Tomás thus mentions only the most common variant line lengths when he says of the two most important fourteenth-century *cuaderna vía* poets:

> ni Juan Ruiz ni López de Ayala [. . .] practicaron el isosilabismo de manera
> rigurosa y constante [. . .] se encuentran a lado de los alejandrinos ordinarios
> variantes de 8 + 7, 7 + 8, 7 + 6, 6 + 7, 8 + 6, 8 + 8.   (1974: 84)

Erratic syllable counting in the *Libro* is not confined to its *cuaderna vía*: in the *verso de arte menor*, which later poets made strictly octosyllabic, Juan Ruiz often includes lines of nine syllables Spanish count, as the following lines (of 8M and 7M respectively) clearly illustrate:

> (11)   El ter-çe-ro cuen-tan las leyes   (26a)
> (12)   quan-do ve-nie-ron los rreyes   (26b)

A similar level of irregularity can be found in Ruiz's lyrics that employ shorter lines: Navarro Tomás says 'entre los hexasílabos, sin orden visible ni apariencia de compensación ni equilibrio métrico, se intercalan algunos heptasílabos y octosílabos de medida clara y segura' (1974: 78). According to Rudolf Baehr's calculation, in Ruiz's *hexasílabos* 'un tercio de los versos son heptasílabos' (1970: 94); both writers might have added that Ruiz also mixes lines of 4F with lines of 5F and 6F, as strophe 1024 illustrates:

(13)	A la de-çida	4F
(14)	di $_{[H]}$ u-na co-rrida;	5F
(15)	fa-llé $_{[H]}$ u-na se-rana	6F
(16)	fer-mo-sa, lo-çana	5F
(17)	e bien co-lo-rada.	5F

The hiatus shown in my scansion of (14) and (15) seems less clumsy than synaloepha; neither treatment can make this strophe syllabically regular, nor do editors have any convincing suggestions for regularizing it.

An irregular syllable count is thus a feature of all the metres that we find in the surviving manuscripts of the *Libro*. The closest we can get to a syllabic formula for Juan Ruiz's verse is: $L = N \pm 2$, where L equals the number of syllables in the line / hemistich and N is the most common number of syllables (in statistics, the *mode*) in the lines / hemistichs of the passage concerned. Both Ruiz's short lines and his hemistichs of *cuaderna vía* contain between five and nine syllables, but we should question whether this is the result of his counting syllables, or whether it simply reflects the structure of phrases in ordinary Castilian speech.

Possible explanations of syllabic irregularity

S. Griswold Morley once argued that syllabic irregularity in medieval Castilian verse may be the result of the poet's aiming at a fixed number of syllables but missing, just as archers often miss their targets (1933: 971–74). This suggestion has found few supporters, and I have argued against Morley's hypothesis in detail elsewhere (Duffell 1999b: 161).[3] It suffices to say here that the idea of a poet setting out to count syllables and still being unable to do so many thousands of lines later is scarcely credible. Today, editors with far less creative talent than the poet have no difficulty in regularizing irregular lines, and even school children can count syllables accurately. This competence was clearly shared by French, Italian, and Catalan speakers of the fourteenth century, and it is difficult to believe that a great Castilian poet could not have made his lines regular, had he wanted to do so.

If we eliminate the possibility of gross incompetence in versifying, then the approximately equal number of syllables in Ruiz's lines must be part of his verse design. Navarro Tomás, who describes the phenomenon of approximate syllable

---

[3] Morley bases his hypothesis on the statistically normal distribution of hemistich lengths in the *Poema de Mio Cid*; but this is a characteristic feature of the lines of a number of non-syllabic metres, and is a strong indication that the *Cid's* metre is non-syllabic.

count as 'fluctuación', argues that it is also a feature of the short lines in which some early *romances* are composed (1974: 75–76). But, although poets have counted syllables in many cultures, from ancient Iranian (see Pighi 1970: 8–9) to modern Japanese (see Brower 1972), I can think of no example where 'approximate counting' is practised or is even allowable. Fluctuation is the distinguishing characteristic not of verse, which John Lotz (1960) defines as 'numerically regulated language', but of prose, language that is not numerically regulated. The rhythm of syllabic verse depends on the regularity of a number of events occurring in time: syllables and, in the case of Romance verse, phrasal stress at the hemistich and line end. Approximate counting produces no such rhythms, and there seems to be no good reason why poets should count approximately. Like the hypothesis of versifying incompetence, that of approximate counting is unsatisfactory and should be rejected.

If the versification of the *Libro de Buen Amor* is based on syllable count, the irregularity of surviving manuscripts can be accounted for only by scribal error; but there are many reasons for doubting that scribal error could have been the principal cause of irregularity on such a scale. Those reasons are psychological, chronological, and practical.

If the syllabic irregularity of the surviving text results from scribal error, then at some stage a scribe with a perfectly regular text in front of him must have produced a text with a very large number of irregular lines. Such behaviour is psychologically unlikely, because metre is an invaluable memory aid for the copyist, helping him retain a whole line in his mind rather than one word at a time. Indeed, metre seems to have originated as a memory aid in preliterate societies (Gaur 1984: 25), and medieval scribes seem to have relied heavily upon it in transcription. I have discussed in detail elsewhere the results of my comparison between the manuscript variants produced by French scribes and those produced by Spanish ones (Duffell 2002: 113–14). One of my most important findings was that only one per cent of variants in the *Chanson d'Antioche* (Duparc-Quioc 1976) change a line's syllable count, but that fifty per cent of those in the *Rimado de Palacio* (Orduna 1981) do. This shows clearly that fourteenth-century French scribes were using the metre as a memory aid in their copying, while their Spanish contemporaries were not. This cannot be explained by linguistic differences, because when the Marqués de Santillana (b. 1398, d. 1458) pioneered his own version of the *verso de arte mayor*, a line of exactly 5F + 5M / F syllables, Spanish scribes captured this regularity very well in their copying (see Duffell 1987: 284 and 2000: 121–22). Only a very tiny proportion of lines in the surviving manuscripts of Santillana's work have the wrong number of syllables.

If, therefore, some copyist of the *Libro* had ignored the syllabic regularity of his original and obliterated its metre, he would have been doing something unparalleled elsewhere in Romance. Nor could his action have escaped detection: as Michel Garcia pointed out, vernacular verse texts of this period were designed for oral performance (1978: 45); the scribe's obliteration of the poem's metre would have rendered a rhythmic delivery of the lines impossible. Phrasal stresses would have fallen at irregular time intervals, and the primary rhythm typical of syllabic verse would have evaporated. Obliterating the metre would have been not only a stupid crime, but also an easily detectable one: that is, of course, if the text was ever regular, and if readers ever read it in such a way as to emphasize the primary rhythms that syllabic regularity creates.[4]

There are also chronological arguments against the scribal-error explanation: the first is that the justification offered by most editors for their regularizing of earlier *cuaderna vía* texts depends on changes in the Castilian language between the thirteenth and fourteenth centuries. There has been a wide acceptance of the hypothesis of John D. Fitz-Gerald (1905) that thirteenth-century poets had used many apocopated forms of words, and that in manuscripts produced when those forms were no longer used scribes had restored the full form of those words, thus destroying the text's syllabic regularity. This argument cannot, however, be applied to fourteenth-century texts like the *Libro* (1330) and the *Rimado de Palacio* (1367–1403), which were composed after the period of the apocopation. This undermines Fitz-Gerald's hypothesis somewhat, since one of its corollaries is that later *cuaderna vía* texts should be more regular than earlier ones, whereas in fact the opposite is the case. The second chronological argument arises from what happened to syllable counting in Castilian at the end of the fourteenth century, and can be observed in the *Rimado de Palacio* itself. Poets simply abandoned counting the syllables in their long-line verse altogether and, for the next century and a half, employed the *verso de arte mayor*, a metre with strong accentual patterns and an irregular line length (except in the hands of a few reforming poets like Santillana). It is difficult to believe that Castilian copyists influenced, or even anticipated, poets in this move away from counting syllables; it is surely much more reasonable to assume that fourteenth-century copyists did not count syllables because they knew that contemporary poets did not.

Finally there are practical reasons for rejecting the idea that copying errors are responsible for the syllabic irregularity found in the manuscripts of Ruiz's text. Many of the irregular lines defy sensible emendation: any proposed regularization is less satisfactory, semantically, syntactically, or aesthetically. As Germán Orduna says in the context of the *Rimado de Palacio*, such lines are 'sin remedio' (1981: 99). An interesting example from the *Libro* is the following line of 5F + 5F, which opens a *cuaderna vía* strophe:

(18)   Dios pa-dre, Dios fijo, Dios Spí-ri-tu santo   (11a)

It can be regularized by inserting the word 'e' after both 'padre' and 'fijo' and by preserving the extra syllable by hiatus. But, in addition to making the line less elegant, the result would destroy a familiar liturgical formula, and might even be

---

[4] Duffell 2003: 117 argues that fourteenth-century *cuaderna vía* texts could never have been read rhythmically, as contemporary French verse was, and subsequent Spanish syllabic verse still is. Three factors combine to make such a delivery impossible: (1) the reader's uncertainty on how to treat adjacent vowels, (2) the frequency of antirhythmic (*ley de Mussafia*) lines in the text, and (3) the presence of many lines with the wrong number of syllables.

held to deny the concept of the Trinity. Editors therefore usually leave it alone, a wholly defective *alejandrino*, but a perfect line of *arte mayor*.

All the arguments examined above confirm G. B. Gybbon-Monypenny's judgment that we should not assume that scribal error is the chief source of syllabic irregularity in the *Libro*. The words with which he concludes the introduction to his edition are excellent advice for future editors:

> en la enmienda de versos por razones puramente métricas, hay que andar con pies de plomo. Sólo en los casos en que un verso es tan defectuoso que resulta imposible creer que el autor lo quería así, y en que se presenta una enmienda más o menos obvia, merece la pena intentar sanarlo.   (1988: 78)

This statement follows almost immediately after an even more important point for researchers seeking to identify Juan Ruiz's metre: 'Me parece que a veces Juan Ruiz se dejaba guiar por el oído, por el ritmo del verso, a costa de la cuenta exacta de las sílabas.' Other writers have gone further than Gybbon-Monypenny in dismissing the importance of syllable count to the *Libro*; thus Ramón Menéndez Pidal believed that Juan Ruiz was 'exento de toda preocupación erudita de las sílabas contadas' (Baehr 1970: 56). The evidence presented above supports this conclusion that Juan Ruiz was not counting syllables; but, if his work is to qualify as verse ('numerically regulated language'), he must have been counting something. Gybbon-Monypenny's insight that 'el oído' and 'el ritmo del verso' were essential to Ruiz's method of versifying lead us to the most likely explanation of the *Libro de Buen Amor*'s metrics, as I shall elaborate.

Rhythm in the 'Libro'

Spanish poets are in a privileged position with regard to rhythm: their language's tendency towards syllable-timing means that they can create primary rhythms by syllabic regularity and phrasal stress (as French poets do), and their language's strong word stress means that they can also create secondary rhythms (as is the custom of English poets). These secondary rhythms are of two types: *simple secondary* rhythms organize word stresses within the line in groups (for example, 2 + 2 in Old English verse), while *complex secondary* rhythms alternate the two events, stress and non-stress (see Chatman 1965: 18–29). In English verse, however, word stress provides regularity, while in most Spanish verse, where syllable count produces primary rhythms, word stress is more often a source of variety (see Domínguez Caparrós 2000: 95–97). Thus English poems tend to be monorhythmic: all their lines are in duple time (stressed and unstressed syllables alternate) or in triple time (stressed on every third syllable); such regular accentual verse is termed stress-syllabic. In contrast Spanish poets usually vary these intervals between stresses: in their poems some lines are in duple time, some in triple, and some in a mixture of the two. Navarro Tomás thus classifies lines in all the metres employed by Juan Ruiz as trochaic (duple-time), dactylic (triple-time),

or mixed (1974: 71–72, 77, and 86). The following hemistichs and lines from the
Libro de Buen Amor offer examples of each of Navarro Tomás's types:[5]

Cuaderna vía
(19)	Trochaic:	pa-**la**-bras **son** de sa**bio**	(44a)
(20)	Dactylic	si que-**re**-des, se-**ño**res	(14a)
(21)	Mixed:	**to**-dos a **tien**-po çier**to**	(74b)

Octosílabos
(22)	Trochaic:	**le**-che, **na**-tas [e] **u**-na tru**cha**	(969d)
(23)	Dactylic:	**mu**-cho ga-**ça**-po de **so**to	(968d)
(24)	Mixed:	man-**te**-ca de **va**-cas **mu**cha	(969b)

Hexasílabos
| (25) | Trochaic: | **Om**-ne **quan**-to **pla**-ze | (1042d) |
| (26) | Dactylic: | le-**vó** me con **si**go | (1029b) |

Note that this line is too short to contain a mixture of these rhythms.

Word stress can thus be seen to provide variety in Juan Ruiz's verse, and that
variety depends on the irregular number of unstressed syllables between the
stresses. This prevents the verse from becoming stress-syllabic, except where the
poet maintains constant intervals between stresses for a series of consecutive
lines. Such series do occur in the *Libro de Buen Amor* (thus, for example, st. 1024
is dactylic and st. 1029 trochaic), but they are usually restricted to no more than
half a dozen lines. Accentual verse, however, is not restricted to the stress-syllabic;
several types allow irregular intervals between stresses (although, as in the *Libro*,
passages with regular intervals may also occur in them). And it seems that in
Castilian just such an accentual metre preceded *cuaderna vía*, and another, somewhat different, accentual metre superseded it. We should therefore study Juan
Ruiz's metrics in the context of Castilian epic metre employed at the beginning
of the thirteenth century, and the *verso de arte mayor* composed at the end of the
fourteenth.

The early history of accentual verse in Castilian

The oldest surviving verse texts in Castilian are popular proverbs first collected and written down in the fifteenth century, but almost certainly composed
and transmitted orally many centuries earlier. The earliest surviving written verse
texts in Castilian are the *Poema de Mio Cid* and the *Libro de Alexandre*, both of

---

[5] In these and the examples that follow I have indicated a prominence peak by placing the
syllable concerned in bold typeface. Note that where stressed syllables are adjacent only the one
bearing phrasal stress becomes a prominence peak. Mark Liberman and Alan Prince 1977
demonstrated decisively that the only aspect of stress that is metrically relevant to English
verse is whether a syllable bears more stress than its neighbours, and Esteban Torre 2002: 32
argues that this is equally true of Spanish.

which date from very early in the thirteenth century. The *Libro de Alexandre* (Willis 1934; MS *O*) begins with a statement to the effect that the poet is counting syllables ('a sylabas contadas') and that this is a technical skill of a high order ('es muy grant maestria'). This statement, without parallel in French poetry, is surely evidence that Castilian poets had not counted syllables before the *Libro de Alexandre*, and this is confirmed by all the surviving texts that may have been composed at an earlier date: the *refranes* collected by the Marqués de Santillana (Canellada 1980), the *Poema de Mio Cid* (Michael 1987), and the surviving fragments of other epics (Alvar and Alvar 1991).[6] Many modern metrists believe that lines in this older type of verse contain two hemistichs, each with two syllables made prominent by having greater stress than their neighbours (Navarro Tomás 1956: 60–61, Maldonado de Guevara 1965, López Estrada 1982: 217–25, Pellen 1985–86, and Goncharenko 1988: 51, all cited in Montaner 1993: 36; more recent support for this view has been provided by Bayo 1999 and Duffell 1999b and 2002). The metre is thus numerically regulated on almost exactly the same principles as Old and Middle English alliterative metre, as can be illustrated by instance (27), which is a Castilian proverb from Santillana's *Refranero*, or by (28)–(31), which are lines 15, 24, 36, and 37 of the *Poema de Mio Cid*:[7]

(27)	A ca-**ba**-llo co-me-**dor**	ca-**bes**-tro **cor**to	7M + 4F
(28)	Mio **Çid** Ruy **Di**-az	por **Bur**-gos en-**tra**va	4F + 5F
(29)	con **grand** rre-**cab**-do	e <u>fuer</u>-te-**mien**-tre se-**lla**da	4F + 7F
(30)	**los** de **dien**tro	non les que-**rién** tor-<u>nar</u> pa-**la**bra	3F + 8F
(31)	A-gui-**ió** Mio **Çid**,	a la **puer**-ta se lle-**ga**va	5M + 7F

Note that in this type of metre (both in Spanish and English) a third syllable in the hemistich may become a (subsidiary) stress peak, in addition to the two metrically prominent syllables; for example, 'fuer-' in (29) and '-nar' in (30). Note also that in some instances an atonic monosyllable, like 'los' in (30), provides the first of the two prominence peaks.[8] A major difference between the Spanish and

---

[6] Baehr notes: 'se puede suponer con seguridad que un período amétrico procedió en Francia y Italia al isosilabismo rigoroso' (1970: 177). French and Occitan poets were composing syllabic verse by the beginning of the eleventh century (see Paris 1933 and Lavaud and Machicot 1950), but the oldest surviving French poem, dating from the end of the ninth, is irregular in syllable count (Purczinsky 1965–66 and Duffell 1999a). For early verse in Italian with an irregular syllable count see Leonetti 1934: 119–27. One surviving Latin poem composed in Spain c.1148, the *Poema de Almería*, is also syllabically irregular, and seems to be in the same metre as the *Poema de Mio Cid* (see Martínez 1975: 223).

[7] In all the examples that follow the two metrically significant prominence peaks, or beats, are indicated by bold typeface, and stressed syllables representing subsidiary peaks are underlined.

[8] Note that the relative stress given to a series of monosyllables in delivery is fixed only in the case of clitic groups like *the man* and *on fire*, where the second syllable must be more prominent than the first. The relative stress of syllables in polysyllabic words, however, is fixed, and it is this fixed relationship (termed *strength* by linguistic metrists) that is regulated in most metres; see Hanson 1995: 66–70.

English metres is that alliteration is unsystematic in the Spanish, and is sometimes entirely absent, and that assonance and rhyme usually supplement or replace it.[9]

The metre that superseded *cuaderna vía*, the *verso de arte mayor*, was also accentual; it differed from epic metre mainly in having greater regularity: intervals between stresses of more than three syllables were avoided, and an interval of two was overwhelmingly preferred. These are the characteristics of the earliest *arte mayor*, as illustrated by the following lines (834e, 829a, 831a, and 838b from the *Rimado de Palacio*'s poem in that metre (st. 818–53); the remainder of the work is in a curious mixture of *cuaderna vía* and *octosílabos* (see Duffell 2003: 116–20)):

(32)	e non **ve**-o nin-**gu**no	que la **quier**ᵃ a-co-**rrer**	6F + 6M
(33)	**Dios** lo de-**man**de	per la **su** sen-**ten**çia	4F + 5F
(34)	con **grant** rre-ue-**rren**çia	**yo** per-don **pi**do	5F + 4F
(35)	To-le-do la **gran**de,	lo-**gar** en Es-**pa**ña	5F + 5F

Later poets adapted the *verso de arte mayor* in different ways: for example, Juan de Mena (b. 1411, d. 1456) and Juan de Padilla (b. 1468, d. ?1522) both composed stress-syllabic *arte mayor* by standardizing the interval between prominences at two syllables; the Marqués de Santillana, on the other hand, converted it into a syllabic metre of 5F + 5M / F, as noted above. In its various forms the *verso de arte mayor* dominated Castilian long-line verse from the last years of the fourteenth century until the advent of the Italianate *endecasílabo* in the second quarter of the sixteenth.

Between epic metre and *arte mayor* comes an interregnum in the history of Castilian long-line verse, the period dominated by *cuaderna vía*. The *Libro de Buen Amor* was composed towards the end of that period. The syllabic irregularity of Ruiz's work (and of the *Rimado de Palacio* somewhat later) can be taken as an indication that the novelty of counting syllables, introduced by *cuaderna vía* poets at the beginning of the thirteenth century, had met its demise by the middle of the fourteenth.[10]

The metric typology of Juan Ruiz's verse

If we assume that Juan Ruiz's verse design was accentual, like epic metre and *arte mayor*, and not syllabic at all, then the lines I have scanned syllabically above should be re-scanned accentually. The verse design of Ruiz's *cuaderna vía* lines

---

[9] Note that rhyme also gradually replaced alliteration in English accentual verse; as late as the sixteenth century a metre very like the *verso de arte mayor*, known as *tumbling verse*, still regulated both these forms of phoneme repetition (see Ker 1898).

[10] Elsewhere I have queried whether Castilian readers and audiences ever appreciated the syllabic regularity of early *cuaderna vía*, and whether that regularity was ever more than a cosmetic exercise, a tidying up after the poetic event (Duffell 2003: 118). Certainly the same accentual structure found in epic metre, the *Libro de Buen Amor*, and the *verso de arte mayor* is present in all *cuaderna vía*.

can then be seen to produce a line of two hemistichs, each with two prominence peaks, or beats, as follows:

(1a)	que **pue**-da de can-**tares**	un li-**bre**-te rri-**mar**	(12c)
(2a)	le-van-**tó** sᵉ el **grie**go:	ten-**dió** la <u>pal</u>-ma **llana**	(57a)
(3a)	le-van-**tó** sᵉ el ve-**lla**co	con fan-ta-**sí**-a **va**na	(57c)
(4a)	qᵘᵉ en **tien**-po de su **vi**da	**nun**-ca la <u>vies</u> ven-**ga**da	(63b)
(5a)	El que **fi**-zº el **çie**lo,	la **tierr**ᵃ e ₍ₕ₎ el **mar**	(12a)
(6a)	Se-ñor **Dios** qᵘᵉ a los jo-**dí**os,	**pue**-blo de per-di-**ción**	(1a)
(7a)	a Da-**niel** sa-**cas**te	del **po**-ço de Ba-bi-**lón**	(1c)
(8a)	<u>Pe</u>-ro **si** las que-**rién**	<u>pa</u>-ra por **e**-llas u-**sar**	(48a)
(9a)	<u>bien</u> o **mal**, qual pun-**ta**res,	<u>tal</u> te di-**rá** cier-ta-**men**te	(70b)
(10a)	a <u>San</u>-ta Ma-**ri**-na li-**bres**-te	del **vien**-tre del **dra**-go	(3c)
(18a)	Dios **pa**-dre, Dios **fi**jo, Dios **Spí**-ri-tu **san**to	(11a)
(19a)	pa-**la**-bras <u>son</u> de **sa**bio	[. . .]	(44a)
(20a)	si que-**re**-des, se-**ño**res	[. . .]	(14a)
(21a)	**to**-dos a <u>tien</u>-po **çier**to	[. . .]	(74b)

Note that optional third prominence peaks appear in the first hemistichs of (8a), (9a), (10a), (19a), and (21a), and in the second of (2a), (4a), (8a), and (9a).

Similarly, the verse design of Juan Ruiz's *arte menor* requires three prominence peaks, or beats, per line, as the following scansions show:

(11a)	El ter-**çe**-ro **cuen**-tan las **leyes**	(26a)
(12a)	**quan**-do ve-**nie**-ron los **rreyes**	(26b)
(22a)	**le**-che, **na**-tas ᵉ <u>u</u>-na **tru**cha	(969d)
(23a)	**mu**-cho ga-**ça**-po de **so**to	(968d)
(24a)	man-**te**-ca de **va**-cas **mu**cha	(969b)

Note that only (22a) contains an optional fourth prominence peak: such lines are rare, perhaps because the poet did not find such a strong trochaic rhythm attractive.

Finally the verse design of Ruiz's putative *hexasílabo* is similar to that of his *cuaderna vía* hemistich, and has two prominence peaks, or beats:

(13a)	**A** la de-**çi**da	(1024a)
(14a)	di ₍ₕ₎ **u**-na co-**rri**da;	(1024b)
(15a)	fa-**llé** ₍ₕ₎ **u**-na se-**rra**na	(1024c)
(16a)	fer-**mo**-sa, lo-**ça**na	(1024d)
(17a)	e **bien** co-lo-**ra**da.	(1024e)
(25a)	**Om**-ne <u>quan</u>-to **pla**-ze	(1042d)
(26a)	le-**vó** me con **si**go	(1029b)

Note that only (25a) contains an optional third prominence peak, and again such lines are rare; more often, as in (13a), an atonic monosyllable is called into service as a beat. As these examples indicate, this line has a greater tendency to become stress-syllabic in Ruiz's hands than either of his longer lines.

In some poems in this metre the lines contain two amphibrachs as often as six syllables, and thus have the same pervasive triple-time rhythm as the *verso de arte mayor*.[10]

Conclusions

All the lines of the *Libro de Buen Amor* are regular according to this hypothesis and all the metres Juan Ruiz employs have the same typology; this double consistency is in sharp contrast to the unpredictable fluctuation that a syllabic interpretation offers. There are, moreover, two great advantages to accepting the suggestion on how Juan Ruiz versified, made by Gybbon-Monypenny in 1988 and elaborated in this chapter. The first is that the history of versifying in Castilian between 1200 and 1500 becomes a story of natural and logical development, not one of oscillation, where poets at first did not count syllables, then suddenly began to do so, and then, almost as suddenly, abandoned the practice. The second is that we can dismiss the charges of metrical incompetence and carelessness made against one of the finest literary craftsmen of medieval Europe. The *Libro de Buen Amor* can then be seen as the poetic achievement it is: a composition of the highest order in every aspect, including its versification.

---

[10] The term *amphibrach* derives from the trisyllabic foot (short / long / long) of Greek quantative verse; modern metrists employ it to describe a rhythmic unit that is weak / strong / weak; see Piera 1980: 122–27.

Exempla and Proverbs in the *Libro de Buen Amor*

BARRY TAYLOR

When Juan Ruiz wrote his *Libro*, he drew on traditions of stories and sayings, Latin and vernacular, written and oral. Their presence throughout the book exemplifies its fusion of popular and learned. This survey of brief sayings and short narratives in the *Libro* is intended to define certain genres, to indicate the traditions underlying Ruiz's use of them, and to point to the coexistence of high and low culture in his work.

'Exempla'

An *exemplum* (plural: *exempla*) is a short story with a message.[1] In the words of J.-Th. Welter:

> Par le mot *exemplum*, on entendait, au sens large du terme, un récit ou une historiette, une fable ou une parabole, une moralité ou une description pouvant servir de preuve à l'appui d'un exposé doctrinal, religieux ou moral.
>
> (Welter 1927: 1)[2]

> (By *exemplum* was understood, in the broad sense of the term, a narrative or short story, a fable or a parable, a morality or a description which could support a doctrinal, religious or moral exposition)

There are thirty-two such tales in the *Libro* (see Table I).

Juan Ruiz uses various names for the *exemplum*. Old Spanish terminology was flexible, and the same term could be used for both of the brief sentential forms, proverb (see pp. 97–100) and *exemplum*. To refer to *exemplum* we find in the *Libro*: 'fabla' (96d, 320d, 407d, 1386d, 1453d), 'muchas fablas e historia paladina' (297c),

---

[1] My references are to Blecua 1992; when I prefer other readings, these are italicized and the manuscript indicated. I also cite notes by Cejador 1913 and Joset edn 1990. For concise overviews of the fable, see Massie 1900 and Jacobs 1912; for medieval animal fables, Ziolkowski 1993 and Gibbs 2002; on the *exemplum* in Ruiz, see Lecoy 1938, Michael 1970, Luis Beltrán 1977, Vasvári 1985–86, Haro Cortés and Aragüés Aldaz 1998, Lacarra 2002.

[2] Welter 1927 remains the classic study of the genre. Where no source is cited, translations are my own.

'enxienplo' (311d, 529d, 1411c; as well as 'enxienplo' passim in the non-authorial rubrics), 'fazaña' (457a, 474a), 'mis fablas e mis fazañas' (908d). On one occasion *fabla* refers unambiguously to animal fable: 'fabla [. . .] de Isopete sacada' (96d; a fable taken from Aesop). The phrase 'Las viejas tras el fuego ya dizen sus pas-trañas' (1273d; The old women now tell their tales round the fire), does not help our investigation, as it refers to a pictorial representation of old women whose *pastrañas* are unrecorded. Not relevant to our purpose is 'romance' (904a), which indicates a longer narrative.[3]

From the earliest written witnesses onwards, the message of the *exemplum* is made explicit either in an introduction (*promythium*) or conclusion (*epimythium*; Perry 1940).[4] A typical structure would be: *promythium*; story proper; message in story; message outside the story (*epimythium*). To take the example of 'The Fox and the Crow':

> *Promythium*: Los que dessean & han gozo en ser alauados por palabras arrepi-enten se dello como se veen engañados, delo qual se pone tal figura
> *Story proper*: Un cuervo, tomando de vna ventana vn queso [. . .]
> *Message in story*: [. . .] Entonçes el cueruo gemio engañado dela vana alauança con gran pesar que auia, el qual non le aprouechaua.
> *Epimythium*: Amonesta esta fabula que ninguno deve oyr njn creer las palabras engañosas [. . .]

> (*Promythium*: Those who desire and take pleasure in being praised in words regret it when they find themselves deceived, of which this image is given.
> *Story proper*: A crow, taking a cheese from a window [. . .] (The fox flatters the crow into singing, the crow drops the cheese and the fox takes it.)
> *Message in story*: [. . .] Then the crow, tricked by the vain praise, groaned, because of the great pain he had, which did not benefit him.
> *Epimythium*: This fable warns that no one must listen to or believe deceitful words)

When the story is inserted in a frame, as it usually is in the *Libro* (see p. 85), the *epimythium* is followed by an application. Thus Don Juan Manuel concludes his version of this story:

> Et vós, señor conde Lucanor, commo quier que Dios vos fizo assaz merced en todo, pues veedes que aquel omne vos quiere fazer entender que avedes mayor poder et mayor onra o más bondades de cuanto vós sabedes que es la verdat, entendet que lo faze por vos engañar [. . .]   (1994: 40)

> (And you, my lord Count Lucanor, although God has shown you sufficient mercy in all things, since you see that that man gives you to understand that

---

[3] See Deyermond 1980a. Compare the usage of Juan Manuel (Orduna 1977) and Ayala (Orduna 1986). On *fazaña*, see Gómez Redondo 1989; for *romance*, see Montaner (1993: 689), and Blecua's note.

[4] Although Perry is concerned only with classical examples, this is true of the genre as a whole.

you have greater power and more advantages than you know is true, understand that he does so to deceive you [. . .])

Despite his reputation for truancy, Ruiz is actually quite conventional in following this arrangement. (His truancy in the use of *exempla* comes elsewhere:
see pp. 93–95.)

The *exempla* of the *Libro* are arranged in five main frames, with the result that
only four tales are told by the Narrator to his audience [1, 4, 5, 22] (see Table I).[5]

Exemplum [1] occupies a prime position and plays the role of a key to the text:
it reinforces the point of the Prose Prologue on the difficulties of interpretation.
Frames A, B, D, and E are the accounts of the Archpriest's courtship of four ladies,
with, in three cases (A, D, and E), debates between the lady and the go-between;
frame C is his debate with Don Amor. In frame E the alternation between narra-
tors is disrupted – possibly by a lacuna –, as two successive tales are told by
Trotaconventos to Garoça [26 and 27].

The tradition of 'exempla' in the frame
Although some books of *exempla* simply arrange their tales in alphabetical order
of subject (in order to facilitate reference), others place their brief narratives in
a frame in which the *exempla* are recounted not by the author but by characters
in a larger structure, either dialogic or narrative (Robinson 1978: 1–2; Taylor
1993, 1995). To cite only works known in Spain, the earliest Western *exemplum*
book, the *Disciplina clericalis* of Petrus Alfonsi (*floruit* 1106), integrates its stories into a series of dialogues between father and son; to this frame tradition
belongs the *Conde Lucanor* (in which we may take it that the adviser Patronio is
named as an allusion to fatherly wisdom). In other cases, the frame is a more
developed narrative, as with the Greek *Barlaam and Joasaph* of John Damascene
and Arabic *Sendebar* and *Kalila and Dimna* (all available in Latin and Old Spanish
versions), and the exemplary romances of Ramon Llull such as *Fèlix o Llibre de
meravelles*. Although not unknown in the Latin classics (a notable example being
the episode of the daughters of Minyas in book IV of Ovid's *Metamorphoses*),
the use of a frame often coincides with a debt to oriental sources: Petrus's work
is explicitly drawn from Arabic sources, and Llull knew the *Kalila*.[6] Critics,
notably María Rosa Lida de Malkiel (1940 and 1959) and Américo Castro (1948),
pointed to Arabic and Hebrew *māqāmat* such as ibn Sabarra's *Book of Delights*
which, like the *Libro*, place tales in a picaresque frame.[7] It is, however, worth
noting that there are works of no apparent oriental affiliation, such as the English
Confessio amantis of John Gower, which place *exempla* in a dialogue frame.
Within the narrative frame, many of Ruiz's *exempla* are used in debate, as in
Kalila and *Fèlix*.

---

[5] References to Ruiz's *exempla*, given in brackets, follow the numeration in Table I.
[6] On Llull and *Kalila*, see Taylor 1995: 648.
[7] For further discussion of the *māqāmat*, see Haywood, this volume.

Animal fables

Most of Ruiz's *exempla* are animal fables, of the tradition of Aesop. (Ruiz himself refers to 'Isopete', 96.) The definitions compiled by Papias, the eleventh-century lexicographer, out of Isidore and Cicero are comprehensive:

1   Fabulas poetae a fando nominaverunt: quia non sunt res factae sed tantum fictae loquendo, ut fictorum [*sic for* ficto] mutorum animalium interloquio imago quedam vitae hominum nosceretur. Sunt autem aut Esopicae aut Libysticae. Aesopice ab Aesopo inventore dictae cum animalia muta vel quae animam non habent inter se sermocinasse finguntur. Libysticae autem cum inter homines et bestias commercium fingitur vocis.

(The poets named fables from *for fari*, 'to speak', as they are not things done but only feigned by speaking, so that by the feigned conversation of dumb animals an image of the life of man might be known. *They are either Aesopic or Libyan* (Aristotle, *Rhetoric*, 2.20.2). They are called 'Aesopic', from their inventor Aesop, when dumb animals or inanimate objects are feigned to have spoken among themselves. They are called 'Libyan' when the exchange of words between man and beasts is feigned.)

2   Fabulae aut delectandi causa fictae sunt ut hae quas vulgo dicunt vel quales Terentius composuit; aut ad naturam rerum ut Vulcanus claudus quia per naturam numquam rectus est ignis; aut ad mores hominum ut apud Horatium mus loquitur muri ut per narrationem fictam ad id quod agitur verax significatio referatur. (Isidore, *Etymologies*, 1.40)

(Fables are invented either to entertain, such as those told by the people, or such as (the plays) of Terence; or (to express) the causes of phenomena, such as (the myth of) limping Vulcan, because in nature fire never goes straight; or to (demonstrate) the ways of men, as when in Horace (*Satires*, 2.6.79–117) the mouse talks to the mouse so that through an invented narrative the true meaning of the action is given.)

3   Fabulae sunt quae nec factae sunt nec fieri possunt quia contra naturam sunt. (Isidore, 1.44)

(Fables are things which have neither happened nor can happen because they are against nature.)

4   Tullius vero fabula ait est quae neque res veras neque verisimiles continet. (Ps-Cicero, *Rhetorica ad Herennium*, 1.8)

(Cicero says: fable is that which contains things neither true nor like the truth.)[8]

It will be noted from these citations that *fabula* had a number of meanings. Quotation 1 is devoted entirely to the animal fable; in quotation 2 the Aesopic fable is the third type of fable, one which is a figurative description of mores; quotations 3–4 do not refer specifically to the Aesopic fable, but it is subsumed

---

[8] Papias 1496, s.v. *fabula*; see also the discussions by Manning 1960, Ziolkowski 1993, and Minnis and Scott 1988. Papias omits Ps-Cicero's identification of this type of fable with tragedy.

into a general account of fictions. St Peter Pascual's condemnation of fable as fiction includes animal fable:[9]

> E amigos, ciertos aced que mejor despenderedes vuestros dias e vuestro tiempo en leer o oyr este libro, que en dezir o oyr fablillas de romances de amor e de otras vanidades, que escrivieron de vestiglos, e de aves que dizen que fablaron en otro tiempo, y çierto es que nunca fablaron, mas escrivieronlo por semejança, e si ay algun buen exemplo, ay muchas malas arterias e engaños para los cuerpos e las animas.

> (And friends, be sure that you will spend your time better in reading this book than in telling or listening to fables of love and other vanities written of animals and birds that are said to have spoken in olden times; and it is certain that they never spoke, but these things were written as a similitude, and if there is any good example in them, there are many tricks and deceptions for body and soul.)

Some aspects of Isidore's treatment, such as the distinction between Aesopic and Libyan fables, were not widely observed by the authors of fables. Other theoreticians who wrote on the *exemplum* usually subsumed the animal fable into the generality of illustrative narratives, *exempla*, whether historical, human, or animal. In his section on the Deadly Sins (218–414), Ruiz interfiles animal fables with brief allusions to historical (chiefly Biblical) episodes. An indication of medieval inclusiveness and Renaissance discrimination is the treatment of fables in *El conde Lucanor*: in the manuscripts the fables are interspersed with other types of tale, while in the princeps of 1575 edited by Gonzalo Argote de Molina they are broadly grouped together.

The animal fable is a classical rather than a Biblical form. The parables of Christ, often cited by medieval authors as a model, or at least a justification, for the *exemplum* (Osgood 1930: 19), have no tales of animals, and the Old Testament includes only two tales with non-human protagonists, and these are drawn from the vegetable kingdom rather than the animal (the fables of the trees in Judges 9: 8–15 and of the thistle and cedar of Lebanon in 2 Kings 14: 9).[10] Presumably animal tales also existed in popular oral tradition in the Middle Ages, but any debt on the part of medieval authors to the traditional animal fable is unverifiable.[11]

Animal fable was also associated with humour. On occasions this is linked with the stigma of being lightweight: Seneca recommends that his friend Polybius should gather 'the tales and fables of Aesop' (fabellas quoque et Aesopeos logos) as a exercise in 'the lighter kind of literature' (haec hilariora studia) to distract

---

[9] *Impugnancia de la seta Mahoma* in Armengol Valenzuela 1904–08: IV, 3; cited by Taylor 2000. Riera i Sans 1986 questions this attribution.

[10] On Biblical fables, see Massie 1900. For citations of these fables by medieval and Renaissance authors, see Manning (1960: 407–09), Sabat de Rivers (1982: 372), Minnis and Scott (1988: 48n48), Wheatley (2000: 39; citing Augustine, *Contra mendacium*).

[11] For discussion of this point, see Lacarra 2000 and Rafael Beltrán in press.

him from his grief.[12] When François Vavasseur (1658) dignified fable with critical attention it was in the significantly named *De ludicra dictione*. The friar Francesc Eiximenis too connects *fabula, trufa* and *risus:*

> Ut ab omni trufa uel risu te omnino preserues in omni tuo sermone et habeas pro certo quod id ad trufas uel fabulas se conuertant predicando, quod Deus tandem reddit eos contemptibiles et miserabiles coram populo suo
>
> (Barcelona 1936: 325)
>
> (Keep from all tales and laughter in all your sermons, and believe that those who turn to tales or fables in preaching, God makes contemptible and wretched among their people.)[13]

Ruiz acknowledges this link by associating an Aesopic fable with a 'toy' or 'trifle' and laughter:

> 'Señora', diz la vieja, 'dirévos un juguete:
> no·m cunta conbusco como al asno con el blanchete
> que él vio con su señora jugar en el tapete;
> dirévos la fablilla si me *dierdes* un risete.'[14]
>
> (1400; 'My lady,' says the old woman, 'I'll tell you a joke: may it not happen to me as happened to the ass who saw the lapdog playing with his mistress on the mat; I'll tell you a fable: go on, laugh')

Doña Garoça ripostes by calling Trotaconventos's fables rubbish: 'La dueña dixo: "Vieja, mañana madrugueste / a dezirme pastrañas" ' (1410; The lady said, 'Old woman, you got up early just to tell me twaddle.'). Similarly Garoça, in 1493, 'fablarme ha buena fabla, non *burlas* (*G*) nin *pastrañas* (*T*), / e dil que non me diga de aquestas tus fazañas.' (He must speak to me well, not tell jokes or stories, and tell him not to tell me these stories of yours; meaning: she will accept her suitor, provided he speaks to her well, *buena fabla*); she does not want Trotaconventos's stories, *pastrañas*, or jokes, *burlas*). Trotaconventos reports this to the Archpriest:

> Mas catad non le digades chufas de pitoflero,
> que las monjas non se pagan del abbad fazañero
>
> (1495; But mind not to tell her lies like a smut-monger, as nuns don't like a story-telling abbot)

He must not tell stories (fazañas) or lies (chufas).

Finally, given the tradition of fable as low-grade, humorous possibly in a stupid way, it is no surprise that animals were seen as truant: indeed, they were often

---

[12] *Ad Polybium* 8.3 (Basore 1932: II, 376–77), cited by Ziolkowski 1993: 23.
[13] See Taylor 1999a: 410.
[14] I prefer *T*'s reading for line d, where, as Cejador 1913 notes, the *si* is optative.

literally marginal, as illustrations of fables appear in the margins of impeccably serious texts such as liturgical books or the Bayeux Tapestry (Herrmann 1964; Randall 1966).[15] For Ruiz the subversive potential of animals was doubtless an attraction.

What was the appeal of such animal stories to the sophisticated medieval reader? Fable is the most transparently false genre, lacking in verisimilitude (as witness Cicero, cited p. 86). It is also the most knowing of genres, and its apparent lack of sophistication is ironic. Anyone who tells a fable is automatically telling something with an underlying message. Although medieval critics do not explicitly regard fable as a type of allegory, nonetheless Walter (see below) uses the terminology of Biblical exegesis (a form of allegoresis) to talk about his fables.[16]

As animal fables belong to both written and oral culture, it is usually difficult to establish the sources of a medieval literary fable: it is always possible that an author, in recreating a received version, might add material from a vaguely recalled oral tradition, or combine remembered versions, as well as making his own conscious contribution to a tale. Rafael Beltrán (in press, part I) has shown that seven of Ruiz's animal fables circulate orally in modern times.[17]

The principal source of Ruiz's fables are the Aesopic fables commonly attributed to Walter the Englishman (c. 1200).[18] These are sixty-two fables in elegiac hexameters. Walter's fables are typically of eight to twelve lines. The *promythium* consists simply of the protagonists; there is also an *epimythium*. Walter's fables are a humorous reworking of the dour prose fables attributed to one Romulus (ninth century?): in Walter the witty Ruiz found a text which was already droll (but not truant). Both Romulus and Walter are in the tradition of Phaedrus, the Roman fabulist whose works were not known in the Middle Ages. Walter impregnated Romulus with an Ovidian wit.[19] Where Romulus clearly articulates the episodes of his narrative, Walter is sometimes so brief as to be oblique, beginning: 'Est lupus, est agnus [. . .]' (Walter 2; There is a wolf, there is a lamb). Walter is also fond of wordplay, especially the use of chiasmus around the caesura, a typically Ovidian figure.

The names 'Romulus' and 'Walter' are not always found in the Latin manuscripts, which sometimes refer to 'Aesop' as the author: Ruiz cites the generic name once: 'fabla de Isopete' (96). The meticulous studies of the fables and their Latin sources by Margherita Morreale (1975a, 1987, 1989–90, 1990, 1991, and 2002), and others, have shown beyond doubt that Walter was Ruiz's principal source. The role of Romulus in the *Libro* is, I think, harder to prove. Morreale is prepared

---

[15] The drawings in MS *S* of a bird (opposite st. 721), bear (870), and ape (1623) do not belong to this tradition; see also the discussion of marginalia in de Looze, below.

[16] For the distinction between fable and allegory, see Strubel 1988.

[17] The assumption of a continuity of medieval and modern narrative traditions is implicit in Michael 1970.

[18] The text of Walter is in Hervieux 1893–94: II, 316–51; there are machine-readable versions by Wright 2002, and Gibbs 2002. The best study is Wheatley 2000.

[19] The text of Romulus is in Hervieux (1893–94: II, 195–233). On Ovid's wit, see Frécaut 1972.

to see Romulus (specifically the Romulus Vulgaris) as a secondary source: Ruiz uses Walter for style, Romulus for story. Elsewhere, as Morreale recognizes, many of the details present in the *Libro* and Romulus but absent from Walter could be simply explained by a common desire by Ruiz and Romulus to clarify the outline of the story.

What version of Walter did Ruiz use? It is possible that he did not know the whole Walter text, as out of sixty-two fables the latest he uses is number 43. (We may note that one Hispanic Walter manuscript, Madrid, Biblioteca Nacional 4245, goes up to Fable 58.) He seems not to have known the version with extra moralizations in Hervieux (1893–94: II, 352–65), and, of course, like many a school text Walter could well have circulated in oral, parodic versions.

Walter, like two other texts used by Ruiz, Cato and *Facetus*, was a school text (Boas 1914; Hunt 1991: I, 66–79). By the twelfth century a corpus of six Latin readers had formed: the *Liber catonianus* or *Auctores sex*, consisting of Cato, the Fables of Avianus, the Eclogues of Theodulus, the Elegies of Maximianus, the *Achilleis* of Statius and the *De raptu Proserpinae* of Claudian.[20] By the thirteenth or fourteenth centuries, this anthology had been replaced by the *Auctores octo* or *Libri minores*, a collection more moral than classicizing: Cato, *Facetus*, *De contemptu mundi*, *Floretus*, the *Tobias* of Matthew of Vendôme, the Fables of Walter, Theodulus, and the *Parabolae* of Alan of Lille. Thus the fables of Romulus were not apparently a school text like those of Walter and Avianus. Of the *Auctores sex*, only the *Disticha* seem to have been translated in the Iberian Peninsula; of the *Auctores octo*, Aesop was available in Catalan, Portuguese, and Spanish before 1500, and there was an Old Catalan adaptation of *Facetus*.[21]

Walter presents various qualities in which Ruiz must have recognized a kindred spirit. Walter's prologue addresses the question of the symbiosis of pleasure and profit, as does Ruiz in his Prose Prologue and the *exemplum* of the Greeks and Romans.

> Vt iuuet, ut prosit, conatur pagina presens:
> Dulcius arrident seria picta iocis.
> Ortulus iste parit fructum cum flore, fauorem
> Flos et fructus emunt; hic nitet, ille sapit.

---

[20] Segovia Cathedral MS B-286 (see Rubio Fernández 1984: no. 558) has three of the *Auctores sex* (Cato, Theodulus, Avianus) plus Ovid's *Remedia amoris* and Alan of Lille's *De planctu Naturae*. BNM 4245 includes Walter (up to Fable 58; f. 93r–121) and *Floretus* (f. 201r–34v), double spaced and glossed in Latin.

[21] On the Hispanic reception of Aesop in Latin and the vernacular, see Keidel 1901. The Old Portuguese Walter is edited by Calado 1994. There is evidence of an Old Catalan Aesop: 'Item, unum librum, in papiro scriptum, in vulgari, qui liber dicitur *Isop*', in a Barcelona inventory of 1340 printed by Hernando 1995: item 90.24. (There are further references to Aesop without indication of language at 331.35 and 393.33.) Walter eventually made his appearance in Spanish in the *Isopete* translated from Steinhöwel's collection and first printed in 1482 (García Craviotto 1989–90: 2316; see also Burrus & Goldberg 1990). The Catalan *Facet* is edited by Morel-Fatio 1886: see bibliography in Taylor 1997. On *Facetus*, see Martínez Torrejón 1978.

Si fructus plus flore placet, fructum lege; si flos 5
   Plus fructu, florem; si duo, carpe duo.
Ne mihi torpentem sopiret inhertia sensum,
   In quo peruigilet, mens mea mouit opus.
Vt messis pretium de uili surgat agello,
   Verbula sicca, Deus, complue rore tuo. 10
Verborum leuitas morum fert pondus honestum,
   Vt nucleum celat arida testa bonum.

(The present page attempts to delight (*pun on* help), to benefit: / Serious things please more sweetly when painted with jests. / This little garden bears fruit with flowers, / The flower and the fruit buy favour: / The first is beautiful, the second is wise (*pun on* tastes good) / (l. 5) If the fruit pleases more than the flower, gather (*pun on* read) the fruit; / If the flower pleases more than the fruit, pick the flower; / If both, take the two. / So that idleness will not make my sluggish senses go to sleep, / My mind has put this work forward, at which it will keep awake. / So that the value of the harvest might rise from lowly land, / (l. 10) Rain on the dry little words, God, with your dew. / The lightness of the words bears the honourable weight of morals, / Just as a dry nutshell conceals a good kernel)

Here may be noted the double intention to delight and to benefit, imaged in the flower and the fruit (line 3). While it was a commonplace for authors to claim to combine instruction with delight, few authors actually refer to 'jokes' rather than a more abstract (or more elevated) 'pleasure'. Walter puns on 'lege' (l. 5); and possibly on 'iuuet' (l. 1), 'sapit' (l. 4). Line 9 invites comparison with Ruizian statements such as 'so mala capa yaze buen bebedor' (18c). The contrast between words and meaning (l. 11) also chimes with a major theme in the *Libro*. Finally, Walter draws on the language of Biblical studies: dew is a Biblical image for God's grace, and the nutshell and kernel are images of surface and underlying meaning.[22]

Strangely, Ruiz does not exploit the literary-critical aspect of Walter's first fable. In the Latin, the tale of the Cock and the pearl follows immediately on Walter's invitation to the reader to take what he wants from his book. Ruiz transfers the story [26] to a much less prominent position within the fifth frame, and misses the literary aspect out entirely.[23]

---

[22] For dew see *Orto do Esposo*, ch. 8 (Maler 1956–64: I, 26–27) and Fray Luis de León (García 1951: 1793); for kernel, Robertson 1951.

[23] This is quite a complicated question. The equivalence of cock and reader is not explicit in Walter, but is made clear by, for instance, *Esopete ystoriado*, I; ed. Burrus and Goldberg 1990: 3: 'Esta fabula rrecuenta el Esopo contra aquellos que leen este libro e non lo entienden' (Aesop tells this fable against those who read this book and do not understand it). Ruiz picks up this interpretation: 'Muchos leen el libro e tiénenlo en poder / que non saben qué leen nin lo pueden entender' (1390ab; Many read the book and have it in their hands who do not know what they are reading and cannot understand it). Curiously, though, these words are put into the mouth of Trotaconventos, who means them metaphorically.

As Morreale's analyses have shown, in his treatment of sources Ruiz largely conforms to standard techniques of the medieval translator, such as localization: Walter's unplaced town and country mice become the 'mures de Monferrado e Guadalajara' [25]. As Ruiz is commonly thought to be a man with New Castile connections, this may be read as familiarization. The animals are also made familiar: Walter's 'hydrus' becomes a crane [7]; Hispanic fauna are introduced in [14]. In many places he adds direct speech [25]. There are cases of increased specificity: 'esca' becomes 'carne' (1437c), although there are cases of the opposite (Morreale 1987: 436). There are examples of added visual detail (202). In some places Ruiz adds an element of lewdness [27].[24] He often renders one Latin word with a Spanish doublet (Morreale 1992: 393); Walter's 'belly' is rendered by four synonymous phrases (204ab). One *exemplum* in which Ruiz is unusually expansive is [15], to which he contributes his legal knowledge (Kelly 1984, and Gybbon-Monypenny's notes 1988).

Francisco Rodríguez Adrados (1986) points out that not all Ruiz's animal fables derive directly from the Latin of Walter. Non-Walterian fables are [2, 11, 21, 22, 28]. In some cases, the resemblance between Ruiz's and other versions is clear but the process of transmission is not. 'The Fox that played dead' [28] is found in the Greek and Hebrew versions of the Seven Sages of Rome, but not apparently in the Latin (Colón 1992; Navarro Peiró 1988: 98–100). In such cases the obvious solution is to invoke oral tradition and conclude that Ruiz heard a version of which there is no extant written record.[25]

Sources from other genres

'Fabliaux'

The *fabliau* is easily recognized: a bawdy tale with human protagonists.[26] There are three such in the *Libro*: the 'Man who wanted three wives' [6], the 'Two lazy suitors' [17], and 'Pitas Payas' [18]. The *fabliau* takes its name from medieval French collections, and it is tempting to think that in giving Pitas Payas a French ambiance Ruiz is alluding to a French genre; moreover, the *fabliaux* seem to be centred (in modern geography) on Northern France and Belgium, and Pitas Payas is set in Brittany, and Flanders. However, tales which modern criticism describes as *fabliaux* are found as early as Petrus Alfonsi (*floruit* 1106). Moreover, to what extent is *fabliau* a valid category? The only difference between the humorous *exemplum* and the *fabliau* is in subject-matter and tone: both are brief tales which use humour to convey a message.[27] The *fabliau* may therefore be legitimately subsumed into the *exemplum*.

---

[24] For lewd readings of the *exempla*, see Vasvári 1990b.

[25] Juan Manuel's version was contaminated by the *Libro* (Blecua 1980: 61). Cf. Dagenais 1994: 202–04.

[26] Nykrog 1973 is the classic study of the genre. On *fabliaux* in the *Libro*, see Vasvári 1989, 1992a, 1995b.

[27] On the message of the *fabliaux*, see Nykrog 1973: 248–49.

Religious tales

Two of Ruiz's *exempla* derive from religious sources. In 'The Drunken hermit' [19], the story itself, showing how one peccadillo leads to ever worse sins and eventually death, conforms perfectly to the conventions of the religious tales of the preachers. Ruiz's truancy is expressed in the application: this tale warns against drunkenness because drunkenness is unattractive in a lover. 'The Devil's vassal' [32], in its presumed original religious context, warned literally against trusting in the Devil. In the *Libro*, because it is told by an earnest narrator, Garoça, it retains the serious warning against gullibility, although it is secularized, the tempter being interpreted first as a generalized 'false friend' (st. 1476) and then specifically as the bawd (st. 1481).

Other sources

The closest source for Ruiz's tale of the Greeks and Romans is in the commentary of Accursius on the *Digest* of Justinian, 1.2.2.24. This was first pointed out by Julio Puyol y Alonso, who found it cited by Nebrija as an example of medieval ignorance which presumed that the ancient Greeks were familiar with the Trinity (1906: 184).[28] Accursius quotes it as a gloss on the invention of the Twelve Tables of Roman law:

> Before this happened, the Greeks sent a sage to Rome to discover whether the Romans were worthy of laws. When he arrived in Rome, the Romans, thinking what could happen, appointed a fool to dispute with the Greek, so that if he lost he would be a laughing stock. The Greek began to dispute with a nod, and raised one finger, signifying one God. The fool, believing that he wanted to blind him in one eye, raised two fingers, and with them raised his thumb too, as naturally happened, as if he wanted to blind him in both; but the Greek thought he was demonstrating the Trinity. Then the Greek opened his hand, to show that all things are laid bare and open to God. But the fool, fearing that he was to be given a slap, raised a closed fist as if to punch. The Greek understood that God enclosed everything in his palm; and so believing that the Romans were worthy of laws, withdrew.

Accursius's purpose is obscure: his introduction is brief, and he draws no moral, so we may assume his purpose was simply historical. As often, Ruiz follows the story itself very closely: drawing on both folk and learned traditions, he contributes folk material on rude gestures and discusses problems of interpretation which belong to Latin learning (Vasvári 1994; Lacarra 2000).[29]

Ruiz's applications

As was noted above, Ruiz is obedient to tradition in (i) adhering closely to his sources (where these can be determined), and (ii) giving each tale an explicit

---

[28] I have used Justinian 1478?: fol. 6^{v}b.
[29] See also Vasvári, below, for discussion of this *exemplum*.

epimythium and application. While the *epimythia* follow his sources, it is in the applications that Ruiz is at his most mischievous. A mismatch between story and interpretation is observable as far back as the Greek Aesop (Chambry 1927: xxxvii). Stories in general can bear different interpretations: 'Mel' in *Sendebar* is told by the vizier in the Syriac and Spanish versions, and by his opponent the odalisk in the Persian (Kantor 1988: 81–83). Medieval exegesis, both of scripture and of classical texts, could accommodate a great variety of interpretations, provided that all such meanings were earnest.[30]

In frame A, the two tales [2 and 3] which the lady tells to the go-between have explicit *epimythia* ('learn from the experience of others' and 'beware of those who promise much') which are in accordance with tradition. In her application, the lady easily presents these recommendations as sexual caution. The message of [4], told by the narrator to the reader, is that man (the Archpriest) cannot over-rule the stars (his amorous nature).

In frame B, tale [5], again told by the narrator to the reader, the story is as in Walter. The difference is that Ruiz draws a parallel between the incorruptible dog and the incorruptible lady. Walter praises incorruptibility; Ruiz just records it, presumably with resignation.

In Frame C, [6] might be read as a literal example rather than a figurative *exemplum*. The debilitating effect of love / sex is stated in the *promythium* and depicted in the tale. In [7] the relationship of tale and application is – as is more normal – figurative. It teaches that freedom is better than subjection (to Love).

In the section on the Deadly Sins [8–16], the structure is simple. There is no argument: the Archpriest simply accuses Amor of being guilty of the Sins and then gives generalized examples of them, with no attempt to apply them to love. Some stories quite clearly and conventionally exemplify the sins in question: [8, 9, 12, 13, 14, 15, 16]. Tale [11] is sensibly applied as a comment on the self-destructive nature of lust. In [10] the problematic reading resides in the *epimythium* (i.e. within the story not in the application), as the conclusion confuses ingratitude with avarice, unless we are to understand that the wolf is mean because he refuses to reward the crane.

In the latter part of Frame C, [17] functions literally. To warn the potential lover that laziness will lose him his woman, Amor tells a story of a lazy man to whom precisely this happens. There is no discrepancy between the story and its application, as both are on the same level. Likewise in [18], Pitas Payas suffers for not paying attention to his wife; the application to the Archpriest is literal (st. 485). [19], in contrast, teaches that drunkenness leads to 'todo mal provecho' (543d), a message which it bears in the religious context from which Ruiz doubtless took it. The Archpriest's truancy is to interpret these evils as sexual failure.

---

[30] On the limits to interpretation, see Augustine, *De doctrina christiana*, III, 27 (Shaw 1952: 191). The *exempla* of the *Gesta romanorum* (see Swan 1894) are made to yield multiple meanings.

In Frame D, Trotaconventos seeks to persuade Endrina to heed (her) good counsel [20–22]. In Frame E, Garoça's five stories all have *epimythia* which teach caution. They are entirely conventional, as they match those of Walter. As in Frame A the lady's applications all interpret caution as equivalent to not being deceived by the Archpriest. Trotaconventos's stories – in accordance with Walter – teach against ingratitude (that is, Garoça's towards Trotaconventos) [24]; that the fool (Garoça) does not appreciate a good thing (the Archpriest) [26]; that one cannot go against nature (i.e. libido) [27]; that a little guy (Trotaconventos) can be useful (to Garoça) [29]; and against timidity (vis-à-vis the Archpriest) [31].

Thus Ruiz's truancy is expressed in the freedom of application afforded by the frame structure.

Proverbs

I use the term 'proverb' to designate the brief statement of a general truth, regardless of origin.[31] While the proverb is grammatically complete, the proverbial phrase is normally only part of a sentence. The proverb in Ruiz has been less studied than the *exemplum*. The two forms have much in common: they therefore share some names; a proverb can be used to summarize or re-express an *exemplum*; in some cases a proverb can be seen as a abbreviated *exemplum*. 929c, 'La liebre del covil sácala la comadreja' (the weasel gets the hare from its form), is hard to define: is it an allusion to a fable, a popular proverb, a false proverb invented by Ruiz, an observation from nature or an old wives' tale? (Rodríguez Adrados 1986: 460).

As with the *exemplum*, there are two traditions of the proverb: the learned *sententia* and the popular proverb (in modern Spanish, *refrán*). Although post-medieval writers came to despise the popular proverb as lazy thinking, Ruiz, like most other medieval authors, values both equally. Don Juan Manuel, for instance, uses popular proverbs alongside learned, and the author of the *Cavallero Zifar* places popular proverbs in the mouths of characters of all social classes (Ynduráin 1969; Piccus 1965–66; Lida de Malkiel 1950–51).[32] The earliest example of an author who apologizes for using a popular proverb appears to be Fernán Pérez de Guzmán around 1450 in his *Diversas virtudes y vicios*:

> El proverbio castellano
> en este lugar enxiero,
> porque a mi pensar es vero
> aunque vulgar, grueso y llano:
> el onbre loco y liviano
> tantas preguntas faría

---

[31] For medieval proverbs, see Taylor 1992; for the popular proverb in medieval Spain, see O'Kane 1959; and *Memorabilia* 2002; for the proverb in Ruiz, see Cejador 1913: II, 323–37; Gella Iturriaga 1973; Vasvári 2000a and in press.

[32] For the European context, Taylor 1992: 31.

que Catón no bastaría
a le dar consejo sano   (Díez Garretas and Diego Lobejón 2000: 193,
                              st. 228)

(I here insert the Castilian proverb, because in my view it is true, although
of the people, gross and plain: *the fool can ask so many questions that
Cato would not be able to give him sane counsel*)

By what features may a popular proverb be identified?[33] To my mind, there
are five criteria for identifying a popular proverb: two of them concern the way in
which a saying is introduced, and three concern the use of comparative material.

a. Anonymity. The presence of a named author (such as Cato, Pr 59, 44bc,
568d) precludes a popular origin.[34]

b. The attribution to 'the people' (as in later authors but not in Ruiz), to 'old
women' ('la vieja ardida' 64a; 'como dize la vieja, quando beve su madexa'
957a; an image of the old wife at her spinning) or simply to an 'old' saying
('proverbio viejo' 93a; 'proverbios antigos' 165c; 'antiguos retráheres' 170c) is
a very strong indication of popular origin.[35]

If these signs are absent, the popular nature of a saying can be verified by comparison with other witnesses. Mere coincidence of content is not sufficient grounds
for identification: there must be some similarity of phrasing, such as the linking
of two prominent words.

c. If a saying used by a medieval author without any of these signs occurs in
another Old Spanish text in which the signs are present, it may be taken that it
is popular (but *cave escriptura* 160, discussed p. 97).[36]

d. If a saying used by a medieval author occurs in a medieval collection of
popular origin (these are a handful of texts) or in a post-medieval collection from
oral sources, I believe it is valid to consider it popular.[37]

e. If a saying has very close parallels in the folk sayings of another Romance
language, this is a possible indicator of a folk origin.[38]

Ruiz has more popular proverbs than learned *sententiae*. Cejador (1913:
323–37) lists 281 'refranes y sentencias proverbiales' and José Gella Iturriaga

[33] Díaz G. Viana 1998. Modern Spanish usage often uses 'tradicional' to indicate circulation
among the people and 'popular' – equivalent to English 'folk-' – to designate origins among
the people.

[34] I depart here from the method of Goldberg 1986. See also her judicious strictures on the
methodology of earlier scholars.

[35] The references to 'vulgar' (presumably in the social sense), as given by O'Kane 1950: 5–6,
are from the fifteenth century; this is possibly indicative of the growing distance between learned
authors and the popular proverb (see n30 and Ynduráin 1969; Piccus 1965–66; Lida de Malkiel
1950–51).

[36] Any future assessment of the popular proverb in the *Libro* must take account of the data
in the 'Indice de refranes' in Dutton (1990–91: VII, 597–609).

[37] The medieval collections are listed by O'Kane 1959: 6. See the numerous parallels with
the *Refranes* attributed to Santillana in, for example, Cejador 1913.

[38] See Jacques Joset's comparisons with French proverbs (edn 1990), and the *Thesaurus
proverbiorum medii aevi* 1995–.

(1973), 377. More conservatively, Eleanor S. O'Kane counts 100 (1959: 18) and Harriet Goldberg 72. Joset's edition is the best for identifying proverbs.

Sententiae are typically introduced by phrases such as 'Como dize el sabio' (166a; as the sage says), 'dízelo sabio enviso' (173d; thus says a shrewd sage); 'Dize un filósofo, en su libro se nota, / que pesar e tristeza el engenio enbota' (1518ab; a philosopher says so, in his book it is noted, that grief and sadness dull the wits), according to Joset a reference to Cato.

There are some cases of a permeability between cultures: see 'Como dize la fabla que del sabio se saca, / que "çedaçuelo nuevo tres días en astaca"' (919ab, and see Cejador's note (1913); as the saying goes, taken from the sage, *a new sieve hangs for three days on the peg*), where a popular proverb is attributed to a sage.

Names

The following seem to be unambiguous terms for the popular proverb: 'pastraña de la vieja ardida' (64a), 'fabla' (80c, 95a, 111a, 942c, 955c, 977a, 994d, 1200a, 1490b, 1622a), 'proverbio viejo' (93a; also 'proverbios antigos' 165c), 'antiguos retráheres' (170c), 'fablilla' (179c, 870a), 'dichos' (378c), 'proverbio' (542a, 869a), 'fazaña' ('fazaña es usada, proverbio non mintroso' 580a), 'parlilla' (921a).[39] 'Suelen' (in the plural) also introduces popular proverbs on two occasions: 'fabla que suelen retraher' (1622a; a proverb which they are used to quote); 'suelen dezir' (1704a).

Derecho is a more ambiguous term. '"Quien mucho fabla yerra", dízelo el derecho' (733b; *He who speaks much errs*, says the proverb) is recorded as a popular proverb by Correas in 1627 (see Joset's note). However, 'Como dize un derecho que "Coita non ha ley"' (928a; As a [sic] law says, *Duress has no law*) is a legal saying, 'Necessitas non habet legem' (necessity knows no law), and is rightly emended by Cejador (1913) to 'Como dize el derecho' (as the law says).[40]

Escriptura is used to introduce a popular proverb at 160b, '[. . .] dize una escriptura / que "buen esfuerço vençe a la mala ventura"' (A writing says: *Good effort overcomes bad luck*). However, the use of such a word to indicate an oral source seems illogical, and does not appear to be attested elsewhere. As the proverb occurs also in a work known to Ruiz, the *Libro de Alexandre* 71 MS P (Willis 1934) – 'Dizen que buen esfuerço vençe mala ventura' (They say that *Good effort overcomes bad luck*) – we may conclude that *escriptura* means 'text'.

Some lines in Ruiz which smack of the popular are actually translated from Latin: for example, 'si el amor da fructo, dando mucho atura' (1364b; if love bears fruit, it lasts long by giving) translates Walter's 'nullus amor durat, nisi fructus seruet amorem' (27: 11; no love lasts unless fruit keeps love).

---

[39] For these names and others, see O'Kane 1950.
[40] For 'Necessitas non habet legem', see Pennington 2002.

Ruiz quotes popular proverbs which he then proceeds to gloss with sententious statements of his own:

> Una fabla lo dize que vos digo agora,
> que '*una ave sola nin bien canta nin bien llora*';
> el mástel sin la vela non puede estar toda ora
> nin las verças non se crían tan bien sin la noria   (111)

> (A proverb says this and I'm telling you now: a solitary bird neither sings well nor weeps well; the mast without the sail cannot stand forever; and sprouts are not grown so well without irrigation)

Here only line b is attested elsewhere as a popular proverb, and it is reasonable to see cd as glosses. Similarly, in 1610 lines a–c are glosses on d, which is a proverb:

> En pequeña girgonça yaze grand resplandor;
> en açúcar muy poco yaze mucho dulçor;
> en la dueña pequeña yaze muy grand amor;
> *pocas palabras cunplen al buen entendedor*

> (In a small jacinth lies great brightness; in very little sugar lies great sweetness; in the small lady lies very great love; a few words suffice for a perceptive man).[41]

Ruiz also reformulates proverbs to fit the *cuaderna vía* line:

> Pero, sí diz la fabla que suelen retraher,
> que '*más val con mal asno* el omne *contender*
> *que solo e cargado faz a cuestas traer*' [. . .]

> (1622; But so says the proverb that they quote, it is better for a man to contend with an awkward ass than alone and laden to carry a burden on his back)

The proverb occurs elsewhere in the shorter form 'Más vale con mal asno contender / que la leña a cuestas traer' (see Joset's note, citing Correas).

Learned 'sententiae'
Of Ruiz's learned sententious sources, the most frequently named is Cato (with three citations at Pr 59 (Blecua 1992: 9), 44bc, and 568d, to *Disticha* I, 5; III, 6; II, 22; respectively). The *Disticha Catonis*, a work of late antiquity (third century?) formerly attributed to a Dionysius Cato or even to Marcus Porcius Cato, consist of fifty-seven monostichs and one hundred and forty-four hexameter

---

[41] Other examples: 17–18 (one popular proverb (18c) and six newly minted); 1612 seems to be all of Ruiz's own invention, as do 66ab, 666.

couplets arranged in four books of approximately equal length, addressed to the author's son. Their message of moderate self-interest and stoicism was not exclusively Roman and proved easily assimilable into medieval Christian culture. Like Aesop, one of the *Auctores octo*, it was one of the most read books of the Latin Middle Ages.[42] Cato appears to enjoy the distinction among authors cited by Ruiz of being exempt from the irony with which he treats authorities.

The other principal body of sententious literature in the Middle Ages was the Biblical wisdom books, attributed to Solomon: Ruiz cites Ecclesiastes at stanza 105 (see pp. 99–100). Among the Ancients, he also names Aristotle (71a: see p. 100) and alludes to him as 'el sabio' (166a; the sage); Ptolemy and Plato (124a); and Hippocrates (303c). In all cases their sayings are divorced from their original ethical or scientific contexts to support an eroticized view of the world.

Truancy

By Ruiz's time there was a body of sententious poems in *cuaderna vía*, including a version of the *Disticha Catonis* known as the *Castigos de Catón*. There is little evidence of the circulation of the *Castigos* in the Middle Ages, but in the print age it was a 'popular' text in the Spanish sense.[43] John K. Walsh (1979–80b) has shown conclusive verbal parallels between the *Libro* and these earnest works, and argued that Ruiz parodies them.[44]

Parallel with Ruiz's application of *exempla* to his amours is his treatment of certain *sententiae*. Although, as was said above, Ruiz does not segregate learned and popular sayings, he does typically manipulate learned material to give it a popular or earthy interpretation: 'Provar todas las cosas el Apóstol lo manda; / fui a provar la sierra e fiz loca demanda' (950ab; Try everything, the Apostle commands; I went to try out the mountains and made a foolish quest; cf. 1 Thessalonians, 5: 21: Omnia autem probate: quod bonum est tenete (Test everything; hold fast what is good)) is a truant reading which traduces the meaning of the original by omitting its second half.

> Como dize Salamón, e dize la verdat,
> que las cosas del mundo todas son vanidat [. . .]
> E yo, desque vi la dueña partida e mudada,
> dixe: 'Querer do non me quieren, faría una nada.'

[42] The standard edition is *Disticha Catonis*, ed. Boas 1952. There is also a transcription with English translation by Jim Marchand in the Labyrinth Latin Bookcase at http://www.georgetown.edu/labyrinth/library/latin/latin-lib.html, 26 March 2002. For a modern English translation see Thomson & Perraud 1990: 49–85. For bibliography on the *Disticha* and their influence, see Taylor 1992: 25, and Thomson & Perraud, 1990: 49–58. For overviews of Cato in medieval Spain see Pietsch 1903; Infantes 1997; Taylor 1999b.

[43] The *Castigos de Catón* are quoted by Abner de Burgos (1270–1349?), but the earliest complete witness is the chapbook *Castigos e exempros de Catom* (Lisboa: Germão Galharde, 1521), in Castilian despite its title (see Infantes 1997).

[44] Walsh's case stands or falls on the closeness of the resemblances between the *Libro* and the background texts he cites.

> (105ab, 106ab; As Solomon says – and he tells the truth – all is vanity
> [. . .] And I, when I saw the lady changed and gone, said, 'To love where
> I'm not loved would be pointless')

cites Ecclesiastes, 1: 2: 'Vanitas vanitatum, dixit Ecclesiastes; Vanitas vanitatum,
et omnia vanitas' (Vanity of vanities, saith the Preacher, Vanity of vanities; all is
vanity). Thus Solomon's existential *vanitas* is turned into sexual frustration.
A phrase originally in Aristotle and transmitted by Cicero (see Blecua's note 1992)
is used for a joke about women, 'del mal tomar lo menos, dízelo el sabidor, / por
ende de las mugeres la mejor es la menor' (1617ab; 'Take the lesser of two evils,'
says the sage, so of women the smallest is the best).

A related phenomenon in Ruiz is the use of an authority as an excuse for
Ruiz's own mischievous thoughts:

> Como dize Aristótiles, cosa es verdadera,
> el mundo por dos cosas trabaja: la primera,
> por aver mantenençia; la otra cosa era
> por aver juntamiento con fenbra plazentera.
>   Si lo dexiés de mío, sería de culpar;
> dízelo grand filósofo, non só yo de rebtar

> (71–72b; As Aristotle says, it is a truth that the world strives for two things:
> the first, to have sustenance; the other is to have union with a pleasing
> female. If I said it of my own accord, I should be blameworthy; a great
> philosopher says it, I'm not to blame)

Here the quotation is brief enough to be sententious, and the sense is in accordance with the original. However, the amoral meaning is immoral in Christian
terms, and Ruiz deflects possible criticism onto the unassailable Aristotle.

Conclusions

To conclude this survey of *exempla* and proverbs in Juan Ruiz, we may recall
B. J. Whiting's encapsulation of the mentality of traditional wisdom:

> [To judge from their proverbs, our ancestors] would seem to be characterized
> by varying degrees of cynicism, cunning, distrust, expediency, suspicion, self-
> interest, misanthropy, despair, frustration, pessimism, secrecy, caution, elitism,
> ingratitude, regional prejudice, and furtiveness [. . .] Proverbs take a dim view of
> humanity, and in them the seamy side prevails over the good.   (1977: xxx, xxxi)

Although Whiting was concerned with the proverbs of early America, his
description is certainly true of the Old Spanish popular proverb corpus, and of
the learned wisdom literature of Ruiz's time: against this background, I believe,
Ruiz emerges as softer in his view of life, and more motivated by fun. We may

conclude from his handling of *exempla* and proverbs that Ruiz, a man with a high education, but sometimes low tastes, uses learned material, both narrative and sententious, to express a popular mentality.

Table I: List of exempla

Stanza	No.	Subject	Type	Source	Motif no.[1]
		Narrator to reader			
47–63	1	Greeks and Romans			H607.1 924A
		¶ A: COURTING OF FIRST LADY			
		Lady to go-between			
82–88	2	Lion's share	Aesopic		J.811.1 J.50+ 51
98–100	3	Earth's labour-pains	Aesopic	Walter 25	U114 K1800
		Narrator to reader			
129–39	4	King Alcaraz			M341.2.4+ 934A
		¶ B: COURTING OF SECOND LADY			
		Narrator to reader			
174–78	5	Incorruptible dog	Libyan	Walter 23	K2062
		¶ C: PELEA CON DON AMOR			
		Narrator to Don Amor			
189–96	6	Man and mill	*Fabliau*		J21.32 910A
199–205	7	Frogs and King Log	Aesopic	Walter 21a	J643.1 277

[1] Figures beginning with a letter are motif numbers from Thompson 1955–58; figures beginning with a number are type numbers from Aarne & Thompson 1964; both are copied from Michael 1970.

Stanza	No.	Subject	Type	Source	Motif no.

'Eight' Deadly Sins

Covetousness, 218–29
  223–25, Fall of Troy and Destruction of Egypt

Stanza	No.	Subject	Type	Source	Motif no.
226–27	8	Dog and reflection of food	Aesopic	Walter 5	J1791.4 34A

Pride, 230–45
  233, Fall of rebel angels

Stanza	No.	Subject	Type	Source	Motif no.
237–44	9	Horse and ass	Aesopic	Walter 43	L452.2 214*

Avarice, 246–56
  247, Dives and Lazarus

Stanza	No.	Subject	Type	Source	Motif no.
252–54	10	Crane and wolf	Aesopic	Walter 8	W154.3 76

Lust, 257–75
  258–59, David and Bathsheba; Destruction of five cities
  261–68, Virgil deceived[2]

Stanza	No.	Subject	Type	Source	Motif no.
270–72	11	Eagle and huntsman	Aesopic		U161

Envy, 276–90
  281–82, Cain and Abel; betrayal of Christ

Stanza	No.	Subject	Type	Source	Motif no.
285–88	12	Peacock and crow	Aesopic	Walter 35	J951.2 244

Greed, 291–303
  294–296 Adam; Lot

Stanza	No.	Subject	Type	Source	Motif no.
298–302	13	Lion and horse	Aesopic	Walter 42	K1121.1 47B

Vainglory and Wrath, 304–16
  305–06, Nebuchadnezzar (Vainglory)
  308–09, Samson, Saul (Wrath)

Stanza	No.	Subject	Type	Source	Motif no.
312–15	14	Lion killed self in rage	Aesopic	Walter 16	W121.2.1

---

[2] Michael here regards 'The Uriah letter' (258–59) and 'Virgil in the basket' (261–68) as tales.

Stanza	No.	Subject	Type	Source	Motif no.
Sloth and hypocrisy, 317–422					
No biblical references					
321–71	15	Court case of Fox vs wolf	Aesopic	Walter 38	U21.4+
408–14	16	Mole and frog	Aesopic	Walter 3	J681.1 278

ADVICE OF DON AMOR TO NARRATOR

Don Amor to Narrator

Stanza	No.	Subject	Type	Source	Motif no.
457–67	17	Two lazy suitors	*Fabliau*		W111.1 1950
474–84	18	Pitas Payas	*Fabliau*		J2301+ 1419
530–43	19	Drunken hermit	Religious		V465.1.1 839+

¶ D: COURTING OF THIRD LADY (DOÑA ENDRINA)

DEBATE OF TROTACONVENTOS AND ENDRINA

Trotaconventos to Endrina

Stanza	No.	Subject	Type	Source	Motif no.
746–53	20	Swallow, farmer, and birds	Libyan	Walter 20	J621.1+ 233C *Lucanor*, 6

Endrina to Trotaconventos

Stanza	No.	Subject	Type	Source	Motif no.
766–79	21	Wolf that sneezed (incomplete)	Aesopic		K1121.2 47B

Narrator to (lady) reader

Stanza	No.	Subject	Type	Source	Motif no.
893–903	22	Lion and ass	Aesopic		K402.3 52

¶ E: COURTING OF FOURTH LADY (DOÑA GAROÇA)

DEBATE OF GAROÇA AND TROTACONVENTOS

Garoça to Trotaconventos

Stanza	No.	Subject	Type	Source	Motif no.
1348–53	23	Peasant and snake	Libyan	Walter 30	J1172.3+ 155

Stanza	No.	Subject	Type	Source	Motif no.
		Trotaconventos to Garoça			
1357–69	24	Greyhound and ungrateful master	Aesopic	Walter 27	W154.4 Cf. 160
		Garoça to Trotaconventos			
1370–83	25	Town mouse and country mouse	Aesopic	Walter 12	J211.2 112
		Trotaconventos to Garoça			
1387–91	26	Cock and sapphire	Aesopic	Walter 1	J1061.1
1401–07	27	Ass and lapdog	Aesopic	Walter 17	J2413.1 214
		Garoça to Trotaconventos			
1412–20	28	Fox that played dead	Aesopic	Syntipas?	J351+ K522 1 33 Lucanor, 29
		Trotaconventos to Garoça			
1425–33	29	Lion and mouse	Aesopic	Walter 18	B371.1 75
		Garoça to Trotaconventos			
1437–41	30	Fox and crow	Aesopic	Walter 15	K334.1 57 Lucanor, 5
		Trotaconventos to Garoça			
1445–49	31	Timid hares	Aesopic	Walter 28	J1812.2 Cf. 1321
		Garoça to Trotaconventos			
1454–75	32	Devil's vassal	Religious		M212.2 Cf. 810, 821 Tubach 1628[3] Lucanor, 45[4]

[3] Tubach 1969.
[4] Michael includes the 'Clérigos de Talavera'.

Part 3: THE DOÑA ENDRINA / DON MELÓN EPISODE

'Was it a Vision or a Waking Dream?': The Anomalous Don Amor and Doña Endrina Episodes Reconsidered

ALAN DEYERMOND

> The juge dremeth how his plees been sped; [. . .]
> The lovere met he hath his lady wonne.
> (Chaucer, *The Parliament of Fowls*, ll. 101 and 105;
> Benson et al. 1988: 386)
>
> Do sheepdogs dream of counting sheep?
> (Connor 2002)

The anomalies

The *Libro de Buen Amor* is a patchwork of anomalies, ambiguities, inconsisten-cies, ironies, and pitfalls for its interpreters. To say that any episode of the *Libro* is anomalous may seem like tautology, but the linked episodes of the debate with Don Amor and the seduction of Doña Endrina, beginning at stanza 180 and continuing to stanza 909, are, even when judged by the high standards of oddity that Juan Ruiz sets himself, notably anomalous. One oddity is apparent at the outset: Don Amor's large size.

> Ca, segund vos he dicho, de tal ventura seo
> que, si lo faz mi signo o si mi mal asseo,
> nunca puedo acabar lo medio que deseo;
> por esto a las vegadas con el Amor peleo.
>
> Dirévos una pelea que una noche me vino,
> pensando en mi ventura, sañudo e non con vino:
> un omne grande, fermoso, mesurado, a mí vino;
> yo le pregunté quién era; dixo: 'Amor, tu vezino'.[1]

This chapter is a considerably revised version of a paper read to the Medieval Hispanic Research Seminar, Queen Mary and Westfield College, on 31 March 2000. I am grateful to those present for comments that have helped in the work of revision, and to those who read drafts of the chapter for a number of useful suggestions.

[1] St. 180–81; Blecua 1992: 50–51. All quotations from the *Libro* will be from this edition, identified by stanza. I regularize the use of c / ç, and silently correct obvious misprints, through-out. These stanzas occur in MS *S* only. They are separated by the rubric 'De cómo el Amor vino al Arcipreste e de la pelea que con él ovo el dicho Arcipreste'. The rubrics are, as Jeremy Lawrance has conclusively demonstrated (1997), not the work of Juan Ruiz. Gybbon-Monypenny (1988) is, as Lawrance says (241n19), right to include them, since he is editing

The personified god of love is traditionally depicted, both in literature and in art, as the young child Cupid. Jacques Joset discusses his anomalous presentation as 'un omne grande, fermoso, mesurado' and considers possible reasons for this (1988: 115–26).[2] Yet however one accounts for this large and imposing figure, both his size and his sudden appearance remain surprising. Even more surprisingly, there is, much later, an indication that Don Amor's size may not be permanent: 'Eres muy grand gigante al tienpo del mandar, / eres enano chico quando lo as de dar' (401ab).[3] These words form part of one of the series of reproaches uttered against Amor, and are a metaphorical amplification of 'prometes grandes cosas, poco e tarde pagas' (400d), but why is this metaphor of shape-changing chosen? Is it possible that it verbalizes a lurking worry about impotence? It may be worth recalling a passage from Gonzalo de Berceo's *Vida de Santo Domingo de Silos*, in which the Devil appears to the young nun Oria (not the protagonist of the *Vida de Santa Oria*) in the form of a snake, which:

> poniéseli delante   el pescueço alçado;
> oras se facié chico,   oras grand desguisado,
> a las veces bien gruesso,   a las veces delgado.
>
> (st. 328b–d; Dutton 1978: 86).

These lines are added by Berceo to Grimaldus's account in chapter 9 of the *Vita Sancti Dominici confessoris Christi et abbatis* (see Deyermond 1975: 85–90). I think it likely that this amplification comes from an authentic dream, possibly one about which Berceo was told in the confessional. The sexual content of Berceo's stanzas is unmistakable, whereas there is room for doubt in the interpretation of Juan Ruiz's lines. Nevertheless, I think it would be rash, especially in view of the passages on which Louise Vasvári 1990a comments, to exclude the possibility that those lines may hint at tumescence and detumescence.

The duplication of amatory doctrine – Don Amor's advice in stanzas 423–574 is in substantial measure repeated by Doña Venus in stanzas 607–48 – has long been recognized, and the explanation in terms of literary sources is equally well known. What Don Amor says is a paraphrase of Ovid's *Ars amatoria* ('Esto que te castigo con Ovidio concuerda', 446c), which is also the source for Venus's advice to Pamphilus in the twelfth-century elegiac comedy *Pamphilus de amore*:

> Si leyeres Ovidio, el que fue mi crïado,
> en él fallarás fablas que le ove yo mostrado,

MS *S* (the same may be said of Blecua, who takes *S* as the base text for his critical edition), but for my purposes it is important to distinguish them from the poet's text.

[2] See also Cherchi 1987 and Di Stefano's note in La Gioia and Di Stefano 1999: 653–54. Joset 1990 is not, as the date would suggest, a later version of his 1988 study, but an earlier one whose publication was delayed. Joset 1988 is therefore the version that should be consulted.

[3] My surprise does not seem to be widely shared. These lines are not singled out for comment in the editions of, for example, Corominas 1967 or Gybbon-Monypenny 1988, and although there is a substantial comment in Zahareas et al. 1990 it does not refer to the aspect that interests me.

muchas buenas maneras para enamorado:
Pánfilo e Nasón yo los ove castigado.   (429)

Since the Endrina episode is an adaptation of *Pamphilus*, the same advice is given twice. That explains how the repetition occurs, but it does not explain why, and, as G. B. Gybbon-Monypenny notes (1988: 231–32n; Blecua 1992 does not comment), Juan Ruiz feels the need to make Venus offer a justification:

Ya fueste consejado del Amor, mi marido;
d'él en muchas maneras fuste apercebido;
porque le fuste sañudo, contigo poco estido;
de lo qu'él non te dixo de mí te será repetido.

Si algo por ventura de mí te fuere mandado
de lo que mi marido te ovo consejado,
serás ende más cierto, irás más segurado:
mejor es el consejo de muchos acordado.   (608–09)

This is not the only case of repetition in the *Libro* (the double narration of the four *serrana* episodes has received a good deal of attention), but it is the most obtrusive.

The narrator-protagonist's name is another surprise. At the end of the debate with Don Amor he names himself as 'Yo, Johan Ruiz, el sobredicho acipreste de Hita' (575a; the stanza is found only in MS *S*), yet in the Endrina episode he is named by Trotaconventos as 'Don Melón de la Uerta, mancebillo de verdat' (727c), and the name recurs several times. It is true that in most cases it is mentioned by Trotaconventos (in 881d she amplifies the name to Don Melón Ortiz), but at the end of the episode the narrator-protagonist says 'Doña Endrina e Don Melón en uno casados son' (891a). Once the episode is over, the name 'Don Melón' is never used again (though it is remembered by readers: see Whinnom 1977–78), and no explanation is offered for this double change. The oddity of this is compounded by the nature of the name: like his beloved Endrina and her mother, Doña Rama, the lover belongs by his name not to the animal but to the vegetable kingdom.[4] This has, understandably, stimulated a good deal of interest (e.g. Vasvari 1988–89). Names in the *Libro* are often unusual (e.g. Doña Cruz), but not to this extent. It is one thing for various kinds of fish and meat to become soldiers in the armies of Cuaresma and Carnal, in an obviously allegorical battle; it is quite another for human characters, in a supposedly realistic love-narrative, to be called Melon, Sloe, and Branch.[5]

---

[4] Joan Corominas argues that *melón* here is more likely to mean 'badger' (1967: 278–82). The possibility cannot be excluded, but the majority opinion that it means 'melon' seems more convincing.
[5] David Hook has discovered that the names or bynames Rama and Melón appear in documents of the period (1993: 158–60); Endrina has not – or, at least, not yet – been documented. Hook rightly advises caution in attributing symbolic or humorous meaning to such names before their historical context is firmly established. However, none of his

The Endrina episode is the narrator-protagonist's only successful courtship (he has hitherto been spectacularly unsuccessful, losing even the clearly available Doña Cruz to his messenger). We are left in doubt about the outcome of his wooing of the nun Garoça, and although it is likely that the 'apuesta dueña' (910b) is seduced after being drugged by Trotaconventos (941–42) she dies within a few days (943c).[6] Only in the case of Endrina is there indisputable success: thanks to Trotaconventos's cunning, Endrina's resistance is overcome (the loss of thirty-two stanzas after 877 prevents us from knowing how), and

> Doña Endrina e Don Melón en uno casados son:
> alégranse las conpañas en las bodas con razón   (891ab)

It is a commonplace of *Libro de Buen Amor* criticism that this success is due to the advice given by Amor and Venus, and that is indeed the impression that the author gives us. Yet that is not quite as satisfactory an explanation as it seems: why, once the narrator-protagonist has learned the lesson and acquired the services of a skilled go-between, does the success not continue? And why does the settled relationship of which we are told in 891ab vanish into thin air, never to be heard of again?[7]

The narrator-protagonist, having presented the conquest of Endrina as his own experience, then denies that it was anything of the sort:

> Entiende bien mi estoria de la fija del endrino:
> díxela por te dar ensienplo, mas non porque a mí vino   (909ab)

This is disconcerting enough, but there is more to come: in the next stanza he says 'Seyendo yo después d'esto sin amor e con coidado' (910a), and the autobiographical narrative continues. What, then, are we to make of 'después d'esto'? After what? It can only be a reference to the Endrina episode.

Putting these anomalies together, we have something very odd indeed: the sudden appearance of a large man (who, we later learn, may become very small), a character whose name changes inexplicably (to one that forms part of an unlikely grouping) and then back again, a long repetition that has no narrative justification, the only successful courtship in a succession of failures (a success that vanishes into thin air), and a sudden disavowal and equally sudden resumption of the first-person narrative. This is, as I said at the outset, notably anomalous

---

documents contains two of the names, so to find all three used for characters in a literary text is so remarkable as to suggest that the author has a special reason for their use.

  [6] I agree with the commentators – for example, Zahareas et al. 1990: 260 – who see the conjunction of the two events as indicating that Trotaconventos had to use such powerful drugs that the 'apuesta dueña' was poisoned. Coromines's doubt (1967: 368) as to how quickly the lady died seems to me to be ill founded.

  [7] The question remains valid even if Coromines is right in interpreting 'casados' not as marriage but as concubinage (1967: 344). But, despite the scorn with which he refers to those who take a contrary view ('como entienden ingenuamente', 'esta incomprensión evidente'), the evidence for his opinion is weak.

even when judged by the high standards of oddity that Juan Ruiz sets himself.[8] Can we account for it? If it were to be read as an extended dream-narrative, all the anomalies would be resolved, but is it reasonable to do so in the absence of an explicit statement by the poet?

Is it a dream?

Over sixty years ago Félix Lecoy said that 'l'Archiprêtre nous raconte qu'il eut un jour un rêve, au cours duquel l'Amour lui apparut' (1938: 209).[9] He makes the point again a little later: 'Juan Ruiz a utilisé, pour introduire le dieu, un procédé banal de la littérature du Moyen Âge, le procédé du songe. Il n'en tire du reste aucun effet particulier' (290n1). After this, he says no more about the matter, and his idea was not taken up. Indeed, because it is mentioned only in passing, and perhaps also because he says that Juan Ruiz made no effective use of the dream element, it seems – although he makes the point three times – to have been largely overlooked.[10]

Lecoy, like Amador de los Ríos before him, was wrong to state as a fact that Juan Ruiz 'nous raconte qu'il eut un jour un rêve': unlike most medieval authors who present dreams in their works, he makes no explicit statement.[11] And since Lecoy gives no reasons for his opinion, it is easier to understand why subsequent criticism did not pursue the matter. Jacques Joset, who has written two interesting articles about dreams and visions in medieval Spanish literature (1995a and b), does not discuss the debate with Don Amor, and his study of the description of Don Amor (1988: 115–26) does not mention the possibility of a dream. This is logical if we accept his strict criterion: an episode is to be read as a dream or vision only if the author explicitly marks it as one. On this basis, Joset concludes that 'El relato de los sueños en la literatura medieval española sigue siendo una tierra si no desconocida por lo menos tan sólo vislumbrada' (1995a: 51).

---

[8] All of this, moreover, is accompanied by a high frequency of source references: there are fourteen explicit references to sources in the verse of the *Libro* (plus another three in the prose prologue), and of these fourteen, ten occur in the Amor and Endrina episodes. It is true that these two episodes occupy 42 per cent of the stanzas, but the source references, at 71 per cent of the total, are disproportionate, and their frequency reminds us that dream visions in late-medieval literature quite often follow the author's reading of a book late at night.

[9] This is more accurate than his previous statement that 'une nuit, le poète a un rêve' (25), a statement that identifies – in Leo Spitzer's classic terms (1946) – the poetic with the empirical I. See also Rey 1979. Lecoy was not the first: José Amador de los Ríos said that 'se le pareció en sueños don Amor' (1861–65: IV, 177), but without further comment, and his words were forgotten.

[10] María Rosa Lida was, Yakov Malkiel tells us (Lida de Malkiel 1973: vii), greatly impressed by Lecoy's book, but although she includes this passage of the *Libro* in the *Selección* that she published in 1941 she does not go any further than a reference to a vision as one of the 'Muchos temas típicos [que] entreteje Juan Ruiz en el largo episodio siguiente' (1973: 49). Walter Holzinger says that 'It could even be argued that [the Don Amor episode] is a dream-vision' (1980: 32), but does not pursue this question.

[11] *Sueño* is used once in the *Libro* to mean 'sleep' (184bc), and never to mean 'dream'.

Julian Palley's study of dreams in medieval Spanish works (1983: 34–63) and the later study by Teresa Gómez Trueba (1999: 50–67) deal mainly with dreams explicitly announced by the authors, though both scholars are willing to go a little beyond that boundary. It is not wholly surprising that neither mentions the *Libro* (Gómez Trueba, in any case, does not begin until the last years of the fourteenth century). Harriet Goldberg, however, is prepared to go further: we owe to her not only a study of the Marqués de Santillana's *Sueño* (1993; on another Santillana poem as a possible dream, see Marino 1985–86) but also the controversial interpretation of the *Razón de amor* and the *Denuestos del agua y el vino* as a 'unified dream report' (1984), so when even she did not think of the *Libro* when preparing her authoritative study of the dream report as a literary device (1983), Félix Lecoy's passing mention seems to be an isolated eccentricity by an otherwise cautious scholar.

In order to make a case for reading these episodes as a dream, I need first to set them in the context of medieval dream theory and of dream visions in late-medieval Castilian, English, and French poetry. This subject has been extensively studied in recent decades, notably in the Proceedings of a conference held in 1983 (Gregory 1985) and a book by Steven F. Kruger (1992).[12] Only the briefest summary is necessary here. The theorists generally divide dreams into those that have some degree of prophetic authority (visions sent directly by God having the highest authority) and those that have a physical or mental cause within the dreamer, and consequently, reflecting only the dreamer's current state, have no prophetic value. These categories are often subdivided: Macrobius establishes three divisions of the authoritative category, and two (*insomnium* and *visum*) of the dreams that lack authority. The *insomnium*, caused by the dreamer's waking preoccupations, is directly relevant to the *Libro*. Below the *visum* – dreams caused by an imbalance of the humours – are those with a temporary and disreputable physical cause, such as an excess of food or wine (they are scarcely thought worthy of comment by the theorists). It is the *insomnium* that is described by Chaucer in *The Parliament of Fowls*:

> The wery huntere, slepynge in his bed,
> 100 To wode ayeyn his mynde goth anon;
> The juge dremeth how his plees been sped;
> The cartere dremeth how his cart is gon;
> The riche, of gold; the knyght fyght with his fon;
> The syke met he drinketh of the tonne;

---

[12] The papers in Gregory 1985 that are of greatest interest for my present subject are those by Marta Fattori (87–109), Tullio Gregory (111–48), Giulio Guidorizzi (149–70), Raoul Manselli (219–44), Christiane Marchello-Nizia (245–59), Franco Michelini Tocci (261–90), and Jean-Claude Schmitt (291–316). C. S. Lewis's summary (1964: 63–65) and Alison M. Peden's article (1985) provide useful introductions to Macrobius's influential work, and Ruth Harvey summarizes the teaching of Avicenna's *De anima* (1975: 49–50). Articles by Peter Burke (1973) and Jacques Le Goff (1977) set dreams in their social context. Most studies of literary dreams in the Middle Ages (e.g. Spearing 1976) include a section on the theory. For medieval Arabic theory, see Irwin 1994: 193–94.

105   The lovere met he hath his lady wonne.

(Benson et al. 1988: 386)

It is so natural for waking preoccupations to carry over into dreams – often, of course, strangely transformed – that it came as no surprise to read, as I was completing the present article, that the 2002 meeting of the American Association for the Advancement of Science had been told that other mammals seem to dream in the same way (Connor 2002).

In the later Middle Ages, many narrative poems – often allegorical ones – have a dream framework, and the number of studies devoted to this kind of poem is large. A. C. Spearing's book (1976), though narrower in scope than its title suggests (apart from twenty-four pages on French poems, he deals only with English texts from the mid-fourteenth to the early sixteenth century), is of particular interest.[13] Some of the texts are earlier than the *Libro*, but most are later. This would rule them out if I were looking for sources for Juan Ruiz's lines, but it does not impair their usefulness in illustrating the ways in which medieval poets handle a tradition.[14] It is, therefore, instructive to compare the ways in which some French, English, and Castilian poets introduce their dream-vision narratives with Juan Ruiz's st. 181 (quoted above).

In the late 1230s, Guillaume de Lorris introduced the *Roman de la Rose* thus:

>   Aucunes genz dient qu'en songes
>   n'a se fables non et mençonges;
>   mes l'en puet tex songes songier
>   qui ne sont mie mençongier,
> 5   ains sont aprés bien aparant,
>   si en puis bien traire a garant
>   un auctor qui ot non Macrobes [. . .]
> 21   El vintieme an de mon aage,
>   el point qu'Amors prent le paage
>   des jones genz, couchier m'aloie
>   une nuit, si con je souloie,
> 25   et me dormoie mout forment,
>   et vi un songe en mon dormant
>   qui mout fu biaus et mout me plot;
>   mes en ce songe onques riens n'ot
>   qui tretot avenu ne soit
> 30   si con li songes recensoit. [. . .]

[13] Other useful studies are those of Hieatt 1967 and Russell 1988 on English, Bodenham 1985 on French, and the wider-ranging book by Lynch (1988, dealing with Latin, French, Italian, and English texts). Boehne 1975 deals with dreams in medieval Catalan prose. For Castilian, see the studies mentioned on pp. 111–12, above.

[14] Gybbon-Monypenny encountered a similar chronological imbalance when trying to establish the *Libro de Buen Amor*'s generic status (1957). If Henry Ansgar Kelly's suggested dating of the *Libro* 'at the forefront of the great burst of poetic activity that occurred in Spain in the 1380s' (1984: 113) were to be accepted, more of the texts would be earlier than Juan Ruiz's work.

> 45   Avis m'iere qu'il estoit mais,
>   il a ja bien .v. anz ou mais,
>   qu'en may estoie, ce sonjoie,
>   el tens enmoreus, plain de joie [. . .]¹⁵

Here there is no doubt that we are to be told about a dream: *songes* occurs five times in the lines quoted (1, 3, 26, 28, and 30), and *songier* once (3). The narrative is set in May (47), and it begins one night (24). The narrator has been reading Macrobius (7), and it is clearly implied that he is suffering the pangs of love (21–23).

Much later, between the 1360s and the early 1380s, we have a cluster of works. Jean Froissart's *Paradis d'Amour* (1360s or early 1370s) opens by telling us (Dembowski 1986: 40–42) that the narrator has been suffering from insomnia (13–18) because of his 'pensees et merancolies' (5–8) – although we are not told what they are, it soon becomes clear –, but finally falls asleep while still thinking (31) of what has been troubling him: Bonne Amour (34). While asleep, he finds himself in a beautiful wood (38–39), and complains to a personified Love, whom he has served faithfully, that his lady will not listen to him (71–75 and 87–93).

Chaucer's *Book of the Duchess* is likely to have been composed in the late 1360s, just after or just before *Le Paradis d'Amour*. Here we again find a sleepless narrator:

>   I have gret wonder, be this lyght,
>   How that I lyve, for day ne nyght
> 3   I may nat slepe wel nygh noght [. . .]   (1988: 330)

The effects of the insomnia, from which the narrator has suffered for eight years (ll. 36–37), are described at some length (ll. 4–29), but we are not told the cause – indeed, the narrator says firmly that he does not know it (ll. 30–35). The waking preoccupation that Guillaume de Lorris describes is thus unknown, but its place is taken by a book:

>   So whan I saw I might not slepe
> 45   Til now late this other night,
>   Upon my bed I sat upright
>   And bad oon reche me a book,

---

¹⁵ Lecoy 1965: 1–2. 'Some folk say that there is nothing in dreams but fancies and lies, but one can dream things that are not false; Macrobius is an authority on this. In my twentieth year, when Love rules the hearts of the young, I went to bed one night and slept soundly. I had a beautiful dream that greatly pleased me, and there was nothing in that dream that did not later come to pass. It was five years ago or more when I dreamed that dream, in May, season of love, full of joy.'

A romaunce, and he it me tok
To rede and drive the night away [. . .]
270 I hadde unneth that worde ysayd
Ryght thus as I have told hit yow,
That sodeynly, I nyste how,
Such a lust anoon me took
To slepe that ryght upon my book
275 Y fil aslepe, and therwith even
Me mette so ynly swete a sweven,
So wonderful that never yit
Y trowe no man had the wyt
To konne wel my sweven rede [. . .][16]

Unlike Guillaume de Lorris, Chaucer does not identify the author, but he later gives enough information about the book's content for it to be identified as Ovid, *Metamorphoses*, II.410–749, probably in a vernacular text (see Chaucer 1988: 967). Like Guillaume, he states that what follows is a dream (*sweven*, ll. 246–49).

A decade later, between 1378 and 1380, Chaucer begins *The House of Fame* with a brief theoretical treatment of types of dream:

God turne us every drem to goode!
For hyt is wonder, be the roode,
To my wyt, what causeth swevens [. . .]
7 Why that is an avision
And why this a revelacion,
Why this a drem, why that a swevene [. . .]   (1988: 348)

The poem's editor, John M. Fyler, comments helpfully on this passage, and concludes that 'Chaucer's use of dream terminology is confusing, apparently on purpose' (1988: 978). The theoretical opening, which is unusual in the dream-vision poetry of the time, continues with a discussion of the causes of dreams:

As yf folkys complexions
Make hem dreme of reflexions
Or ellys thus, as other sayn,
For to gret febleness of her brayn,
25 By abstinence or by seknesse,
Prison-stewe or gret distresse,
Or ellys by dysordynaunce
Of natural acustumaunce [. . .]

---

[16] Both 'sweven' and 'drem' mean a dream, and 'mette' is the past tense of *meten* 'to dream' (Davis et al. 1979: 94 and 149 and Chaucer 1988: 1269).

35   Causeth suche dremes ofte;
      Or that the cruel lyf unsofte
      Which these ylke lovers leden
      That hopen over-muche or dreden,
      That purely her impressions
40   Causeth hem avisions [. . .]   (348–49)

Chaucer here follows the progression from physical causes to the lover's waking preoccupations (and then to external and authoritative inspiration – not quoted here because it is not relevant to the Don Amor episode). The narrator goes to sleep (ll. 112–14) and has a 'wonderful [. . .] drem' (62, also 79–80 and 119–20). Here again, then, there is an explicit statement that what follows is a dream. We are not, however, told what was on the narrator's mind before he fell asleep, and there is no suggestion that he was reading at that point. In *The Parliament of Fowls* (written a couple of years after *The House of Fame*), on the other hand, there is preoccupation with love at the outset (ll. 1–7), and a book, Cicero's *Somnium Scipionis*, plays a dominant part (ll. 17–32). Then, as in *The Book of the Duchess* and *The House of Fame*, the narrator falls asleep and we are told that he dreams (ll. 85–98; 1988: 385–86). Thus the book is represented in the dream by its author, rather as love is, in the *Libro* episode, represented by the personified Don Amor.

It is unnecessary to quote any further fourteenth-century examples, such as Chaucer's Prologue to *The Legend of Good Women* or William Langland, *Piers Plowman*. The tradition continues in the fifteenth century, both in English and in Castilian. King James I of Scotland wrote in *The Kingis Quair*, perhaps in the mid-1420s:

st. 2   Quhen as I lay in bed allone waking,
         New partit out of slepe a lyte tofore,
         [I] toke a boke to rede apon a quhile.

st. 3   Of quhich the name is clepit properly
         Boece (efter him that was the compiloure),
         Schewing the counsele of Philosophye [. . .]

st. 8   The longe night beholding (as I saide),
         My eyen gan to smert for studying.
         My buke I schet and at me hede it laide,
         And doun I lay bot ony tarying,
         The mater newe in my mind rolling [. . .]

st. 11   And sone I herd the bell to matyns ryng
         And up I rase, no langer wald I lye.
         Bot now (how trow ye) suich a fantasye
         Fell me to mind that ay me thoght the bell
         Said to me: 'tell on, man, quhat thee befell.'
                                        (Norton-Smith 1971: 1–3)

The narrator's situation here is unusual: he has been asleep, has woken, and cannot get to sleep again. There is no mention of his waking preoccupations (it is within the dream that he falls in love), and the book that he reads, Boethius's *De consolatione Philosophiae* ('the counsele of Philosophye', 3c), is therefore even more dominant than the *Somnium Scipionis* at the beginning of *The Parliament of Fowls*. Neither Boethius nor Philosophy appears to him in person, and the voice that speaks to him is that of the bell for Matins (11c and fg).

Perhaps a decade after *The Kingis Quair*, the Marqués de Santillana wrote *El sueño* (it is very unusual for 'dream' or a cognate word to appear in the title). We are told what is troubling the narrator (ll. 25–32; Rohland de Langbehn 1997: 100–01). He has not been reading a book, though it is possible that the classical allusions that follow in lines 43–48 are prompted by Santillana's awareness that a book often appears at this point in dream-vision poetry (the allusions derive from Lucan's *Pharsalia*, as scholars have long been aware: see Rohland de Langbehn 1997: 101n and 320). Then we move directly into an account of the dream (ll. 57–64).

In 1444, about a decade after *El sueño*, Juan de Mena finished the *Laberinto de Fortuna*. The presentation of the dream vision is quite unlike any of those that we have so far encountered: there is no preparation (the first twelve stanzas are a general introduction to the poem), and stanza 13 takes us straight into the vision (De Nigris 1994: 70).[17] A very similar presentation of a dream is to be found a generation or so later, in Scotland, in Robert Henryson's Prologue to 'The Taill off the Lyon and the Mous' (one of *The Morall Fabillis of Esope the Phrygian*) (st. 192–96; Wood 1958: 49–50). The difference is, of course, that Aesop appears to the dreamer (like Don Amor, he is 'off stature large'), but he is not presented as the cause of the dream. The similarity between Mena and Henryson suggests that the traditional form of introduction to a dream vision has been superseded, but that is not the case: Henryson's most famous poem, *The Testament of Cresseid* (the chronology of his works is obscure), introduces the subject-matter of the poem in almost the same way as the *Roman de la Rose* and, in all but one respect, *The Book of the Duchess* and *The Kingis Quair*:

> st. 1   Ane doolie sessoun to ane cairfull dyte
> Suld correspond, and be equivalent.
> Richt sa it wes quhen I began to wryte
> This tragedie, the wedder richt fervent,
> Quhen Aries, in middis of the Lent,
> Schouris of haill can fra the north discend,
> That scantlie fra the cauld I micht defend. [. . .]

> st. 4   For I traistit that Venus, luifis Quene,
> To quhome sum tyme I hecht obedience,
> My faidit hart of lufe scho wald mak grene [. . .]

---

[17] Some twenty years after the *Laberinto*, a dream vision is used to provide a frame for allegory in an early sentimental romance, *Triste deleytación* (see Haywood 2000a: 418–20 and 2000b: 16).

st. 6 I mend the fyre and beikit me about,
      Than tuik ane drink my spreitis to comfort,
      And armit me weill fra the cauld thairout:
      To cut the winter nicht and mak it schort,
      I tuik ane Quair, and left all uther sport,
      Writtin be worthie Chaucer glorious,
      Of fair Cresseid, and worthie Troylus. [. . .]

st. 9 To brek my sleip ane uther quair I tuik,
      In quhilk I fand the fatall destenie
      Of fair Cresseid, that endit wretchitlie.   (Wood 1958: 105–07)

The mention of the narrator's waking preoccupation with love, present in the *Roman de la Rose* but absent from *The Book of the Duchess* and *The Kingis Quair*, is found in stanza 4.

In the poems quoted and discussed above, four features recur (though only one poem, *The Parliament of Fowls*, exhibits all four):

A.   'Dream' or its equivalent ('songe', 'sueño') occurs.
B.   We are told of the narrator's waking preoccupation with love.
C.   The narrator is reading a book.
D.   An imposing figure appears to the narrator.

It is convenient to represent their distribution in these poems, and in the *Libro*, in tabular form, though some qualifications are needed (a letter in parentheses means that the feature is displaced):

Roman de la Rose	A	B	C*	
Paradis d'Amour		B		
Book of the Duchess	A	‡	C*	
House of Fame	A			
Parliament of Fowls	A	B	C*	D†
Kingis Quair			C*	
Sueño	A	B		
Laberinto de Fortuna				D†
Morall Fabillis	A			D†
Testament of Cresseid	(A)§		C*	(D)§†
Libro de Buen Amor		B	(C)§	D†

* The books / authors are, respectively, Macrobius, Ovid *Metamorphoses* (not named), Cicero *Somnium Scipionis*, Boethius *De consolatione Philosophiae*, and Chaucer *Troilus and Criseyde*.

‡ We are told that there are waking preoccupations, but the narrator says he does not know what has caused his insomnia.

† The figures are, respectively, Scipio, Bellona, Aesop, Cupid, and Don Amor.

§ In *The Testament of Cresseid* it is Cresseid, not the narrator, of whom the word 'dream' is used and to whom Cupid appears. In the *Libro* no book or author is mentioned before the appearance of Don Amor, but Ovid and *Pamphilus* are mentioned during the narrative (429a, 429d, 698c, and 891d).

How does the Don Amor episode of the *Libro de Buen Amor* match the pattern of the other texts? The absence of the word 'sueño' separates it from six of the texts (from seven if the displaced use of 'dream' in *The Testament of Cresseid* is included), but the same is true of the *Paradis d'Amour*, *The Kingis Quair*, and the *Laberinto de Fortuna*, so the word's absence is no obstacle to seeing this episode as a dream vision. By prefacing Don Amor's appearance with a reference to waking preoccupation with love, Juan Ruiz puts his episode in the same group as the *Roman de la Rose*, the *Paradis d'Amour*, *The Parliament of Fowls*, and *El sueño*.[18] Don Amor's appearance puts the episode into the same group as *The Parliament of Fowls*, the *Laberinto de Fortuna*, the *Morall Fabillis*, and, in a displaced form, *The Testament of Cresseid*. Finally, five of the poems show the narrator reading a book, but the *Libro*, like five other poems, does not, so even if we attach no importance to the displaced references to Ovid and *Pamphilus* the *Libro* is by no means an oddity.

Consequences of the dream-vision hypothesis

Thus the Don Amor episode, and with it the episode of Doña Endrina, fit comfortably into the pattern of dream-vision narratives, and since the anomalies discussed above are no longer anomalous if seen in a dream context, it is, I suggest, reasonable to categorize the episodes, at least provisionally, as a dream vision. This would make sense of the otherwise rather puzzling reference to wine in 181b, 'pensando en mi ventura, sañudo e non con vino': the narrator seems to be telling us that his *insomnium* is caused by his preoccupation with love, not by a physical cause such as drunkenness.

If this is a dream, when does it end? The earliest point at which we might regard it as having ended is Don Amor's departure:

> Partióse Amor de mí e dexóme dormir;[19]
> desque vino el alva, pensé de comedir
> en lo que me castigó e, por verdat dezir,
> fallé que en sus castigos usé sienpre bevir.
> Maravilléme mucho, desque en ello pensé,
> de cómo en servir dueñas todo tiempo non cansé:
> mucho las guardé siempre, nunca me alabé;
> – quál fue la raçón negra por que non recabdé?   (576–77)

José Miguel Martínez Torrejón says that the Don Amor episode's 'independencia formal está marcada por un exordio (181) y un *explicit* (575), así como por la falta de referencias a otros momentos del *Libro*' (1993: 197). The first statement

---

[18] Torres-Alcalá 1990 does not deal with dream visions.
[19] This line does not invalidate the dream hypothesis. It is quite common for sleeping and waking to occur within the action of a dream.

is correct, but the second does not take account of the fact that the following section is signalled in the penultimate stanza of this episode:

> Pánfilo mi criado, que se está bien de vagar,
> con mi muger doña Venus te verná a castigar.   (574cd; *G* only)

A few stanzas later it is clear that we are still within the dream, because the narrator-protagonist is talking with Venus:

> fui me a Doña Venus que le levase mensaje,
> ca ella es comienço e fin d'este vïaje.   (583cd; *G* only)

Does Venus's departure make a more convincing end to the dream?

> Fue se Doña Venus, a mí dexó en fadiga.
> Si le conortan no lo sanan al doliente los joglares,
> el dolor crece e non mengua oyendo dulces cantares;
> consejóme Doña Venus, mas non me tiró pesares:
> ayuda otra non me queda, sinon lengua e parlares.
>
> (648d–49; *S* only)

This could mark a return to the waking state, but we are soon told that the successful courtship of Doña Endrina is a re-enactment of the plot of *Pamphilus*:

> Fallé una tal vieja qual avía mester,
> artera e maestra e de mucho saber;
> Doña Venus por Pánfilo non pudo más fazer
> de quanto fizo aquésta por me fazer plazer.   (698)[20]

and the point is made again at the end of the episode:

> Doña Endrina e Don Melón en uno casados son:
> alégranse las conpañas en las bodas con rrazón;
> si villanía he dicho, aya de vós perdón,
> que lo feo de la estoria diz Pánfilo e Nasón.   (891)

The narrator seems to draw an even firmer line under the Endrina story when he says that he narrated it as an *exemplum*, not because it really happened to him ('non porque a mí vino', 909b).[21] Since stanza 910 takes us back into realistic narrative (the episode of the 'apuesta dueña'), it makes sense to see the dream-vision

---

[20] The extent to which it re-enacts *Pamphilus* is demonstrated by Lecoy (1938: 307–27); his analysis is refined by Gybbon-Monypenny 1970b.

[21] The use of 'vino' here echoes that in st. 181, which begins the dream-vision episode. This repetition provides a verbal marker for the beginning and end of the dream.

narrative as ending with stanza 909. That is not, however, the last narrative of its kind in the *Libro*, as we shall see.

The statement that the Endrina story was 'por te dar ensienplo, mas non porque a mí vino' (909b) is, as I have already noted, hard to reconcile with 'Seyendo yo después d'esto sin amor e con coidado' (910a; MS *S* only) if we take this as a realistic, waking narrative. It does, however, make sense if we regard the Endrina episode as part of a dream: we have all experienced the dejection that comes on waking from a pleasant dream (not necessarily an erotic one) and realizing that the pleasure was illusory – 'in sleep a king, but, waking, no such matter', as Shakespeare says (Sonnet 87).

Endrina was the narrator's one genuine sexual conquest. The fact that it was achieved under a different name, Don Melón de la Huerta, is odd, but does not in itself invalidate the conquest – it still, within the bounds of the fiction created by Juan Ruiz, happened in the real world. If, however, we accept that it happened in a dream, we see the narrator-protagonist as experiencing sexual intercourse only with a woman who has been drugged (see st. 941–43, discussed earlier) and with *serranas* who are sexual predators and who, in effect, rape him. The picture is complete: a sexual incompetent, stumbling from one disaster to another, and able to find consolation only in a dream.

The place of dream-vision elements within the *Libro*'s structure should now be set out schematically:

> {Prologues; unsuccessful pursuits of women}
>
> I   180–575   Night: Don Amor arrives; debate
> II   576–83   Amor leaves before dawn; meditation on I
> III 583–649   Doña Venus
> IV   650–52   Meditation on III
> V   653–891   The conquest of Doña Endrina
> VI   892–909   Meditation on V

This accounts for 730 stanzas (42.2% of the *Libro*). Is that the end of the matter? I think not: after a 157-stanza interval occupied by the 'dueña apuesta', the *serranas*, and religious lyrics, we move out of the realistic narrative into allegory. We have already met personification allegory – the appearance of Don Amor – within the dream. Now we read of two further substantial allegories, the battle of Carnival and Lent and the triumph of Love.[22] In the second of these, the dream figure of Don Amor reappears, riding in triumph through the city as a 'grand enperante' (1245a). In due course, he departs, much as he had in 576a:

> Otro día mañana, antes que fues de día,
> movió con su mesnada Amor e fue su vía;
> dexó me con cuidado, pero con allegría:
> este mi señor sienpre tal costunbre avía.   (1313)

---

[22] A similar movement, out of the allegorical Prison of Love and back again, occurs a century and a half later, in Diego de San Pedro's *Cárcel de Amor*.

We again need a schematic summary:

VII	1067–1209	Carnal and Cuaresma
VIII	1210–63	Triumphal entry of Carnal and Amor
IX	1264–1303	Amor's tent
X	1304–13	Amor speaks and, before dawn, departs

I do not maintain that these sections, which occupy 247 stanzas (14.3% of the *Libro*), constitute a dream, but they continue the dream-vision material, so that it reaches a total of 977 stanzas out of 1728 (56.5%). More than half of the *Libro* is taken up by a narrative that, to state the case very cautiously, strongly resembles a dream vision and by a second, allegorical, narrative that is clearly linked to the first one. This is not the way in which we have been accustomed to read the *Libro*. I am embarrassed that it was only after decades of lecturing on the *Libro* and intermittently writing about it that I noticed what now seems obvious (and what was so obvious to Amador de los Ríos and Lecoy that they mentioned it only in a passing overstatement).

The Relationship between the *Libro de Buen Amor* and *Celestina*: Does Trotaconventos Perform a *Philocaptio* Spell on Doña Endrina?

DOROTHY SHERMAN SEVERIN

Keith Whinnom, in his University of Exeter inaugural lecture of 1967, 'Spanish Literary Historiography: Three Forms of Distortion' (publ. 1968), poured cold water on the notion that the *Libro de Buen Amor* might have had any influence on *Celestina*, as argued by, for example, F. Castro Guisasola (1924). The case for seeing such an influence has been argued again by Samuel G. Armistead (1973, 1976–77), which leads us to wonder if any of the situational and verbal coincidences could possibly indicate a link, other than their common source in the *Pamphilus*.[1] One area of difference has seemed clear enough, however; unlike Trotaconventos, Rojas's creation was definitely an *hechicera* or sorceress and, as I think I have proved in a monograph, *Witchcraft in 'Celestina'* (1995), also a *bruja* or witch. She performs a *philocaptio* spell to capture Melibea's love, but exceeds the usual bounds of white magic for these spells and enters the realms of black magic by conjuring up a demon to help her in her enterprise. As María Rosa Lida de Malkiel pointed out in *La originalidad artística de 'La Celestina'* (1962: 560), although Juan Ruiz's creation Trotaconventos mentions her *escantos* or enchantments a number of times, the text seems to show her trying to seduce Doña Endrina on behalf of Don Melón by her arts of persuasion alone. This, however, was written before Peter Russell's seminal article on magic in *Celestina* (1963), in which he explained the basis of Celestina's *philocaptio* spell.

Celestina appears at Melibea's house selling a skein of thread which has already been anointed with snake oil and into which a devil has been conjured. After touching the skein, Alisa leaves her daughter alone to conclude bargaining for it with Celestina, who procures from Melibea her girdle or *cordón*. This is more than sufficient to capture Melibea's love for Calisto. As Alan Deyermond has argued persuasively (1977), the Devil is unleashed in the text through

---

[1] See Gybbon-Monypenny 1970b and Jenaro-MacLennan 1988 on the relationship between the *Libro* and *Pamphilus*; and Haywood, above, for a short discussion of *Pamphilus* and other Latin analogues.

the conjuration, and infects everyone who touches the *cordón*, and by extension the gold chain with which Calisto rewards Celestina, with the tragic result of the deaths of most of the principals in the work.

What is remarkable about this *philocaptio* spell is that it far exceeds the usual procedure, which was not to enter the realm of black magic and summon up demons, but simply to use charms, love philtres, wax figures, and the usual paraphernalia of white magic, according to Richard Kieckhefer in his latest work *Forbidden Rites*; he also points out that from the early fourteenth century the possession and use of magical writing becomes a recurrent theme in the records of persecution (1997: 1). Let us examine the *Libro* text in the light of our improved knowledge about magic procedures in the Middle Ages. When Trotaconventos is first introduced to us, the reader is warned that 'éstas dan la maçada; sy as orejas, oyas' (699d), to listen carefully, because these women are dangerous.[2] A 'maçada' can be a blow of the mace but can also be an illness (Joset 1974: 253), or extreme harm (Corominas 1967: 270). Trotaconventos agrees to visit Doña Endrina at home: 'Dixo: "Yo iré a su casa de esa vuestra vezina / e le faré tal escanto e le daré tal atalvina, / por que esa vuestra llaga sane por mi melezina"'(709a–c).[3] She says that she will go to Doña Endrina and enchant her and give her an *atalvina*, a drink made of almond milk and flour (Cejador 1913: I, 248–49), or alternatively and even worse, flour, water, garlic, bacon, and fried bread (Corominas 1967: 277), in order to cure Don Melón's love malady. Then Trotaconventos uses a metaphor:

> La çera que es mucho dura e mucho brozna e elada,
> desque ya entre las manos una vez está maznada,
> después con el poco fuego cient vezes será doblada;
> doblar se ha toda dueña que sea bien escantada   (711)

> (The wax which is hard and frozen, once kneaded between the hands then heated a bit, can be folded a hundred times; all ladies who are well enchanted can be bent [over] thus).

Is this merely a metaphor, and why has it been chosen? In fact a basic part of most *philocaptio* spells was dolls made by warming wax and making a human form which could then be used for enchantment, often with a piece of clothing from the victim attached. The metaphor is not casual, but to the contemporary audience would call up an image of the magical use of wax. Nor is the drink of *atalvina* a casual note, rather a reminder of the love potions which were

---

[2] Quotations are from Gybbon-Monypenny 1988, with an occasional variant reading in brackets if the alternative is particularly relevant, and translations are my own. In my analysis I shall refer to several editions of *Libro* and to Morreale 1963 and 1979. Citations to *Celestina* are to Rojas 1987.

[3] *Escanto* also seems to be used in the sense of *descanto* or 'spiel' at stanza 756, and at 764 we also get *ledanía*, literally an ecclesiastical term, 'litany', with the possible meaning of enchantment or spell.

frequently administered in *philocaptio* spells. Editors are surprisingly unanimous on this point, and Joset even calls Trotaconventos a *bruja*.[4] Trotaconventos then concludes:

> Esta dueña que dezides, mucho es en mi poder:
> si non por mí, non la puede omne del mundo aver;
> yo sé toda su fazienda e quanto ha de fazer;
> por mi conssejo la faze, más que non por su querer.   (716)

> (This lady whom you speak of is in my power, and no man can have her except through me; I know her actions and what she is planning to do; she acts more on account of my advice than on her own desires.)

Doña Endrina is in Trotaconventos's power and does what the *alcahueta* wants almost against her own will. Finally Trotaconventos offers to get Don Melón this girl and others, saying 'yo faré con mi escanto que se vengan paso a pasillo; / en aqueste mi farnero las traeré al sarçillo' (718cd). She will bring them all round with her enchantments and into the weave of her sieve or basket, *farnero*, used for casting lots, as well as for carrying the cheap jewellery and gewgaws which she sells to gain admission to the girls' houses. Margherita Morreale (1979: section A, 1-44) lists the magical uses of the *harnero*, and also thinks that Trotaconventos wants to make an exchange with Doña Endrina (1963: 299), just as Celestina will trade the skein of thread for Melibea's girdle. Indeed, when Trotaconventos does enter Doña Endrina's house with her wares, her first words are:

> [...] Señora fija,
> para esa mano bendicha quered esta sortija;
> si vós non me descobrierdes, dezir vos he una past[r]ija
> que penssé aquesta noche [...]   (724)

> (My lady, daughter, take this jewel from me; if you don't give me away I'll tell you a tale that I made up tonight.)

Interestingly, one of the earliest editors, Julio Cejador y Frauca (1913: I, 254n), thought that this jewel accepted by Doña Endrina was in fact enchanted. We might also wonder whether the 'past[r]ija' is merely an amusing story, or words which might be connected with a spell. The word has not been extensively researched but is simply accepted as a variant of *pastraña*.

The *sortija* does not disappear from the text. Rather it is the means of luring Doña Endrina's mother Doña Rama from the house on Trotaconventos's second visit. Before we get to that point we are faced with the first of two large lacunae in the text: a 25-line gap between 765c and 766a, and a 32-stanza one between 781d and 782a. The second one was obviously the result of an expurgation, since

---

[4] See Corominas 1967: 272, Joset 1974: 257, Blecua edn 1983: 110, and Gybbon-Monypenny 1988: 479.

it must have shown Don Melón forcing Doña Endrina, while the first lacuna features at the end of the first interview with Doña Endrina and the beginning of the subsequent interview with don Melón, and must have been lost as the result of the censoring of the later rape scene.[5] There is therefore a missing component of the *philocaptio* spell. So far we have had a love potion, a wax effigy, a magic sieve, an enchanted ring, and possibly a magical incantation. What is conspicuously absent is a piece of clothing or other personal *prenda* from Doña Endrina. Whether this was obtained we shall never know. Nonetheless, Morreale believes that Trotaconventos was aiming to make an exchange of the jewel for some possession of Doña Endrina's.

However, it is worth noting that she has touched the girl's hand, which could be just as effective for magic purposes. Certainly this exchange does not feature in the subsequent Don Melón passage, which opens *in medias res* with Trotaconventos telling him to abandon hope and Melón complaining that he will die of love malady. Trotaconventos suddenly intervenes and cuts him short with the assurance that she has the girl in her power: 'Doña Endrina es vuestra e fará mi mandado' (798a). The lady is in your power and will do my will. On her subsequent visit to Endrina's house she lures her mother Doña Rama away with a story about the ring; the patron for whom she sold the jewel now wants it back because it is full of flaws. The quarrelsome Doña Rama rushes from the house to find out more from the neighbours, but her action is not logical, as surely she could have learned more from the *alcahueta* herself. As Trotaconventos rather tellingly remarks, the devil take her: 'Ya levase el uerco [diablo] a la vieja rriñosa [. . .]'(828a). This is reminiscent of *Celestina* and Alisa's sudden disappearance from the scene to tend a sick relative, which Celestina attributes in an aside to the devil. The *alcahueta* returns triumphant to Don Melón with the assurance that Doña Endrina has agreed to visit Trotaconventos's house and that 'encantador malo saca la culebra del forado' (868c), the evil enchanter lures the snake from its hole.

Tellingly, the episode of the enchantment does not feature in the common source, the *Pamphilus*.[6] This could indicate a direct link between the two texts, in other words, that Juan Ruiz introduced the *philocaptio* idea to the story, and that Rojas knew the *Libro*. It is noteworthy that the text of *Celestina* is extremely explicit about the *philocaptio* spell and that Celestina herself goes to the extreme of calling up a demon, while the *philocaptio* components of the *Libro* are merely

---

[5] See de Looze, below, for an alternative explanation. There is a twenty-five line gap between 765c and 766a (fols li and lii), and a second gap at 781d–782a (fols lix and lx). Folios li and lix formed a single folded sheet which produced two folios (four pages), as did folios lii and lx. Tearing out one folio would cause the eventual loss of the other side of the sheet (Vàrvaro 1968–69: 136 and n14).

[6] According to G. B. Gybbon-Monypenny, Juan Ruiz abandons the *Pamphilus* text at 709–12, 717–18, 723–25, and from 737 ceases to follow it closely, and introduces substantive material (1988: 253–92); see Burkard's English version of this portion of the *Pamphilus* (1999: 164–65).

suggested in passing, as though the audience would pick up the clues without more exact explanation. The expectation would be that once Trotaconventos had given Endrina the enchanted ring and extracted some item from her (she does in fact seem to touch her on the hand), she would complete the spell with a wax doll and incantations. Even Celestina is not explicit on this point; she warns Calisto that he must give back the *cordón* because she needs to do more with it, but we do not hear what this might be.

Unlike the Celestina story, Melón / Endrina will have a happy ending. Trotaconventos has not indulged in black magic, and despite the (missing) rape scene, all is reconciled in the end and Melón and Endrina are married. But the text, even in its fragmentary state, provides us with ample evidence that, like her literary heir Celestina, Trotaconventos was an *hechicera* well versed in the white arts of *philocaptio*.[7]

---

[7] Michael J. Ruggerio is one of the first to call Celestina a *bruja* rather than a mere *hechicera*, but he sees no magical qualities in Trotaconventos (1966: 8).

Part 4: THEORETICAL APPROACHES

Text, Author, Reader, Reception: The Reflections of Theory and the *Libro de Buen Amor*

LAURENCE DE LOOZE

If theory implies a stepping back in an act of observation, as its etymology suggests, encouraging us to reflect on our acts of interpretation, then surely the term is not out of place here; I submit that theory already has a large hold on the critical reception of the *Libro*, but that its role has not usually been made explicit.[1] I hope to show that the *Libro* – or the three or four *Libro*s, as the late Paul Zumthor would have said (1972), insisting on the *mouvance* of the text – invites us to be mindful of theory when we approach the work.

If criticism on the *Libro* ineluctably leads us back to the undecidable, then our interest in most of the critical discussions of the work must be as much in the process of criticism as in its product. That is, the final result will in some respects matter less than the path by which a particular critic has passed; in almost every instance another theoretical path would lead to a different set of results. As with the historical Juan Ruiz, for whom we have either too many candidates or none at all, so also for many of the crucial questions about the *Libro* we have numerous (and contradictory) answers, depending on the evidence selected – and, often enough, we simply have no answers at all.[2] The conclusions of any scholarly investigation will be those made possible by the theoretical approach being used. As a famous crux of the *Libro* seems to suggest, the work can say what one wishes to make it say: 'bien o mal, qual puntares, tal te dirá çiertamente' (70b).[3] The fingers of one's theory simply pluck the melody of the critical approach.

We are, fortunately, past the period when critics held that they had no theory. They may not always have been conscious of their theory, but even a 'common-sensical' approach to any work determined what was common-sensical according

---

[1] The word 'theory' derives from the Greek *theoria* (θεωρία), which means 'sight', 'contemplation', and 'speculation'. While the term is often used 'to mean a system of concepts that aims to give a global explanation to an area of knowledge' (Godzich 1986: xiii), especially since Kant, the Greeks did not set praxis in opposition to speculative knowledge: the *theoros* (θεωρός) was a publicly sanctioned observer who acted as a mediator between the event and subsequent discussions (xiv–xv).

[2] See, for example, the debate between Hernández 1988 and Kelly 1988; also Orduna 1988, and Joset's overview (1988: 19–26).

[3] On st. 69–70, see Drayson, and Vasvári, this volume.

to a complex system of theoretical presuppositions. The area of critical study that was earliest codified in theoretical terms was textual criticism, forming as it did the basis for editions of the work.

One of the problems inherent in opening the floodgates of theory is that the possibilities for what should constitute the text (and therefore the meaning) of the *Libro* multiply very rapidly. Once the sluices are open, the *Libro* almost immediately becomes Protean, or perhaps I should say Hydra-like; certainly one advantage of embracing a particular theory, whatever that might be, is that it prevents the generation of endless possibilities and reduces the field to a manageable size. This is also one of the reasons why unproven suppositions have a way of hardening over time until they come to be treated as though they were proven fact. Instead of viewing the potentiality of unlimited possibilities (in terms of the texts and their meanings) as a menace that threatens to overwhelm the critic, we could simply choose to view a hundred-headed *Libro* as a vast and rich field for critical work. Many critics, however, and in particular those hunting a single meaning until, like a frightened deer, it can finally be bagged, would have to abandon long-cherished opinions regarding the prerogatives and privileges of their scholarly work.

John Dagenais (1994) is an example of the degree to which a change in theory – in textual theory only, in fact – has dramatically altered the *Libro*'s text. Dagenais re-approached the matter of the three main manuscripts of the *Libro* from a standpoint drawn from Paul Zumthor's theory of the *mouvance* (1972) of medieval works, and developed as *variance* by Bernard Cerquiglini (1989). The result was a radical change in terms of the text(s) produced. We have only sketchy reconstructions of what a full *mouvance / variance* edition à la Dagenais would look like typographically, but it would be quite different. Here, for example, Dagenais quotes a section of text in which a reader adds a marginal count of the fourteen flaws which prevent Don Furón being the best go-between:[4]

iiij°	¶	era mintroso beodo ladron E mesturero
iiij°		tahur pelador goloso / ⌐ rrefertero
iiij°		rreñidor adeuino susio E agurero
ij		neçio / ⌐ peresoso tal es mi escudero

(Dagenais 1994: 155, 1620; ms T 36ʳ)

The manuscript evidence has not changed at all; the shift in re-presentation of the *Libro* to modern readers, right down to how one presents manuscript passages on the printed page of a modern book, merely reflects again a change in theory.

---

[4] There have been very few *mouvance* editions to date; but see Pickens 1978. For *mouvance* and *variance* in Ancient Greek literature, see Nagy 1996. Parkes 1993 and Saenger 1997 also show that the text is far more than the words organized on a page in a modern print edition.

Each time the theory changes, then, the *Libro* (that is, our conception of what the *Libro* is) changes along with it.[5]

In our evocations of the author and the reader (or audience), the reflections of theory can greatly aid us. Leo Spitzer did a great service to medievalists when he wrote a brief but seminal note on what he called 'the empirical "I"' (1946), in which he underscored the importance of recognizing that the first-person author-narrator in medieval literature generally has two levels: the particular 'I' who speaks also occupies a universalizing position as a kind of Everyman figure.[6] Nevertheless, this teasing-out of the various levels of narration has been developed much further by modern literary theorists. Wayne C. Booth (1961) set forth a typology of authorial and narratorial roles that can be applied to any literary work. Using modern examples, Booth distinguished between the flesh-and-blood historical Author, the Implied Author, and the Narrator. The distinction between the first two is crucial for avoiding facile judgments about authorial intention. Booth's argument is that even in the closest of relationships between the actual historical author and the portrait that is gradually built up of the author in a literary work, the two will still never be exactly the same. The image of the author presented in a literary work will always be a construction of the literary text and of artifice – usually a less complex or a less contradictory self than the real author. Even the most faithful attempt to recreate a real authorial self will still always remain a somewhat altered, somewhat cleaned-up version of the historical author, with many troubling or irrelevant aspects not apparent. The narrator is, of course, the actual speaking voice, which may be identified more or less closely with the implied author. In many first-person narratives, we are given to understand that the narrator gradually grows into the implied author figure; much will depend on whether the narrator depicts his tale as he viewed it during the supposed events or as he sees it from the end. Indeed, the protagonist who acts in the story may not yet have the (wiser) point of view that the narrator develops towards the end of the story.[7] In the criticism of Dante's *Divina commedia* it is a commonplace that the implied authorial Dante (Dante-the-Author) greatly disagrees with his earlier protagonist-self travelling through the first circles of Hell (Dante-the-Pilgrim); the narrating voice is sometimes more distant from, and sometimes closer to, the point of view of the protagonist. Clearly, the degree of overlap between these selves may vary greatly; for this reason some juanruizian critics differentiate between Juan Ruiz (the Author) and the Archpriest (the Narrator; see Introduction and the article by Haywood, this volume).

There have been subsequent modifications of Booth's typology, the best known of which is Gérard Genette's reinterpretation of Booth's levels of narrative (1972),

---

[5] I am indebted here (and at many other points) to Pearsall 1984.

[6] For further discussion on the relevance of Spitzer to the *Libro*, see Haywood in this volume.

[7] In the plot of a tale narrated in the first-person the point to which the narrator evolves must be prior to the beginning of the narrated story (Todorov 1967: 49).

not in terms of selves but entirely in terms of the narrative's spatial-temporal universe ('diegesis', Genette 1972: 280). For Genette, the key distinctions are plotted on two axes, 'level' and 'relation': the first refers to whether the narration takes place from within or without the world of the story (in Genette's terms, *intradiegesis* vs *extradiegesis*), and the second to whether the narrating voice is the principal actor in the tale or whether the tale happens to others (*homodiegesis* vs *heterodiegesis*). *The Great Gatsby*, for Genette, is an example of intradiegetic heterodiegesis since Nick, the narrator, is part of the diegetic world of the tale although he is a bystander to the main story, which is about Gatsby.[8]

In literary studies, especially those that focus on narratorial issues, Genette's terms have eclipsed Booth's, partly because of the prestige of French theoretical formulations in general, and partly because of Genette's personal prestige as a theorist. However, Booth's typology is easier to manipulate and remains more useful. Moreover, the seemingly objective precision of Genette's terms is somewhat misleading, since for any intradiegetic narrator the distinction between homodiegesis and heterodiegesis is one of degrees for the simple reason that the story happens to any narrator who is within the world of the story. It will often be difficult to say whether the story is primarily that of the narrator's relationship to the events or that of the events themselves. There is also slippage in Genette's terminology, depending on the starting point of the framing (diegetic) situation. For example, Genette lists (1972: 256) Homer as an extradiegetic and heterodiegetic narrator, which indeed he is, but then casts Ulysses as an intradiegetic and homodiegetic narrator (in *Odyssey*, Books 9–12), which is also true, but this time only within the narration of the Homeric narrator. Booth's terms make it clear that Ulysses becomes a narrator only within the already-narrating voice, and his terminology clarifies to whom we are referring when we say 'Homer' – the unknown author, the implied author (whose values and attitudes do not coincide entirely with those of Odysseus), or the third-person voice that narrates the work as a whole.

Regardless of the terminology adopted, a typology of authorial and narratorial voices has much to offer *Libro* studies. It would be edifying to go back through the scholarship to see to what extent perceptions about the implied author have been transferred onto the historical author(s); whilst repeated attempts to read the *Libro* as autobiography conflate all three levels. The rejection of naïve readings of the *Libro* as autobiography was deftly carried out by María Rosa Lida de Malkiel (1959 and 1961, chap. 2), and seconded by Francisco Rico (1967). The former's interest in doing away with autobiography was entirely in the hopes of demonstrating direct literary influence, not in studying the narratological aspects of the *Libro*, and the same can be said for Américo Castro (1948 and 1954) and Rico: while Lida de Malkiel was determined to make a case for the *Libro* as descended from the *maqāmāt*, and for that reason followed on Castro's arguments, Rico's study of the influence of Ovid and the *Pamphilus* is nevertheless the more convincing. In a major article on autobiographical aspects in the *Libro*

---

[8] For these questions, see Genette (1972: 225–67), with a diagrammatic scheme at p. 256.

G. B. Gybbon-Monypenny (1957), while taking Castro as starting point, veered toward specifically narratological questions when he argued that the autobiographical dimension in the *Libro* should be understood as a matter of adherence to literary codes and not as a reflection of lived reality.[9]

The *Libro* is particularly fascinating for its slippages between narrator and protagonist. Rico elegantly underscores (1967: 308 and n18) the way it has anticipated our own critical dilemmas; just as there is slippage between the implied author / narrator / protagonist in the *Libro*, the work also treats 'Pánfilo y Nasón', as Rico puts it, 'como si faltara la copulativa' (308). Now, over thirty years later, it would be interesting to have Rico rearticulate his observations in the light of Booth's or Genette's typology since there are times at which we do not know whether the narrator overlaps with the implied author or with the protagonist, or with both. The Doña Endrina episode is particularly notable in that what seems to be an experience of narrator / implied author, the Archpriest, turns out to be an episode in the life of Don Melón de la Huerta, protagonist and, it seems, narrator of the events. How should we relate this Don Melón to the implied author? Is this simply a change of name (but why? and when?), or is there a slippage from an overlapping implied author and narrator to a narrator who overlaps with the protagonist but who no longer has any tie to the Implied Author?[10]

I have made reference to the study of literary influence in the *Libro*. Here again, critical theory offers new avenues to critics. Most work on influence has been of the most traditional sort – imitation of specific literary forms (for example, Arabic *maqāmāt*, goliardic poetry, Aesop's Fables) and specific writers and works (Ovid, *Pamphilus*). Almost three-quarters of a century after Félix Lecoy published his *Recherches sur le 'Libro de Buen Amor'* (1938), it is still invaluable for contextualizing the *Libro*. Still, there has been much theoretical work done in other fields on the full range of literary relations that link, explicitly or implicitly, discrete works, and we might wish to avail ourselves of some of it. Some scholars, without dressing their studies in the terminological robes of theory, have nevertheless moved in new directions. Both G. B. Gybbon-Monypenny (1957) and Jeremy Lawrance (1984) look at the ways in which literary, intellectual, and social codes have passed into and through the *Libro* without the author

---

[9] Gybbon-Monypenny has also gone further than any other critic in emphasizing the pan-European literary context for the *Libro*. He is, for example, one of the very few critics to have considered the intertextual importance of the *Roman de la Rose*. I am deeply indebted to his discussion (1957; 1973) for my 1997 book on fourteenth-century pseudo-autobiographical works, including the *Libro*. He also notes (1957) the confusion in the *Libro* between author and protagonist, or what we might call, à la Booth, a slippage between protagonist and narrator / implied author.

[10] Raymond S. Willis mentioned that 'the author's *yo* dissolves into don Melón's' (1963–64: 362). John K. Walsh 1979–80a has seen the name slippage as evidence of an earlier, performative version that consisted only of the Doña Endrina episode, to which the first-person Archpriest's voice was added. Marina Scordilis Brownlee 1981–82 also argues that there is a shift in levels; which she associates with the midpoint name-changes in medieval romances; also see Deyermond, this volume.

(or authors) ever having given them much conscious thought; these studies thus separate questions of influence from that of authorial intention.[11] Lawrance, working from C. S. Lewis (1964), argues that a kind of 'watered-down' scholasticism made its way into much late-medieval writing, whether the author was aware of it or not, and 'came to form the subconscious mental furniture of the educated man in the Middle Ages' (1984: 223). This argument moves the question of literary influence out of the realm of conscious imitation. The author does not consciously reflect on values that seem self-evident, yet they pass from a source – or more likely a wide diffusion of sources – into a given written work.

In recent years theoreticians have given considerable thought to widening the scope of what constitutes influence; that is, the intertextual relationship between a given work and a whole range of predecessors. If our knowledge (and that of any author) regarding what constitutes a narrative is built up from the narratives we have (he or she has) already had contact with, then any given narrative carries within it the traces of prior codes of writing, even when reference is not made to specific works (Genette 1982: 7). To take a modern example, a detective novel can be a detective novel only if the writer and reader already have an idea of what a detective novel is; and this comes from prior reading. The same is true for medieval forms of writing, whether scholastic commentary, romance, lyric, *pastourelle*, beast fable, *fabliaux*, epic. . . . When Lawrance shows the subtle ways in which the *Libro* plays with the forms of writing and the intellectual currents of Juan Ruiz's day in the expectation that the audience would get most or all of the allusions, he is setting forth the intertextuality of the *Libro*. And while Lawrance's interest may be only in demonstrating the literate nature of the *Libro* audience, as opposed to romantic notions of a 'público callejero', the implications of his arguments go far beyond his overt conclusions.

In a manner similar to that adopted by Gybbon-Monypenny (1965, 1973), I wish to suggest that critics of the *Libro* should show more willingness to cross the Pyrenees (intellectually) and give attention to developments in the criticism on French medieval literature. The lack of communication between medievalists working on French and Spanish is stunning, and the critics who have worked on both literatures can be counted on one's hands (Gybbon-Monypenny, Lecoy, Spitzer, and Zink 1985 come immediately to mind). Some intellectual battles are still being fought arduously in Madrid that have long been laid to rest in Paris. There were similar debates in France about the admixture of oral and written culture in both the epics and the romances, and most critics of French late-medieval literature would embrace Lawrance's assertion of a sophisticated reading public that detected and appreciated a wide range of registers. I would add only that what we call oral literature can never be more than a written version of oral style and one that has been produced, received, and read within the literary environment of *manuscriptura*.

Studies of intertextuality and certain aspects of post-structuralist theory can be of considerable use to us here. Let us recall the structuralist position on

---

[11] See also Walsh 1979–80a and Jenaro-MacLennan 1974–79.

énonciation – that is, the trace left in the text of the process that created it. There was already, among the structuralists, debate as to whether the term 'enunciation' should refer merely to the traces left in the text or also to the enunciating act that produced it.[12] If the latter, then a crack was opened through which the pressure of all the features that had gone into producing the text could pass: systems and institutions of literary production, patronage control, the technology of manuscript production, readers' expectations, range of licence, generic expectations, social codes, ideologies, and the role of the unconscious.[13] Many of these features, particularly the last, were ones of which the author might be partially or completely unaware in any conscious way. Part of what a text said or meant would necessarily escape from authorial intention; or rather 'intention', assuming we were absolutely correct about the intentions we attributed to an author, could only tell us what the author may have consciously wanted to produce, not what the text actually implied.

If we reapproach the *Libro* via these routes, one of the biggest dilemmas of all becomes irrelevant, namely the inability to pinpoint who Juan Ruiz was or even determine whether more than one author contributed to the *Libro*. There has always been uneasiness about attributing authorial intentions to an unknown person (or at least there should have been), but whether or not we know exactly who Juan Ruiz was we can reconstruct à la Lawrance the world of the clerical discourses in which he moved and delineate à la Jenaro-MacLennan (1974–79) the intellectual issues that found expression in his writings. But there is still more to do. I would not go so far as to define intertextuality in the wide terms associated with Julia Kristeva (1969), in which intertext just means text, but the theoretical work of Hans Robert Jauss (1970a, 1970b), Harold Bloom (1973), Genette (1982), and even some portions of Kristeva's work (1969), would certainly be useful. Both Bloom and Jauss address the question of how writers respond to previous writing, and Jauss specifically considers how genres thrive and change; that is, how a literary work also faces toward the future. One's first response to Bloom's Freudian approach to literary creation might be to state simply that Juan Ruiz shows no Bloomian anxiety as such; and it is perhaps true that in the *Libro* the anxiety about predecessors and the need to clear the ground for new artistic creation do not leap forth in the way that, say, they might seem to in the case of Juan Ruiz's contemporary, Don Juan Manuel.

Nevertheless, a case could be made that the *Libro* reveals a profound need to unshackle itself from past writing, and that the parodic aspects, and even the serious recapitulations of pre-existing forms of writing (particularly in MS *S*), are ways of arm-wrestling with past creations in order to move beyond them. In that moving beyond we are already into the terrain investigated by Jauss,

---

[12] For Émile Benveniste (1974: II, 80) 'enunciation' referred to an extralinguistic act, whereas for Algirdas Julien Greimas and Joseph Courtés (1979: 127) it was only the textual trace of that act. See also Todorov 1970: 3.

[13] Michael Riffaterre has called this *La Production du texte* (1979).

whose theories are not Freudian, but are based rather in questions of reception. For Jauss, the paramount works of literature challenge the 'horizon of expectation' of their readers. To these works he contrasts lesser 'stereotypes' (1970b: 86) which merely redeploy pre-existing codes. The new, provocative aspects of major works – that is, the elements that cannot be assimilated to already-existent literary codes – actually cause genres to change. Though Jauss never quite says so, it also follows that these provocatory works are also always generically mixed, since whatever elements challenge the reader's horizon and do not conform to the codes of a particular genre can be read only as something else; that is, as some other kind / genre of writing.[14]

It is easy to see the value of these approaches for a work so obviously generically mixed as the *Libro*. Rather than needing to resolve whether the *Libro* is unified or not, the critic is freed from the pressure of forcing the evidence to bow before theories of organic unity. The centrifugal forces of the work, especially in the second half, and the *Libro*'s eclecticism are the markers of horizon-provocation, and in this sense the *Libro* is a kind of fourteenth-century *Pantagruel* or *Don Quixote* or even *Ulysses*: a triumphant work that both re-deploys and moves beyond the forms of contemporary narrative.

Our discussion has begun to bridge the gap from author to reader, and from creation to reception. Jauss is one of the fathers of 'reception theory' or 'reader-response theory'. There is an intimate relationship between the cluster of three elements: the author, the reader, and the meanings that are considered legitimate for a text. The question that often goes unanswered in discussions of legitimacy is: legitimate to whom in this triad? In the case of the *Libro*, to shift the burden off the shoulders of an unrecoverable author or authors and onto readers can prove to be a considerable boon. Bound up with decisions regarding which interpretations to accept are many aspects of power, whether we speak of the world of medieval institutions or modern ones.

There are, currently, many strands to reception theory, but all share the idea that the meaning of a literary text is impossible without the meeting of the written word with the reader / audience who receives it. 'Meaning' therefore always means 'meaning for' a particular reader or group of readers.[15] The question of what the *Libro* means – or should be taken as meaning, or can mean – has received much attenion: I shall defer these questions for the moment and concentrate first on the audience or readership of Juan Ruiz, for the simple reason that the disagreements about meaning often gloss over many unspoken assumptions about readerships and the role of the reader in the construction of the text.

Dayle Seidenspinner-Núñez's essay (1988–89) specifically deals with reader-response theory. She uses the notion of an 'implied reader' as set forth by

[14] I have taken this up elsewhere (1997: 20–21); see also Gravdal 1993.
[15] The best introduction in English to reception theory remains Tomkins 1980.

Wolfgang Iser (1974; later refined, 1978), and she characterizes the problem nicely:[16]

> yet to focus on the author's intention, the social and historical meaning, or the way in which a work is constructed without considering the addressee or receptor is to overlook the fact that literary texts are *processes* of signification actualized only in the practice of reading.   (1988–89: 260)

As reception theory develops, including in Iser's own reworkings, the implied reader comes to mean the reader implied by the text; that is, by the author's created work rather than by the creating author himself. As Seidenspinner-Nuñez notes, the Iserian approach relieves us of the problem of 'the lack of available data' (1988–89: 261n10) for Juan Ruiz.[17] Much of what Lawrance (1984) has argued about Juan Ruiz's historical audience also describes the reader implied by the text, and the literary and literate worlds the *Libro* presupposes are those of both the unknown author(s) and the implied readers.

Iser also describes the active role taken by readers in completing or filling-in the gaps left in a text: 'The gaps are those very points at which the reader can enter into the text, forming his own connections and conceptions and so creating the configurative meaning of what he is reading' (1974: 40).[18] Poststructuralism, particularly deconstruction, has shown that there are always gaps in any discourse, and that in those gaps the reader can tease out the things that the text tries not to say, refuses to acknowledge, suppresses. As Seidenspinner-Núñez seems aware, there will therefore be gaps even in a work that seems to present a seamless discourse. In comparing the *Libro* to Don Juan Manuel's *Conde Lucanor* (Part I), she speaks of how:

> the shifting perspectives of the Archpriest's parody maximize the possibilities of play, variant interpretations, and the reader's participation [. . .] In the *Conde Lucanor*, in contrast, Juan Manuel is constantly struggling to impose order, to establish hierarchies and rules, to encapsulate and control human experience within several narrative frames [. . .] In so doing, he represents an aristocratic reaction to the 14th-c. crisis   (1988–89: 263–64).

Everything in this passage points to a desperate attempt in the *Conde Lucanor* to keep from surfacing in the literary text the cracks that have already appeared in the social fabric.

---

[16] Seidenspinner-Núñez also alludes to the comments on Iser in Eagleton 1983, which provides an excellent introduction to literary theory (the novice should be warned that he saves Marxist criticism, 'political criticism', as a kind of final-chapter panacea to the ills present in other approaches).

[17] Of an 'implied reader', Iser says that 'this term incorporates both the prestructuring of the potential meaning by the text, and the reader's actualization of this potential through the reading process' (1974: xii).

[18] He also comments that in such gaps 'the reader is stimulated into forming his own connections' (1974: 208).

In the case of the *Libro*, there are gaps galore. To name just a few: how does the *serrana* section relate to the preceding Doña Endrina episode? How do the *Gozos de Santa María* relate to the rest of the work? How should a reader bridge from the prose prologue to the *cuaderna vía*? How might we view passages that occur only in manuscript *S*? How should we construe portions, such as the 'Cántiga de Talavera', which might be accretions? How can we interpret what are quite literally gaps in the text, the most obvious of which is the culminating scene of the Doña Endrina episode?[19] The history of the reception of the *Libro* is that of filling in these, and other, gaps. Depending on which gaps a reader fills in, and how this is done, the *Libro* can be made to say many different things. Once again, as the text says: 'bien o mal, qual puntares, tal te dirá çiertamente' (70b); or, as Seidenspinner-Núñez puts it: 'different readers are free to actualize the *Libro* in different ways and [. . .] no single interpretation will exhaust the semantic potential of this open text' (1988–89: 263).

The upshot of the reader-response approach, is, once again, that a literary work can mean more than its author ever consciously intended and can even circumvent, contest, undermine, or subvert the author's own conscious intentions. Since the publication of Iser's book, there have been numerous lines of enquiry into the ways in which a literary work speaks not because of authorial intention but because of the social, unconscious, and political pressures, the relations of power in both the writing and reception of works, and the institutions that regulate literary taste and the range of meanings deemed acceptable. Meaning can always be found if it must be. Stanley Fish (often considered one of the more radical figures in reader-response criticism) has argued that consensus regarding literary interpretation may be more a 'testimony to the power of an interpretive community' than 'proof of the stability of objects' to be interpreted (1980: 338), and he gives the example of how his students managed to find Christological significance in writing on the blackboard simply because he told them it was a poem for them to interpret, when in fact it was a list of early twentieth-century linguists left over from the class that preceded Fish's own (1980: 322–37). This may be an abuse of what university educators generally conceive of as their benevolent guiding role (Fish would probably contest this view), but it shows well the role of power in determining interpretation.

This does not mean a text can just mean anything, however, as even Fish acknowledges (1980: 338–55). There are two approaches, in addition to Fish's, which usefully counter the potentially centrifugal forces of some reader-response criticism. First, Peter J. Rabinowitz (1977) has proposed a typology of reception, which elegantly complements Booth, and is of particular interest to those concerned with the range of meanings that would have been available to readers contemporary with the author and with which meanings can be legitimately actualized by modern

---

[19] I have considered this last 'gap' from a reader-response standpoint (1997: 49–56).

readers.[20] Rabinowitz is himself indebted to Booth, Walker Gibson (1949–50), and Walter J. Ong (1975).

Rabinowitz's typology is fourfold, delineating: 1) the *actual audience* that has read or will read the work; 2) the *authorial audience*, that is, the specific hypothetical audience for which the work is rhetorically designed; 3) the *narrator's audience*, the readership that the narrator supposedly believes he is addressing; and finally 4) the *ideal narrative audience* – 'ideal from the narrator's point of view' (1977: 134) in that its members would unquestioningly agree with everything the narrator says. These roles may overlap, as, for example, when the actual audience that consumes a novel is identical with the one to whom the author seems to be speaking. For the modern medievalist, however, there will always be a distinction in that for any medieval work the actual audience of readers over time most likely includes centuries of readers who were not conceived of in the author's audience; with the exception of works that seem to address all future generations, the actual audience of any older work of literature has always greatly outstripped the reach inscribed in the text. As for the narrator's audience, it may occasionally overlap with the authorial audience, although in virtually all fictional narrative there will be a distinction in that the narrator narrates as though his addressee believed in the historical veracity of all the events recounted, whereas the author's audience knows it is reading a fictional work. Finally the ideal narrative audience will often be slightly different from the narrator's audience in terms of the extent of its resistance to the rhetoric of the narrative voice. Following Booth, Rabinowitz returns to the example of Jason from the third section of William Faulkner's *The Sound and the Fury* in which 'the ideal narrative audience believes that Jason has been victimized and sympathizes with his whining misery, although the narrative audience despises him' (1977: 134).

For the medievalist, and specifically for readers of the *Libro*, this typology can make for greater precision. The actual audience comprises two very distinct groups, medieval and modern readers, as well as readers from many intervening centuries; only the medieval readers can overlap with the authorial audience, since the *Libro* in no wise could anticipate twentieth- or twenty-first-century mentalities. I leave to others to decide to what extent the authorial audience overlaps with the narrative audience, but presumably the ideal narrative audience was one who responded, whether because nonplussed or because joyfully perplexed, to the twists and turns, the contradictions, the halts and hiccups of the narrator's voice; the narrator certainly narrates as though his swerves were entirely commonplace. What is more, the judgments we make as modern readers can be separated from our analysis of the authorial audience, the narrator's audience, or the medieval members of the actual audience. Lawrance's analysis (1984) is a superb study of

---

[20] Very few of our critical pronouncements are anything like what medieval readers might have said about contemporary works. Even the most traditional philological and historical scholarship places emphasis on details of which most medieval readers would have been entirely unaware.

the authorial audience, and we can probably assume that many fourteenth- and fifteenth-century members of the actual audience closely corresponded to the authorial audience. But when Lawrance mentions that *coplas* 1162–70 and 1579–1605 are 'as near as Juan Ruiz ever comes to writing rubbish' (1984: 224), he is quite clearly speaking in terms of the sensibilities of the modern actual readers.

The second approach that can serve modern readers of a medieval text such as the *Libro* quite well is that of Umberto Eco. His explorations in semiotics led him to consider the reader and the reader's role in constructing the meaning of a work (1962, 1979, 1989). Despite taking a different approach to these questions from that of Rabinowitz and Iser, Eco says quite similar things. He makes a distinction – which, nevertheless, can never be hard and fast – between 'closed' and 'open' works. Iser would describe Eco's 'open' works as those with many gaps that the reader needs to fill; Eco prefers to speak in terms of 'textes de jouissance' (Barthes 1973), which are texts that demand an active, performative role of the reader in the construction of their meaning. Since all texts are communicative, an addressee or, as Eco prefers, a Model Reader is always presupposed by a literary work; in the case of an 'open' text such as James Joyce's *Ulysses* (Jauss would call this a text that provokes the horizon of expectation), the reader must actively participate in the construction of meaning, whereas a 'closed' work, such as a James Bond novel (Jauss's stereotyped literary work), simply pulls the reader along a familiar 'and predetermined path' (Eco 1979: 8). What interests Eco is the relationship between a reader's competence and the indeterminacy of meaning in the open work. Like Fish, Eco takes pains to make clear that open texts are not without limits on their meaning.

Some of Eco's formulations (1979) now appear somewhat dated but he is surely correct that the 'ideal reader' of an 'open' work such as *Finnegan's Wake* cannot be a Greek reader of the second century BC; however, is not this is also true of a 'closed' work such as an Ian Fleming novel? In the same book Eco gives only cursory attention to the problems that arise when the model reader specified by a text is very different from the actual readership because of either social or historical differences (1979: 8, 50–52). However, Eco (1980) returns to the question of finding meanings that could not have been anticipated by the author, the 'author' being understood as 'a mere metaphor for "textual strategy"' (Eco 1979: 11).[21] This is of considerable interest for modern readers of medieval literature, aware that we constitute neither the authorial audience, nor part of the actual audience known to the world into which the medieval text was born. Is it legitimate to 'find [. . .] in the text what the author was unaware of but which the text in some way conveyed'? (1980: 157). Eco gives a qualified yes to this

---

[21] Eco also establishes a typology for examining whether multiple interpretations are contradictory or complementary (1980: 148–53). A. A. Parker's insightful comments (1976) on the 'Greeks and Romans' intuitively perceived the problematics Eco formalized. Parker's study is fundamental for its balanced approach and for how it modifies the earlier comments of Lida de Malkiel 1961 and Zahareas 1965; also see de Looze 1998 and Vasvári 1994.

question, and offers several examples, one of which is Freud's reading of Sophocles' *Oedipus Rex*:

> it appears that this type of inference is an essential part of the actualization of the message. We posit that there does exist a text in which the author could clearly not have been aware of encyclopedic data through which a whole series of actions or relations express given psychic contents, and yet it appears quite evident that the entire textual strategy leads inexorably to invest it with contents of that nature. A typical case would be Sophocles' *Oedipus Rex*, at least the way Freud read it [. . . This] leads us to say (or reiterate) that the Model Reader of *Oedipus Rex* was not the one Sophocles was thinking of, but the one Sophocles' text postulates.   (1980: 158–59)

For the *Libro*, then, the 'model reader' is the one who actualizes potentialities in the text and who completes its gaps, and as such the model reader includes more than simply the people, or the type of intellectual outlook, that the author might have consciously anticipated. It also can include meanings that the author could not possibly have anticipated. The critical approaches outlined here, and others, all have a part to play.

As yet, the number of critics who have taken up 'new philological' tools to study the *Libro* has not been large.[22] To Seidenspinner-Núñez's reader-response approach, I might add my own reception-based analysis of a few portions of the *Libro* (de Looze 1997). There is also interesting work by Cesáreo Bandera, including an article on the *Libro* and deconstruction (1977), and many of the publications of the last decade by Louise Vasvári show the imprint of conscious reflection on the methodological approach taken (for example, Vasvári 1988–89; also see Burke 1998).

The scholarly work on the *Libro* that has generated the most debate in the last decade about how critics should view the text has undoubtedly been that of Dagenais (1994; see my discussion above), which demonstrates the degree to which our image of the *Libro* is a product of modern editorial techniques, the actual medieval work being very different in texture, look, and culture. Dagenais convincingly establishes that what most critics study is a modern rewriting of the *Libro*. In response, Dagenais turns to French theories of *mouvance* and *variance* (also see Lawrance, this volume, for a discussion of these terms).

It should be noted that to this day most discussions, including very good ones of the possibilities digital technologies hold for the editing of medieval texts, tend to scrutinize the distortions inherent in the ideologies that formed earlier, print-based editions while simply lauding the virtues of the new modes being championed (Lerer 1996, Richard and Partridge in press). To be sure, the God-like power of the modern researcher who, with a click of a mouse, can move back and

---

[22] For articles on New Philology in general, see Nichols 1990; particularly that by Siegfried Wenzel.

forth between manuscript versions is profoundly un-medieval and runs the risk of greatly distorting our impression of what the medieval textual experience was like every bit as much as did earlier scholarly editions. Moreover, most new technologies assume that all students of medieval literature have their laptop always at the ready, an assumption implicitly favouring wealthier, Western researchers. By comparison, a traditional edition, for all its flaws, is far more democratic in global terms, because a single book does not begin to compare in terms of cost to a computer nor does it need the same infrastructure of high-speed access to the Web from home or office (let us remember that the third world depends largely on internet cafés where one pays for an hour of time in order to take care of e-mail correspondence, rather than on individual possession of computers).

Dagenais's study has the virtue of returning to the *Libro* manuscripts, and, while there are only three, what he discovers is that the variance from one to another is great. He also builds on twenty years of *mouvance* and *variance* study of French and English medieval literature which has concentrated on the whole *mise en scène* and *mise en page* of medieval texts – on how, in fact, the whole culture of manuscript reproduction and presentation differs from modern modes.

There is a fascinating wrinkle in Dagenais's book, however, and one that has had serious consequences for how *mouvance* and *variance* have been viewed in *Libro* studies and by hispanomedievalists more generally. The study of *mouvance* and *variance* in medieval French studies has inevitably stressed the plurality of meaning since a variant manuscript, or variances in a passage, necessarily imply that the text of one manuscript will not mean exactly the same thing as that of another. The centrifugal nature of meaning in manuscript culture has been very much forefronted, and few scholars working in Old French or Occitan would propose that a work means quite the same thing – or, more importantly, means in quite the same ways – from one manuscript to another. In their emphasis on the how of meaning more than the what of meaning – an emphasis that ultimately derives from structuralism – scholars of French would stress that each manuscript is the product of slightly different pressures, interests, peoples, and places, and that its text will always be slightly different. *Variance* refers to more than mere difference in words: a luxurious presentation manuscript and a student copy of a text may contain the same words in a particular passage, but differences in presentation, parchment or paper quality, margins, concentration of abbreviations, illustrations (or lack thereof), doodlings, glosses, binding, etc., will all be part of what the text meant in its time and continues to mean in ours.

However, because there is so little communication between medievalists, most hispanomedievalists have depended heavily on Dagenais for their access to questions of *mouvance* and *variance*, and one of the striking features (which is decidedly unlike *variance* studies of other literatures) of Dagenais's study is that he has somewhat incongruously yoked *variance* to what he calls the 'ethical reading' of the Middle Ages. Now, ethical reading is a reductive, neo-Robertsonian approach that has had particular success in England and North America, especially since

Judson Boyce Allen's 1982 book.[23] Ostensibly, Dagenais proposes to use the *vari-ance* of manuscripts to show that readers read 'ethically' (and in no other fashion) in the Middle Ages – and therefore that all texts meant the same thing to all read-ers. Rather incongruously, then, precisely at the moment that multiplicity in terms of presentation is embraced, multiplicity in terms of reception is denied, despite the obvious fact that differences in the text must inevitably make for differences in how / what that text means. One might say that, yoked to *variance*, ethical reading seeks to replace the neatness of the standard scholarly edition with a new neatness of reception / meaning. This strategy makes *variance* a purely cosmetic feature and uses the dazzling visual multiplicity of presentation to mask the fact that the same *variance* is being declared, quite literally, meaningless (because no matter what differences there are in the texts, they will all always mean the same thing).

The monolithic construction of medieval reading raises problems in both Allen and Dagenais; indeed the most debated aspect of Dagenais's book is the question of whether or not all readers read ethically, and the range of scholars' reactions is great, varying in quality and detail (Martínez 1997, Dagenais 1998, Martínez 1998, Montaner Frutos & Montaner Frutos 1998, Greenia 1999). Lawrance, in particular, makes some important points: he cleaves ethical reading from *variance* (1998: 159), and notes that 'the material paleographic remains of marginalia are likely to preserve only a fragment, and perhaps a highly unrepresentative frag-ment, of the range of medieval reading practices' (160).[24] The semi-public nature of the medieval manuscript might have prevented some readers from leaving evi-dence of unethical reading practices in the manuscripts, and caused others to leave evidence that their reading was 'charitable', not 'concupiscent'.[25]

Curiously, one of the characteristics of Dagenais's book that has been almost completely masked by the controversy over ethical reading and the seeming strangeness of his representations of the *Libro* text is that he does not adduce much manuscript evidence for ethical reading. In fact, marginal annotation and marking does not point clearly to ethical reading, and Dagenais acknowledges as much. The scantiness of the evidence and the problems surrounding the manipulation of the data is evident in reading the book. For example, if one glances at Dagenais's sec-tion on marginalia (1994, chap. 5) – where one would expect to find evidence of ethical reading – one finds him struggling with the evidence. In his discussion of 'Marginalia in G' (156–58), he acknowledges that 'vino' in the margin of folio 73[r] has not annotated a passage that refers to 'a topical critique of overindulgence in

---

[23] Robertsonian refers to the work of D. W. Robertson who generalized a reading approach based on *caritas* and *cupiditas* from St Augustine's *De doctrina christiana* from scriptural exegesis to medieval secular culture (Robertson 1962; esp. 25 and 60). For Augustine *cupiditas* or *concupiscentia* is a loving of the sign for the sign's sake, whereas *caritas* refers to a loving of the divine signified (God) through the signs of the world / text.

[24] See particularly Alberto and Fernando Montaner Frutos 1998; also Dyer 1998: 162, and Martínez 1998: 174–75.

[25] The latter group of readers take pleasure in the sign (Augustine's *fruor*) whereas the former make use of (*utor*) the signifying text.

wine' but rather a passage 'extolling [. . .] the fine wines enjoyed by nuns'.
Determined to resist 'this gloss [. . . which is] seemingly so inappropriate to the
passage' (157), Dagenais concludes that it must be registering the reader's (ethical)
'indignation at the text's casual treatment of the problem' (Does not this interpretation contravene Dagenais's view of the *Libro* as an 'ethical' text?). What we
find, then, in Dagenais's approach is that marginal marks accompanying 'ethical'
passages and marginal marks accompanying non-ethical passages will always
be interpreted as 'ethical' responses. The Montaner Frutos brothers have concisely
expressed the problem of this circularity in Dagenais's arguments: 'su explicación
de estas marcas de lectura no se encamina a apoyar la tesis de la lectura ética, pese
a sus declaraciones, sino que se apoya en esta tesis' (1998: 164–65). In the thirteenth century, Stephen Langton raised similar objections to such interpretative
strategies: faced with an interpretation of a red cow in Numbers 19: 2 as prefigur-
ing the red blood of the Passion, he pointed out that 'it would be all the same if the
cow had been black; the allegory is worthless; whatever the colour of the cow,
some sort of allegory could be found for it' (quoted in Smalley 1978: 261). In his
book Dagenais fares no better with the evidence of manuscript *S*. The sketches in
the margins are, he concedes, 'puzzling' (163) and the best he can do is suggest a
parallel between the mouse / bear / rat on folio 51^v and 'the modern English
metaphorization of "rat"' (163). But surely modern English colloquial uses of 'rat'
tell us little about medieval Spanish readers' responses.

In the final analysis, it will be impossible to prove, in any definitive way, the
extent to which medieval reading practice was 'ethical'. If, however, Dagenais
had historicized his understanding of the 'gloss', he would be aware that it signified not only 'comment, explanation, description' but also 'specious or sophis-
tical interpretation, the pursuit of favor by adulation, flattering or deceitful
speech' (Hanning 1987: 31) and that glossing was somewhat suspiciously
viewed as a means of manipulating as much as explaining texts (29).[26] In the end,
the yoking of ethical reading and *variance* has obscured the fact that *variance*
tends toward a multiplicity, not a uniqueness, of meaning in manuscript texts.

If we return to the *Libro* from the standpoint of *variance* as francophone
critics practise it, the *Libro* will be free to speak in different ways, depending on
the manuscript version we are reading. For, as Zumthor would say, there are
at least three *Libros de Buen Amor*, and four if one wishes to count the extant
medieval fragment of the Portuguese translation. Each represents a reception
and reperformance of the work, whether or not one or more is a revision specifically authorized by an author(s). If the two-version theory were not, in fact,
correct, we should nevertheless still have an extraordinary example of reader
response, and this *variance* in terms of the text, and thus its meaning, would be
sufficient to occupy scholars for years to come.[27] Finally, we certainly do have
what is potentially an instance of concupiscent reader response in the curiously

---

[26] For other pertinent essays see Finke and Shichtman 1987.
[27] On the two-recension hypothesis see Haywood, and Lawrance, both this volume.

missing folios on which the culmination of the Doña Endrina episode evidently took place. I have discussed elsewhere the centrality, both literal and metaphorical, of this missing passage (1997: 55–56). We are reasonably, if not entirely, sure that the folios disappeared early on (Castro 1954: 358, 363–64). Naturally, if someone did intentionally remove the pages, they may have considered themselves to be acting ethically in removing the temptation of an erotic scene, thereby averting a situation in which other readers might fall in moral terms (nevertheless, the refusal to cede to a concupiscent reading could also become a means of strengthening oneself as a 'charitable' reader). I think, however, that the odds are against this. When I was working on the relevant portion of my 1997 book, I went to see the head of the manuscript collection at Harvard's Houghton library. When I outlined the situation, he was quite unequivocal. Someone stole it, he told me, and he went on to say that in all periods erotic literature and erotic episodes are always the first to disappear from manuscripts and from libraries; even at the Houghton, he said, they have to keep all erotic literature under lock and key.

In the end, the very lack of manuscript text for the erotic culmination of the Doña Endrina episode becomes a hermeneutic challenge to the modern reader, and a reminder both of earlier readers' reactions and of our own inability to fully understand manuscript texts. To a certain extent nothing is lost in the economy of the text, not even the absence of the text, for that very absence becomes part of what and how the text must mean.

The underlying message of everything I have written above is largely that there is a need for diversity in terms of theoretical approaches to the *Libro*. I do not have the space to consider all strands of current literary theory, and of necessity I have left out many important approaches – Marxist, psychoanalytic, and socio-political, for example – and I have made only brief reference to certain others. Rather than parade critical theories, I wish instead to return briefly to a well-known study of the *Libro* and reconsider it from the standpoint of its theory.

It may come as a surprise that the work I have in mind is Thomas R. Hart's 1959 book on the *Libro*. Most critics either remember or have been made aware that Lida de Malkiel (1960–61) gave Hart's book a scathing reception, and as a result it has been little consulted since. They probably remember as well that Hart attempted to read each and every portion of the *Libro* in an entirely 'ethical' or Robertsonian manner.

I do not intend to rehabilitate Hart's book here; but I do wish to stress that he reads in a tried and true medieval fashion. His far-fetched allegorizing analogies are probably not correct in the sense of according with either authorial intention or, in terms I prefer, the meanings available to a Model Reader. For Lida de Malkiel, Hart's interpretations are 'arbitraria' and therefore 'errónea' (1960–61: 343). None the less it is worth pointing out that his readings are almost textbook examples of the sort of 'artificial conceptual correspondences' and 'far-fetched comparison' that, as Lawrance has noted (1984: 226), were typical of the medieval scholastic tradition. In fact, we really should scrutinize the theoretical basis of the objections to Hart's proposals, because to the degree that they appeal to authorial intention, about which we know virtually nothing, the objections are not really legitimate (this does not, of course, make Hart's readings any more correct). I do not mean to be obtuse here, nor to suggest that I agree with Hart's views – indeed, I do not – but since Hart (mis)reads the *Libro* no more outrageously than the *Ovide moralisé* misread Ovid's *Metamorphoses*, it is not unreasonable to think either that medieval readers might have made similarly artificial correspondences or that they would not have been put off by such readings. Lida de Malkiel acknowledges as much when she comments that 'cualquier obra puede alegorizarse en cualquier sentido, y ahí está el *Ovidio moralizado*' (1960–61: 343). This mode of reading may be of little interest to modern readers, but, as the reference to the *Ovide moralisé* makes clear, medieval readers might well have been intrigued by such interpretations.[28] Underpinning the practices of both medieval readers and Hart is the notion of the arbitrary relationship between sign and signified, as most powerfully set forth by Saint Augustine. The fourfold exegetical approach to biblical texts acknowledged that one could establish typological connections between the Old Testament type and an antitype (for example, Moses and Christ) which was considered to be grounded in the historical reality of the type, the portrayal of the textual antitype, the pragmatic situation of the discourses, and the historical authors' presumed intentions (see Auerbach 1984). The challenge to medieval readers was to learn to make (to our mind arbitrary) rapprochements between very different concepts on the basis of analogy. These clerical practices seeped into secular reading and interpretation, as many examples make clear, including ones from the *Libro* (see Cantarino 1974 and Lawrance 1984).

As already stated, I believe that we must scrutinize the basis of the rejection of Hart's interpretations. To the extent that the rejection is based in our projections of authorial intentions, we are merely favouring a post-medieval form of reading over a medieval, scholastic one, since Hart has a clear theory of the text, which is very much a medieval one. In the rejection of Hart's interpretations, then, we utter our preference for modern theories of textuality and meaning. The need to be explicit regarding these preferences is therefore crucial, and our refusal to accept an obvious case of 'misreading', even if it is the sort of misreading in which medieval readers might have delighted, should put us on guard against the misreading that characterizes all interpretation. Paul de Man has been among the most

---

[28] A good fourteenth-century example of the delight readers could have in such allegorizing is Jean Froissart's *Prison amoureuse*. When the first-person narrator is asked to write book based on his patron's dream material, he does so according to 'artificial conceptual correspondences', glossing the whole dream as a love allegory. Then, when the patron's lover asks for a further gloss on one section, the narrator provides an allegorical gloss of an entirely different (and equally artificial) sort, and neither narrator nor patron seems troubled by either the arbitrary nature of the first gloss or the fact that the second allegorical interpretation develops in an entirely different direction from the terms of the first gloss; see Froissart 1994: 200–09, and for discussion, de Looze 1997: 124–25.

unrelenting in pointing out that every reading is always a misreading, but the lesson needs periodic reiteration.[29] There is perhaps nothing more dangerous for modern readers than to believe, as Hart and Dagenais did, that they can actually read as medieval readers; we can never do more than read a medieval work as a modern mentality would have medieval readers do. A putative medieval reading through modern eyes will never be the same as an actual medieval reading.

Theory helps clarify the relationship between our modes of reading and the meanings we discover in the medieval text. Hart's interpretations of the *Libro* represent an extreme case, but they derive quite easily from the presuppositions of his theoretical approach. Many instances of the symbiosis between critical theory and critical results are less clear, but this is not necessarily an advantage. At least with Hart's book we know quite well the ways in which, and the standard according to which, its readings may be considered legitimate or illegitimate.

I began this essay by asking what critical theory contributes to our understanding of the *Libro*. The answer, I think, is: 'everything'. I maintain that we should welcome theoretically diverse approaches to this work – and in fact to all medieval writing. Each methodology will have its contribution to make, and each contributes to an ever incomplete patchwork of meaning. To a plurality of texts let us marry a plurality of methodologies. We shall probably never exhaust the full complexity of the writers, readers, and texts that the medieval world produced.

As the *Libro* puts it, 'faré / punto a mi librete, mas non lo çerraré' (1626cd). The last time I held the *S* manuscript of the *Libro* in my hands, in the reading room at the Biblioteca Antigua of the Universidad de Salamanca, I turned to the final pages of the codex, reluctant indeed to *cerrar* the book. There, scribbled after the end of the *Libro*, are several medicinal recipes. Who were these readers / writers, I wondered, who used the final portions of parchment as a medicinal miscellany (a common practice, as we know well)? What did it say, if anything, about their view of the *Libro* as text, as book, about the limits of the text, and about what constituted *entendimiento*?[30] For a work that seems to begin in more than one spot, depending on the manuscript, and end in more than one way, according to which manuscript reading one follows, these salubrious scribblings seemed a wonderful way for the book to trail off. The manuscript that has been wounded by a violation at its very centre (in the Doña Endrina episode) finishes with recipes for the reader's health. We learn what is good for a pain in one's molars, and also that capers are good for liver problems.[31] I would add only that theory is good for the pains and joys of literary interpretation.

---

[29] This is most forcefully argued in de Man 1971.

[30] Germán Orduna 1988 argued that a distinction needed to be made between the *Libro* and the Archpriest's book, since the totality of the one was not necessarily synonymous with the totality of the other.

[31] These passages are reproduced in the 1975 facsimile edition of MS *S*, which powerfully conveys Orduna's distinction between the *Libro* and the manuscript codex: volume I, the facsimile of the manuscript codex, reproduces the pages at the end with their medicinal recipes, but volume II, which is a transcription only of the *Libro*, does not include them.

Chaotics, Complexity, and the *Libro de buen amor*

ELIZABETH DRAYSON

The beautiful swirling shape known as the Lorenz attractor is a visual image of a strange attractor, a term coined by twentieth-century chaos theorists to illustrate the stability and hidden structure in supposedly patternless systems. In this essay, I should like to suggest ways in which a modern interdisciplinary approach can enrich critical reading, by exploring the metaphorical and literal relevance of both the term 'strange attractor' and the concept of chaos to the study of a fourteenth-century Castilian poem.

Faced with the complexity and apparent disorder of Juan Ruiz's *Libro de buen amor*, critics have tried hard to smooth out the structures of the *Libro* in a more rigidly linear fashion, notably in terms of its overall design, attempting to impose unity in a way which exemplifies what Roland Barthes calls a 'centrist philosophy to control texts, language and power structures within society' (Hayles 1990: 187). The *Libro* has sometimes been characterized as anthological in structure. In the nineteenth-century, José Amador de los Ríos emphasized this aspect in his long discussion of the diverse aspects of fourteenth-century Castilian life encompassed by the text (1861–65: IV, 155–204), underlining the amorphous nature of 'el variado conjunto que constituye tan peregrina obra' (160). Later critics, such as Gonzalo Sobejano (1973) echoed this opinion, but tried to impose the idea of a formal structure by stating that at close range the reader is aware of the juxtaposition of apparently disparate sections of text, yet only when the text is viewed as a whole can any coherence be seen. The proposition that perception of the text varies according to scale bears directly upon chaos theory.

In spite of the predominantly European sources for the *Libro*, Américo Castro believed the work to be strongly influenced by Hispano-Arabic literature precisely because of its complex and fluid structure:

> Ni en el *Pamphilus* ni en la *Bataille de Caresme et de Charnage*, ni en todo lo demás, se encuentra la forma flúida y deslizante característica del estilo del Arcipreste. Ahora bien, este modo de entrar el poeta en su realidad literaria, y de instalarse en ella, es propio de la manera árabe de estar en la vida.   (1954: 406)

The form of the *Libro* is, in Castro's eyes, typified by movement and change: 'una continua e interna transición estructura el *Libro*' (1954: 397). In a similar way, María Rosa Lida de Malkiel (1961) saw resemblances between the Hebrew literature of medieval Spain and the *Libro*, but there is no reason to believe that the Archpriest knew Hebrew. Later, Oliver T. Myers (1972) and Philip O. Gericke (1981) searched for symmetry in the two halves of the text and for order in terms of compilation. Yet attempts to impose symmetry on the amorphous structure fail, for the text has more than one beginning and no fixed end or conclusion. The matter is further complicated by the incompleteness of all the extant manuscripts and by the question of the number of redactions. Alberto Blecua describes his view of the disordered nature of the work:

> Obra de acción episódica, auténtico rosario de episodios con algunos cuentos mayores; la repetición de las situaciones con un similar principio, medio y desenlace; el abrupto fluir del sistema narrativo, con cortes y tajos en su desarrollo, que se alterna con la morosidad de las argumentaciones a través de ejemplos, comparaciones y digresiones perpetuas; los cambios bruscos de tono [. . .] producen en el lector actual, educado en otros sistemas narrativos cultos o populares, la sensación de andar perdido en un universo literario que le es ajeno.   (1983: xix)

Not only does Blecua feel the *Libro* belongs to an alien literary world, he also believes it to be strange and unintelligible in its originality (1983: xx). These comments arise because of the essentially amorphous nature of the work. It is a text in a state of what chaos theorists call permanent instability both in terms of the divergences between the extant manuscripts and in terms of the mutability of critical opinion in relation to virtually every aspect of the text. The *Libro* does not conform to conventional expectations of structuring or plot, hence the widely divergent interpretations of its meaning. Harriet Hawkins points out that:

> the signature of a complex 'irregular' (non-linear) work may be that its internal dynamics (order containing chaos, regular irregularities and so on), inevitably (as it were deterministically) evoke artistic and critical responses that are themselves unpredictable, chaotic, contradictory and uncontrollable either by the author or by the critical tradition.   (1995: 87)

I propose that a reading of the text in the light of chaos theory, while perhaps constituting an unpredictable critical response in itself, can rescue the *Libro* from alienating unintelligibility by uncovering structures and meanings which have resonance within contemporary modes of investigation.

Chaos theory in relation to art and literature

Chaos theory and its sequel, complexity, have been at the heart of the scientific revolution of the last forty years. For James Gleick, and other scientists, where chaos begins, classical mathematical science stops, because 'the shapes of classical geometry are lines and planes, circles and spheres, triangles and cones. They represent a powerful abstraction of reality, and they inspired a powerful philosophy of Platonic harmony' (1989: 94). In this philosophy, order is privileged over disorder; but chaos theory relates to the irregular side of nature, the discontinuous and erratic areas, which traditionally have been sources of puzzlement outside the reductive Newtonian view of the world. It is a science of the global nature of systems, in which order masquerades as randomness, and fantastic and delicate structures underlie complexity.

One essential feature of chaos theory is that apparently random phenomena observed in various branches of science result from complex dynamic underlying principles. Central to this is the paradoxical 'random pattern', where patterns in systems such as weather, mathematical fractals, and ecology occur as if haphazardly, although these patterns are, in fact, repeated, with slight variations each time. The new pattern is almost the same as the previous one, but is randomly different and therefore constantly evolving. In his now famous work *Chaos: Making a New Science*, Gleick describes how researchers into chaotic dynamics discovered that the 'disorderly behaviour of simple systems acted as a creative process. It generated complexity: richly organized patterns, sometimes stable and sometimes unstable' (1989: 43). It is the dissolution of order into turbulence, the very essence of the strange attractor, which paradoxically signals the profound interconnectedness of the system: 'a complex system can give rise to turbulence and coherence at the same time' (Gleick 1989: 56).

In the last decade, writers, critics, and artists have tapped a rich new source of analogy and convergence between scientific chaos and the humanities. Peter Stoicheff's essay on the chaos of metafiction underlines this interchange when he states that science and fiction have been influenced by 'a revolution in contemporary thought that examines similar roles of narrative and of investigative procedure, in our reading or knowledge of the world' (1991: 85). Such an enterprise has a vigorous philosophical underpinning in the thought of the French philosopher Michel Serres whose major interest lies in the parallel development of scientific, philosophical, and literary trends. Of particular interest to this essay are Serres's views on the concept of disorder, through which he invites rethinking of 'the relations between order and disorder in such a way as to show how everything begins, ends and begins again according to a universal principle of disorder' (1982: xxvii). His statement that the world needs to be rethought, not in terms of its laws and regularities, but rather 'in terms of perturbations and turbulences, in order to bring out its multiple forms, uneven structures and fluctuating organizations' (1982: xxvii) might apply equally well to certain literary texts. The productive nature of perturbation, the power of disorder to modify reality and reveal its complexities, are ideas essential to the analysis of the *Libro*.

Perhaps a caveat is necessary at this point. Literature and its criticism are not sciences, and it would clearly be inappropriate to consider texts according to the literal principles of non-linear dynamics. Scientific terms can be used only as metaphors, but these metaphors can nevertheless offer fresh critical perspectives on literary works. Interaction between science and the arts is nothing new, and at its best can be mutually enriching. Gleick notes that the planes, circles, and spheres of Euclid (c. 300 BC) and later Pythagorean mathematics provided an ideal model of beauty for many artists. Contemporary chaos scientists constantly draw on images from literature and art to describe their own new concepts.

Benoit Mandelbrot links art and chaos theory in his seminal *Fractals: Form, Chance and Dimension* (1977). 'Fractal' is a word coined by Mandelbrot to describe what is broken, irregular, or fragmented, and it is a key term in the new geometry of chaos. It came to stand for a way of describing irregular shapes which do not fit the limitations of classical geometry. Mitchell Feigenbaum, another founding father of chaos theory, reinforces the links between art and science when he discusses how Turner paints turbulent fluids, echoing Mandelbrot's thoughts on human perception through art, which, he says, is 'a theory about the way the world looks to human beings' (Gleick 1989: 186).

This interchange between art and science is particularly stimulating for writers and critics because the metaphors of chaos theory can be applied in extremely diverse ways, and to both modern and earlier literature. Chaos, disruption, and fragmentation are terms clearly appropriate to post-modernism and contemporary literature. They also have relevance to medieval texts which are amorphous and lack classical unity and proportion, creating an impression of structural and thematic disorder. It is precisely this unstructured quality which was long ago identified by the French medievalist Edmond Faral as a feature of some of the greatest medieval romances: 'Beaucoup de romans, et des plus réputés, manquent totalement d'unité et de proportions' (1924: 60). Forty years later, Eugène Vinaver developed this further in his discussion of Arthurian romance, in which the interlacing of several separate themes on a large scale creates a narrative of vast dimensions and subtle coherence, multiple and varied, in which everything is 'part of a wider canvas, of a work still unwritten, of a design still unfulfilled' (1966: 15). No anachronism exists in using new scientific paradigms to interpret works written before those paradigms emerged: the laws and precepts of chaos theory and complexity have always existed, but have only recently become measurable and found expression in scientific language. In fact, Serres argues that great literature constitutes a 'reservoir of knowledge' for scientists, and can at times prefigure the insights of science (1982: xxxix). Therefore, to read a medieval text in terms of chaotics is to set free aspects of the text which have lain imprisoned or unnoticed by previous modes of interpretation.

One such approach to Early Modern works is that of Hawkins, who examines what she describes as the 'persistent instability that characterizes the dynamical interaction between order and disorder in both canonical and popular fictions' (1995: ix). Her main examples come from Shakespeare and Milton, and show that premodern works also contain, as she puts it, 'symmetries, asymmetries, ruptures, iterations, recursions and bifurcations'. She feels that the use of chaos theory confirms modern critical arguments that canonical works show how subversion and resistance are still present within containment (Hawkins 1995: 11).

Hawkins's study forms part of a growing body of scholarly work that investigates literary texts, both early and modern, in terms of chaos theory.[1] James W. Earl's study of the Old English poem *Beowulf* (1994) is of particular interest in

---

[1] See Cheever 1989, Reed 1994, and Zants 1996.

its application of chaos theory to a medieval work. His approach establishes the connection between the fractal coastlines of what is known as the Mandelbrot set, which become more indefinable and complex the more they are magnified, and an equivalent process in poetry, whereby the closer one looks, the more one sees. What at first sight appears simple, branches into complex symmetries and repeating structures when viewed at close quarters, a phenomenon which, Earl suggests, was already well understood in the Middle Ages.

Chaos and complexity in the structure of the 'Libro'

In no great poem of the medieval era can this phenomenon be seen more clearly than in the *Libro*.[2] It is a text in a permanent state of instability, with random patterns repeated at unpredictable points, but never repeated in quite the same way. In terms of the poem's overall shape, this is clearly illustrated in the structural position of *exempla*, of allegory, and of Marian lyrics. One group of exemplary fables occurs between stanzas 226 and 371 and is used at first sight to illustrate the seven deadly sins, though their apparently pious purpose is subverted by their context, since they fall within Don Amor's advice to the Archpriest on how to be successful in love. A second group of fables appears asymmetrically in the later part of the text in relation to the first group, between stanzas 1348 and 1484, and one might suppose that these would have a similar pseudo-didactic purpose, but at this point they are used as part of a dialectical battle between Doña Garoça and Trotaconventos, in a dialogue which paves the way for the amorous relationship between the nun and the Archpriest (also see Taylor, this volume). The pattern is similar in that both groups of fables relate to the love theme, though this is again subversive when set against the familiar use of exemplary fables in popular sermons. Each group of stories is used as a means of proving an argument, but the interlocutors and the context differ, while the structural ordering of the *exempla* is not predictable within the scope of the whole. Both groups are similar in purpose and almost symmetrical in each half of the *Libro*, yet not identical in function.

Likewise, the sections of allegory are not symmetrically structured in the text as we have it, since the introduction of the allegorical figure of Don Amor begins at stanza 181 and ends at 575, while the main allegorical battle between Carnal and Cuaresma spans 1067–1314. Nor does the purpose of the allegorical figures of Don Amor and Venus as counsellors of love to the Archpriest prepare the reader or audience for the function of the great central allegory, which epitomizes in mock-epic style the fundamental conflict in the *Libro* between religious love and sexual love.

A third example, the Marian lyrics, might be considered to form the structural backbone of the work (Myers 1972; also see Haywood and Lawrance, both in this volume), being placed near the beginning, middle, and end of the extant text, but these locations are approximate, the text is incomplete, and in each case the

---

[2] All references and citations are to Criado de Val and Naylor 1972, and are to stanzas.

function not only of the lyrics but also of the versification differs, since these are examples of metrical variety and virtuosity, not of homogeneity.

If we move in from the global to the local and tighten the focus on the imagery of the poem, certain images disclose a similar type of chaotic pattern.[3] The text is rich in imagery, which is diffused throughout the seven thousand lines of the poem, with little clustering or impression of density. The spread of the imagery is unstructured throughout the poem, which may dilute its impact on initial reading, though its use is far more frequent than that of any other poetic devices. There are many image groups in the *Libro*, of which three will serve as illustrations.

One of the numerous images of food in the *Libro*, that of honey, appears in lines 514c, 1065c, 1379c, and 1380c, the last two of which can be viewed together. The pattern of image repetition reflects the inevitable disorder of a diffuse and complicated text. What is especially intriguing, however, is that the image is repeated for different purposes, rather than relating to the same referent. In 514c, 'quien non tiene miel en la orça tengala en la boca' is an allusion to the power of sweet but deceptive words, which links to the major theme of the illusory nature of language itself. In 1065c, 'las llagas quel llagaron son mas dulçes que miel' is an image which paradoxically contrasts the physical pain of Christ's wounds with sweetness, and reminds the reader of the symbolism of honey in medieval art, where it represents the ministry of Christ. Lines 1379c and 1380c, 'el que teme la muerte, el panal le sabe fiel' and 'con miedo de la muerte la miel non es sabrosa', spoken by the country mouse after he and his friend – the town mouse – have almost been caught feasting on the remains of the dining table, contrast the sweetness of life with bitter death, as even honey tastes of gall to those who fear for their lives. By its repetition with different referents, the image of honey correlates language, deception, religious suffering and death.

Musical imagery and references are equally randomly distributed in the text. Juan Ruiz was clearly very knowledgeable about music, as his poem contains one of the first Castilian lists of instruments (the only similar example can be found in the early-thirteenth-century *Libro de Alexandre*). The cluster of musical images in the parody of the canonical hours has overtly sexual meanings. Line 375c, '*primo dierum onium*, los estormentos tocar' relates to both sexual and musical instruments, as does the bell and clapper image in line 383d, '*justus est domine*; tañe a nona la canpana', while at evening prayer 'Nunca vy sancristan que a visperas mejor tanga, / todos los jnstrumentos toca con la chica manga' (384ab; see Vasvári below). Here the priest is skilled at playing both musical and sexual instruments. An ironic echo of this sacrilegious ambiguity comes nearer the end, in line 1537b, where the approach of death is signified by the ringing of the church bells: 'non coydan ver la ora que tangan las campanas'. In contrast, the mood of this passage is sombre and threatening. Through a common image, love and death are again linked, as they were by the imagery of honey.

A musical image also lies at the complex and ambiguous heart of stanzas 69 and 70, where the *Libro* itself is compared to a musical instrument which will respond

---

[3] For a full study of the imagery of the *Libro*, see Phillips 1983.

to the skill of the reader / player: 'dicha buena o mala por puntos la juzgat, / las coplas con los puntos load o denostat' (69cd). 'Por puntos' is a pun on 'por momentos' and also 'according to the notes of the musical scale'.[4] The imagery of music therefore equates the text of the poem itself with sexual love, reinforcing the displacement of desire from woman to language elsewhere in the work.

The third extensive group of images relates to journeys, often by sea, some of which are suggestive of sexual adventure. When Don Amor is exhorting the narrator to pluck up courage, he uses the image of the turbulent sea and frightened sailor:

> Si la primera onda del mar ayrada
> espantase al marynero quando vyene torbada,
> nunca en la mar entrarie con su nave ferrada.   (614abc)

The vast power of the sea and its fearsome waves are ironically humorous in their hint of the potential power of sexual love, for the lover is equated with a small ship engulfed by the ocean. In lines 650cd, the narrator is again metaphorically helpless at sea, without oars, on the uncharted waters of sexual love: 'puso me el marinero ayna en la mar fonda, / dexo me solo e señero, syn Remos, con la blaua onda'.

The image of the Virgin Mary as a port or haven used in the *Gozos*, 'Estrella del mar, puerto de folgura' (1681a), and her presence to aid the helpless narrator, 'que me saque a puerto' (1683d), echo his plight in the amorous context of line 651b: 'oteo a todas partes e non puedo fallar puerto'. Once again, images are repeated with varying referents, in this case linking worldly and divine love in a way which parallels the linking of sexual and religious love in mystical writing. Imagery of paths and travelling work in the same way. Lines 116cd 'tome senda por carrera / commo andaluz' refers to the narrator's deception in sexual love by Cruz the baker woman and his go-between, Ferrand Garçia. In lines 186cd, the Archpriest reprimands Don Amor because of the difficulty of the journey to sexual experience: 'fazes al que te cree lazar en tu mesnada / E por plazer poquillo andar luenga jornada'. Yet the image of a path is also used to represent the road to death in 1569d: 'nunca torna con nuevas quien anda esta carrera'. Repetition with variation within the range of images of journeying firmly links major themes of sexual and religious love and death.

This subtle manifestation of consistency within chaos is equally discernible in the poem's preoccupation with the phrase 'buen amor'.[5] Jacques Derrida (1967) discusses the importance of keywords and contexts when he describes books as reservoirs of chaos (unlike Serres, who sees them as reservoirs of knowledge). He employs the scientific term 'iteration', whose meaning he later adapts to express the idea that any word acquires a slightly different meaning each time it

---

[4] Joset (1974: I, 34–35n) discusses this interpretation of stanzas 69 and 70 with reference to other critical opinion; also on this passage see de Looze, above, and Vasvári 1983–84 and below.

[5] On this phrase, see Gybbon-Monypenny 1961 and Dutton 1966; also see Vasvári and de Looze, in this volume.

appears in a new context. He suggests that repetition of words in unpredictable contexts produces continually evolving meanings (Derrida 1967: 226–34).

In his unpublished thesis, Jacques Joset makes a similar point about transitions of meaning on the level of individual words. While the repetition of words can be considered as an archaic trait attributable to the oral presentation of much medieval literature, Joset notes that in the *Libro* between one stanza and another a word may change its meaning, giving the impression that the book progresses, as he explains, 'par vagues successives, que chaque strophe apporte une nouveauté qui modifie la copla antérieure et lance la suivante' (1970: 394).

If the text is viewed at this level of magnification, the metaphors of chaos theory are equally illuminating, because individual key words and terms, scattered liberally and unpredictably, are repeated progressively and with variation. The pivotal term 'buen amor' merits special attention, for its essential ambiguity derives from its repetitive yet divergent usage. It appears altogether fifteen times in the text, in lines 37 and 48 of the prose prologue, and in stanzas 13, 18, 66, 68, 443, 932, 933, 1331, 1452, 1507, 1578, and twice in 1630. The stanza numbers show that the pattern is random, with a tendency to clustering at the beginning and end of the work. The initial meaning of the good love of God, 'el buen Amor, que es el de dios' (Prose Prologue 37), later carries the implication of sexual love, for example in line 1331d 'fe a que buen amor qual buen amiga buscolo', and also denotes good will and friendliness in line 443b (in Ms *G*) 'rruegal que te non mienta, muestral buen amor'. 'Buen amor' is used to describe both the book itself, and the go-between, Trotaconventos. A. Bonilla y San Martín makes the acute observation that equating the term 'buen amor' with the bawd renders the term synonymous with 'alcahueta' itself, and therefore the author's designation of the book as 'libro de buen amor' (933b) is the same as calling it 'libro de alcahuetería' (1906: 377n2; also see Márquez Villanueva 1993). Each time the context varies to produce richer associative levels of signification, built on the now familiar structure of random repetition which is never exactly the same twice, a structure which evinces an underlying kaleidoscopic cohesion, hitherto obscured by critical attempts to discover conventional kinds of order in the poem.

Love as chaos

The overarching theme of love in the *Libro* can also be viewed as a source of significant instability and chaos in the narrative, which through its disorderly effects disrupts the ideological and psychological orders implicit in the text. One of the most striking expressions of the idea of chaotic disruption occurs in *The Strange Attractor*, a detective novel by Desmond Cory in which the fictional scientist describes this phenomenon:

> Maybe for a while things can go round in a nice smooth orbit . . . But then some unknown factor interferes and attracts the particles – pulls them out of the pattern. And it all goes haywire. We call that factor a 'strange attractor'.
> (Hawkins 1995: 126)

In the *Libro*, sexual love may be seen as the chaotic element which disturbs the order of religious love. The various women who are the objects of the Archpriest's amorous attention act as 'strange attractors', creating chaos in personal terms for the narrator, and also in terms of the implicit religious establishment.

The powerfully chaotic nature of love is forcefully expressed by the narrator when he is admonishing Don Amor for his lack of success in love affairs. Love drives people mad: 'Traes enloquecidos a muchos con tu saber' (184a). According to the Archpriest, Love is responsible for eight, not seven, deadly sins, causing man to betray his original, unsullied nature.[6] Juan Ruiz illustrates the sin of lust with a story about the poet Virgil which demonstrates the topsy-turvy, chaotic effect of sexual passion on men, as it reverses the status quo and destabilizes the natural order. First, the Archpriest shows how lust leads to the ultimate chaos, murder: 'Por amor de berssabe, la mujer de vrias, / fue el Rey dauid omeçida e fizo a dios falliaz' (259b), and how it is capable of destroying entire cities: 'ffueron por la loxuria çinco nobles çibdades / quemadas e destruydas' (260a), a direct reference to the destruction of cities including Sodom and Gomorrah in Genesis 19. Virgil, magus and wise man, 'sabidor', and therefore the fount of reason and rationality, is thrown into disorder by the strange attractor, 'la dueña', who deceives and dishonours him. So great is the power of sexual passion to disrupt both man and the natural order that it leads Virgil to turn the riverbed of the Tiber in Rome to copper by way of revenge:

> Todo el suelo del Ryo de la çibdad de Roma,
> tiberio, agua cabdal, que muchas aguas toma,
> fizol suelo de cobre, Reluze mas que goma.   (266abc)

A further example of how sexual desire leads to murder is embedded in Don Amor's advice to the Archpriest to avoid drinking too much wine. A hermit, who had lived forty years without ever tasting wine, is tempted by the devil, over-indulges and, in a state of heightened excitation, rapes a woman in the village. Fearing retribution, he murders her:

> desçendyo de la hermita, forço a vna muger,
> ella dando muchas bozes non se pudo defender,
> desque peco con ella temio mesturado ser,
> matola el mesquino e ovo se de perder.   (541)

In this tale, the chaos unleashed by lust is prefigured by the shattering of religious order as the devil corrupts the pious hermit, so that the episode might be viewed as a microcosm of the main narrative, in which the narrator, as priest, suffers the psychological turbulence of sexual love and overturns the ecclesiastical order in his abandonment of celibacy.

The idea of the 'strange attractor' is described by the physicists who coined the phrase as 'psychologically suggestive' (Gleick 1989: 133). To describe the female characters in the *Libro* as strange attractors implies that they act as elements

---

6 See Joset (1974: I, 85), notes to 218ab for further discussion of the deadly sins.

of unpredictability. When the Archpriest is first attracted to Doña Endrina, with whom he conducts one of the two major love affairs in the narrative, he finds himself in a state of mental and emotional agitation:

> la llaga non se me dexa a mi catar nin ver,
> ende mayores peligros espera que an de seer,
> Reçelo he que mayores dapnos me padran rrecreçer,
> fisica nin melesina non me puede pro tener.   (589, MS *G*)

Yet in spite of his declarations of love, 'muchas vezes gelo dixe que fynque mal denostado; / non preçia nada, muerto me trae coytado' (602bc), he cannot be sure how she will react. She rebuffs him each time. It is only with the help of the procuress Trotaconventos's enchantment that his anguish can be appeased by Endrina's acquiescence (see Severin, this volume).

However, the chaos of sexual passion which culminates in the apparent seduction or rape of Endrina (an episode missing from the manuscripts, but presumably originally present and modelled upon the rape scene in the Latin source, *Pamphilus* 669–740) brings potential disaster to her as well as to the narrator, as she describes the fate of the dishonoured woman:

> vase perder por el mundo, pues otro cobro non tyene,
> pyerde el cuerpo e el alma, a muchos esto aviene;
> pues otro cobro yo non he, asy fazer me convyene.   (885bcd)

Both Endrina and the Archpriest have acted outside the bounds of the social and religious status quo, and order can be re-established only when she forms a stable marriage with the protagonist, who earlier metamorphosed into Don Melón de la Huerta, 'doña endrina e don melon en vno casados son' (891a), thus humorously sidestepping the dilemma of the Church's prohibition of marriage for priests.[7]

Like a fractal pattern, the cycle of abstinence and passion is repeated with variations in the narrative, as each encounter the narrator has with women destabilizes him and disrupts the ecclesiastical order. The natural sexual order is also disrupted during the Archpriest's adventures with the *serranas* or wild mountain women. At the start of his travels in the mountains, he acknowledges that he is not acting in a rational manner in undertaking such a journey: 'fuy a prouar la syerra e fiz loca demanda' (950b). The adjective 'loco' is consistently set against the natural order of reason and of religious love often signified by 'buen amor'. In this wild mountain terrain, nothing is harmonious. Not only does the Archpriest lose his mule, but neither can he find food, and snow and hail are falling. In this frightening scenario he encounters the mountain women who usurp the masculine role of guides and providers of food and shelter, and the sexual status quo is also upturned, as the *serrana* known as La Chata demands sexual favours of the

---

[7] Joset (1974: I, 310–11n891a) discusses this interpretation, with reference to other critical opinion.

narrator, telling him to get up quickly and get his clothes off: 'la vaquera trauiessa diz: "luchemos vn Rato, / lyeua te dende apriesa, desbuelue te de aques hato"' (971). Harmony and normality are not restored until the Archpriest leaves the *sierra* and finds a shrine to the Virgin Mary at Santa María del Vado, where he offers up prayers. This skilful parody of the *pastourelle* in which shepherdesses are metamorphosed into mountain women and courtship rituals are inverted (950–1042; Tate 1970) is a comic variant of the love theme in which the *serranas*, as strange attractors, once again present sexual love as instigating chaos and disharmony.[8] This disharmony is set strikingly against the narrator's relationship with another female character, the Virgin Mary, who constitutes the only stable female force in the poem.

While Hawkins argues that the political order, as evidenced in Shakespeare's history plays, is often portrayed as precarious and on the edge of chaos (1995: 134), the same might be said of the religious order underlying the *Libro*. Elements of latent dissent within the religious system break through at certain points in the narrative, notably in the discussion of confession which forms part of the allegory of the battle between Cuaresma and Carnal, in the description of corrupt priests in the section on the properties of money, and in the episode of the Talavera clergy at the end of the Salamanca manuscript (1690–1709). The discourse on confession (1128–60) is delivered by the friar, who has come to confess Don Carnal, itself a hollow exercise, for Don Carnal pretends to be contrite and then escapes from prison immediately afterwards. The instruction to priests not to hear the confession of those outside their parishes, and not to accept written confessions, indicates that both these deviations from the procedure stipulated by ecclesiastical authority were commonplace and that clergy did not always obey the rules.[9] More extreme than this is the satire on ecclesiastical corruption in stanzas 493 and 494, in which the priests at the Papal court in Rome worship money instead of God:

> Yo vy en corte de Roma, do es la santidad,
> que todos al dinero fazen grand homildat,
> grand onrra le fazian con grand solepnidat,
> todos a el se omillan, commo a la magestat.   (493)

Finally, the rebellion of the clergy of Talavera against the Papal bull forbidding them to have concubines (1690–1709) addresses an issue of burning importance to priests in fourteenth-century Castile, and further underlines the incipient anarchy threatening the apparently stable structures of ecclesiastical doctrine and practices (Linehan 1971 and 1997).

Although he may purport to be a conscious spokesman for the religious establishment and ideology of his time, the Archpriest is in fact a subversive figure within whom the orderly role of the priest and the chaotic persona of the lover

---

[8] See Joset (1974: II, 33n).
[9] To explore this aspect further, see Lecoy 1938, Joset (1974: II, 108n1128), Hamilton 1970.

are in conflict. He himself is a force of chaos and instability in the context of the fourteenth-century Catholic Church; his choice of life and love over the repressive power of Catholicism sets him against the institution which he represents as a priest. His primary duty to religion and moral order is flouted by his role as a romantic lover who wreaks havoc both in personal relationships and vis-à-vis ecclesiastical doctrine. We might note, as Hawkins points out (1995: 149), that in religious mythology order is normally personified by male figures and disrupted by chaos embodied in women, such as Pandora, Eve, and Kali. The Church and its representative, the priest, exemplify masculine order, law, and discipline, while women are feminine forces of disruption, a duality symbolized by the association of Latin with Church authority and power and of the vernacular with women and disempowerment. In this respect, Juan Ruiz sloughs off the narrator's normative masculine role, which becomes aligned with the feminine and the chaotic as lover and sympathizer with his female characters. This is further reinforced by his parody of Latin ecclesiastical texts such as the canonical hours (372–87), which undermines the authority of Latin religious discourse and asserts the vernacular over and above it.

In the light of this, the Archpriest's second significant love affair, with the nun Garoça, becomes a final statement of the supremacy of love and chaos over religious authority and law. As a nun, Doña Garoça ought to be an asexual female figure similar to the Virgin Mary, yet the narrator wrests her from this role and casts her in that of lover and human mother: 'mas valdrie a la fermosa tener fijos e nieto, / que atal velo prieto, nin que abitos çiento' (1500cd). Both nun and archpriest reject Catholic morality in favour of the passion of love, epitomizing a subtext of the *Libro*, which is a defiance of subordination to masculine religious authority. The disruptive effects of the chaos caused by love reveal the overthrow of the order imposed by religious ideology and by medieval male psychology.

What are the implications of using the metaphors of chaos theory for the study of the *Libro*? Mandelbrot states that our feeling for beauty is inspired by the harmonious arrangement of order and disorder as it occurs in natural objects – in clouds, trees, mountain ranges, the structure of human blood vessels and lungs, for example. This is an idea which can be extended to literary works, and here the concept of scale is important, for to be effective and enduring, art must exhibit the same characteristics at every level. The *Libro* reveals both pattern and change throughout, bringing to mind Gleick's comment that a complex system may give rise to turbulence and coherence at the same time.

C. S. Lewis (1936: 141) wondered likewise whether a work of art can be of the highest calibre without unity and proportion. Perhaps he had in mind the kind of unity and proportion equally evident in classical geometry and in the formal conventions of classical drama. The question of how a canonical work like the *Libro* can last through the centuries and elicit a complex and divergent range of critical responses is a fascinating one. The comments of chaos theorists such as Mandelbrot on the subject of art suggest that audiences and readers may somehow perceive in great art a fusion of harmony and disorder comparable to that which they perceive not only in everyday human life, but also in the biological structures of their own physical being. If this is so, then it may be that enduring literary works like the *Libro* are neither unified and proportional in the classical sense, nor entirely fragmented and disjointed, but hermeneutically intricate and contingent, unpredictable in terms of reader and critic response, yet with an underlying deep patterning built on disruption and randomness.

The Novelness of the *Libro de Buen Amor*

LOUISE O. VASVÁRI

The *Libro de Buen Amor* belongs to those perverse narratives of early vernacular literary production that satirize or mix generic conventions and thus do not fit conventional nineteenth-century generic designations to which surveys of literature still tend to adhere. In his 1992 edition of the *Libro* Alberto Blecua succinctly summarizes over a half a century of scholarly opinions regarding the structure and genre of this very complex work, on initial reading apparently a kind of miscellany of episodes, which has been dubbed everything from a moralizing narrative poem to a *cancionero* or a goliardesque compendium.[1] But Blecua, like his predecessors, still drawing on these same conventional generic categories, can conclude no more than that the work is 'una anomalía literaria', a work of great originality, but whose literary tradition, motives of composition, and literary coordinates are ultimately unknowable to us, lost in a nebulous tradition (1992: xxv). That this is a problem of criticism rather than some sort of generic confusion within the work itself is evident when we consider that other works, both earlier and later than the *Libro*, have been described in similar terms. Blecua does add the helpful insight that this generic problem is a creation of the medieval scholastic system, into which virtually all medieval literary traditions flow, but he does not develop this idea further.[2]

In this chapter I shall propose, rather, that the *Libro* exemplifies the extremely heterogeneous nature of some medieval texts, characterized by permeability of generic boundaries and intertextual relationships that cross discrete genres. Although such works tend to be marginalized as unclassifiable, they are structurally and generically fully retrievable within the context of the prehistory of the novel as examples of novelized discourse. With this aim, I shall first attempt to outline briefly such a prehistory of the novel, proposing a counter-model that seeks to discredit traditional, received models of literary history, primary among them György Lukács's *Theory of the Novel* (first publ. 1922), and Ian Watt's

---

[1] All quotations and references are from this edition (Blecua 1992), and to stanzas.

[2] On medieval generic indeterminacy see Dragonetti 1980, Bakhtin (1981: 113–117), Payne 1981, Arrathoon 1984, Smith 1990, and Relihan 1993, on this aspect of the *Libro*, see Whinnom (1968: 17), Asensio 1973, and Morreale (1969–71: 307); and on the *Libro* as miscellany or *cancionero* see Haywood, this volume, Joset (1981: I, 296–97), Sevilla Arroyo 1988, and Barra Jover 1990, and Di Camillo (1990: 253n).

The Rise of the Novel (1957). Then I shall apply this model to the *Libro*, with the aim of showing that work's 'novelness' in two senses of the term, as a novel, original work, and as a part of the prehistory of the novel. Following Jeffrey Mehlman (1977: 69), my aim will also be to suggest that a reading of the *Libro* be valued in particular in its capacity to 'read' other texts, and thus to liberate energies otherwise contained in those earlier works. Or, to use Mikhail Bakhtin's much more blunt, sexually-charged terminology, how novelness 'penetrates' or invades (*proniknovenie*) privileged discourses.

The approach adopted here derives primarily from Bakhtin's essays (1981). Very briefly stated, he argues for the absolute novelty of the novel as the only genre that is not only a later creation than other genres, but that is new in each period that it is created. He defines the novel as a fundamentally anti-canonical literary form of expression, with a new orientation towards language and an acute sensitivity to the place of otherness in subject formation. It insists on a dialogue between the literary canon and those other discourses in which culture is inscribed, such as legal, religious, sub-literary. Bakhtin makes an important distinction between novels and novelness (*romannost*), that is, between examples of a genre recognized as such, and a broader range of cultural activities that share their central characteristic of treating language as dialogic.

Bakhtin does not form a comprehensive system; rather his essays constitute an innovative series of studies on the history and development of the novel, and the reoccurrence of ideas at different times leads to inconsistency in the definition of key terms, complicated by a lack of adequate bibliographical apparatus. While I find his theoretical work to be the single most useful framework for understanding the history and prehistory of the novel, he can be faulted for general theorizing without exemplification from a concrete corpus of literature, and for neglect of the medieval period: he jumps from a rather cursory analysis of Apuleius's *Golden Ass* to Dostoevsky, giving epic only a passing mention. Here I aim to contribute to Bakhtin's framework by locating the the *Libro de Buen Amor*, a work that he never mentions, within the theoretical scheme of the novel.

The Prehistory of novelistic discourse

Margaret Anne Doody (1996), in a polemic against traditional literary history, attacks the assumption that there is something modern and new about the narratives called novels produced in Europe, and most specially in England, since the early eighteenth century, and which are held to supersede older kinds of storytelling, such as epic, ballad, and romance. Doody proposes that the novel's origins date to the ancient novel (often called 'Greek romance'), such as *Daphnis and Chloe*, and to two Roman narratives, the fragmentary *Satyricon* of Petronius Arbiter and *The Golden Ass* of Apuleius, which is based on a lost Greek original. Doody emphasizes the historical continuities of novelistic discourse as an intertextual verbal construct. This approach also stresses elements of linguistic playfulness, self-consciousness, artifice, and parody.

The Hungarian Marxist Lukács, the first modern theoretician of the novel, considered it to be the representative genre and typical product of capitalist modernity. He also saw it as a transitory form, with its ultimate dissolution foreseen in a future communist society. For Lukács, although the epic and the novel are the two major forms of great literature, the latter supersedes former in an age in which the extensive totality of life is no longer a given, and where the transcendental, that is, the world of God, has been abandoned. Although epic verse at once creates distance and embraces all life in a mythology, only prose can depict life realistically. However, Lukács struggles to deal with the complex structure and parodic character of *Don Quijote*. Although he acknowledges that, in Antiquity and the Middle Ages, novel-like texts existed, he never returns to this idea, positing instead five stages for the novel, beginning with Rabelais and Cervantes. The second stage, the 'conquest of everyday reality', was marked by the creation of a positive bourgeois hero by authors like Defoe, Fielding, and Smollett.[3]

Watt's *Rise of the Novel* probably remains the most influential work on the subject studied in English departments.[4] Watt relates the emergence of the eighteenth-century novel to the increasing social and literary power of the commercial and middle class, and to the rise of individualism, arguing that the main tradition of the novel was realism, starting with Defoe and Richardson, authors whom Lukács had posited for his second stage of novelistic development. Watt's analysis is decidedly Anglo-centric, and sees the novel's emergence as an English phenomenon. His first chapter, 'Realism and the Novel Form', presents the essence of what he terms *formal realism*: the absence of formal conventions and the rejection of traditional plots, and the placing of unprecedented value on originality. The novelist's primary task is to convey the impression of fidelity to human experience, that is, realism. To sustain this opinion, Watt ignores, among other factors, the absolute penetration of these realist novels with innumerable conventions of romance, such as the name symbolism of characters and romance-type plots based on an endless series of unbelievable and sentimental or melodramatic adventures, including birth tokens, kidnappings, mistaken identities and disguises, and the postponement of the union of the hero and heroine until the conclusion.

Less than a decade after Lukács's influential work, Bakhtin (1895–1975) originally published his study of Dostoevsky (1929, first translated to English 1973), in which he described the author's role as innovator through a study of Dostoevsky's poetics, rather than through stylistic analysis. In this study Bakhtin introduced the term polyphony: the novel, perceived as a musical score, is seen as the complete register of all social voices of an era. Polyphony can be compared to the sacred and secular juxtapositions in the medieval misericords

---

[3] Some of Lukács's ideas on the novel were fully developed only in his contributions to the later Russian 1934–35 debates on the novel (Tihanov 2000).

[4] McKeon 1987, which I shall not discuss here, is a great improvement since his title refers explicitly to the rise of the 'English' novel.

(*sillerías*) in churches, which often have a scatological and obscene underside (see Mateo Gómez 1979).[5]

He argued that Dostoevsky inaugurated a new 'polyphonic' type of fiction in which a variety of discourses expressing different ideological positions are set in play without being judged by a totalizing authorial discourse; that is, because of its polyphonic character the novel could not be reduced to the 'author's voice', or to any particular viewpoint, but rather the characters speak for themselves in their own voices, registers, and dialects, thus creating a dialogic rather than mono-logic work. Later Bakhtin came to realize that this was not a unique discovery of Dostoevsky's but an inherent characteristic of novelistic discourse – one that he traced back to its origins in the parodic genres of classical and medieval culture – the satyr play, Menippean satire, and the popular culture of carnival. Bakhtin's initial ideas on the novel were expounded in a revised and expanded edition of the Dostoevsky book in 1963.

In his *Rabelais and his World*, written in the 1940s (Bakhtin 1968), Bakhtin's goal was an ironic de-crowning of authoritative discourse. He studied the anti-culture and anti-language of the medieval and Renaissance 'folk culture of laugh-ter', which he called the carnivalesque, and attempted to reconstruct its verbal, gestural, and ritual manifestations. The Rabelais book was the first of his stud-ies to become available in Western languages, and it has had the widest impact. In my own publications, it is the text on which I have relied most heavily for theoretical support in my attempt to reconstruct the *Libro*'s carnivalesque semi-otic system. However, of particular interest here is the group of articles written between 1934 and 1941, first published in Moscow in 1975, and titled, in the English-language edition, *The Dialogic Imagination* (1981). Here Bakhtin delivers his full account of the origins of the novel, its distinct discourse, and its unique role in the system of all genres. The English-language volume consists of four essays, which do not appear in the order in which they were written: 'Epic and the Novel', 'From the Prehistory of Novelistic Discourse', 'Forms of Time and of the Chronotope in the Novel', and 'Discourse in the Novel'. No compre-hensive system emerges from these studies, but rather he presents a kind of anti-poetics, centred on the idea of discourse as a social phenomenon. In his view of the social nature of discourse the echoes of Lukács's work are most apparent.

Bakhtin calls the novel a 'metagenre', which 'swallows' all other established rule-governed genres, and the language styles peculiar to them. He cites Xenophon, Menippus, Petronius, and Apuleius as representatives of the earliest examples of novelization. As with Lukács, the novel is particularly suited to our post-lapsarian civilization, since it thrives on the kind of diversity that the epic, and other traditional narrative forms, aims to purge from its world. However, in absolute opposition to Lukács, according to Bakhtin, the novel is not the modern continu-ation of the epic but, rather, its reverse because in the novel 'the entire world

---

[5] See Holquist 1990, Morson and Emerson 1990, Danow 1991, Todorov 1998, and Brancham 1999 for some guidance on these issues.

and everything sacred in it is offered to us without distancing at all, in a zone of crude contact'. Bakhtin thus destroys Lukács's theory with the insight that epic distance is abolished by the laughter inherent in carnivalesque novelistic discourse.

Bakhtin laid great stress on the generic uniqueness and autonomy of the novel, which arose from its openness to continual change, its ability to criticize itself, its use of parody and of different languages, and especially its heteroglossia and dialogic character. Heteroglossia is for Bakhtin the master trope of the novel as a genre. It consists of a multiplicity of voices, the coexistence and competition among a diversity of mixed social registers within any language, and, in particular, the struggle between official and non-official registers. In Bakhtin's terms, the dialogic, a particular instance of the polyphony of social and discursive forces, involves an interplay between multiple voices, each the embodiment of a social context and a way of understanding the world, including the voices of the author, the narrator(s), or characters, and of other texts and styles imitated or quoted within the novelistic text. In short, Bakhtin stressed that the novel is inherently intertextual and parodic; it is a subversion not only of all mainstream as well as folk discourses but, ultimately, of itself as well. For Bakhtin *novel* is precisely that fundamentally anti-canonical force in any literary system that reveals the artificiality and the constraints of the monologic canon of the time. It insists on the dialogue between what is admitted as 'literature' and those discourses that are excluded.

In his characteristically corporeal terminology, Bakhtin defines the novel as being able to 'ingest' other genres and still retain its status as a novel. Other genres cannot include novelistic elements without undermining their own generic identity. Throughout *Rabelais and his World* he utilizes the same imagery, drawing on the human body's creative functions – defecation, copulation, giving birth, among the many functions of the grotesque 'lower bodily stratum' – to analyse the carnivalesque. He sees the body as inter-corporeal in much the same way as the novel is intertextual. Like the novel, the body cannot be envisaged outside a world of interrelationships of which it is a living part.

Bakhtin's oeuvre, when taken together, constitutes a cohesive group of ideas on the nature of literature, but individually each major book offers a different perspective and somewhat different terminology. Bakhtin actually developed three major theories of the novel and its relation to other genres: (i) he describes the novel's special use of language, its dialogized heteroglossia; (ii) he classifies genres according to an increasingly historical, concrete use of what he dubbed the chronotope (literally, 'time-space'), a unit of narrative analysis of space and time patterns; chronotope, metaphorically derived from Einstein's theory of relativity, refers to the inseparability and interdependence of time and space as organizing centres of narrative events in literary genres; and (iii) he emphasizes the carnivalesque, which is indebted to parodic genres and to folkloric oral carnival. Dostoesvsky is an example of the first, Goethe of the second, and Rabelais of the third. All, however, can be applied to the *Libro de Buen Amor*, thus helping to historicize further the theory of the origins of the novel.

The novelness of the 'Libro de Buen Amor'

If we consider the intertwined conceptual models that Bakhtin used to charac-
terize novelization, heteroglossia (and polyphony), dialogic discourse, the novelistic chronotopes, and the carnivalization of pre-existing discourses, we can see
that the *Libro* exemplifies all of them.[6]

The *Libro* is the perfect example of the polyphonic text, right from its key words,
buen amor, which can function – alternately or simultaneously – in religious
discourse (as the love of God or as Augustinian *caritas*), in the discourse of eroticism, as love, courtly or base, and can even serve to name the old bawd Trotaconventos. Critics have expended much philological erudition in grappling with
the problem of pinning down this shifting term. Most have been preoccupied
with teasing out more and more possible meanings according to the context; but
the game is rather in the constant play with the simultaneous meanings, high and
low. No later studies have bettered Anthony N. Zahareas's conclusion that 'the
term *buen amor*, like the equivocal *intellectum* or *entendimiento* that the author
proposes to impart to the reader in the Prose Prologue, is alternately distinct and
blurred, but mostly ambiguous' (1965: 25).[7]

Although too much scholarly ink has already been spilled on *buen amor*, it is
nevertheless useful to begin this analysis of the *Libro* by examining it once again
to see how it sheds light on the polyphonic nature of the whole work. Critical
discussion has centred on the term's religious versus erotic meanings, but with
little consideration about why both the bawd Trotaconventos and the book itself
are also jokingly christened *buen amor*. And, yet, understanding this enigmatic
onomastic game becomes central in understanding the *Libro*'s programme of
novelization. There are two passages in the text of this most heterodox use of
buen amor which we must consider.

In my discussion of these and other passages I shall not follow the sequence
of episodes as they appear in the book but rather, for the sake of clarity, according to the interrelatedness of key words, and embedded discourses that I want to
trace. In st. 919–33, the second and less complex of the two passages, after a
failed love adventure in which Trotaconventos had been the procuress, the protagonist hurls some forty demeaning but humorous insult words at her, all of

---

[6] *Heteroglossia* is a general term which encompasses *polyglossia*, the simultaneous presence
of two or more national languages interacting within a single cultural system, and the former
is often used for the latter. An example in the *Libro* of polyglossia is the fable of the mock
legal court of *Don Ximio* (321–65), replete with burlesque Latin legalisms, usually placed in
rhyme position.

[7] Beginning with Sobejano 1983 (see also Gybbon-Monypenny 1961, Dutton 1966), a
number of scholars have attempted to elucidate the meaning of *buen amor*. For the best overview
of the question, see Orduna (1991; but to his bibliography add Márquez Villanueva 1965, Joset
1971, Edwards 1974, Aubrun 1980, Gerli 1981–82). Morales Faedo (1997) treats separately
those occurrences that appear only in the longer MS *S*. While in this article I treat all existing
(and possible) versions as one open-ended text, this distinction is nevertheless important since
the most outrageously polysemous uses of the term occur in the longer version.

which connote prostitute and/or pimp. Those nicknames, as well as the bawd's Christian name, Urraca 'magpie', and the other three names applied to her in the text: *picaza parlera* 'gossipping magpie', *troya* 'pig / whore / cunt', and *buen amor* belong to a special category of invective that is characteristic of the familiar language of the marketplace.[8] *Troya* was the most common medieval word for prostitute, while the *p-p-* of *picaza parlera* suggests both *pícara* and numerous sexually-charged words, just as they do in the phonosymbolic name of that unfortunate cuckold *Pitas Pajas*.[9] Notice also that Urraca's insult names over-determine her status as a loose woman: a too-open and active mouth or, in topsy-turvy fashion, a too active 'lower mouth', as well as, in the name *Trotaconventos*, running about out of bounds.

In traditional culture spoken words carried a great deal more authority than they do now, with evil words considered equal to evil deeds. Invective is a cat-egory of ritual insult, grammatically and semantically isolated from context, that functions as a complete unit, something like a proverb; it follows its own 'gram-mar of insult', with its rules as restricted as those of a sonnet (Labov 1972). The humour resides in the excessive accumulation of vulgar epithets, oaths, and curses, and exaggerated stereotyped abusive terms about the grotesque physical and moral defects of the victim, all with ludic intent. Such grotesque debasement often reduces the victim to the bestial level, as in the example of *troya*, above, or to the material lower bodily stratum, the zone of genital organs.

Other examples of ritualized insulting in the text are of the two other pimp characters, Ferránd Garçía and Furón, the former the predecessor of Trotaconventos in the Cruz episode, and the latter the inappropriate successor after her death. The protagonist accuses Furón, who ruined his love affair with a girl for the sake of playing a practical joke on him, of being a *rapaz trainel*, which he follows up with a harangue of *catorce cosas*, fourteen and more invec-tives, *mintoroso, beodo, ladrón, peleador, goloso* among them. In line with the carnivalesque focus on the lower bodily stratum it is not a surprise that the youth's name Furón 'weasel' also connotes penis in many European languages (Vasvári 1995a).

The *trova cazurra* is another poetic form related to the invective. In the 'Cruz cruzada' episode, where the protagonist takes his revenge on Ferránd Garçía, the other rogue pimp who committed the 'gran escarnio' against him of 'tasting the wares' of the baker-girl Cruz he was supposed to procure for his master, leaving him to chew his own cud. The protagonist, who, as he says, has been royally 'screwed' ('súpome el clavo echar'), can take his revenge only with snappy invectives, calling Ferrán García *traidor, falso, marfuz* 'male fox', *escolar goloso, compañero de cucaña* and, most cleverly, *conejero* 'cony catcher', whose 'cunning'

---

[8] John K. Walsh (1983) studies the list of Trotaconventos's joke nicknames from the perspective of legal discourse. See Vasvári 1995c on Trotaconventos's three other names; and, for an anthropological-linguistic perspective on invective, Ayoub & Barnett 1965, Murray 1979.

[9] See Vasvári 1992a on phonosymbolism and on Pitas Pajas's unfortunately connotative name, which might be rendered in English something like 'wanking weenie'.

implications are already obvious, but which can in performance be made even more hilarious if delivered with a slight pseudo-Freudian slip of the tongue, as *coñejero* (Vasvári 1985).

The insults hurled at Trotaconventos, Furón, and Ferránd Garçía are also related to the *escarnio*, a personal invective in poetic form. The protagonist's long harangue or *recuesta* against Don Amor (182–422) is essentially one long *escarnio*. Embedded within the longer diatribe are insult terms similar to those used against the two male pimps, in particular the term *goloso laminero*, where Amor is accused of always wanting to be the first one to 'taste' any girl he sees.[10]

After this excursus into other invective episodes, let us get back to the bawd. In spite of having so grossly insulted her, the protagonist immediately asks again for her help in finding a new girl. The old woman pretends to take the insults not as a game but as slander, and on one level she is right because one of the features that is supposed to distinguish ritual insults from free-floating verbal abuse is that its implausibility must be patently obvious. And slandering someone as *puta* (or *gafo, cornudo, fudidincul, traydor, herege*) was a serious offence which could be severely penalized by Alfonsine legislation (Craddock 1990). But the protagonist was, after all, just telling the truth by calling a whore a whore. And while it was slander to insult someone of higher rank with such terms, to insult a professional or even a loose woman (defined as someone who has 'known' five or more men) was not a punishable offence. Prostitutes, both because they were socially marginal and because the charges were true, could be insulted with impunity. It was said that to call a prostitute in a whorehouse a whore was as natural as praying in church (Huston 1980: 97). Finally, the *fueros*, which strictly punish such insults, give free rein to them during carnival festivities. Even today during carnival victims of such public verbal aggression are forced to endure their humiliation in silence (Gilmore 1998).

Trotaconventos does not suffer the protagonist's harangue in silence; she retorts that it costs no more to speak nicely than to be insulting. She immediately exacts a price for the offence, warning the Archpriest that only if he addresses her properly, by the presumably euphemistic *buen amor*, will she once again do his bidding: 'Nunca diga[de]s nonbre malo nin de fealdat, / llamatme 'buen amor' e fare yo lealtat' (932ab). Although she pretends to be insulted, she actually knows the rules of the game, one of which is, don't get hurt – get even. Understanding that the Archpriest's stream of sexual insults was the ultimate monologic attempt to finalize her, to freeze her identity, and to pre-empt possible rejoinders, she replies: 'Either you speak *my* language, call me what *I* want to be called, or you don't get anything from me.' The desperate suitor, forced to do her bidding, goes one better, re-christening both the old woman and the book

---

[10] Gluttony and drunkenness could both be topics for insults (Madero 1992: 144); both are also related to loss of sexual control, as is demonstrated in the *exemplum* of the hermit whose drunkenness leads to rape and murder.

buen amor: 'Por amor de la vieja e por dezir razón, / "buen amor" dixe al libro e a ella toda saçón' (933ab). That is, in topsy-turvy carnivalesque fashion he has conceded defeat in the match and the old whore has at least temporarily taken over the text.

Another way to look at this episode is with the help of terminology developed in film theory, where Trotaconventos speaks within the narrative's diegesis, or story world, where extradiagesis refers to material outside the story, such as introductory and title sequences. This is important because readers are inclined to give more authority to the latter. At the same time Juan Ruiz functions here simultaneously as a character speaking within the diegesis and as a voice-over narrator or omniscient authorial voice outside the story. However, by naming both the old woman and the book *buen amor* he is confounding the two levels, text and gloss.

The importance of naming both the bawd and the book with the same sense-shifting key word becomes further clarified if we examine an earlier occurrence of *buen amor* in the text in the enigmatic '*yo libro*' passage (strophes 65–70). The placement of this passage as a kind of coda to the *exemplum* of the debate in sign language between the Greek and the Roman, which is the liminal episode between the complex of preliminary materials and the main body of the text, indicates that the two passages together (with the Prose Prologue) serve as a kind of built-in guide to the reader.

The passage begins by apologizing for the potentially offensive surface meaning of the book, under which is supposedly hidden the allegorical kernel of moral knowledge:

> que saber *bien*, e mal *dezir encobierto* e doñeguil
> Lo que *buen amor dize*, con *razón* te lo pruevo.
> Las del *buen amor* son *razones encubiertas*
>
> (65c, 66d, 68a; my emphasis)

A little further on, in 70a it appears that it is the book itself – '*yo, libro*' – that is addressing its readers. As is evident by their structure, the following two strophes, with the inanimate book speaking in the first person, are the textualization of a riddle from oral tradition. The riddle is an oral sub-literary discourse which plays with levels of meaning of language. It is a comparison, or a metaphor with one term concealed, whose function is both to lead and mislead; it describes one thing in terms of another (inanimate in terms of animate and vice versa), through a vocabulary of *double entendres*.[11]

To engage in riddling is to become involved in verbal contest with the aim of confounding an adversary to gain power. The riddle is a two-part genre, one of the few literary forms in which the roles of both speaker and hearer are

---

[11] For a detailed analysis of this episode, see Vasvári 2000b. Relevant studies on the riddle include Roy 1977 and 1992, Brandes 1980: 128–36, Stewart 1983a, and 1983b, McGrady 1984, Hasan-Rokem and Shulman 1996, and Vasvári 1998.

incorporated. The speech roles that the riddle demands are clear – the speaker deceives; the hearer deciphers – and the riddle's content and meaning are rule-bound. The riddler says one thing but intends another, and his adversary decipherer assumes the existence of a contract underlying the exchange in which the adversary will do everything possible to mislead the hearer by describing a harmless non-sexual referent in terms that lead away from the solution, and towards sexual content. Riddles follow a formal and very limited structure; one common type manipulates the normal borders of referential speech, and has an inanimate object speak in the first person. By breaching the normative limits of language through the confusion of linguistic categories, the riddler controls the answer, which is always overdetermined; that is, the initial act of obfuscation permits multiple answers to each of the elements which comprise the riddle. The solution is constructed so as to satisfy the conditions for two solutions simultan-eously: the straight but naïve answer, and the sexual one for those who possess adequate folkloric competence.

What kind of knowledge, or self-knowledge, does the answer to a riddle imply? The riddle is an agonistic folkloric genre structured as an exercise in intelligence proposed by the riddler to the listener, where the ultimate pur-pose of the game is to reveal rather than to conceal the supposed hidden mean-ing. Take, as an example, the English 'so round, so firm, so fully packed, so free and easy on the draw', a cigarette advertisement devised to associate smoking with virility. Or, to cite one Spanish example in a similar vein: 'De día colgado, de noche apretado'; answer, 'La tranca de una puerta' (Brandes 1980: 133). Keith Whinnom (1981: 63–72) called this technique the festive 'defraudación' by the malicious author of the reader's smutty expectations. He gave the example of the endless definitions of obscene riddles whose sup-posed clean surface solution is 'the candle'. In both obscene and supposedly clean riddles the game is that there can be only the illusion of hermeneutic closure.

The *Libro* instructs that one must read it 'por puntos', repeating *puntos* and *puntar* six times in eight lines, in a linguistic game of paronomasia, a common stylistic feature of puns. On the denotative level it instructs readers to punctu-ate properly, or perhaps to modulate by musical punctuation, pausing according to their own desires; thus suggesting that careful and measured reading is neces-sary to decipher the 'razones encubiertas', or allegorical sense, which lies hid-den in the 'palabras feas' of the surface text. However, the passage also lends itself to an obscene counter-reading for those with the appropriate folkloric competence in riddle solving, which proposes that one has to seek the love of 'encubiertas [. . .] por puntos', where 'encubiertas' is the street name referring to a higher class of prostitute who wears a *mantilla*, and 'puntos' connotes pene-trative sex acts.

The I who declares itself a book, in order to function as a riddle, must be some-thing other than what it purports to be, but what? In erotic riddling the answer is obvious: there is a rich tradition of riddles which equate the open[ed] book, written upon by a pointed pen, and the like, with the receptive female sexual organ.[12] The 'yo libro' riddle is an example of the work's self-conscious textuality, which juxtaposes the learned and the lewd, alerting us to the poet's playful artistry in constructing a poetics of the riddle for the whole book.

If we now compare the two passages, the onomastic *buen amor* punch-line in the insults of the Trotaconventos episode, followed by the *yo libro* riddle, we see that in typical heteroglossic style both the old bawd and the book have claimed their own narrative voice, in competition with that of that 'yo' of the confused narrator-protagonist. And they have spoken out precisely in those sections of the book that belong structurally to its interpretative system of signposts. Both declare themselves to be 'buen amor'. I should dare to go further and claim that, in fact, in carnivalesque discourse these two oft opened bodies – the alternate animate and inanimate solutions to the riddle of *buen amor*, whore and book – are equated.[13]

Bakhtin insisted on the opposition between the classical – finished, closed – body and the grotesque open carnivalesque body, which he, in turn, equated with the female, locating it in a system of grotesque images of pregnancy, birth, growth, old age, and disintegration. Bakhtin actually found his model of the grotesque body in terra-cotta figures of pregnant hags which bring together the two most grotesque aspects of the body: birth and death (see also Russo 1986). The aging Trotaconventos is the prototypical image of this Bakhtinian unruly woman, her grotesque body set loose in the public sphere, *la mujer pública*, in every sense. In one scene, pretending to be insane, she exposes herself naked in the public square. Since death is also a part of this image, at a later point in the text her death is also carnivalized: the episode begins with the protagonist's absurd funeral lament, that, like the Prose Prologue, is parodic. It begins with an unsurpassable alliterative invective against death: '¡Ay, Muerte! ¡Muerta seas, muerta e malandante!'. In the typical perversity of carnivalized genres, with its

---

[12] Compare the following example, for which the official answer is actually a book, which plays with the opposite effect, making itself sound animate and sexual:

> Soy una grande memoria
> Y tambien soy un talento
> Es mi cuerpo muy chiquito
> Y en cualquier parte quepo;
> De comer no necesito
> Y de beber mucho menos;
> Dinero tampoco gasto,
> Vestido tampoco tengo,
> Y sin pensar ni saber
> Grandes cosas en mi encierro.   (Demófilo 1880: 173, no. 607)

[13] It is impossible to offer sufficient examples here to support what may seem to be an outrageous reading of the text. For a detailed analysis of the whole episode, see Vasvári 2000b. But let one succinct seventeenth-century English proverb suffice: 'a book is like a whore, by day-light, or by candle . . . it is ever free for every knave to penetrate'.

That the whole *Libro* is a riddle has been suggested before in a metaphorical sense by Zahareas 1965, and by Raymond S. Willis, who observed that it is 'spangled with lexical riddles that must have first teased, then amused, the auditors who solved [these] verbal puzzles' (1983: 85).

constant tension between form and irreverent content, the go-between is then described in heaven as a sanctified martyr. The episode ends with the now disembodied voice of the newly minted saint, speaking from beyond the grave, blessing those who visit her grave and say a *paternoster* for her, and praying that they should find 'buen amor e plazer de amiga' (1518–78). In heaven Trota-conventos has joined many other carnivalesque saints, such as the French Saint Jambon 'ham / backside' and Sainte Andouille 'tripe sausage / penis', Saint Cauillebault Confesseur 'Nice Balls', his sister, Sainte Velue 'Hairy', and her male namesake, Saint Velu, from a phallic hagiography by the same name.[14] The sanctified bawd's erotic powers are also akin to those performed by Sainte Velue, whose celestinesque miracles included the ability to give back to women their virginity.

But let us return once more to the earlier image of the equivalence of the whore and the book, both promiscuously open to manipulation. If the pregnant hag, unit-ing birth and death, a woman breaking out of bounds, represents the core image of grotesque realism, the 'yo libro' riddle, at the margin of the text proper, is the same sort of 'pregnant page' as in medieval marginal art, signifying nothing in order to give birth to meaning at the centre.[15]

This point is substantiated by Juan Ruiz's use of the proverb in which the syn-tagm 'buen amor' occurs frequently; however, I can mention only one instance here (see further Vasvári 2000a and in press). Like the riddle, the proverb is a micro-discourse integrated into a larger discourse, and like slogans and maxims, is in its straight application a monologic oral discourse of popular pedagogy. Hence, throughout the *Libro* Juan Ruiz delights in deflating the book's authority by twisting proverbs, most often in the context of agonistic dialogic exchanges in the mouth of potentially subversive speakers, very frequently of that mouth-piece of oral culture, Trotaconventos. Many of these proverbs distort the author-ity of the adjectives, *buen* and *mal*, and that of 'buen amor'. They may be strung together in strophe-long paremiological chains or in strophe-initial or strophe-final position, thus creating a circulatory discourse. Most importantly, Juan Ruiz aims to pervert and abuse the proverb's popular authority and its pre-established modes of thinking by humorous and obscene re-contextualization, so that, in effect, many of the *Libro*'s proverbs no longer function as bits of inherited wis-dom, but turn into another oral genre, the joke. Juan Ruiz's excessive manipula-tion, his travestying of proverbs, can only be derisive.

Here I shall examine only one of the *Libro*'s hundreds of chains of proverbs: Don Amor, the protagonist's allegorical pimp, whom along with the two real-life pimps he had termed 'goloso', recommends that he seek the services of a go-between and show her 'buen amor' (443b) to ensure that she serve him well,

---

[14] See Koopmans 1984 and 1985 on the carnivalization of stereotyped genres of religious discourse, including the lament.

[15] See Camille 1992 for marginal illustrations which deflate the message of the authoritative text at the centre of the page with caricaturesque figures in sexual and scatological poses.

'que mucha mala bestia vende buen corridor / e mucha mala ropa cubre buen cobertor' (443cd). Part of the joke is that the Archpriest is a bad student because he will get in trouble with Trotaconventos, in the scene analysed above, precisely because he does not follow his preceptor's advice. No surprise, then, that Amor warns him at one point that he is trying to 'maestro ante que discípulo ser' (427a). The linguistic joke is that while, as popular wisdom the proverb says 'a lot of bad horses are sold by good, that is, unscrupulous salesmen', as perverted proverb it reiterates the view that 'many a crafty pimp ('corredor', 'cobertor') has sold a bad whore ('mala bestia', 'mala ropa')'.[16] Unsurprisingly, the majority of the perverted proverbs in the *Libro* are aptly put into the mouth of Trotaconventos, who represents orality. It is one of the ways in which with her situational comprehension of reality, and the lack of abstractions in her mentality, permit her voice to talk back and constantly threaten to take over the text.

I have spoken in some detail about the invective onomastics of the Trotaconventos and related episodes, and about the 'yo libro' riddle, with a sideways glance at proverbs. My aim in weaving together a somewhat circular narrative about these episodes has been to propose that such an alternate, carnivalized reading, which confounds animate and inanimate and reduces all to the lower bodily sphere, suggests the formula: Trotaconventos = open body = open book = 'yo, libro' = 'libro de buen amor'. From this perspective the book can be seen as the textualization of popular oral culture, an open, heteroglossic voice in opposition to the monologic, closed, canonized textual discourses it parodies. Such a reading makes the *Libro de Buen Amor* descend to the grotesque corporeal level posited by Bakhtin as the sphere of festive carnivalesque parody. It also makes the *Libro de Buen Amor* into the *Libro de alcahuetería*, the 'Prostitute's Guidebook' (see Drayson, this volume). This polysemy of *buen amor* is intimately interwoven with the oral-textual dialogism of the book, as we can also see from the many other proverbs and lyric verses in the work, taken from oral tradition where *buen amor* occurs with this debased sense. On a more theoretical level, we can say that such 'playing with words' involves far more than jongleuresque juggling. Rather, it reorients the relationship between high and low culture, compromising its very status as linguistic sign. If Trotaconventos is the embodiment of the grotesque body of folk culture and of the agonistic conflict between high culture and low, she also has, as we have seen, embryonic male equivalents in the two roguish pimps, Ferránd García and Furón.

I have discussed in some detail the liminal episode of the *yo libro* talking book-riddle in order to begin to demonstrate the rich interplay of polyphony, heteroglossia, dialogism, and the carnivalesque parody of literary and folkloric discourses that, following Bakhtin, I posited as characteristics of novelistic discourse. At the same time, this episode, because of its strategic placement in the text, offers a further metatextual commentary on the necessity of reading the

---

[16] 'Mala bestia' is documented in Latin for 'prostitute' (Huston 1980: 100). See also Cantarino 1974 on the deliberate *equivocatio* between different senses of 'good'.

whole *Libro* within the 'form-shaping' or 'genre-shaping' grotesque realism of carnivalesque folk humour, which seeks to deny everyday reality, replacing it with a deliberately distorting mimesis, reducing with its joco-serious hilarity all that is held in high esteem to the concrete level of the body. In the last section, let us look at the *Libro*'s carnivalesque manipulation of inherited discourses.

The episodes of the *Libro de Buen Amor* continue to be studied primarily in a literary context, even though, as I have repeated here, it is a work that reflects the medieval heteroglossia between literary and sub-literary discourses.[17] The *Libro* incorporates a plurality of the discourses of its time, including a mock Aesopic fable (featuring bestiality), both the learned and the popular sermon, a funeral lament, love lyrics and obscene songs, proverbs, riddles, ritual insults, the dream vision, the *exemplum*, an *ars amandi*, debate poetry, Latin comedy, rule books for clergy, the lying tale, *fabliaux*, the joke, parodic or burlesqued legal, religious, and medical discourse, epitaph, letters, among others.[18] And here I have further discussed the riddle, ritual insults, proverbs, and the epithet. In the space remaining I can do no more than offer a schematic overview and exemplification of how such variety is ingested and, through carnivalization, novelized by the *Libro*.

Carnivalization can be defined as an effort to liminalize groups of texts that are usually considered central to their respective traditions by wrenching them from their usual surroundings and placing them through parodic perspectivism into an entirely different text-milieu in confrontation with 'liminal genres of popular consumption'. The carnivalesque provides a mirror of carnival; it is a carnival reflected and refracted through the multi-perspective prism of verbal art, the transposition of carnival into the language of literature (Seidenspinner-Núñez 1981; Pérez Firmat 1986: xvi, Danow 1995: 4). Bakhtin divided the carnivalesque into the three forms of folk humour that circulated widely in the medieval world: ritual spectacle, such as carnival pageants and comic shows of the marketplace; comic verbal compositions, parodies, both oral and written, in Latin and the vernacular; and various genres of billingsgate, that is, abuse and violent invective, such as curses, oaths, and profanation. They have in common that they contain protocols of high culture from a position of debasement, as if the carnivalesque grotesque body politic had, through grotesque realism, ingested the corpus of high culture and excreted it out in recombined, inverted, mockery. Of these forms of folk humour Bakhtin paid special attention to carnival because within its complex system of images it concentrates all the features of comic popular culture, becoming its fullest expression. Hence, the term carnivalesque, or its synonym 'grotesque realism', came to be applied by synecdoche to the whole of this culture.

---

[17] The first book-length study taking into account carnivalization in the *Libro* was Monique De Lope 1984, which considered only the two obvious episodes in this regard, the 'Batalla de doña Cuaresma y don Carnal' and *serrana* episodes (Vasvári 1986–87).

[18] This list is not exhaustive nor have I had occasion to discuss all of those discourses mentioned; for further studies see my 1985–86, 1988–89, 1989, 1990a, 1990b, 1992a, 1992b, 1995b.

Bakhtin considered that his concept of the carnivalesque as present in literature had its origins in actual carnival, which existed on the borderline of art and life. And, although in his *Rabelais and his World* he did not employ the same vocabulary of dialogism that permeates the essays in *The Dialogic Imagination*, it is clear that Bakhtin's concept of carnival is an inherently dialogized concept, both polyphonic and heteroglossic, where voices and languages break free from hierarchical control. Of the three forms of carnivalized folk humour posited by Bakhtin I have already analysed several ritual invectives and have also discussed the textualization of some folk discourses. Here, then, I shall end by speaking briefly about the textualization of carnival spectacle itself, that is, 'carnivalized carnival'.

Lent and Carnival epitomizes in mock-epic style the same fundamental conflict between high and low that is seen illustrated in the intellectually constipated Greek and the gesticulating Roman rogue (Vasvári 1994; or, say, long and lean and humourless Don Quijote and proverb-spouting Sancho Panza). It also epitomizes the conflict, knotted up in the riddle of 'buen amor', between religious love and sexual love. The episode in the *Libro* which most neatly exemplifies this concept is the extremely long episode of the Battle of Carnival and Lent, an elegant textualization that, although it has its ultimate roots in actual carnival performances, manages to stylize the fundamental conflict of 'letting go and restraint' – to steal a title from Philip Roth – into ingestion and non-ingestion, both sexual and of food. Further, since carnival is a performative happening, its textualization in the *Libro* also epitomizes the ingestion of oral culture, and specifically of spectacle, by textual culture. In other terms, the Carnal and Cuaresma episode is an example of folk narrative of the public square (itself the symbolic zone, or central chronotope, of debasing contact between high and low social and literary hierarchies) that compresses many of the discrete categories of bodily human experience – food, sex, death, and rebirth – by carnivalesque levelling of epic through compression and parodic stylization of themes and language. The episode is a precise example of a point I discussed in the context of comparing Lukács and Bakhtin, how epic distance is destroyed by the creation of comical heroes, here turning them into edible sides of pork and the like, thus making it impossible to imagine a non-dialogic reading. But degradation and death in carnival time do not mean absolute destruction but rather a push into the reproductive lower stratum, where conception and new birth take place: the birth of novelistic discourse.

The Carnal-Cuaresma episode also illustrates beautifully the equation on the semantic level, that is, in everyday speech, of what to Bakhtin was the very spine and structure of the novel: penetration, ingestion, and excretion. The mock-epic alimentary battle of Carnal and Cuaresma in the *Libro* is fought with both live animals and prepared meats and ludicrous, though appropriate, weapons like pots and platters. Central to the carnivalesque verbal games of the episode is the creation of an anti-language, whose basic form is the relexicalization or semantic reinterpretation of central metaphors of the three major symbolic levels of carnival: food, sex, and violence, which I once dubbed the 'gastro-genital' (Vasvári 1991;

cf. Gilmore 1998: 44–45 on these same features in modern carnival in Spain).
These semantic fields can exist simultaneously, superimposed, alternating, or
intermingled with one another. For example, edible soldiers of the two armies of
Carnal and Cuaresma, such as *gruesso tocino* 'fatty bacon', *pixota* 'hake', *puerco*
'piggy', *ostra* 'oyster', *liebre* 'hare', *conejo* 'cony', and others, function simultaneously in the three semantic fields, violence, gastronomy, and sexuality, as,
respectively, combatants or cadavers (depending on the stage of the battle), prepared foods and/or live animals, and sex organs of one or the other sex. In this
episode of 'carnival as rape' the violent sexual relexicalization revolves around
the key terms *luchar / lidiar* 'do battle / copulate', and *matar* 'kill / copulate / rape.'
Male sharks 'kill' female partridges and castrate capons, while the acoustically
phallic *pixota* 'hake' (which recalls *pija* 'penis') threatens the *puerco* 'piggy /
female sex organ' with rape. Victory in Carnival consists in the act of 'stuffing'
the enemy like a carnival sausage, preferably anally. The most important of Don
Carnal's vassals is the personified Don Jueves Lardero 'Fat Thursday', but whose
name also suggests 'Ritual Carnival Bugger', as in the French carnival terms
larder 'stuff strips of fatback into a piece of meat with a wide needle / copulate',
and hence *lardeur* 'active homosexual'.

Calendar rites make it obligatory for Don Carnal to be vanquished in the first
round of the battle with Lent. In the *Libro*, for his further derision, Carnal is placed
in singular combat with a series of phallic fish and vegetables because anal rape
was considered the worst possible form of humiliation and, therefore, naturally,
a popular carnival topic. Poor Carnal is attacked, among others, by a leek, commonly cultivated as an aphrodisiac in medieval Europe for its supposed ability
to produce semen, a belief due to its formal similarity to the male organ, with its
elongated shape with its white 'head' and green, that is, lusty, 'tail', and hard texture when fresh, which, however, quickly goes limp when heated. Ritual battles
between Carnal and Cuaresma normally must end with the judgment, execution,
and often burial of Flesh or one of his fleshy representatives, most commonly,
the cock. In the *Libro*, however, he is only imprisoned and forced to do penance,
and in his triumphant return, which takes place at the proper liturgical moment,
he is accompanied by his double, Don Amor. In a combined liturgical parody of
the risen Christ and epic parody of the return of the victorious military leader,
the revitalized, blood-splattered Carnal returns in a triumphant procession at the
end of Lent as King of the Flesh. The degradation enacted in carnival and in
carnivalized writing is the incessant reminder that we are all creatures of flesh
and thus of food and faeces also. But this degradation is simultaneously an affirm-
ation linked to regeneration and renewal. And this was essentially Bakhtin's
definition of novelization, the constant being born anew in each period.

Conclusion

As Walter Haug (2000) emphasizes, we must consider the great significance
of the heightened awareness of fictionality in the High Middle Ages, which

liberated previous literary endeavours from their traditional narrow functionality for society (moral, social, didactic, political, etc.). It is this concept of fictionality, fused with the dethroning voice of orality, which creates a polyphonic / dialogic novelistic discourse, which 'ingests, masticates, and excretes' all existing literary, paraliterary, and nonliterary discourses, turning all of them into parodic sexual antidiscourses by the superior communicative power of the streetwise spoken vernacular.

I have argued here that the polyphonic perverse corpus that is the *Libro de Buen Amor*, that results from this fusion of high and low, is like the open body of grotesque realism, transforming topsy-turvy all inherited genres and thus representing the regenerative victory of a novelistic *Weltanschaung* over inherited moribund genres and the ideals they embody.[19] As I have argued elsewhere (Dangler 2002), the *Libro* has overturned the expected relationships of power. Just as the Roman rogue bests the stuffy Greek scholar, Pitas Pajas gets routed by his better endowed apprentice, and Don Carnal always comes back to vanquish Cuaresma, so the *Libro* outdoes the *mester de clerecía*.[20]

As Bakhtin said, popular and heterogenous tradition has been largely ignored because traditional philology partakes of the same official, serious ideology. Hence it has obstructed issues about sexuality and orality of the written text. I have attempted to illustrate how such an literary archaeology of sexuality might be undertaken.[21] Although this approach could be attacked on the grounds of anachronism or impropriety, it is essential that we labour to understand the spoken language of medieval culture. This is clearly a difficult task since we have access to it primarily through textuality. It is precisely because of this that we must make use of other tantalizing remains of the past, from folklore, visual images, and bits of ritual, combined with a study of linguistic archaeology. Our philological task is to give birth again to a living, vital, sexually charged language from a dead textual body. It is only through this process that we can apprehend the 'novelness' of the *Libro de Buen Amor*.

---

[19] Contrast the roughly contemporary *Canterbury Tales* and the *Decameron*, which are both replete with carnivalization, but where each individual tale is oriented to one of the two models of discourse, the written or the oral (Cook 1986).

[20] See Vasvári 1994, where I comment on five episodes in the *Libro* where sex is portrayed as a game of dominance and submission, reinterpreted as insertive and receptive sexual – and linguistic – roles.

[21] I am extending Michel Foucault's 1979 notion of literary archaeology, which he defined as the need for diachronic rules of discursive formation.

ABBREVIATIONS

AEM	*Anuario de Estudios Medievales*
AFE	*El Crotalón: Anuario de Filología Española*
AHLM	Asociación Hispánica de Literatura Medieval
AIH	Asociación Internacional de Hispanists
AM	*Anuario Medieval*
AS	Acta Salmanticensia
BC	Biblioteca Clásica (Barcelona)
BHS	*Bulletin of Hispanic Studies*
BRAE	*Boletín de la Real Academia Española*
BRH	Biblioteca Románica Hispánica
C	*La Corónica*
CCa	Clásicos Castalia
CCs	Clásicos Castellanos
CL	*Comparative Literature*
CSIC	Consejo Superior de Investigaciones Científicas
CT	Colección Támesis
FMLS	*Forum for Modern Language Studies*
HR	*Hispanic Review*
HSMS	Hispanic Seminary of Medieval Studies, Madison
In	*Incipit*
JHP	*Journal of Hispanic Philology*
KRQ	*Kentucky Romance Quarterly*
LH	Letras Hispánicas
MLN	*Modern Language Notes*
MLR	*Modern Language Review*
MR	*Medioevo Romanzo*
MS(S)	Manuscript(s)
NRFH	*Nueva Revista de Filología Hispánica*
PMHRS	Papers of the Medieval Hispanic Research Seminar
PMLA	*Publications of the Modern Language Association of America*
RAE	Real Academia Española
REH	*Revista de Estudios Hispánicos* (USA)
RF	*Romanische Forschungen*
RFE	*Revista de Filología Española*
RPh	*Romance Philology*
RPM	*Revista de Poética Medieval*

Sp	*Speculum*
SpS	Spanish Series
UCPMP	Univ. of California Publications in Modern Philology
UP	University Press
ZRP	*Zeitschrift für romanische Philologie*

WORKS CITED

Editions and translations

BLECUA, Alberto, ed., 1983. Arcipreste de Hita, *Libro de Buen Amor*, Clásicos Universales, 57 (Barcelona: Planeta).

——, 1992. Juan Ruiz, Arcipreste de Hita, *Libro de buen amor*, LH, 70 (Madrid: Cátedra).

——, 2001. Arcipreste de Hita, *Libro de buen amor*, Clásicos y Modernos, 7 (Barcelona: Crítica).

BREY MARIÑO, María, trans., 1966. Arcipreste de Hita, *Libro de buen amor*, Odres Nuevos, 5th edn (Madrid: Castalia). 1st edn 1954.

CEJADOR Y FRAUCA, Julio, ed., 1913. Arcipreste de Hita, *Libro de Buen Amor*, CCs, 14 and 17 (Madrid: La Lectura) ('Arcipreste de Hita' on cover, 'Juan Ruiz, Arcipreste de Hita' on title page).

CHIARINI, Giorgio, ed., 1964. Juan Ruiz, Arcipreste de Hita, *Libro de Buen Amor*, Documenti di Filologia, 8 (Milan: Ricciardi).

COROMINAS, Joan, ed., 1967. Juan Ruiz, Arcipreste de Hita, *Libro de Buen Amor*, BRH, 4.4 (Madrid: Gredos).

CRIADO DE VAL, Manuel, & Eric W. NAYLOR, ed., 1972. Arcipreste de Hita, *Libro de buen amor: edición crítica*, Clásicos Hispánicos, 2.9 (Madrid: CSIC). 1st edn 1965.

DUCAMIN, Jean, ed., 1901. Juan Ruiz, Arcipreste de Hita, *'Libro de buen amor': texte du XIVe siècle publié pour la première fois avec les leçons des trois manuscrits connus*, Bibliothèque Méridionale, 1st ser., 6 (Toulouse: Édouard Privat).

GYBBON-MONYPENNY, G. B., ed., 1988. Arcipreste de Hita, *Libro de buen amor*, CCa, 161 (Madrid: Castalia).

JANER, Florencio, ed., 1864. 'Libro de cantares de Joan Roiz', in *Poetas castellanos anteriores al siglo XV: colección hecha por Don Tomás Antonio Sánchez, continuada por el Excelentísimo Señor Don Pedro José Pidal, y considerablemente aumentada e ilustrada a vista de los códices y manuscritos antiguos*, Biblioteca de Autores Españoles, 57 (Madrid: Rivadaneyra; repr. Madrid: Atlas, 1952), pp. 225–82 and 582–88.

JOSET, Jacques, ed., 1974. Juan Ruiz, *Libro de buen amor*, CCa, 14 and 17 (Madrid: Espasa-Calpe).

——, 1981. Juan Ruiz, *El Libro de Buen Amor*, CCa, 14 and 17 (Madrid: Espasa-Calpe).

——, 1990. Juan Ruiz, Arcipreste de Hita, *Libro de buen amor*, Clásicos Taurus, 1 (Madrid: Taurus).

KANE, Elisha K., trans., 1968. *The Book of Good by Juan Ruiz*, 2nd edn, ed. John E. Keller (Chapel Hill: University of North Carolina Press). 1st edn 1933.

LA GIOIA, Vincenzo, and Giuseppe DI STEFANO, ed. & trans., 1999. Juan Ruiz, *Libro del Buon Amore* (Milan: Rizzoli).

PONS GRIERA, Lidia, ed. and trans., 1971. Arcipreste de Hita, *Libro de buen amor* (Barcelona: Bruguera).

RUIZ, Juan, Arcipreste de Hita, 1974. *Libro de buen amor: edición facsímil del manuscrito Gayoso (1389) propiedad de la Real Academia Española* (Madrid: RAE).

——, 1975. *Libro de Buen Amor: edición facsímil del códice de Salamanca, Ms. 2.663*, Códices Literarios, A1 (Madrid: Edilan).

——, 1977. *Libro de buen amor*, I: *Facsímil*, II: *Introducción y transcripción del Códice de Toledo (Biblioteca Nacional Madrid Vª-6-1)*, ed. Manuel Criado de Val & Eric W. Naylor (Madrid: Espasa-Calpe).

SALVADOR MIGUEL, Nicasio, trans., 1985. Juan Ruiz, Arcipreste de Hita, *Libro de buen amor*, Clásicos Modernizados Alhambra, 1 (Madrid: Alhambra).

SINGLETON, Mack, trans., 1975. *The Book of the Archpriest of Hita (Libro de Buen Amor)* (Madison: HSMS).

WILLIS, Raymond W., ed. and trans., 1972. Juan Ruiz, *Libro de Buen Amor* (Princeton: UP).

Secondary works

AARNE, Antti, & Stith THOMPSON, 1964. *The Types of the Folktale: A Classification and Bibliography*, 2nd edn, FF Communications, 184 (Helsinki: Academia Scientiarum Fennica).

ADAMS, Kenneth W. J., 1970. 'Juan Ruiz's Manipulation of Rhyme: Some Linguistic and Stylistic Consequences', in Gybbon-Monypenny 1970a: 1–28.

——, 1989. '"Plogome otrosí oír muchas vegadas libros de devaneos": Did Pero López de Ayala Know the *Libro de buen amor*?', in *Essays on Hispanic Themes in Honour of Edward C. Riley*, ed. Jennifer Lowe and Philip Swanson (Edinburgh: Dept of Hispanic Studies, Univ.), pp. 9–40.

AGUADO, José María, 1929. *Glosario sobre Juan Ruiz, poeta castellano del siglo XIV* (Madrid: the author, ptd Espasa-Calpe).

ALLEN, Judson Boyce, 1982. *The Ethical Poetic of the Later Middle Ages: A Decorum of Convenient Distinction* (Toronto: Univ. of Toronto Press).

ALLEN, Peter L., 1992. *The Art of Love: Amatory Fiction from Ovid to the 'Romance of the Rose'* (Philadelphia: Univ. of Pennsylvania Press).

ALONSO, Dámaso, 1957. 'Crítica de noticias literarias transmitidas por Argote', *BRAE*, 37: 63–81.

ALTMAN, Charles F., 1986. 'The Medieval Marquee: Church Portal Sculpture as Publicity', in *Popular Culture in the Middle Ages*, ed. Josie P. Campbell (Bowling Green, OH: Bowling Green Univ. Popular Press), pp. 6–15.

ALVAR, Carlos, and Manuel ALVAR, ed., 1991. *Épica medieval española*, LH, 330 (Madrid: Cátedra).

AMADOR DE LOS RÍOS, José, 1861–65. *Historia crítica de la literatura española*, 7 vols (Madrid: the autor, ptd José Fernández Cancela et al.; repr. Madrid: Gredos, 1969).

AMASUNO, Marcelino V., in press. 'El arciprestre como *homo astrologicus* en el *Libro de buen amor*', *Hispanic Research Journal*.

ARGOTE DE MOLINA, Gonzalo, ed., 1575. Don Juan Manuel, *El conde Lucanor* (Seville: Hernando Díaz).

ARMENGOL VALENZUELA, Pedro de, ed., 1904–08. *Obras de San Pedro Pascual* (Rome: Tipografia della Pace di F. Cuggiani; Imprenta Salustiana).

ARMISTEAD, Samuel G., 1973. 'An Unnoticed Fifteenth-Century Citation of the *Libro de buen amor*', *HR*, 41: 88–91.

——, 1976–77. 'Two Further Citations of the *Libro de Buen Amor* in Lope García de Salazar's *Bienandanzas e fortunas*', C, 5: 75–77.

ARNOLD, H. H., 1940. Review of Lecoy 1938, *HR*, 8: 166–70.

ARRATHOON, Leigh A., 1984. 'Jacques de Vitry, the Tale of Calogrenant, *La Chastelaine de Vergi*, and the Genres of Medieval Narrative Fiction', in her ed. *The Craft of Fiction: Essays in Medieval Poetics* (Rochester, MI: Solaris), pp. 281–368.

ASENSIO, Eugenio, 1973. 'Dos obras dialogadas con influencias del *Lazarillo de Tormes, Colloquios*, de Collazos, y Anónimos, *Diálogo del capón*', *Cuadernos Hispanoamericanos*, 280–82: 385–98.

ASKINS, Arthur L-F., 1986–87. 'A New Manuscript of the *Libro de buen amor*?', C, 15: 72–76.

AUBRUN, Charles V., 1980. ' "Buen Amor": Approximation', in *Homenaje a Don Agapito Rey*, ed. Josep Roca-Pons (Bloomington: Dept of Spanish and Portuguese, Indiana Univ.), pp. 73–89.

AUERBACH, Erich, 1984. 'Figura', *Scenes from the Drama of European Literature*, Theory and History of Literature, 9 (Minneapolis: Univ. of Minnesota Press), pp. 11–76.

AYOUB, Millicent R., and Stephen A. BARNETT, 1965. 'Ritualized Verbal Insult in White High School Culture', *Journal of American Folk-Lore*, 78: 337–44.

BAEHR, Rudolf, 1970. *Manual de versificación española*, trans. K. Wagner and F. López Estrada, BRH, 3.25 (Madrid: Gredos).

BAKHTIN, Mikhail, 1929. *Problemy tvorchestva Dostoevskogo* (Leningrad: Priboi). Trans. R. W. Rotsel, *Problems of Dostoevsky's Poetics* (Ann Arbor: Ardis, 1973). Caryl Emerson, trans. of expanded edn, introd. Wayne C. Booth (Minneapolis: Univ. of Minnesota Press, 1984).

——, 1968. *Rabelais and his World*, trans. Hélène Iswolsky (Cambridge, MA: MIT Press).

——, 1981. *The Dialogic Imagination: Four Essays*, ed. Michael Holquist and trans. Caryl Emerson & Holquist (Austin: Univ. of Texas Press).

BALDWIN, John W., 1994. *The Language of Sex: Five Voices from Northern France around 1200* (Chicago: Univ. of Chicago Press).

BANDERA, Cesáreo, 1977. 'De la apertura del *Libro* de Juan Ruiz a Derrida y viceversa', *Dispositio*, 2: 54–66.

BARCELONA, Martí de, 1936. 'L'*Ars praedicandi* de Francesc Eiximenis', *Analecta Sacra Tarraconensia*, 12: 301–40.

BARRA JOVER, Mario, 1990. 'El *Libro de buen amor* como "cancionero" ', *Revista de Literatura Medieval*, 2: 159–64.

BARTHES, Roland, 1973. *Le Plaisir du texte* (Paris: Seuil).

BASORE, John W., trans., 1932. Seneca, *Moral Essays*, II (London: Heinemann).

BATAILLON, Louis-J., 1993. *La Prédication au XIIIème siècle en France et Italie: études et documents* (Aldershot, Hants: Variorum).

BAYO, Juan Carlos, 1999. 'La teoría del verso desde el punto de vista lingüístico (el sistema de versificación del *Cantar de Mio Cid*)', doctoral thesis, Univ. de Barcelona.

BELTRÁN, Luis, 1977. *Razones de buen amor: oposiciones y convergencias en el libro del arcipreste de Hita*, Pensamiento Literario Español, 5 (Madrid: Fundación March & Castalia).

BELTRÁN, Rafael, in press. 'Cuentos populares del *Libro de buen amor* en la tradición oral moderna: I (las fábulas); pérdidas, pervivencias, y ¿recuperaciones?', in *Actas del IX Congreso de la AHLM, La Coruña 2001*; 'II: religiosos, novelescos, de matrimonios y mentiras', in *Actes del X Congrés de la AHLM, Alacant 2003*.

BENSON, Larry D., F. N. Robinson, et al., ed., 1988. *The Riverside Chaucer*, 3rd edn (Oxford: UP).

BENVENISTE, Émile, 1974. *Problèmes de linguistique générale* (Paris: Gallimard), II.

BERMEJO CABRERO, José Luis, 1973. 'El saber jurídico del Arcipreste', in Criado de Val 1973a: 409–15.

BIHLER, Heinrich, 1955–56. Review of 1st edn (1954) of Brey Mariño 1966, *Romanistisches Jahrbuch*, 7: 374–76.

BIZZARRI, Hugo O., 1999. 'Algunas consideraciones sobre la rama *G* del *Libro de buen amor*', *In*, 19: 13–33.

BLACKMORE, Josiah, and Gregory S. HUTCHESON, ed., 1999. *Queer Iberia: Sexualities, Cultures, and Crossings from the Middle Ages to the Renaissance* (Durham, NC: Duke UP).

BLAKE, N. F., 1979. *The English Language in Medieval Literature*, University Paperbacks, 670 (London: Methuen).

BLECUA, Alberto, 1980. *La transmisión textual de 'El Conde Lucanor'* (Bellaterra: Seminario de Literatura Medieval y Humanística, Universidad Autónoma de Barcelona).

——, 1983. *Manual de crítica textual*, Literatura y Sociedad, 33 (Madrid: Castalia).

——, 1991–92. 'Los textos medievales castellanos y sus ediciones', *RPh*, 45: 73–88.

BLOOM, Harold, 1973. *The Anxiety of Influence: A Theory of Poetry* (Oxford: UP).

BOAS, M., 1914. 'De librorum Catonianorum historia atque compositione', *Mnemosyne*, n.s., 42: 17–46.

——, ed., 1952. *Disticha Catonis* (Amsterdam: North-Holland).

BODENHAM, C. H. L., 1985. 'The Nature of the Dream in Late Mediaeval French Literature', *Medium Ævum*, 54: 59–73.

BOEHNE, Patricia J., 1975. *Dream and Fantasy in 14th- and 15th-Century Catalan Prose* (Barcelona: Hispam).

BONILLA Y SAN MARTÍN, A., 1906. 'Antecedentes del tipo celestinesco en la literatura latina', *Revue Hispanique*, 15: 372–86.

BOOTH, Wayne C., 1961. *The Rhetoric of Fiction* (Chicago: Univ. of Chicago Press).

BRAIDOTTI, Erminio, 1981. 'Eroticism in the *Libro de Buen Amor*', unpubl. doctoral dissertation, University of Pennsylvania; *Dissertation Abstracts International*, 42 (1981–82): 2698; abstract at http://wwwlib.umi.com/dissertations/fullcit/8127005 (2 July 2003).

BRANCHAM, Bracht R., 1999. 'Inventing the Novel', in *Critical Essays on Mikhail Bakhtin*, ed. Caryl Emerson (New York: G. K. Hall), pp. 202–11.

BRANDES, Stanley, 1980. *Metaphors of Masculinity: Sex and Status in Andalusian Folklore* (Philadelphia: Univ. of Pennsylvania Press).

BROCKELMANN, C., 1999. 'Makāma', in *Encyclopaedia of Islam*, CD-ROM Edition v.1.10 (Leiden: Brill).

BROWER, Robert H., 1972. 'Japanese', in *Versification: Major Language Types*, ed. W. K. Wimsatt (New York: MLA & New York UP), pp. 38–51.

BROWN, Catherine, 1998. *Contrary Things: Exegesis, Dialectic, and the Poetics of Didacticism* (Stanford: UP).

BROWNLEE, Marina Scordilis, 1981–82. 'Permutations of the Narrator-Protagonist', *Romance Notes*, 22: 98–101.

——, 1982. 'Autobiography as Self-(Re)presentation: The Augustinian Paradigm and Juan Ruiz's Theory of Reading', in *Mimesis: From Mirror to Method, Augustine to Descartes*, ed. John D. Lyons and Stephen G. Nichols (Hanover, NH: UP of New England for Dartmouth College), pp. 71–82.

——, 1994. 'Discursive Parameters of the Picaresque', in *The Picaresque: A Symposium on the Rogue's Tale*, ed. Carmen Benito-Vessels and Michael Zappala (Newark: Univ. of Delaware Press), pp. 26–35.

BUENO, Julián L., 1983. *La sotana de Juan Ruiz: elementos eclesiásticos en el 'Libro de buen amor'* (York, SC: Spanish Literature Publications).

BULLOCH, Vern L., & James A. BRUNDAGE, 1996. *Handbook of Medieval Sexuality*, Garland Reference Library of the Humanities, 1696 (New York: Garland).

BURKARD, Richard, 1995. 'The Ordering of Stanzas 436–443 in the *Libro de buen amor*', *Hispanófila*, 113: 1–10.

——, 1999. *The Archpriest of Hita and the Imitators of Ovid: A Study of the Ovidian and Pseudo-Ovidian Background of the 'Libro de buen amor'*, Estudios de Literatura Medieval John E. Keller, 1 (Newark, DE: Juan de la Cuesta).

BURKE, James F., 1981–82. 'The *Libro de buen amor* and the Medieval Meditative Sermon Tradition', *C*, 9: 122–27.

——, 1998. *Desire Against the Law: The Juxtaposition of Contraries in Early Medieval Spanish Literature* (Stanford: UP).

BURKE, Peter, 1973. 'L'histoire sociale des rêves', *Annales: Économies, Sociétés, Civilisations*, 28: 329–42.

BURRUS, Victoria A., and Harriet GOLDBERG, ed., 1990. *Esopete ystoriado (Toulouse 1488)*, SpS, 61 (Madison: HSMS).

CALADO, Adelino Almeida, 1994. '*Livro de Exopo*: edição crítica com introdução e notas', *Boletim da Biblioteca da Universidade de Coimbra*, 42: 1–99.

CAMILLE, Michael, 1992. *Image on the Edge: The Margins of Medieval Art* (Cambridge, MA: Harvard UP).

CANELLADA, María Josefa, ed., 1980. Marqués de Santillana, *Refranero* (Madrid: Magisterio Español).

CANTARINO, Vicente, 1974. 'La lógica falaz de don Juan Ruiz', *Thesaurus* (Bogotá), 29: 435–56.

——, 1989. 'Juan Ruiz: reflexiones sobre doña Endrina', *AM*, 1: 46–61.

CANTERA BURGOS, Francisco, 1973. 'La judería de Hita en el cuadro de los núcleos judíos de Guadalajara', in Criado de Val 1973a: 439–46.

CASTELLANOS, Luis Arturo, 1973. 'La estructura del *Libro de Buen Amor*', in Criado de Val 1973a: 30–37.

CASTRO, Américo, 1948. *España en su historia: cristianos, moros y judíos* (Buenos Aires: Losada); 2ⁿᵈ edn (Barcelona: Crítica, 1983).

——, 1952. 'El *Libro de Buen Amor* del Arcipreste de Hita', *CL*, 4: 193–213.

——, 1954. *La realidad histórica de España*, Biblioteca Porrúa, 4 (Mexico City: Porrúa).

CASTRO GUISASOLA, F., 1924. *Observaciones sobre las fuentes literarias de 'La Celestina'*, Anejos de la *RFE*, 5 (Madrid: Centro de Estudios Históricos).

CATALÁN, Diego, with Suzy PETERSEN, 1970. ' "Aunque omne non goste la pera del peral . . . ": sobre la "sentencia" de Juan Ruiz y la de su *Buen Amor*', *HR*, 38.5 (Extraordinary Number: *Studies in Memory of Ramón Menéndez Pidal*): 56–96.

CÁTEDRA, Pedro M., 1982. *Dos estudios sobre el sermón en la España medieval* (Bellaterra: Univ. Autónoma de Barcelona, 1981 [1982]).

——, 1989. *Amor y pedagogía en la Edad Media: estudios de doctrina amorosa y práctica literaria*, AS: Estudios Filológicos, 212 (Salamanca: Univ).

CERQUIGLINI, Bernard, 1989. *Éloge de la variante: histoire critique de la philologie* (Paris: Seuil).

CHAMBRY, Émile, ed. and trans., 1927. *Ésope, Fables* (Paris: Les Belles Lettres).

CHAPMAN, Janet A., 1970. 'Juan Ruiz's "Learned Sermon" ', in Gybbon-Monypenny 1970a: 29–51.

CHATMAN, Seymour B., 1965. *A Theory of Meter*, Janua Linguarum, Ser. Minor, 36 (The Hague: Mouton).

CHAYTOR, H. J., 1966. *From Script to Print: An Introduction to Medieval Vernacular Literature* (London: Sidgwick & Jackson). 1st edn Cambridge, UP, 1945.

CHEEVER, Leonard A., 1989. 'Orderly Disorder: Chaos in One Hundred Years of Solitude', *Publications of the Arkansas Philological Association*, 15: 11–27.

CHERCHI, Paolo, 1987. 'El retrato de don Amor', *C*, 16.1: 132–37. Also in *RFE*, 66 (1986): 313–17.

——, 1993. 'Il prologo di Juan Ruiz e il *Decretum Gratiani*', *MR*, 18: 257–60.

CLARKE, Dorothy Clotelle, 1947–48. 'Hiatus, Synalepha, and Line Length in López de Ayala's Octosyllables', *RPh*, 1: 347–56.

——, 1971. 'A Passage in Juan Ruiz's Prologue: Anacoluthon – or Composite Art?', *MLN*, 86: 254–63.

——, 1972. 'Juan Ruiz and Andreas Capellanus', *HR*, 40, 390–411.

——, 1984. 'Juan Ruiz: A *romance viejo* in the *Libro de buen amor* (*la mora*)?', *KRQ*, 31: 391–402.

COBBAN, A. B., 1975. *The Medieval Universities: Their Development and Organization* (London: Methuen).

COLEMAN, Janet, 1981. *English Literature in History, 1350–1400: Medieval Readers and Writers* (London: Hutchinson).

COLÓN, Germán, 1992. 'La fábula "Vulpes" del *Syntipas* griego, el Arcipreste y don Juan Manuel', in *Estudios de literatura y lingüística españolas: miscelánea en honor de Luis López Molina* (Lausanne: Sociedad Suiza de Estudios Hispánicos), pp. 181–93.

CONNOLLY, Jane E., ed., 1987. *Translation and Poetization in the 'Quaderna vía': Study and Edition of the 'Libro de miseria d'omne'*, SpS, 33 (Madison: HSMS).

CONNOR, Steve, 2002. 'The Big Question Is, Do Sheepdogs Dream of Counting Sheep?', *The Independent* (20 February): 12.

COOK, Jan, 1986. 'Carnival and the *Canterbury Tales*', in *Medieval Literature: Criticism, Ideology, and History*, ed. David Aers (New York: St Martin's Press), pp. 169–91.

CORNULIER, Benoît de, 1995. *Art poëtique: notions et problèmes de métrique* (Lyon: Presses Universitaires de Lyon).

CORTIJO OCAÑA, Antonio, 2000. 'Hacia la ficción sentimental: la *Rota Veneris* de Boncompagno da Signa', *C*, 29.1: 53–74.

COX, Catherine S., 1997. *Gender and Language in Chaucer* (Gainesville: Univ. Press of Florida).

CRADDOCK, Jerry R., 1990. 'La legislación alfonsí ante el pecado y las transgresiones civiles', unpubl. lecture, Cursos de Verano de la Universidad Complutense: Amor, pecado y muerte en la Edad Media, El Escorial, 30 July-3 Aug.

CRIADO DE VAL, Manuel, 1960a. *Doña Endrina: adaptación escénica del 'Libro de Buen Amor' del Arcipreste de Hita* (Madrid: Oficina Gráfica Madrileña).

——, 1960b. *Teoría de Castilla la Nueva: la dualidad castellana en los orígenes del español*, BRH, 2.46 (Madrid: Gredos).

——, 1973a. *El Arcipreste de Hita: el libro, el autor, la tierra, la época: Actas del I Congreso Internacional sobre el Arcipreste de Hita* (Barcelona: SERESA).

——, 1973b. 'La Tierra de Hita: el contorno mozárabe del *Libro de Buen Amor*', in Criado de Val 1973a: 447–55.

——, 1978. 'El *Libro de Buen Amor*, ¿fue escrito en versión "cortesana" gallego-portuguesa, por el "taller" de las *cantigas alfonsíes*?', *Revista de Literatura*, 40: 31–45.

CROSBY, Ruth, 1936. 'Oral Delivery in the Middle Ages', *Sp*, 11: 88–110.

CUARTERO SANCHO, M. P., in press. 'La paremiología en el *Libro de buen amor*', in Toro Ceballos in press.

DAGENAIS, John, 1986–87a, ' "Avrás dueña garrida": Language of the Margins in the *Libro de buen amor*', *C*, 15: 38–45.

——, 1986–87b. 'A Further Source for the Literary Ideas in Juan Ruiz's Prologue', *JHP*, 11: 23–52.

——, 1989. ' "Se usa e se faz": Naturalist Truth in a *Pamphilus* Explicit and the *Libro de buen amor*', *HR*, 57: 417–36.

——, 1991. '*Cantigas d'escarnho* and *serranillas*: The Allegory of Careless Love', *BHS*, 68: 247–63.

——, 1992a. 'Mulberries, Sloe Berries; Or, Was Doña Endrina a *Mora*?' *MLN*, 107: 396–405.

——, 1992b. ' "Cálame y e conocerme as": On the Name of Don Melón', *C*, 21.1: 1–14.

——, 1994. *The Ethics of Reading in Manuscript Culture: Glossing the 'Libro de buen amor'* (Princeton: UP).

——, 1998. 'Forum: A Reader's Response', *C*, 26.2: 257–69.

DANGLER, Jean, 2002. 'Response to "Using Literary Texts in a History of Sexuality" ', *C*, 30.1: 244–47.

DANOW, David K., 1991. *The Thought of Mikhail Bakhtin: From Word to Culture* (Basingstoke: Macmillan).

——, 1995. *The Spirit of Carnival: Magical Realism and the Grotesque* (Lexington: UP of Kentucky).

DANTE ALIGHIERI, 1979. *La Divina commedia*, ed. Umberto Bosco and Giovanni Reggio, 3 vols (Florence: Le Monnier).

DAVIS, Norman, Douglas GRAY, Patricia INGHAM, and Anne WALLACE-HADRILL, 1979. *A Chaucer Glossary* (Oxford: Clarendon Press).

DE LOOZE, Laurence, 1997. *Pseudo-Autobiography in the Fourteenth Century: Juan Ruiz, Guillaume de Machaut, Jean Froissart, and Geoffrey Chaucer* (Gainesville: UP of Florida).

——, 1998. 'To Understand Perfectly Is to Misunderstand Completely: "The Debate in Signs" in France, Iceland, Italy and Spain', *CL*, 50: 136–54.

DE LOPE, Monique, [1984]. *Traditions populaires et textualité dans le 'Libro de Buen Amor'* (Montpellier: Centre d'Études et de Recherches Sociocritiques).

DE MAN, Paul, 1971. *Blindness and Insight: Essays in the Rhetoric of Contemporary Criticism* (Oxford: UP).

DE NIGRIS, Carla, ed., 1994. Juan de Mena, *'Laberinto de Fortuna' y otros poemas*, introd. Guillermo Séres, BC, 14 (Barcelona: Crítica).

DEMBOWSKI, Peter F., ed., 1986. Jean Froissart, *La Paradis d'Amour; L'Orloge amoureus*, Textes Littéraires Français, 339 (Geneva: Droz).

DEMÓFILO [pseud.], 1880. *Colección de enigmas y adivinanzas en forma de diccionario* (Seville: R. Balderaque).

DERRIDA, Jacques, 1967. *De la grammatologie* (Paris: Minuit).

DEYERMOND, Alan, 1970. 'Some Aspects of Parody in the *Libro de buen amor*', in Gybbon-Monypenny 1970a: 53–78.

——, 1973. 'Early Allusions to the *Libro de Buen Amor*: A Postscript to Moffatt', *MLN*, 88: 317–21.

——, 1974. '*Juglar*'s Repertoire or Sermon Notebook? – The *Libro de Buen Amor* and a Manuscript Miscellany', *BHS*, 51: 217–27.

——, 1975. 'Berceo, el diablo y los animales', in *Homenaje al Instituto de Filología y Literaturas Hispánicas Dr. Amado Alonso en su cincuentenario 1923–1973* (Buenos Aires: Comisión de Homenaje), pp. 82–90.

——, 1977. '*Hilado – cordón – cadena*: Symbolic Equivalence in *La Celestina*', *Celestinesca*, 1.1: 6–12.

——, 1979–80. 'The Sermon and its Uses in Medieval Castilian Literature', *C*, 8: 127–45.

——, 1980a. 'Juan Ruiz's Attitude to Literature', in *Medieval, Renaissance and Folklore Studies in Honor of John Esten Keller*, ed. Joseph R. Jones (Newark, DE: Juan de la Cuesta), pp. 113–25.

——, ed., 1980b. *Historia y crítica de la literatura española*: I, *Edad Media* (Barcelona: Crítica).

——, 1994. 'De las categorías de las letras: problemas de género, autor y título en la literatura medieval española', in *Actas del III Congreso de la AHLM (Salamanca, 3 al 6 de octubre de 1989)*, ed. María Isabel Toro Pascua (Salamanca: Biblioteca del Siglo XV and Departamento de Literatura Española e Hispanoamericana, Univ. de Salamanca), I, 15–39.

——, 2004. *The 'Libro de Buen Amor' in England: A Tribute to Gerald Gybbon-Monypenny*, Manchester Spanish and Portuguese Studies, 17 (Manchester: Manchester Spanish and Portuguese Studies).

DI CAMILLO, Ottavio, 1990. '*Libro de buen amor* 70a: What Are the *Libro*'s Instruments?' *Viator*, 21: 239–71.

DIAS, João José Alves, ed., 1982. *Livro dos Conselhos de El-Rei D. Duarte: Livro da Cartuxa* (Lisbon: Estampa).

DÍAZ G. VIANA, Luis, 1998. *Una voz continuada: estudios históricos y antropológicos sobre la literatura oral* (Oyarzun: Sendoa).

DÍEZ GARRETAS, María Jesús, and María Wenceslada de DIEGO LOBEJÓN, ed., 2000. Fernán Pérez de Guzmán, *Un cancionero para Alvar García de Santamaría: 'Diversas virtudes y vicios' de Fernán Pérez de Guzmán*, Estudios y Ediciones, 1 (Tordesillas: Instituto de Estudios de Iberoamérica y Portugal, Univ. de Valladolid).

DILLARD, Heath, 1984. *Daughters of the Reconquest: Women in Castilian Town Society, 1100–1300* (Cambridge: UP).

DODDS, Jerrilynn D., 1990. *Architecture and Ideology in Early Medieval Spain* (University Park: Pennsylvania State UP).

DOMÍNGUEZ, César, 1997. '*Ordinatio* y rubricación en la tradición manuscrita: el *Libro de buen amor* y las *cánticas de serrana* en el MS *S*', *RPM*, 1: 71–112.

DOMÍNGUEZ CAPARRÓS, José, 2000. *Métrica española*, 2nd edn (Madrid: Síntesis).

DONNELL, Sidney, and Gregory S. HUTCHESON, ed., 2002. 'Return to Queer Iberia', *C*, 30.1: 215–65.

DOODY, Margaret Anne, 1996. *The True Story of the Novel* (New Brunswick, NJ: Rutgers UP).

DRAGONETTI, Roger, 1980. *La Vie de la lettre au Moyen Âge: 'Le conte du Graal'* (Paris: Seuil).

DRORY, Rina, 2000. 'The Maqama', in *The Literature of Al-Andalus*, ed. María Rosa Menocal, Raymond P. Scheindlin, and Michael Sells (Cambridge: UP), pp. 190–210.

DUFFELL, Martin J., 1987. 'The Metre of Santillana's Sonnets', *Medium Aevum*, 56: 276–303.

——, 1999a. 'Accentual Regularity in the *Sainte Eulalie*', *Rivista di Studi Testuali*, n.s., 1: 81–108.

——, 1999b. 'The Metric Cleansing of Hispanic Verse', *BHS* (Liverpool), 76: 151–68.

——, 2000. 'The Santillana Factor: The Development of Double Audition in Castilian', in *Santillana: A Symposium*, ed. Alan Deyermond, PMHRS, 28 (London: Dept of Hispanic Studies, Queen Mary and Westfield College), pp. 113–28.

——, 2002. 'Don Rodrigo and Sir Gawain: Family Likeness or Convergent Development?', in *'Mio Cid' Studies: 'Some Problems of Diplomatic' Fifty Years On*, ed. Alan Deyermond, David G. Pattison, and Eric Southworth, PMHRS, 42 (London: Dept of Hispanic Studies, Queen Mary and Westfield College), pp. 129–49.

——, 2003. 'French Symmetry, Germanic Rhythm, and Spanish Meter', in *Chaucer and the Challenges of Medievalism: Essays in Honor of H. A. Kelly*, ed. Donna Minkova & Theresa Tinkle, Studies in English Medieval Language and Literature, 5 (Bern: Peter Lang), pp. 105–27.

DUNN, Peter N., 1970. '"De las figuras del arçipreste"', in Gybbon-Monypenny 1970a: 79–93.

DUPARC-QUIOC, Suzanne, ed., 1976. *La Chanson d'Antioche*, Documents Relatifs a l'Histoire des Croisades, 9 (Paris: Académie des Inscriptions et Belles Lettres).

DUTTON, Brian, 1966. '"Con Dios en buen amor": A Semantic Analysis of the Title of the *Libro de buen amor*', *BHS*, 43: 161–76.

——, 1970. '"Buen Amor": Its Meaning and Uses in Some Medieval Texts', in Gybbon-Monypenny 1970a: 95–121.

——, ed., 1978. Gonzalo de Berceo, *Obras completas*, IV: *La vida de Santo Domingo de Silos*, CT, A74 (London: Tamesis).

——, with Jineen KROGSTAD, ed., 1990–91. *El cancionero del siglo XV, c. 1360–1520*, Biblioteca Española del Siglo XV, Maior, 1–7 (Salamanca: Univ. & Biblioteca Española del Siglo XV).

DYER, Nancy Joe, 1988. In Martínez 1998: 161–71.

EAGLETON, Terry, 1983. *Literary Theory: An Introduction* (Minneapolis: Univ. of Minnesota Press).

EARL, James W., 1994. *Thinking about Beowulf* (Stanford: UP).

ECHARD, Siân, and Stephen PARTRIDGE, ed., in press. *The Book Unbound: Manuscript Studies and Editorial Theory for the 21st Century*.

ECO, Umberto, 1962. *Opera aperta* (Milan: Bompiani).

ECO, Umberto, 1979. *The Role of the Reader: Explorations in the Semiotics of Texts* (Bloomington: Indiana UP).

——, 1980. 'Two Problems in Textual Interpretation', *Poetics Today*, 2: 145–61.

ECO, Umberto, 1989. *The Open Work*, trans. Anna Cancogni (Cambridge, MA: Harvard UP).

EDWARDS, Robert, 1974. 'Narrative Technique in Juan Ruiz's History of Doña Garoza', *MLN*, 89: 265–73.

EDWARDS, Viv, and Thomas J. SIENKEWICZ, 1990. *Oral Cultures Past and Present: Rappin' and Homer* (Cambridge, MA: Blackwell).

ELLIOTT, Alison Goddard, 1984. *Seven Medieval Latin Comedies*, Garland Library of Medieval Literature, B20 (New York: Garland).

ENCINA, Juan del, 1978–83. *Obras completas*, ed. Ana María Rambaldo, CCs, 218–20 and 227 (Madrid: Espasa-Calpe).

EUGENIO Y DÍAZ, Francisco, 1973. 'El lenguaje jurídico del *Libro de Buen Amor*', in Criado de Val 1973a: 422–33.

FARAL, Edmond, 1924. *Les Arts poétiques latins du XIIᵉ et du XIIIᵉ siècle: recherches et documents sur la technique littéraire du Moyen Âge*, Bibliothèque de l'École des Hautes Études, 238 (Paris: Honoré Champion); repr. Geneva: Slatkine, 1982.

FAULHABER, Charles B., 1972. *Latin Rhetorical Theory in Thirteenth- and Fourteenth-Century Castile*, UCPMP, 103 (Berkeley: Univ. of California Press).

——, 1974–75. 'The Date of Stanzas 553 and 1450 of the *Libro de buen amor* in MS 9589 of the Biblioteca Nacional, Madrid', *RPh*, 28: 31–34.

FERRÁN, Jaime, 1973. 'La música en el *Libro de Buen Amor*', in Criado de Val 1973a: 391–97.

FILGUEIRA VALVERDE, José, 1973, 'Juan Ruiz en Burgos', in Criado de Val 1973a: 369–70.

FINKE, Laurie A., and Martin B. SHICHTMAN, ed., 1987. *Medieval Texts and Contemporary Readers* (Ithaca: Cornell UP).

FISH, Stanley, 1980. *Is There a Text in this Class? The Authority of Interpretive Communities* (Cambridge, MA: Harvard UP).

FITZ-GERALD, John D., 1905. *Versification of the 'Cuaderna vía' as Found in Berceo's 'Vida de Santo Domingo'* (New York: Columbia Univ.).

FLEISCHMAN, Suzanne, 1982–83. Review of Juan Ruiz, Archpriest of Hita, *The Book of True Love*, ed. Anthony N. Zahareas, trans. Saralyn R. Daly (University Park: Pennsylvania State UP, 1978), *RPh*, 36: 280–89.

——, 1990. 'Philology, Linguistics, and the Discourse of the Medieval Text', *Sp*, 65: 19–37.

FOUCAULT, Michel, 1979. 'What Is an Author?', in *Textual Strategies: Perspectives in Post-Structuralism Criticism*, ed. Josué V. Harari (Ithaca: Cornell UP), pp. 141–60.

FRÉCAUT, Jean-Marc, 1972. *L'Esprit et l'humour chez Ovide* (Grenoble: Presses Universitaires de Grenoble).

FREEDBERG, David, 1989. *The Power of Images: Studies in the History and Theory of Response* (Chicago: UP).

FROISSART, Jean, 1994. *La Prison amoureuse (The Prison of Love)*, ed. Laurence de Looze (New York: Garland).

GABRIEL, Astrik L., 1989. 'Universities', in *The Dictionary of the Middle Ages*, ed. Joseph R. Strayer (New York: Scribner's, 1982–89), XII, 282–300.

GÁMEZ MONTALVO, María Francisca, 1996. 'El procedimiento judicial en el *Libro de Buen Amor*', in Toro Ceballos and Rodríguez Molina 1996: 203–10.

GARCIA, Michel, 1978. 'La versificación', in his ed., Pero López de Ayala, *Libro de poemas, o Rimado de Palacio*, BRH, 4.12 (Madrid: Gredos), I, 41–58.

——, 1988–89. 'Le *Livre de Bon Amour* avant Tomás Antonio Sánchez', *Cahiers de Linguistique Hispanique Médiévale*, 22: 53–81.

GARCÍA, Félix, ed., 1951. *Obras completas castellanas de Fray Luis de León*, Biblioteca de Autores Cristianos, 3 (Madrid: Editorial Católica).

GARCÍA CRAVIOTTO, Francisco, ed., 1989–90. *Catálogo general de incunables en bibliotecas españolas*, 2 vols (Madrid: Ministerio de Cultura, Dirección General del Libro y Bibliotecas).

GARCÍA GÓMEZ, Emilio, trans., 1952. *El collar de la paloma: Tratado sobre el amor y los amantes de Ibn Hazm de Córdoba* (Madrid: Sociedad de Estudios y Publicaciones), 3rd edn, Libro de Bolsillo, Clásicos, 351 (Madrid: Alianza, 1971).

——, 1956. 'La canción famosa *calvi vi calvi, calvi aravi*', *Al-Andalus*, 21: 1–18, and 'Adición', 215–16.

GAUNT, Simon, 1995. *Gender and Genre in Medieval French Literature*, Cambridge Studies in French (Cambridge: UP).

GAUR, Albertine, 1984. *A History of Writing* (London: British Library).

GAUTIER, Léon, 1878–82. *Les Épopées françaises: étude sur les origines et l'histoire de la littérature nationale*, 2nd edn, 4 vols (Paris: Société Générale de Librairie Catholique).

GAUTIER-DALCHÉ, J., 1970–71. 'L'Histoire castillane dans la première moitié du XIVe siècle', *AEM*, 7: 239–52.

GELLA ITURRIAGA, José, 1973. 'Refranero del Arcipreste de Hita', in Criado de Val 1973a: 251–69.

GENETTE, Gérard, 1972. *Figures III* (Paris: Seuil).

——, 1982. *Palimpsestes: la littérature au second degré* (Paris: Seuil).

——, 1987. *Seuils* (Paris: Seuil).

GERICKE, Philip O., 1981. 'On the Structure of the *Libro de buen amor*: A Question of Method', *KRQ*, 28: 13–21.

GERLI, E. Michael, 1976. *Alfonso Martínez de Toledo*, Twayne's World Authors Series, 398 (Boston: Twayne).

——, 1981–82. '"Recta voluntas est bonus amor": St Augustine and the Didactic Structure of the *Libro de buen amor*', *RPh*, 35: 500–08.

——, 1982. 'Don Amor, the Devil, and the Devil's Brood: Love and the Seven Deadly Sins in the *Libro de Buen Amor*', *REH*, 16: 67–80.

——, ed., 1985. Gonzalo de Berceo, *Milagros de Nuestra Señora*, LH, 224 (Madrid: Cátedra).

——, 1990. 'Fernán Pérez de Guzmán, *Cancionero de Baena* 119, and the *Libro de buen amor*', *MLN*, 105: 367–72.

——, 1992. 'El silencio en el *Libro de buen amor*: ¿lagunas textuales o lectura dramática?', in *Actas del X Congreso de la AIH: Barcelona, 21–26 de agosto de 1989*, ed. Antonio Vilanova (Barcelona: PPU), I, 207–14.

——, 1995. 'Carvajal's *serranas*: Reading, Glossing, and Rewriting the *Libro de buen amor* in the *Cancionero de Estúñiga*', in *Studies on Medieval Spanish Literature in Honor of Charles F. Fraker*, ed. Mercedes Vaquero and Alan Deyermond (Madison: HSMS), pp. 159–71.

——, 2001–02. 'On the Edge: Envisioning the *Libro de buen amor* in the *Cancionero de Palacio*', *eHumanista* 1, http://www.spanport.ucsb.edu/projects/ehumanista.

GERLI, E. Michael, 2002. 'The Greeks, the Romans, and the Ambiguity of Signs: *De doctrina Christiana*, the Fall, and the Hermaneutics of the *Libro de buen amor*', *Bulletin of Spanish Studies*, 79: 411–28.

GIBBS, Laura, ed., 2002. 'The Aesop Text Project', at http://casweb.cas.ou.edu/lgibbs/aesop/texts/AesopTexts.html (26 March 2002).

GIBSON, Walker, 1949–50. 'Authors, Speakers, Readers, and Mock Readers', *College English*, 11: 265–69.

GILMAN, Sander L., 1974. *The Parodic Sermon in European Perspective: Aspects of Liturgical Parody from the Middle Ages to the Twentieth Century*, Beiträge zur Literatur des XV bis XVIII Jahrhunderts, 6 (Wiesbaden: Steiner).

GILMAN, Stephen, 1983. 'Doña Endrina in Mourning', in *Homenaje a José Manuel Blecua ofrecido por sus discípulos, colegas y amigos* (Madrid: Gredos), pp. 247–55.

GILMORE, David D., 1998. *Carnival and Culture: Sex, Symbol, and Status in Spain* (New Haven: Yale UP).

GINZBURG, Carlo, 1989. *The Cheese and the Worms: The Cosmos of a Sixteenth-Century Miller* (New York: Dorset); original Italian edn 1976.

GITTES, Katherine S., 1990. *Framing the Canterbury Tales: Chaucer and the Medieval Frame Tale Tradition*, Contributions to the Study of World Literature, 41 (New York: Greenwood).

GLEICK, James, 1988. *Chaos: Making a New Science* (London: Cardinal).

GODZICH, Wlad, 1986. 'Foreword', in Paul de Man, *The Resistance to Theory*, Theory and History of Literature, 33 (Minneapolis: Univ. of Minnesota Press), pp. ix–xviii.

GOLDBERG, Harriet, 1983. 'The Dream Report as a Literary Device in Medieval Hispanic Literature', *Hispania* (USA), 66: 21–31.

——, 1984. 'The *Razón de amor* and *Los denuestos del agua y el vino* as a Unified Dream Report', *KRQ*, 31: 41–49.

——, 1986. 'The Proverb in *Cuaderna vía* Poetry: A Procedure for Identification', in *Hispanic Studies in Honor of Alan D. Deyermond: A North American Tribute*, ed. John S. Miletich (Madison: HSMS), pp. 119–33.

——, 1993. 'The Marqués de Santillana: Master Dreamer', in *The Dream and the Text: Essays on Literature and Language*, ed. Carol Schreier Rupprecht (Albany: SUNY Press), pp. 245–64.

GÓMEZ-BRAVO, Ana M., 1999. 'Cantar decires y decir canciones: género y lectura de la poesía cuatrocentista castellana', *BHS* (Liverpool), 76: 169–87.

GÓMEZ MORENO, Ángel, 1983–84. 'Una forma especial del tópico de modestia', *C*, 12: 71–83.

GÓMEZ REDONDO, Fernando, 1989. 'Terminología genérica en la *Estoria de España* alfonsí', *Revista de Literatura Medieval*, 1: 53–75.

GÓMEZ TRUEBA, Teresa, 1999. *El sueño literario en España: consolidación y desarrollo del género* (Madrid: Cátedra).

GONCHARENKO, S. F., 1988. *Stilisticheskiï analiz ispanskogo stijotvomogo teksta: osnovy teoriï ispanskoï poeticheskoï rechi* (Moscow: Vysshaïa Shkola).

GONZÁLEZ PALENCIA, Ángel, 1930. *Los mozárabes de Toledo en los siglos XII y XIII: volumen preliminar; estudios e indices* (Madrid: Instituto de Valencia).

GONZÁLVEZ RUIZ, Ramón, in press. 'La persona de Juan Ruiz y la fecha del *Libro de Buen Amor*', in Toro Ceballos in press.

GOYTISOLO, Juan, 2001. 'Contra una lectura anémica de nuestra literatura: a propósito de *Queer Iberia*', *ABC Cultural* (10 February): 7–10.

GRAVDAL, Kathryn, 1993. 'Poem Unlimited: Medieval Genre Theory and the Fabliau', *L'Esprit Créateur*, 33: 10–17.

GREEN, Otis H., 1963. 'Medieval Laughter: The *Book of Good Love*', in his *Spain and the Western Tradition: The Castilian Mind in Literature from 'El Cid' to Calderón* (Madison: Univ. of Wisconsin Press), I, 27–71.

GREENIA, George, ed., 1998. 'Forum: Letters and Responses on "Manuscript Culture in Medieval Spain"', *C*, 27.1: 123–247 (Contributors: Keith Busby, Daniel Eisenberg, Noel Fallows, Francisco J. Hernández, Jeremy Lawrance, Alberto and Fernando Montaner Frutos, René Pellen, Carlos Sáez, Michael Solomon, José Luis Suárez, Lillian von der Walde Moheno, Aengus Ward; Anthony J. Cardenas, John Dagenais, H. Salvador Martínez).

——, ed., 1999. 'Forum: Letters on "Manuscript Culture in Medieval Spain"', *C*, 27.2: 171–232 (Contributors: Leonardo Funes, Michel Garcia, José Manuel Lucía Megías, Germán Orduna, Pedro Sánchez-Prieto Borja).

GREGORY, Tullio, ed., 1985. *I sogni nel medioevo: Seminario Internazionale, Roma, 2–4 ottobre 1983* (Roma: Edizioni dell'Ateneo).

GREIMAS, Algirdas Julien, and Joseph COURTÉS, 1979. *Sémiotique: dictionnaire raisonné de la théorie du langage* (Paris: Hachette).

GUILLAUME DE LORRIS and JEAN DE MEUN, 1974. *Le Roman de la Rose*, ed. Daniel Poirion (Paris: Garnier-Flammarion).

GUMBRECHT, Hans Ulrich, 1973. 'Aspectos de una historia recepcional del *Libro de Buen Amor*', *Cuadernos Hispanoamericanos*, 280–82: 598–610.

GUREVICH, A. IA., 1988. *Medieval Popular Culture: Problems of Belief and Perception*, trans. János M. Bak and Paul A. Hollingsworth, Cambridge Studies in Oral and Literate Culture, 14 (Cambridge: UP). 1st Russian edn Moscow, 1981.

GYBBON-MONYPENNY, G. B., 1957. 'Autobiography in the *Libro de buen amor* in the Light of Some Literary Comparisons', *BHS*, 34: 63–78.

——, 1961. 'Lo que buen amor dize con rrazon te lo prueuo', *BHS*, 38: 13–24.

——, 1962. 'The Two Versions of the *Libro de buen amor*: The Extent and Nature of the Author's Revision', *BHS*, 39: 205–21.

——, 1965. 'The Spanish *Mester de Clerecía* and its Intended Public: Remarks Concerning the Validity as Evidence of Passages of Direct Address to the Audience', in *Medieval Miscellany Presented to Eugène Vinaver by Pupils, Colleagues and Friends*, ed. F. Whitehead et al. (Manchester: UP), pp. 230–44.

——, ed., 1970a. *'Libro de buen amor' Studies*, CT, A12 (London: Tamesis).

——, 1970b. '"Dixe la por te dar ensienpro": Juan Ruiz's Adaptation of the *Pamphilus*', in Gybbon-Monypenny 1970a: 123–47.

——, 1972. 'The Text of the *Libro de buen amor*: Recent Editions and their Critics', *BHS*, 49: 217–35.

——, 1973. 'Guillaume de Machaut's Erotic "Autobiography": Precedents for the Form of the *Voir-Dit*', in *Studies in Medieval Literature and Languages in Memory of Frederick Whitehead*, ed. W. Rothwell, W. R. J. Barron, David Blamires, and Lewis Thorpe (Manchester: UP), pp. 133–52.

HAMILTON, Rita, 1970. 'The Digression on Confession in the *Libro de buen amor*', in Gybbon-Monypenny 1970a: 149–57.

HANNING, Robert W., 1987. '"I Shal Finde it in a Maner Glose": Versions of Textual Harassment in Medieval Literature', in Finke & Shichtman 1987: 27–50.

HANSEN, Elaine Tuttle, 1992. *Chaucer and the Fictions of Gender* (Berkeley: Univ. of California Press).

HANSON, Kristin, 1995. 'Prosodic Constituents of Poetic Meter', *Proceedings of the West Coast Conference on Formal Linguistics*, 13: 62–77.

HARO CORTÉS, Marta, and José ARAGÜÉS ALDAZ, 1998. 'El *exemplum* medieval castellano: una aproximación bibliográfica', *Boletín Bibliográfico de la AHLM*, 12: 385–457.

HART, Thomas R., 1959. *La alegoría en el 'Libro de buen amor'* (Madrid: Revista de Occidente).

——, 1998. *'En maneira de proençal': The Medieval Galician-Portuguese Lyric*, PMHRS, 14 (London: Dept of Hispanic Studies, Queen Mary and Westfield College).

HARVEY, E. Ruth, 1975. *The Inward Wits: Psychological Theory in the Middle Ages and the Renaissance*, Warburg Institute Surveys, 6 (London: Warburg Institute).

HASAN-ROKEM, Galit, and David SHULMAN, 1996. *Untying the Knot: On Riddles and Other Enigmatic Modes* (Oxford: UP).

HAUG, Walter, 2000. *Der Tristanroman im Horizont der erotischen Diskurse des Mittelalters und der frühen Neuzeit* (Freiburg: Universitätsverlag).

HAWKINS, Harriet, 1995. *Strange Attractors: Literature, Culture and Chaos Theory* (London: Prentice Hall).

HAYLES, N. Katherine, 1990. *Chaos Bound: Orderly Disorder in Contemporary Literature and Science* (Ithaca: Cornell UP).

HAYWOOD, Louise M., 1997. 'Lyric in Medieval Secular Narrative', in *Proceedings of the Eighth Colloquium*, ed. Andrew M. Beresford and Alan Deyermond, PMHRS, 5 (London: Department of Hispanic Studies, Queen Mary and Westfield College), pp. 61–73.

——, 2000a. '"La escura selva": Allegory in Early Sentimental Romance', *HR*, 68: 415–28.

——, 2000b. 'Narrative and Structural Strategies in Early Spanish Sentimental Romance', *Fifteenth-Century Studies*, 25 (1999 [2000]): 11–24.

——, 2000c. 'Pasiones, Angustias y Dolores en el *Libro de buen amor*', in *Actas del VIII Congreso Internacional de la AHLM (Santander, 22–26 de septiembre, 1999)*, ed. Margarita Freixas and Silvia Iriso (Santander: Consejería de Cultura del Gobierno de Cantabria, Año Jubilar Lebaniego, and AHML), II, 935–44.

——, 2000d. 'Reading Song in Sentimental Romance: A Case Study of Juan de Flores's *Grimalte y Gradissa*', *C*, 29.1: 129–46.

——, in press. 'El cuerpo grotesco en el *Libro de buen amor* de Juan Ruiz', in Toro Ceballos, in press.

HEINRICHS, Wolfhart, 1997. 'Prosimetrical Genres in Classical Arabic Literature', in *Prosimetrum: Crosscultural Perspectives on Narrative in Prose and Verse*, ed. Joseph Harris and Karl Reichl (Cambridge: D. S. Brewer), pp. 249–75.

HEMPEL, Wido, 2000. 'Textinterne und paratextuelle Datierung von Dichtung: zwei Beispiele (*El Libro de buen amor*, *Les Contemplations*)', in *Zur Überlieferung, Kritik und Edition alter und neuerer Texte: Beiträge des Colloquiums zum 85. Geburtstag von Werner Schröder am 12. und 13. März 1999 in Mainz*, ed. Kurt Gärtner and Hans-Henrik Krummacher, Abhandlungen der Geistes- und sozialwissenschaftlichen Klasse, Jahrgang 2000.2 (Mainz: Akademie der Wissenschaften und der Literatur), pp. 223–41.

HERNÁNDEZ, Francisco J., 1984–85. 'The Venerable Juan Ruiz, Archpriest of Hita', *C*, 13: 10–22.

——, 1988. 'Juan Ruiz y otros arciprestes, de Hita y aledaños', *C*, 16.1: 1–31.

HERNANDO, Josep, 1995. *Llibres i lectors a la Barcelona del s. XIV*, Textos i Documents, 30–31 (Barcelona: Fundació Noguera).

HERRMANN, Léon, 1964. *Les Fables antiques de la broderie de Bayeux*, Coll. Latomus, 69 (Brussels: Latomus).

HERVIEUX, Léopold, ed., 1893–94. *Les Fabulistes latins, depuis le siècle d'Auguste jusqu'à la fin du Moyen Âge*, I & II: *Phèdre et ses anciens imitateurs directs et indirects* (Paris: Firmin-Didot); repr. Burt Franklin Research and Source Works, 99 (New York: Franklin, 1964).

HIEATT, Constance B., 1967. *The Realism of Dream Visions: The Poetic Exploitation of the Dream Experience in Chaucer and his Contemporaries*, De Proprietatibus Litterarum: Series Practica, 2 (The Hague: Mouton).

HINDLEY, A., 1967. 'Une pièce inéditée du seizième siècle: la farce de Ragot, Musarde et Babille', *Revue d'Histoire du Thêatre*, 19: 7–23.

HOLQUIST, Michael, 1990. *Dialogism: Bakhtin and his World* (London: Routledge).

HOLZINGER, Walter, 1980. 'Imagery, Iconography and Thematic Exposition in the *Libro de Buen Amor*', *Iberoromania*, ns, 6 (1977 [1980]): 1–34.

HOOK, David, 1993. 'Further Onomastic Footnotes for the *Libro de buen amor*', *FMLS*, 29: 156–64.

HUNT, Tony, 1991. *Teaching and Learning Latin in Thirteenth-Century England*, 3 vols (Cambridge: Brewer).

HUSTON, Nancy, 1980. *Dire et interdire: éléments de jurologie* (Paris: Payot).

INFANTES, Víctor, 1997. 'El *Catón* hispánico: versiones, ediciones y transmisiones', in Lucía Megías 1997: II, 839–46.

IRWIN, Robert, 1994. *The Arabian Nights: A Companion* (London: Allen Lane, The Penguin Press).

ISER, Wolfgang, 1974. *The Implied Reader: Patterns of Communication in Prose Fiction from Bunyan to Beckett* (Baltimore: Johns Hopkins UP).

——, 1978. *The Act of Reading: A Theory of Aesthetic Response* (Baltimore: Johns Hopkins UP).

IVY, G. S., 1958. 'The Bibliography of the Manuscript Book', in *The English Library Before 1700: Studies in its History*, ed. Francis Wormald and C. E. Wright (London: Athlone Press), pp. 32–65.

JACOBS, Joseph, 1912. 'Fable', in *Encyclopaedia of Religion and Ethics*, ed. James Hastings (Edinburgh: Clark), V, 676–78.

JAUSS, Hans Robert, 1970a. *Literaturgeschichte als Provokation* (Frankfurt: Suhrkamp).

——, 1970b. 'Littérature médiévale et théorie des genres', *Poétique*, 1: 79–101.

——, 1977. 'Alterität und Modernität der mittelalterlichen Literatur', in his *Alterität und Modernität der mittelalterlichen Literatur: Gesammelte Aufsätze 1956–1976* (Munich: Fink), pp. 9–47.

——, 1982. 'Literary History as a Challenge to Literary Theory', in his *Toward an Aesthetic of Reception*, trans. Timothy Bahti, Theory and History of Literature, 2 (Brighton: Harvester), pp. 3–45.

JENARO-MACLENNAN, L., 1974–79. 'Los presupuestos intelectuales del prólogo al *Libro de buen amor*', *AEM*, 9: 151–86.

——, 1988. 'Sobre el texto del *Pamphilus* en el *Libro de buen amor*', *RFE*, 68: 143–51.

JOHNSON, Leonard W., 1990. *Poets as Players: Theme and Variation in Late Medieval French Poetry* (Stanford: UP).

JOSET, Jacques, 1970. 'Le *Libro de buen amor* de Juan Ruiz, Archiprêtre de Hita: essai de lecture critique', unpubl. doctoral thesis, Univ. of Liège.

——, 1971. 'Le "bon amors" occitan et le "buen amor" de Jean Ruiz, Arcipreste de Hita (réflexions sur le destin d'une expression "courtoise")', in *Actes du Seizième Congrès International de Langue et Littérature d'Oc et d'Études Franco-Provençales, Montpellier, 1970* (Montpellier: Centre d'Études Occitanes), II, 349–68.

——, 1988. *Nuevas investigaciones sobre el 'Libro de buen amor'* (Madrid: Cátedra).

——, 1990. '"Un omne grande, fermoso, mesurado, a mí vino" (*LBA*, 181c)', *Dicenda*, 6 (1987 [1990]: *Arcadia: estudios y textos dedicados a Francisco López Estrada*, I): 155–63. (Already revised in Joset 1988: 115–26.)

——, 1995a. 'Sueños y visiones medievales: razones de sinrazones', *Atalaya*, 6 (*Les Transgressions de l'Ordre au Moyen Âge*): 51–70.

——, 1995b. 'Cuatro sueños más en la literatura medieval española (Berceo, un "sueño" anónimo del siglo XVI, el Arcipreste de Talavera, doña Leonor López de Córdoba)', in *Medioevo y literatura: Actas del V Congreso de la AHLM (Granada, 27 septiembre-1 octubre 1993)*, ed. Juan Paredes (Granada: Univ.), II, 499–507.

JUAN MANUEL, Don, 1991. *El libro de los estados*, ed. Ian R. Macpherson and Robert Brian Tate, CCa, 192 (Madrid: Castalia).

——, 1994. *El conde Lucanor*, ed. Guillermo Serés, introd. Germán Orduna, BC, 6 (Barcelona: Crítica).

JURADO, José, 1988. '*Libro de Buen Amor*, 881c: la alusión a la *cocatriz*', *BRAE*, 68: 433–54.

JUSTINIAN, 1478? *Digestum vetus* (Venice: Jenson) (British Library, IC.19747).

KANE, Elisha K., 1930. 'The Personal Appearance of Juan Ruiz', *MLN*, 45: 103–09.

KANTOR, Sofía, 1988. *El 'Libro de Sindbād': variaciones en torno al eje temático 'engaño-error'*, Anejos del *BRAE*, 42 (Madrid: RAE).

KEIDEL, George C., 1901. 'Notes on Æsopic Fable Literature in Spain and Portugal during the Middle Ages', *ZRP*, 25: 721–30.

KELLERMANN, Wilhelm, 1951. 'Zur Charakteristik des *Libro del Arcipreste de Hita*', *ZRP*, 67: 225–54.

KELLY, Henry Ansgar, 1984. *Canon Law and the Archpriest of Hita*, Medieval and Renaissance Texts and Studies, 27 (Binghamton: Center for Medieval and Early Renaissance Studies).

——, 1985–86. 'Archpriests, Apostles, and Episcopal Epistles', *C*, 14: 1–5.

——, 1988. 'Juan Ruiz and Archpriests: Novel Reports', *C*, 16.2: 32–54.

KER, W. P., 1898. 'Analogies between English and Spanish Verse (*Arte mayor*)', *Transactions of the Philological Society* (1899–1902): 113–28.

KERKHOF, Maxim P. A. M., 1993. 'Las filigranas del manuscrito *S* del *Libro de Buen Amor*', *In*, 13: 15–20.

KIECKHEFER, Richard, 1997. *Forbidden Rites: A Necromancer's Manual of the Fifteenth Century* (Stroud, Glos.: Sutton).

KINKADE, Richard P., 1970. '"Intellectum tibi dabo . . . ": The Function of Free Will in the *Libro de buen amor*', *BHS*, 47: 296–315.

——, 1973. '*Ioculatores Dei*: el *Libro de Buen Amor* y la rivalidad entre juglares y predicadores', in Criado de Val 1973a: 115–28.

——, 1996. 'A Thirteenth-Century Precursor of the *Libro de Buen Amor*: The *Art d'Amors*', *C*: 24.2: 123–39.

KIRBY, Steven D., 1986. 'Juan Ruiz's *Serranas*: The Archpriest-Pilgrim and Medieval Wild Women', in *Hispanic Studies in Honor of Alan D. Deyermond: A North American Tribute*, ed. John S. Miletich (Madison: HSMS), pp. 151–69.

KOCH, Friedrich Georg, 1957. 'Virgil im Korbe', in *Festschrift für Erich Meyer zum sechzigsten Geburtstag 29. oktober 1957: Studien zu Werken in den Sammlungen des Museums für Kunst und Gewerbe* (Hamburg: [no publisher's details]), pp. 105–09.

KOLVE, V. A., 1984. *Chaucer and the Imagery of Narrative: The First Five Canterbury Tales* (Stanford: UP).

KOOPMANS, Jelle, ed., 1984. *Quatre sermons joyeux* (Geneva: Droz).

——, 1985. 'Sermon joyeux et théâtre profane (XVᵉᵐᵉ et XVIᵉᵐᵉ siécles)', *Rapports: Het Franske Boek*, 55: 97–110.

KOOPMANS, Jelle, and Paul VERHUEYCK, 1987. *Sermon joyeux et truanderie: Villon, Nemo, Ulespiègle*, Faux Titre, 29 (Amsterdam: Rodopi).

KRISTEVA, Julia, 1969. *Semiotikè: recherches pour une sémanalyse* (Paris: Seuil).

KRUGER, Steven F., 1992. *Dreaming in the Middle Ages*, Cambridge Studies in Medieval Literature, 14 (Cambridge: UP).

LABOV, William, 1972. 'Rules for Ritual Insults', in *Studies in Social Interaction*, ed. David Sudnow (New York: Free Press), pp. 120–69.

LABRADOR HERRAIZ, José J., and Ralph A. DIFRANCO, 1989. 'Otra alusión al *Libro de Buen Amor* en el *Cancionero* de Pedro de Rojas (1582), BNM Ms. 3924', in *Imago Hispaniae: lengua, literatura, historia y fisonomía del español (Actas del Simposio-homenaje a Manuel Criado de Val en Pastrana, Guadalajara, del 7 al 10 julio 1987)*, ed. Ángel Montero Herreros, Ciriaco Morón Arroyo, and José Carlos de Torres, Problemata Literaria, 3 (Cassel: Reichenberger), pp. 401–07.

LACARRA, María Jesús, 2000. 'Tipos y motivos folclóricos en la literatura medieval española: "La disputa de los griegos y los romanos" entre la tradición oral y la escrita', in *Actas del VIII Congreso Internacional de la AHLM (Santander, 22–26 de septiembre, 1999)*, ed. Margarita Freixas and Silvia Iriso (Santander: Consejería de Cultura del Gobierno de Cantabria, Año Jubilar Lebaniego & AHLM), II, 1039–50.

——, 2002. 'El *Libro de buen amor*, ejemplario de fábulas a lo profano', *Interletras* 4:4, at http://fyl.unizar.es/gcorona/critica4.htm, 26 March 2002.

LANOUE, Daniel G., 1980–81. 'Divine and Carnal Music in the *Libro de buen amor*', *JHP*, 5: 85–100.

LAURENCE, Kemlin M., 1970. 'The Battle of Don Carnal and Doña Cuaresma in the Light of Medieval Tradition', in Gybbon-Monypenny 1970a: 159–76.

LAVAUD, René, and Georges MACHICOT, ed. and trans., 1950. *Boecis: poème sur Boèce (fragment): le plus ancien texte littéraire occitan* (Toulouse: Institut d'Études Occitanes).

LAWRANCE, Jeremy N. H., 1984. 'The Audience of the *Libro de buen amor*', *CL*, 36: 220–37.

——, 1985. 'The Spread of Lay Literacy in Late Medieval Castile', *BHS*, 62: 79–94.

——, 1998. Letter in Greenia 1998: 149–61.

——, 1997. 'The Rubrics in MS *S* of the *Libro de buen amor*', in *The Medieval Mind: Hispanic Studies in Honour of Alan Deyermond*, ed. Ian Macpherson and Ralph Penny, CT, A170 (London: Tamesis), pp. 223–52.

LE GENTIL, Pierre, 1949. *La Poésie lyrique espagnole et portugaise à la fin du Moyen Âge*: I, *Les Thèmes et les genres* (Rennes: Plihon).

LE GOFF, Jacques, 1977. 'Les rêves dans la culture et la psychologie collective de l'Occident médiéval', in his *Pour un autre Moyen Âge: temps, travail et culture en Occident: 18 essais*, Collection Tel, 181 (Paris: Gallimard), pp. 299–306. 1ˢᵗ publ. in *Scolies*, 1 (1971): 123–30.

LECOY, Félix, 1938. *Recherches sur le 'Libro de Buen Amor' de Juan Ruiz, Archiprêtre de Hita* (Paris: E. Droz); 2nd edn, A. D. Deyermond (Farnborough, Hants: Gregg International, 1974).

LECOY, Félix, ed., 1965. Guillaume de Lorris and Jean de Meun, *Le Roman de la Rose*, I, Classiques Français du Moyen Âge, 92 (Paris: Honoré Champion).

LEES, Clare A., with Thelma FENSTER and Jo Ann MCNAMARA, ed., 1994. *Medieval Masculinities: Regarding Men in the Middle Ages*, Medieval Culture, 7 (Minneapolis: University of Minnesota Press).

LEONETTI, Pasquale, 1934. *Storia della tecnica del verso italiano*, II.1: *La tecnica del verso dialettale popolaresco dei primordi* (Naples: Morano).

LERER, Seth, ed., 1996. *Literary History and the Challenge of Philology: The Legacy of Erich Auerbach* (Stanford: UP).

LEWIS, C. S., 1936. *The Allegory of Love: A Study in Medieval Tradition* (London: Oxford UP).

——, 1964. *The Discarded Image: An Introduction to Medieval and Renaissance Literature* (Cambridge: UP).

LIBERMAN, Mark, and Alan PRINCE, 1977. 'On Stress and Linguistic Rhythm', *Linguistic Inquiry*, 8: 249–336.

LIDA (DE MALKIEL), María Rosa, 1940. 'Notas para la interpretación, influencia, fuentes y texto del *Libro de buen amor*', *Revista de Filología Hispánica*, 2: 105–50. Repr. in Lida de Malkiel 1973: 153–202.

——, 1950–51. 'Tres notas sobre don Juan Manuel', *RPh*, 4: 155–94.

——, 1959. 'Nuevas notas para la interpretación del *Libro de buen amor*', *NRFH*, 13: 17–82.

——, 1960–61. Review of Hart 1959, *RPh*, 14: 340–43.

——, 1961. *Two Spanish Masterpieces: The 'Book of Good Love' and 'The Celestina'*, Illinois Studies in Language and Literature, 49 (Urbana: Univ. of Illinois Press).

——, 1962. *La originalidad artística de 'La Celestina'* (Buenos Aires: Eudeba).

——, 1966. *Dos obras maestras españolas: el 'Libro de buen amor' y 'La Celestina'*, (Buenos Aires: Eudeba).

——, 1973. *Juan Ruiz: selección del 'Libro de Buen Amor' y estudios críticos*, ed. Yakov Malkiel (Buenos Aires: Eudeba).

LINEHAN, Peter, 1971. *The Spanish Church and the Papacy in the Thirteenth Century*, Cambridge Studies in Medieval Life and Thought, 3rd series, 4 (Cambridge: UP).

——, 1986–87. 'The Archpriest of Hita and Canon Law', *C*, 15: 120–26.

——, 1997. *The Ladies of Zamora* (Manchester: UP).

LÓPEZ-BARALT, Luce, 1992. *Islam in Spanish Literature from the Middle Ages to the Present*, trans. Andrew Hurley (Leiden: E. J. Brill; San Juan: Editorial de la Univ. de Puerto Rico).

LÓPEZ ESTRADA, Francisco, 1982. *Panorama crítico sobre el 'Poema del Cid'*, Literatura y Sociedad, 30 (Madrid: Castalia).

LOTZ, John, 1960. 'Metric Typology', in *Style and Language*, ed. Thomas A. Sebeok (Boston: MIT Press and Wiley), pp. 135–48.

LUCÍA MEGÍAS, José Manuel, ed., 1997. *Actas del VI Congreso Internacional de la AHLM (Alcalá de Henares, 12–16 de septiembre de 1995)*, 2 vols (Alcalá de Henares: Univ. de Alcalá).

LUKÁCS, György, 1971. *The Theory of the Novel: A Historico-Philosophical Essay in the Forms of Great Epic Literature*, trans. Anna Bostock (Cambridge, MA: MIT Press). First publ. 1922.

LY, Nadine, 1993. 'L'art de la *dispositio* dans le *Libro de buen amor* de Juan Ruiz, Archiprêtre de Hita', *Bulletin Hispanique*, 95: 379–452.

LYNCH, Kathryn, 1988. *The High Medieval Dream Vision: Poetry, Philosophy, and Literary Form* (Stanford: UP).

MACCHI, Giuliano, 1968. 'La tradizione manoscritta del *Libro de Buen Amor*: a proposito di recenti edizioni ruiziane', *Cultura Neolatina*, 28: 264–98.

MCDOWELL, John H., 1985. 'Verbal Duelling', in *Handbook of Discourse Analysis*, III: *Discourse and Dialogue*, ed. Teun A. Van Dijk (New York: Academic Press), pp. 203–11.

MCGRADY, Donald, 1984. 'Notas sobre el enigma erótico, con especial referencia a los *Cuarenta enigmas en lengua española*', *Criticón*, 27: 71–108.

MCKEON, Michael, 1987. *The Origins of the English Novel (1600–1740)* (Baltimore: Johns Hopkins UP).

MADERO, Marta, 1992. *Manos violentas, palabras vedadas: la injuria en Castilla y León (siglos XIII–XV)* (Madrid: Taurus).

MALDONADO DE GUEVARA, F., 1965. 'Knittelvers "verso nudoso"', *RFE*, 48: 34–59.

MALER, Bertil, ed., 1956–64. *Orto do Esposo: texto inédito do fim do século XIV ou começo do XV*, 3 vols (Rio de Janeiro: Ministério da Educação e Cultura, Instituto Nacional do Livro), I and II; Acta Univ. Stolkholmiensis, Romanica Stolkholmiensia, 1 (Stockholm: Almquist & Wiksell), III.

MANDELBROT, Benoit B., 1977. *Fractals: Form, Chance, and Dimension* (San Francisco: Freeman).

MANNING, Stephen, 1960. 'The Nun's Priest's Morality and the Medieval Attitude toward Fables', *Journal of English and Germanic Philology*, 59: 403–16.

MARINO, Nancy F., 1985–86. 'The *Vaquera de la Finojosa*: Was she a Vision?', *Romance Notes*, 26: 261–68.

MÁRQUEZ VILLANUEVA, F., 1965. 'El buen amor', *Revista de Occidente*, 9: 269–91.

——, 1973. 'Nuevos arabismos en un pasaje del *Libro de Buen Amor* (941ab)', in Criado de Val 1973a: 202–07.

——, 1990. 'El carnaval de Juan Ruiz', *Dicenda: Cuadernos de Filología Hispánica*, 6 (1987 [1990]: *Arcadia: Homenaje a Francisco López Estrada*): 177–88.

——, 1993. *Orígenes y sociología del tema celestinesco* (Barcelona: Anthropos).

——, 2002. 'La nueva biografía de Juan Ruiz', in *Morada de la palabra: homenaje a Luce y Mercedes López-Baralt*, ed. William Mejías López (San Juan: Editorial de la Univ. de Puerto Rico), I, 33–51.

MARTÍN MARTÍN, José L., 1996. 'La iglesia de frontera y el Arcipreste de Hita', in Toro Ceballos and Rodríguez Molina 1996: 383–403.

MARTÍNEZ, H. Salvador, 1975. *El 'Poema de Almería' y la épica románica*, BRH, 2.219 (Madrid: Gredos).

——, ed., 1998. 'Critical Cluster: Manuscript Culture in Medieval Spain', *C*, 26.2: 131–94.

MARTÍNEZ RUIZ, Juan, 1973. 'La tradición hispano-árabe en el *Libro de Buen Amor*', in Criado de Val 1973a: 187–201.

MARTÍNEZ TORREJÓN, J. M., 1978. 'El *Libro de Buen Amor* y un manual de cortesía: el *Facetus* "Moribus et vita"', *Anuario de Letras*, 13: 184–200.

——, 1993. 'Lectura retórica de la "Pelea" entre Don Amor y el Arcipreste (*Libro de buen amor*, cs.181–575)', in *Literatura Medieval: Actas do IV Congresso da Associação Hispânica de Literatura Medieval (Lisboa, 1–5 Outubro 1991)*, ed. Aires A. Nascimento and Cristina Almeida Ribeiro (Lisbon: Edições Cosmos), III, 197–201.

MASSIE, J., 1900. 'Fable', in *A Dictionary of the Bible*, ed. James Hastings (Edinburgh: Clark), I, 825.

MATEO GÓMEZ, Isabel, 1979. *Temas profanos en la escultura gótica española: las sillerías de coro* (Madrid: Instituto Diego Velázquez, CSIC).

MEDCALF, Stephen, 1981. 'On Reading Books from a Half-Alien Culture', in his ed. *The Later Middle Ages* (London: Methuen), pp. 1–55.

MEHLMAN, Jeffrey, 1977. *Revolution and Repetition: Marx / Hugo / Balzac* (Berkeley: Univ. of California Press).

Memorabilia: Boletín de Literatura Sapiencial, at http://parnaseo.uv.es/ Memorabilia.htm, 26 March 2002.

MENÉNDEZ PIDAL, Ramón, ed., 1908–11. *Cantar de Mio Cid: texto, gramática y vocabulario*, 3 vols (Madrid: Bailly-Baillière).

——, 1941. 'Notas al libro del Arcipreste de Hita, I: Título que el Arcipreste de Hita dió al libro de sus poesías', 'II: Un copista ilustre del *Libro de buen amor* y dos redacciones de esta obra', in his *Poesía árabe y poesía española, con otros estudios de literatura medieval*, Colección Austral, 190 (Madrid: Espasa-Calpe), pp. 117–28. Repr. from *Revista de Archivos, Bibliotecas y Museos*, 2 (1898): 106–09, and *Romania*, 30 (1901): 434–40.

——, 1957. *Poesía juglaresca y orígenes de las literaturas románicas*: *problemas de historia literaria y cultural*, Biblioteca de Cuestiones Actuales, 6 (Madrid: Instituto de Estudios Políticos); 2nd edn of his *Poesía juglaresca y juglares: aspectos de la historia literaria y cultural de España*, Publicaciones de la *RFE*, 7 (Madrid: Centro de Estudios Históricos, 1924).

MENÉNDEZ Y PELAYO, Marcelino, 1923. *Antología de poetas líricos castellanos desde la formación del idioma hasta nuestros días*, Biblioteca Clásica, 160 (Madrid: Librería de Perlados, Paez), III.

MENOCAL, María Rosa, 1987. *The Arabic Role in Medieval Literary History: A Forgotten Heritage* (Philadelphia: Univ. of Pennsylvania Press).

MICHAEL, Ian, 1970. 'The Function of the Popular Tale in the *Libro de buen amor*', in Gybbon-Monypenny 1970a: 177–218.

——, 1985–86. 'Epic to Romance to Novel: Problems of Genre Identification', *Bulletin of the John Rylands Library*, 68: 498–527.

——, ed., 1987. *Poema de Mio Cid*, CCa, 75, 2nd edn (Madrid: Castalia).

——, in press. 'The Survival of Mozarabic Culture and its Literary Products: *El libro del cavallero Zifar* and *El lubro de buen amor*', *RPh*.

MICHALSKI, André Stanislaw, 1964. 'Description in Mediaeval Spanish Poetry', Ph.D. dissertation (Princeton Univ.); abstract in *Dissertation Abstracts*, 25 (1964–65): 5933.

——, 1973. 'La parodia hagiográfica y el dualismo Eros-Thanatos en el *Libro de Buen Amor*', in Criado de Val 1973a: 57–77.

MIGNANI, R., 1969. 'Le due redazioni del *Libro de Buen Amor*', *Quaderni Ibero-Americani*, 5, fasc. 37: 1–7.

MILLARES CARLO, Agustín, 1923. 'La biblioteca de Gonzalo Argote de Molina', *RFE*, 10: 137–52.

MINNIS, A. J., and A. B. SCOTT, with David WALLACE, 1988. *Medieval Literary Theory and Criticism, c. 1100–c. 1375: The Commentary Tradition* (Oxford: Clarendon Press).

MINTZ, Jerome R., 1997. *Carnival Song and Society: Gossip, Sexuality, and Creativity in Andalusia* (Oxford: Berg).

MOFFATT, Lucius Gaston, 1956. 'An Evaluation of the Portuguese Fragments of the *Libro de Buen Amor*', *Symposium*, 10: 107–11.

——, 1957. 'Alvar Gómez de Castro's Verses from the *Libro de buen amor*', *HR*, 25: 247–51.

MOFFATT, Lucius Gaston, 1960. 'The Evidence of Early Mentions of the Archpriest of Hita or of his Work', *MLN*, 75: 33–44.

MONEDERO, Carmen, ed., 1987. *Libro de Apolonio*, CCa, 157 (Madrid: Castalia).

MONFRIN, Jacques, 1964. 'La bibliothèque Sánchez Muñoz et les inventaires de la bibliothèque pontificale à Peñíscola', in *Studi di bibliografia e di storia in onore di Tammaro de Marinis*, 4 vols (The Vatican: Biblioteca Apostolica Vaticana), III, 229–69.

MONTANER (FRUTOS), Alberto, ed., 1993. *Cantar de Mio Cid*, introd. Francisco Rico, BC, 1 (Barcelona: Crítica).

——, & Fernando MONTANER FRUTOS, 1998. Letter in Greenia 1998: 162–82.

MORALES FAEDO, Mayuli, 1997. 'El "buen amor" en Juan Ruiz a la luz del plurilingüismo bajtiniano', *Medievalia,* 25: 52–62.

MOREL-FATIO, A., 1886. 'Mélanges de littérature catalane, II: *Le Livre de courtoisie*', *Romania*, 15: 192–235.

MORLEY, S. Griswold, 1933. 'Recent Theories about the Meter of the *Cid*', *PMLA*, 48: 965–80.

MORREALE, Margherita, 1963. 'Apuntes para un comentario literal del *Libro de buen amor*', *BRAE,* 43: 249–371.

——, 1967. 'Más apuntes para un comentario literal del *Libro de buen amor*, con otras observaciones al margen de la reciente edición de G. Chiarini', *BRAE*, 47: 213–86 & 417–97.

——, 1969–71. 'Más apuntes para un comentario literal del *Libro de buen amor*, sugeridos por la edición de Joan Corominas', *HR*, 37 (1969): 131–63, and 39 (1971): 271–313.

——, 1975a. ' "Falló çafir golpado', 1387c: análisis de la adaptación de una fábula esópica en el *Libro de buen amor*', in *Studia hispanica in honorem R. Lapesa* (Madrid: Gredos and Cátedra-Seminario Menéndez Pidal), III, 369–74.

——, 1975b. 'Una lectura de las "pasiones" de Juan Ruiz (*Libro de buen amor*, 1043–1066)', *BRAE*, 55: 331–81.

——, 1979. 'Sobre la reciente edición del *LBA* por Jacques Joset para Clásicos Castalia', *Thesaurus*, 34: 1–44.

——, 1983–84. 'Los "gozos" de la Virgen en el *Libro* de Juan Ruiz, I y II', *RFE*, 63: 223–90 and 64: 1–69.

——, 1987. 'La fábula de las liebres en el *Libro* del Arcipreste de Hita', *MR*, 12: 403–42.

——, 1989–90. 'La fábula "del alano que llevava la pieça de carne en la boca" en el *Libro* del Arcipreste: lectura sincrónica y diacrónica contra el fondo en la tradición latina', *Cahiers de Linguistique Hispanique Médiévale*, 14–15: 207–33.

——, 1990. ' "Enxiemplo de la raposa e del cuervo" o "la zorra y la corneja" en el *Libro* del Arcipreste de Hita (1437–1443)', *RLM*, 2: 49–83.

——, 1991. 'La fábula del caballo y el asno en el *Libro* del Arcipreste de Hita', *RFE*, 71: 23–78.

MORREALE, Margherita, 1992. 'La fábula del asno y el blanchete en el *Libro* del Arcipreste (1401–1408)', in *Scripta philologica in honorem Juan M. Lope Blanch* (Mexico City: UNAM), III, 351–84.

——, 2001. 'Importancia relativa del estudio de la lengua y de la ecdótica en la lectura del *Libro* de Juan Ruiz', in *Los orígenes del español y los grandes textos medievales Mio Cid, Buen Amor y Celestina*, ed. Manuel Criado de Val, Biblioteca de Filología Hispánica, 26 (Madrid: CSIC), pp. 191–205.

MORREALE, Margherita, 2002. 'La fábula en la Edad Media: el *Libro* de Juan Ruiz como representante castellano del *Isopete*', in *'Y así dijo la zorra': la tradición fabulística en los pueblos del Mediterráneo*, ed. A. Pérez Jiménez and G. Cruz Andreotti (Madrid: Ediciones Clásicas; Málaga: Charta Antiqua), pp. 209–38.

MORROS, Bienvenido, 2003. 'La comedia elegíaca y el *Libro de Buen Amor*', *Troianalexandrina*, 3: 77–121.

——, in press. 'La figura del arçipreste de Hita', in Toro Ceballos, in press.

MORSON, Gary Saul, and Caryl EMERSON, 1990. *Mikhail Bakhtin: Creation of a Prosaics* (Stanford: UP).

MUÑOZ GARRIGÓS, José, 1977. 'El manuscrito *T* del *Libro de Buen Amor*: estudio fonético-evolutivo', *Anales de la Universidad de Murcia*, 35: 147–225.

MURILLO RUBIERA, Fernando, 1973. 'Jueces, escribanos y letrados en el *Libro de Buen Amor*', in Criado de Val 1973a: 416–21.

MURRAY, Stephen, 1979. 'The Art of Gay Insulting', *Anthropological Linguistics*, 21: 211–23.

MYERS, Oliver T., 1972. 'Symmetry of Form in the *Libro de buen amor*', *Philological Quarterly*, 51: 74–84.

NAGY, Gregory, 1996. *Poetry as Performance: Homer and Beyond* (Cambridge: UP).

NAVARRO PEIRÓ, Angeles, trans., 1988. *Los cuentos de Sendebar* (Sabadell: Ausa).

NAVARRO (TOMÁS), Tomás, 1956. *Métrica española* (Madrid: Guadarrama).

——, 1974. *Métrica española*, 4th ed. (Madrid: Guadarrama).

NEPAULSINGH, Colbert I., 1974. 'The Rhetorical Structure of the Prologues to the *Libro de buen amor* and the *Celestina*', *BHS*, 51: 325–45.

——, 1977. 'The Structure of the *Libro de Buen Amor*', *Neophilologus*, 61: 58–73.

——, 1986. *Towards a History of Literary Composition in Medieval Spain*, Univ. of Toronto Romance Series, 54 (Toronto: Univ. of Toronto Press).

NICHOLS, Stephen G., ed., 1990. *Sp*, 65.1 (*The New Philology*).

NORTON-SMITH, John, ed., 1971. James I of Scotland, *The Kingis Quair* (Oxford: Clarendon Press).

NYKROG, Per, 1973. *Les Fabliaux*, Publications Romanes et Françaises, 123 (Geneva: Droz).

O'KANE, Eleanor S., 1950. 'On the Names of the *Refrán*', *HR*, 18: 1–14.

——, 1959. *Refranes y frases proverbiales españolas de la Edad Media*, Anejos del *BRAE*, 2 (Madrid: RAE).

OCTAVIO DE TOLEDO, José M., 1878. 'Vision de Filiberto', *ZRP*, 2: 40–69.

OLIVER ASÍN, Jaime, 1956. 'La expresión *ala ud* en el *Libro de Buen Amor*', *Al-Andalus*, 21: 212–14.

ONG, Walter J., 1975. 'The Writer's Audience Is Always a Fiction', *PMLA*, 90: 9–21.

——, 1981. *Fighting for Life: Contest, Sexuality, and Consciousness* (Ithaca: Cornell UP).

ORDUNA, Germán, 1977. 'El *exemplo* en la obra literaria de don Juan Manuel', in *Juan Manuel Studies*, ed. Ian Macpherson, CT, A60 (London: Tamesis), pp. 119–42.

ORDUNA, Germán, ed., 1981. Pero López de Ayala, *Rimado de Palacio*, Collani di Testi Ispanici: Testi Critici, 1, 2 vols (Pisa: Giardini).

——, 1986. 'El concepto de enxienplo en la obra del canciller Ayala', in *Philologica hispaniensia in honorem Manuel Alvar*: III, *Literatura* (Madrid: Gredos), pp. 305–08.

——, 1988. 'El *libro de buen amor* y el libro del arcipreste', *C*, 17.1: 1–7.

——, 1991. 'Lectura del "buen amor" ', *Incipit*, 11: 11–22.

OSGOOD, Charles G., 1930. *Boccaccio on Poetry: Being the Preface to the Fourteenth and Fifteenth Books of 'Genealogia deorum gentilium' in an English Verse Translation* (Princeton: UP).

PAIEWONSKY CONDE, Edgar, 1972. 'Polarización erótica medieval y estructura del *Libro de buen amor*', *Bulletin Hispanique*, 74: 331–52.

PALLEY, Julian, 1983. *The Ambiguous Mirror: Dreams in Spanish Literature*, Albatros Hispanófila, 27 (Valencia: Albatros; Chapel Hill: Hispanófila).

PAPIAS, 1496. *Vocabularium* (Venice: Philippus Pincius) (British Library, IB.23664).

PARIS, Gaston, ed., 1933. *La Vie de Sainte Alexis, poème du XIe siècle: texte critique*, 7th ed. (Paris: Champion).

PARKER, A. A., 1976. 'The Parable of the Greeks and the Romans in the *Libro de Buen Amor*', in *Medieval Hispanic Studies Presented to Rita Hamilton*, ed. A. D. Deyermond, CT, A42 (London: Tamesis), pp. 139–47.

PARKER, Margaret, 1991. 'The Text as Mediator: Ovid and Juan Ruiz', *Comparative Literature Studies*, 28: 341–55.

PARKES, M. B., 1993. *Pause and Effect: An Introduction to the History of Punctuation in the West* (Berkeley: Univ. of California Press).

PARKINSON, Stephen, in press. 'Concurrent Patterns of Verse Design in the Galician-Portuguese Lyric', in *Proceedings of the Thirteenth Colloquium*, ed. Alan Deyermond, PMHRS (London: Dept of Hispanic Studies, Queen Mary, Univ. of London).

PAYNE, F. Anne, 1981. *Chaucer and Menippean Satire* (Madison: Univ. of Wisconsin Press).

PEARSALL, Derek, 1984. 'Texts, Textual Criticism, and Fifteenth-Century Manuscript Production', in *Fifteenth-Century Studies: Recent Essays*, ed. Robert F. Yeager (New Haven: Yale UP), pp. 121–36.

PEDEN, Alison M., 1985. 'Macrobius and Mediaeval Dream Literature', *Medium Ævum*, 54: 74–86.

PELLEN, René, 1985–86. 'Le modèle du vers épique espagnol à partir de la formule cidienne ('el que en buena hora . . . '): exploitation des concordances pour l'analyse des structures textuelles', *Cahiers de Linguistique Hispanique Médiévale*, 10: 5–37 and 11: 5–132.

PENNINGTON, Ken, 2002. 'Innocent III and the *Ius commune*', at http://classes.maxwell. syr.edu/his311/Maxims1.html, 26 March 2002.

PERALES DE LA CAL, Ramón, 1973. 'Organografía medieval en la obra del Arcipreste', in Criado de Val 1973a: 398–406.

PÉREZ FIRMAT, Gustavo, 1986. *Literature and Liminality: Festive Readings in the Hispanic Tradition* (Durham, NC: Duke UP).

PÉREZ LÓPEZ, José Luis, 2002. 'La fecha del *Libro de buen* amor', *In*, 22: 105–42.

——, in press. 'Investigaciones sobre el *Libro de buen amor* en el archivo y biblioteca de la catedral de Toledo', in Toro Ceballos in press.

PERRY, B. E., 1940. 'The Origins of the *Epimythium*', *Transactions of the American Philological Society*, 71: 391–419.

PHILLIPS, Gail, 1983. *The Imagery of the Libro de 'Buen Amor'*, SpS, 9 (Madison: HSMS).

PICCUS, Jules, 1965–66. 'Refranes y frases proverbiales el en *Libro del Cavallero Zifar*', *NRFH*, 18: 1–24.

PICKENS, Rupert T., ed., 1978. *The Songs of Jaufré Rudel*, Studies and Texts, 41 (Toronto: Pontifical Institute of Mediaeval Studies).

PICONE, Michelangelo, 1988. 'Tre tipi di cornice novellistica: modelli orientali e tradizione narrativa medievale', *Filologia e Critica*, 13: 3–26.

PIERRUGUES, Pierre, 1908. *Glossarium eroticum linguae Latinae* (Berlin: Herman Barsdorf).

PIETSCH, Karl, 1903. 'Preliminary Notes on Two Old Spanish Versions of the *Disticha Catonis*', *Decennial Publications of the University of Chicago*, 1st ser., 7: 193–221.

PIGHI, Giovanni Battista, 1970. *Studi di ritmica e metrica* (Torino: Bottega d'Erasmo).

POLÍN, Ricardo, 1994. *A poesía lírica galego-castelá, 1350–1450*, Biblioteca de Divulgación, Serie Galicia, 16 (Santiago de Compostela: Univ.).

PRIETO, Antonio, 1980. 'Con la titulación del *Libro* del Arcipreste de Hita', in his *Coherencia y relevancia textual: de Berceo a Baroja*, Estudios, 9 (Madrid: Alhambra), pp. 77–114.

PURCZINSKY, Julius, 1965–66. 'Germanic Influence in the *Saint Eulalia*', *RPh*, 19: 271–75.

PUYMAIGRE, Théodore Joseph Boudet, comte de, 1861–62. *Les Vieux Auteurs castillans*, 2 vols (Paris: Didier; Metz: Rousseau-Pallez).

PUYOL Y ALONSO, Julio, 1906. *El Arcipreste de Hita: estudio crítico* (Madrid: Imp. de los Sucesores de M. Minuesa de los Ríos).

RABINOWITZ, Peter J., 1977. 'Truth in Fiction: A Reexamination of Audiences', *Critical Inquiry*, 4: 121–41.

RABY, F. J. E., 1934. *A History of Secular Latin Poetry in the Middle Ages* (Oxford: Clarendon Press; repr. Oxford: UP for Sandpiper, 1997), II.

RAMÍREZ PIMIENTA, Juan Carlos, 1998. 'La aventura de doña Endrina y Don Melón de la Uerta: el matrimonio de la viuda como control social', *Hispanic Journal*, 19: 169–82.

RANDALL, Lilian M. C., 1966. *Images in the Margins of Gothic Manuscripts*, California Studies in the History of Art, 4 (Berkeley: Univ. of California Press).

REED, Cory A., 1994. 'Chaotic Quijote: Complexity, Nonlinearity, and Perspectivism', *Hispania* (USA), 77: 738–49.

RELIHAN, Joel, 1993. *Ancient Menippean Satire* (Baltimore: Johns Hopkins UP).

REY, Alfonso, 1979. 'Juan Ruiz, don Melón de la Huerta y el yo poético medieval', *BHS*, 56: 103–16.

RICHARDSON, Henry B., 1930. *An Etymological Vocabulary to the 'Libro de buen amor' of Juan Ruiz, Archpriest of Hita*, Yale Romanic Studies, 2 (New Haven: Yale UP).

RICO, Francisco, 1967. 'Sobre el origen de la autobiografía en el *Libro de buen amor*', *AEM*, 4: 301–25.

——, 1985. ' "Por aver mantenencia": el aristotelismo heterodoxo en el *Libro de buen amor*', *AFE*, 2: 169–98.

RIEGER, Dietmar, 1987. ' "Senes breu de parguamina"? Zum Problem des gelesenen Lied im Mittelalter', *RF*, 99: 1–18.

RIERA I SANS, Jaume, 1986. 'La invenció literària de Sant Pere Pascual', *Caplletra*, 1: 45–60.

RIFFATERRE, Michael, 1979. *La Production du texte* (Paris: Seuil).

ROBERTSON, D. W., 1951. 'Some Mediaeval Literary Terminology, with Special Reference to Chrétien de Troyes', *Studies in Philology*, 48: 669–92.

——, 1962, *A Preface to Chaucer: Studies in Medieval Perspectives* (Princeton: UP).

ROBINSON, F. N., ed., 1978. *The Complete Works of Geoffrey Chaucer* (Oxford: UP).

RODRÍGUEZ ADRADOS, Francisco, 1986. 'Aportaciones al estudio de las fuentes de las fábulas del Arcipreste', in *Philologica hispaniensia in honorem Manuel Alvar*, ed. Humberto López Morales et al. (Madrid: Gredos), III, 459–73.

RODRÍGUEZ-PUÉRTOLAS, Julio, 1976. 'Juan Manuel y la crisis castellana del siglo XIV', in his *Literatura, historia, alienación* (Barcelona: Labor), pp. 45–69.

——, 1996. 'Horizonte literario en torno al Arcipreste de Hita: un hombre y un libro fronterizos', in Toro Ceballos and Rodríguez Molina 1996: 561–67.

ROHLAND DE LANGBEHN, Regula, ed., 1997. Marqués de Santillana, *'Comedieta de Ponza', sonetos, serranillas y otras obras*, introd. Vicente Beltrán, BC, 12 (Barcelona: Crítica).

ROJAS, Fernando de, 1987. *La Celestina*, ed. Dorothy S. Severin with Maite Cabello, LH, 4 (Madrid: Cátedra).

RÖSSNER, Michael, 1984. 'Rezeptionsästhetische Lektüre im Werk des Arcipreste de Hita: zu den Leerstellen im *Libro de Buen Amor*', *Archiv für das Studium der neueren Sprachen und Literaturen*, 221: 113–29.

ROUHI, Leyla, 1999. *Mediation and Love: A Study of the Medieval Go-Between in Key Romance and Near-Eastern Texts*, Brill's Studies in Intellectual History, 93 (Leiden: Brill).

ROY, Bruno, 1977. *Devinettes français du Moyen Âge*, Cahiers d'Études Médiévales, 3 (Montreal: Bellarmin).

——, 1992. *Une culture de l'équivoque* (Montreal: Presses de l'Université de Montréal; Paris: Champion).

RUBIO FERNÁNDEZ, Lisardo, 1984. *Catálogo de los manuscritos clásicos existentes en España* (Madrid: Universidad Complutense).

RUGGERIO, Michael J., 1966. *The Evolution of the Go-Between in Spanish Literature through the Sixteenth Century*, UCPMP, 78 (Berkeley: Univ. of California Press).

RUSSELL, Ian, 1991. 'My Dear, Dear Friends: The Parodic Sermon in Oral Tradition', in *Spoken in Jest*, ed. Gillian Bennett, Folklore Society Mistletoe Series, 21 (Sheffield: Sheffield Academic Press), pp. 23–56.

RUSSELL, J. Stephen, 1988. *The English Dream Vision: Anatomy of a Form* (Columbus: Ohio State UP).

RUSSELL, Peter, 1963. 'La magia como tema integral de la *La Tragicomedia de Calisto y Melibea*', in *Studia philologica: homenaje a Dámaso Alonso por sus amigos y discípulos con ocasión de su 60º aniversario*, III (Madrid: Gredos), pp. 337–54. Repr. and expanded in his *Temas de 'La Celestina' y otros estudios del 'Cid' al 'Quijote'*, Letras e Ideas, Maior, 14 (Barcelona: Ariel, 1978), pp. 241–76.

RUSSO, Mary, 1986. 'Female Grotesques: Carnival and Theory', in *Feminist Studies; Critical Studies*, ed. Teresa de Lauretis (Bloomington: Indiana UP), pp. 213–29.

RYCHNER, Jean, 1955. *La Chanson de geste: essai sur l'art épique des jongleurs*, Société de Publications Romanes et Françaises, 53 (Geneva: Droz).

SABAT DE RIVERS, Georgina, ed., 1982. Juana Inés de la Cruz, *Inundación Castálida*, CCa, 117 (Madrid: Castalia).

SAENGER, Paul, 1997. *Space Between Words: The Origins of Silent Reading* (Stanford: UP).

SÁEZ, Emilio, and José TRENCHS, 1973. 'Juan Ruiz de Cisneros (1295/ 1296–1351/1352), autor del *Buen Amor*', in Criado de Val 1973a: 365–68.

SÁNCHEZ, Thomás Antonio, ed., 1779–90. *Coleccion de poesías castellanas anteriores al siglo XV*, 4 vols (Madrid: Antonio de Sancha).

SÁNCHEZ CANTÓN, F. J., 1918. 'Siete versos inéditos del *Libro de buen amor*', *RFE*, 5: 43–45.

——, 1950. *Libros, tapices y cuadros que coleccionó Isabel la Católica* (Madrid: CSIC).

SANTILLANA, Íñigo López de Mendoza, marqués de, 1988. *Obras completas*, ed. Ángel Gómez Moreno and Maximilian P. A. M. Kerkhof, Autores Hispánicos, 146 (Barcelona: Planeta).

SAPERSTEIN, Marc, 2000. 'The Sermon as Oral Performance', in *Transmitting Jewish Traditions: Orality, Textuality and Cultural Diffusion*, ed. Yaakov Elman and Israel Gershoni (New Haven: Yale UP), pp. 248–77.

SCHAFFER, Martha E., 1989–90. '*Poema* or *Cantar de Mio Cid*: More on the Explicit', *RPh*, 43: 113–53.

SCHWARZBAUM, Haim. 1989. 'International Folklore Motifs in Petrus Alphonsi's *Disciplina clericalis*', in his ed. *Jewish Folklore between East and West: Collected Papers* (Beer-Sheva: Ben Gurion Univ.), pp. 239–71.

SEAGAR, Dennis, 1991. *Stories Within Stories: An Ecosystemic Theory of Metadiagetic Narrative* (New York: Peter Lang).

SEIDENSPINNER-NÚÑEZ, Dayle, 1981. *The Allegory of Good Love: Parodic Perspectivism in the 'Libro de Buen Amor'*, UCPMP, 112 (Berkeley: Univ. of California Press).

——, 1988–89. 'On "Dios y el mundo": Author and Reader Response in Juan Ruiz and Juan Manuel', *RPh*, 42: 251–66.

——, 1990. 'Readers, Response, and Repertoires: *Rezeptionstheorie* and the Archpriest's Text', *C*, 19.1: 96–111.

SERRES, Michel, 1982. *Hermes: Literature, Science, Philosophy*, ed. Josué V. Harari and David F. Bell (Baltimore: Johns Hopkins UP).

SEVERIN, Dorothy S., 1994. '"*Cancionero*": un género mal nombrado', *Cultura Neolatina*, 54: 95–105.

——, 1995. *Witchcraft in 'Celestina'*, PMHRS, 1 (London: Dept of Hispanic Studies, Queen Mary and Westfield College); 2nd edn, 1997.

SEVILLA ARROYO, Florencio, 1988. 'El cancionero de Juan Ruiz', *Epos*, 4: 163–81.

SHAW, J. F., trans., 1952. St Augustine, *On Christian Doctrine*, in *The Confessions, The City of God, On Christian Doctrine* (Chicago: Encyclopaedia Britannica).

SMALLEY, Beryl, 1978. *The Study of the Bible in the Middle Ages*, 2nd edn (Notre Dame: Univ. of Notre Dame Press).

SMITH, Frederik N., 1990. *The Genesis of Gulliver's Travels* (Newark: Univ. of Delaware Press).

SOBEJANO, Gonzalo, 1963. 'Escolios al *Buen Amor* de Juan Ruiz', in *Studia philologica: homenaje ofrecido a Dámaso Alonso* (Madrid: Gredos), III, 431–58.

——, 1973. 'Consecuencia y diversidad en el *Libro de buen amor*', in Criado de Val 1973a: 7–17.

SOLALINDE, Antonio G., 1914. 'Fragmentos de una traducción portuguesa del *Libro de buen amor*', *RFE*, 1: 162–72.

SPEARING, A. C., 1976. *Medieval Dream-Poetry* (Cambridge: UP).

SPITZER, Leo, 1934. 'Zur Auffassung der Kunst des Arcipreste de Hita', *ZRP*, 54: 237–70.

——, 1939. Review [in Spanish] of Lecoy 1938, *Revista de Filología Hispánica*, 1: 266–74.

——, 1946. 'Note on the Poetic and the Empirical "I" in Medieval Authors', *Traditio*, 4: 414–22. Repr. in his *Romanische Literaturstudien 1936–1956* (Tübingen: Niemeyer, 1959), pp. 100–12.

STEIGER, Arnald, 1964. 'Überlieferungsgeschichte der spanischen Literatur des Mittelalters', in ed. Karl Lang et al. *Geschichte der Textüberlieferung der antiken und mittelalterlichen Literatur*, II: *Überlieferungsgeschichte der mittelalterlichen Literatur* (Zurich: Atlantis), pp. 439–597.

STEWART, Ann Harleman, 1983a. 'Double Entendre in the Old English Riddles', *Lore and Language*, 3.8: 39–52.

——, 1983b. 'The Diachronic Study of Communicative Competence', in *Current Topics in English Historical Linguistics: Proceedings of the Second International Conference on English Historical Linguistics held at Odense University, 13–15 April, 1981*, ed. Michael Davenport, Erik Hansen, & Hans Frede Nielsen, Odense University Studies in English, 4 (Odense: UP), pp. 123–36.

STOCK, Brian, 1983. *The Implications of Literacy: Written Language and Models of Interpretation in the Eleventh and Twelfth Centuries* (Princeton: UP).

STOICHEFF, Peter, 1991. 'The Chaos of Metafiction', in *Chaos and Order: Complex Dynamics in Literature and Science*, ed. N. Katherine Hayles (Chicago: Univ. of Chicago Press), pp. 85–99.

STRUBEL, Armand, 1988. 'Exemple, fable, parabole: le récit bref figuré au Moyen Âge', *Le Moyen Âge*, ser. 5.2, 94: 341–61.

SWAN, Charles, trans., 1894. *Gesta romanorum* (London: Bell).

TATE, R. B., 1970. 'Adventures in the *Sierra*', in Gybbon-Monypenny 1970a: 219–29.

TAYLOR, Andrew, 1991. 'The Myth of a Minstrel Manuscript', *Sp*, 66: 43–73.

TAYLOR, Barry, 1992. 'Medieval Proverb Collections: The West European Tradition', *Journal of the Warburg and Courtauld Institutes*, 55: 19–35, plates 5–6.

——, 1993. 'Wisdom Forms in the *Disciplina clericalis* of Petrus Alfonsi', *C*, 22.1: 24–40.

——, 1995. 'Some Complexities of the *Exemplum* in Ramon Llull's *Llibre de les bèsties*', *MLR*, 90: 646–58.

——, 1997. 'Un texto breve catalán sobre cortesía', in Lucía Megías 1997: II, 1491–99.

——, 1999a. 'The Fables of Eiximenis: Norm and Abnormality', *MLR*, 94: 409–14.

——, 1999b. 'Michael Verinus and the *Distichs* of Cato in Spain: A Comparative Study in Reception', in *Latin and Vernacular in Renaissance Spain*, ed. Barry Taylor and Alejandro Coroleu, Cañada Blanch Monographs, 3 (Manchester: Manchester Spanish and Portuguese Studies), pp. 73–82.

——, 2000. 'La *fabliella* de don Juan Manuel', *RPM*, 4: 187–200.

TERREROS Y PANDO, Estevan de, 1758. *Paleografia española, que contiene todos los modos conocidos, que ha habido de escribir en España desde su principio y fundacion, hasta el presente*, Espectaculo de Naturaleza, 13 (Madrid: Joachin Ibarra).

Thesaurus, 1995–. *Thesaurus proverbiorum medii aevi: Lexikon der Sprichwörter des romanisch-germanischen Mittelalters*, begun by Samuel Singer; ed. Kuratorium Singer der Schweizerischen Akademie der Geistes- und Sozialwissenschaften (Berlin: De Gruyter).

THOMPSON, Stith, 1955–58. *Motif-Index of Folk-Literature: A Classification of Narrative Elements in Folktales, Ballads, Myths, Fables, Mediaeval Romances, Exempla, Fabliaux, Jest-Books, and Local Legends*, 2nd edn (Copenhagen: Rosenkilde & Bagger; Bloomington: Indiana UP).

THOMSON, Ian, and Louis PERRAUD, ed., 1990. *Ten Latin Schooltexts of the Later Middle Ages: Translated Selections*, Mediaeval Studies, 6 (Lewiston: Edwin Mellen).

TICKNOR, George, 1849. *History of Spanish Literature*, 3 vols (London: John Murray).

TIKHANO, Galin, 2000. *The Master and the Slave: Lukács, Bakhtin, and the Ideas of their Time* (Oxford: Clarendon Press).

TODOROV, Tzvetan, 1967. *Littérature et signification* (Paris: Larousse).

——, 1970. 'Problèmes de l'énonciation', *Langages*, 17: 3–11.

——, 1998. *Mikhail Bakhtin: The Dialogic Principle*, trans. Wlad Godzich, Theory and History of Literature, 13 (Minneapolis: Univ. of Minnesota Press); 1ˢᵗ publ. 1981.

TOLEDO, Alfonso Martínez de, 1970. *Arcipreste de Talavera, o Corbacho*, ed. Joaquín González Muela, CCa, 24 (Madrid: Castalia).

TOMASSINI, Giovanni Battista, 1990. *Il racconto nel racconto: analisis teorica dei procedimenti d'inserzione narrativa*. (Rome: Bulzoni).

TOMKINS, Jane P., ed., 1980. *Reader-Response Criticism from Formalism to Post-Structuralism* (Baltimore: John Hopkins UP).

TORO CEBALLOS, Francisco, ed., in press. *Estudios de frontera: Alcalá la Real y el Arcipreste de Hita: II Congreso Internacional celebrado en Alcalá la Real, del 9 al 11 de mayo de 2002* (Jaén: Diputación Provincial).

——, and José RODRÍGUEZ MOLINA, ed., 1996. *Estudios de frontera: Alcalá la Real y el Arcipreste de Hita: Congreso Internacional celebrado en Alcalá la Real, del 22 al 25 de noviembre de 1995* (Jaén: Diputación Provincial).

TORRE, Esteban, 2002. *El ritmo del verso: estudios sobre el cómputo silábico y la disposición acentual, a la luz de la métrica comparada, en el verso español moderno* (Murcia: Univ.).

TORRES-ALCALÁ, Antonio, 1990. 'El *Libro de buen amor* y el *Roman de la rose*: algunas analogías', *AM*, 2: 172–83.

TUBACH, Frederic C., 1969. *Index exemplorum: A Handbook of Medieval Religious Tales,* FF Communications, 204 (Helsinki: Academia Scientiarum Fennica).

ULLMAN, Pierre L., 1967. 'Juan Ruiz's Prologue', *MLN*, 82: 149–70.

VALDEÓN BARUQUE, Julio, 1975. *Los conflictos sociales en el reino de Castilla en los siglos XIV y XV* (Madrid: Siglo Veintiuno).

——, 1977. 'Las tensiones sociales en Castilla en tiempos de don Juan Manuel', in *Juan Manuel Studies*, ed. Ian Macpherson, CT, A60 (London: Tamesis), pp. 181–92.

VÀRVARO, Alberto, 1968–69. 'Nuovi studi sul *Libro de buen amor*: problemi testuali', *RPh*, 22: 133–57.

——, 1969–70. 'Lo stato originale del ms. *G.* del *Libro de buen amor* di Juan Ruiz', *RPh*, 23: 549–56.

VASVÁRI, Louise O., 1983–84. 'An Example of *Parodia Sacra* in the *Libro de buen amor*: *Quoniam*, "Pudenda" ', *C*, 12: 195–203.

——, 1985. 'La semiología de la connotación: lectura polisémica de "Cruz cruzada panadera" ', *NRFH*, 32 (1983 [1985]): 299–324.

——, 1985–86. 'La digresión sobre los pecados mortales y la estructura del *Libro de Buen Amor*', *NRFH*, 34: 156–80.

——, 1986–87. 'Erotic Polysemy in the *Libro de Buen Amor*: Àpropos Monique de Lope's *Traditions populaires et textualité*', *C*, 15: 127–34.

——, 1988–89. 'Vegetal-Genital Onomastics in the *Libro de buen amor*', *RPh*, 42: 1–29.

——, 1989. 'The Two Lazy Suitors in the *Libro de Buen Amor*: Popular Tradition and Literary Game of Love', *AM*, 1: 181–205.

——, 1990a. ' "Chica cosa es dos nuezes": Lost Sexual Humor in the *Libro del Arcipreste*', *REH*, 24: 1–22.

——, 1990b. 'A Tale of "Taillying": Aesop Topsy-Turvy in the *Libro del Arcipreste*', *Journal of Interdisciplinary Literary Studies / Cuadernos Interdisciplinarios de Estudios Literarios*, 2: 13–41.

——, 1991. 'Gastro-Genital Rites of Reversal: The Battle of Flesh and Lent in the *Libro del Arcipreste*', *C*, 20.1: 1–15.

——, 1992a. 'Pitas Pajas: Carnivalesque Phonosymbolism', *REH*, 26: 135–62.

——, 1992b. 'Why Is Doña Endrina a Widow? Traditional Culture and Textuality in the *Libro de Buen Amor*', in *Upon My Husband's Death: Widows in the Literature and Histories of Medieval Europe*, ed. Louise Mirrer (Ann Arbor: Univ. of Michigan Press), pp. 259–87.

——, 1994. 'Festive Phallic Discourse in the *Libro del Arcipreste*', *C*, 22.2: 89–117. Repr. as 'The Semiotics of Phallic Aggression and Anal Penetration as Male Agonistic Ritual in the *Libro de buen amor*', in Blackmore & Hutcheson 1999: 130–56.

——, 1995a. '*Don Hurón* como *trickster*: un arquetipo psico-folklórico', in *Actas del Tercer Congreso de la AHLM (Salamanca, 3 al 6 de octubre de 1989)*, ed. María Isabel Toro Pascua, 2 vols (Salamanca: Biblioteca Española del Siglo XV & Dpto. de Literatura Española e Hispanoamericana), II, 1121–26.

——, 1995b. 'El hijo del molinero: para la polisemia popular del *Libro del Arcipreste*', in *Erotismo en las letras hispánicas: aspectos, modos y fronteras*, ed. Luce López-Baralt and Francisco Márquez Villanueva, Publicaciones de la *NRFH*, 7 (Mexico City: Colegio de México), 461–77.

——, 1995c. 'Múltiple transparencia semántica de los nombres de la alcahueta en el *Libro del Arcipreste*', in *Medioevo y literatura: Actas del V Congreso de la AHLM (Granada, 27 septiembre-1 de octubre, 1993)*, ed. Juan Paredes (Granada: Univ.), IV, 453–63.

——, 1997. 'Peregrinaciones por topografías pornográficas en el *Libro de Buen Amor*', in Lucía Megías 1997: II, 1563–72.

——, 2000a. 'El refranero polisémico del buen amor: "so mal tabardo está el buen amor" ', in *Actas del XIII Congreso de la AIH, Madrid, 6–11 de julio de 1998*, ed. Florencio Sevilla and Carlos Alvar (Madrid: Castalia), I, 238–43.

——, 2000b. ' "De todos instrumentos, yo, libro, só pariente" (*LBA* 70): el texto liminal como cuerpo sexual', in *Actas del VIII Congreso Internacional de la AHLM, Santander, 22–26 de septiembre de 1999*, ed. Margarita Freixas and Silvia Iriso (Santander: Consejería de Cultura del Gobierno de Cantabria, Año Jubilar Lebaniego, and AHLM), II, 1769–79.

VASVÁRI, Louise O., in press. 'The Perverted Proverb in the *Libro de Buen Amor*', in *Under the Influence: Re-thinking the Comparative in Medieval Iberia*, ed. Cynthia Robinson and Leyla Rouhi (Leiden: Brill).

[VAVASSEUR, François], 1658. Francisci Vavassoris, *De ludicra dictione liber in quo tota iocandi ratio ex veterum scriptis aestimatur* (Paris: Cramoisy).

VETTERLING, Mary-Anne, 1981. 'The Rediscovery of the *Libro de buen amor* in the Eighteenth Century', *Dieciocho: Hispanic Enlightenment Aesthetics & Literary Theory*, 4: 24–33.

——, 1981–82. 'Film Review: *Libro de buen amor*', *C*, 10.1: 110–11.

VILLENA, Enrique de, 1994. *Obras completas*, ed. Pedro M. Cátedra, 2 vols, Biblioteca Castro (Madrid: Turner).

VINAVER, Eugène, 1966. *Form and Meaning in Medieval Romance*, Presidential Address of the Modern Humanities Research Association (Cambridge: MHRA).

VRIES, Henk de, 1985–86. 'Sobre "dos cantigas marianas" de Juan Ruiz', *C*, 14: 268–71.

WALKER, Mary F., 1990. *Lovesickness in the Middle Ages: The Viaticum and its Commentaries* (Philadelphia: Univ. of Pennsylvania Press).

WALKER, Roger M., 1966. 'Towards an Interpretation of the *Libro de buen amor*', *BHS*, 43: 1–10.

——, 1970. ' "Con miedo de la muerte la miel non es sabrosa": Love, Sin and Death in the *Libro de buen amor*', in Gybbon-Monypenny 1970a: 231–52.

——, 1971. 'Oral Delivery or Private Reading? A Contribution to the Debate on the Dissemination of Medieval Literature', *FMLS*, 7: 36–42.

——, 1974. *Tradition and Technique in the 'Libro del cavallero Zifar'*, CT, A36 (London: Tamesis).

WALSH, John K., 1979–80a. 'The Genesis of the *Libro de buen amor* (from Performance Text to *Libro* or *Cancionero*)', paper read to the Modern Language Association of America Special Session as 'The *Libro de Buen Amor*: Perspectives and Directions' (29 December); abstract, 'The *Libro de buen amor* as a Performance-Text', in *C*, 8: 5–6; in press, with a study by Nicholas G. Round, PMHRS.

——, 1979–80b. 'Juan Ruiz and the *mester de clerezía*: Lost Context and Lost Parody in the *Libro de buen amor*', *RPh*, 33: 62–86.

——, 1983. 'The Names of the Bawd in the *Libro de buen amor*', in *Florilegium Hispanicum: Medieval and Golden Age Studies Presented to Dorothy Clotelle Clarke*, ed. John S. Geary, with Charles B. Faulhaber and Dwayne E. Carpenter (Madison: HSMS), pp. 151–64.

WATT, Ian, 1957. *The Rise of the Novel: Studies in Defoe, Richardson and Fielding* (Berkeley: Univ. of California Press).

WELTER, J.-Th., 1927. *L'Exemplum dans la littérature religieuse et didactique du Moyen Âge* (Paris: Occitania).

WENZEL, Siegfried, 1990. 'Reflections on (New) Philology', in Nichols 1990: 11–18.

WHEATLEY, Edward, 2000. *Mastering Aesop: Medieval Education, Chaucer, and his Followers* (Gainesville: UP of Florida).

WHINNOM, Keith, 1968. *Spanish Literary Historiography: Three Forms of Distortion* (Exeter: Univ., 1967 [1968]). Repr. in his *Medieval and Renaissance Spanish Literature: Selected Essays*, ed. Alan Deyermond, W. F. Hunter, and Joseph T. Snow (Exeter: Univ. of Exeter Press, with the *JHP*, 1994), pp. 96–113.

——, 1977–78. 'A Fifteenth-Century Reference to Don Melón and Doña Endrina', *JHP*, 2: 91–101.

WHINNOM, Keith, 1981. *La poesía amatoria de la época de los Reyes Católicos*, Durham Modern Languages Series, HM2 (Durham: Univ.).

WHITING, Bartlett Jere, 1977. *Early American Proverbs and Proverbial Phrases* (Cambridge, MA: Belknap Press).

WHITTEM, Arthur F., 1931. 'Some Data on Juan Ruiz, Archpriest of Hita', *MLN*, 46: 363–67.

WILLIS, Raymond S., ed., 1934. *'El libro de Alexandre': Texts of the Paris and Madrid Manuscripts*, Elliott Monographs in Romance Languages and Literatures, 32 (Princeton: UP; Paris: Presses Universitaires de France).

——, 1963–64. 'Two Trotaconventos', *RPh*, 17: 353–62.

——, 1974. 'Thirteen Years: Seedbed of Riddles in the *Libro de Buen Amor*', *KRQ*, 21: 215–27.

——, 1983. 'An Archpriest and an Abbess?', in *Essays on Hispanic Literature in Honor of Edmund L. King*, ed. Sylvia Molloy and Luis Fernández Cifuentes, CT, A98 (London: Tamesis), pp. 245–54.

WINROTH, Anders, 2000. *The Making of Gratian's 'Decretum'* (Cambridge: UP).

WOLF, Ferdinand, 1859. 'Zur Geschichte der spanischen Literatur im Mittelalter', in his *Studien zur Geschichte der spanischen und portugiesischen Nationalliteratur* (Berlin: A. Asher), pp. 1–302. Repr. from a review 1st publ. 1831–32.

WOOD, H. Harvey, ed., 1958. *The Poems and Fables of Robert Henryson, Schoolmaster of Dunfermline*, 2nd edn (Edinburgh: Oliver and Boyd).

WRIGHT, A. E., 2002. 'Aesopus', at http://ccat.sas.upenn.edu/jod/texts/aesop.html, 26 March.

YNDURÁIN, Francisco, 1969. 'Refranes y "frases hechas" en la estimativa literaria del siglo XVII', in his *Relección de clásicos* (Madrid: Prensa Española), pp. 299–331.

——, 1973. 'Una nota sobre la composición del *Libro de buen amor*', in Criado de Val 1973a: 217–31.

ZAHAREAS, Anthony N., 1964. 'Juan Ruiz's *Envoi*: The Moral and Artistic Pose', *MLN*, 79: 206–11.

——, 1964–65. 'Parody of the Canonical Hours: Juan Ruiz's Art of Satire', *Modern Philology*, 62: 105–09.

——, 1965. *The Art of Juan Ruiz, Archpriest of Hita* (Madrid: Estudios de Literatura Española).

——, 1978–79. 'Structure and Ideology in the *Libro de buen amor*', *C*, 7: 92–104.

——, and Óscar PEREIRA, with Thomas MCCALLUM, 1990. *Itinerario del 'Libro del Arcipreste': glosas críticas al 'Libro de buen amor'*, SpS, 56 (Madison: HSMS).

ZANTS, Emily, 1996. *Chaos Theory, Complexity, Cinema, and the Evolution of the French Novel*, Studies in French Literature, 25 (Lampeter: Edwin Mellen).

ZINK, Michel, 1976. *La Prédication en langue romane avant 1300* (Paris: Champion).

——, 1985. *La Subjectivité littéraire autour du siècle de saint Louis* (Paris: Presses Universitaires de France).

ZIOLKOWSKI, Jan M., 1993. *Talking Animals: Medieval Latin Beast Poetry, 750–1150* (Philadelphia: Univ. of Pennsylvania Press).

ZUMTHOR, Paul, 1972. *Essai de poétique médiévale* (Paris: Seuil).

SUBJECT INDEX

STANZA INDEX